COLLABORATIVE CONSULTATION IN THE SCHOOLS

Effective Practices for Students with Learning and Behavior Problems

Third Edition

Thomas J. Kampwirth
Professor Emeritus
California State University, Long Beach

Upper Saddle River, New Jersey
Columbus, Ohio

Library of Congress Cataloging-in-Publication Data
Kampwirth, Thomas J.
Collaborative consultation in the schools: effective practices for students with learning and behavior problems / Thomas J. Kampwirth.—3rd ed.
p. cm.
Includes bibliographical references and index.
ISBN 0-13-117810-5
1. Educational counseling—United States. 2. Group work in education—United States. 3. Learning disabled children—Services for—United States. 4. Problem children—Services for—United States. 5. School management and organization—United States. I. Title.

LB1027.5.K285 2006
371.9--dc22

2004059738

Vice President and Executive Publisher: Jeffery W. Johnston
Acquisitions Editor: Allyson P. Sharp
Editorial Assistant: Kathleen S. Burk
Production Editor: Sheryl Glicker Langner
Production Coordination: Carlisle Publishers Services
Design Coordinator: Diane C. Lorenzo
Cover Designer: Ali Mohrman
Cover Image: Superstock
Production Manager: Laura Messerly
Director of Marketing: Ann Castel Davis
Marketing Manager: Autumn Purdy
Marketing Coordinator: Tyra Poole

This book was set in Garamond by Carlisle Publishers Services, Ltd.
The cover was printed by Phoenix Color Corp.

Pearson Education Ltd.
Pearson Education Singapore Pte. Ltd.
Pearson Education Canada, Ltd.
Pearson Education—Japan
Pearson Education Australia Pty. Limited
Pearson Education North Asia Ltd.
Pearson Educación de Mexico, S.A. de C.V.
Pearson Education Malaysia Pte. Ltd.

10
ISBN: 0-13-117810-5

This text is dedicated to our children: Kathy, Tom, and Ed;
and to our grandchildren:
Alyssa Strom, Shane Strom, Conor Roche, and Elise Roche.

May their dreams come true.

Educator Learning Center: An Invaluable Online Resource

Merrill Education and the Association for Supervision and Curriculum Development (ASCD) invite you to take advantage of a new online resource, one that provides access to the top research and proven strategies associated with ASCD and Merrill—the Educator Learning Center. At **www.educatorlearningcenter.com,** you will find resources that will enhance your students' understanding of course topics and of current issues, in addition to being invaluable for further research.

HOW THE EDUCATOR LEARNING CENTER WILL HELP YOUR STUDENTS BECOME BETTER TEACHERS

With the combined resources of Merrill Education and ASCD, you and your students will find a wealth of tools and materials to better prepare them for the classroom.

Research

- More than 600 articles from the ASCD journal *Educational Leadership* discuss everyday issues faced by practicing teachers.
- A direct link on the site to Research Navigator™ gives students access to many of the leading education journals, as well as extensive content detailing the research process.
- Excerpts from Merrill Education texts give your students insights on important topics of instructional methods, diverse populations, assessment, classroom management, technology, and refining classroom practice.

Classroom practice

- Hundreds of lesson plans and teaching strategies are categorized by content area and age range.
- Case studies and classroom video footage provide virtual field experience for student reflection.
- Computer simulations and other electronic tools keep your students abreast of today's classrooms and current technologies.

LOOK INTO THE VALUE OF THE EDUCATOR LEARNING CENTER YOURSELF

A 4-month subscription to Educator Learning Center is $25 but is **FREE** when packaged with any Merrill Education text. In order for your students to have access to this site, you must use this special value-pack ISBN number **WHEN** placing your textbook order with the bookstore: 0-13-186208-1. Your students will then receive a copy of the text packaged with a free ASCD pincode. To preview the value of this website to you and your students, please go to **www.educatorlearningcenter.com** and click on "Demo."

About the Author

Thomas Kampwirth is Professor Emeritus in the Department of Educational Psychology, Administration, and Counseling at California State University, Long Beach. He taught in the areas of special education and school psychology from 1971 to 2004, and was coordinator of the school psychology program at CSULB for 25 years. He is a consulting school psychologist for the special education system operated by the Orange County Department of Education in California.

He has served as a special education teacher and a school psychologist in numerous districts in Illinois, Arizona, and California. His research interests include aptitude-treatment interactions and consultation processes. Dr. Kampwirth received his doctorate in school psychology from the University of Illinois in 1968. In 2003 he was given the Lifetime Achievement Award by the National Association of School Psychologists.

Preface

This book was written to fill the needs of two different groups: university students and practitioners in the schools. The students are likely to be doing advanced work in special education, school psychology, school counseling, or educational administration. The practitioners are currently employed in these professions and are being asked increasingly to help others, usually teachers or parents, solve teaching/learning and behavior management problems. In this book, I present the consultation process as a collaborative, problem-solving endeavor designed to assist consultees in their work with students who have, or are at risk for, school adjustment or learning problems. In addition, I include a chapter on ethics and advocacy and a chapter on systems-level consultation designed to improve service delivery to students and teachers in a whole school or district.

Consultation as a service delivery system in the public schools has increased in popularity over the last several years. Prior to 1990, most special and general educators were still expected to deal on their own with whatever problems they experienced in their teaching or management of children; indeed, those who sought help may have been regarded as unable to deal with the job of teaching and subtly, or overtly, rejected by their peers or supervisors. To an even greater extent, parents in the United States, since the decline of the extended family configurations that were prevalent before World War II, have been expected to raise their children without much assistance from others. The "village" that it takes to raise a child had disappeared and been replaced by neighbors known only slightly and relatives who lived far away. Only people with large financial resources could access relatively expensive professional help for their children who needed it. Most parents, including those with children with disabilities, were left to their own resources.

In today's schools, we are fortunate to have experienced a change in attitudes about the value of collaborative assistance and teamwork. Part of the credit for this change should be given to the field of special education, which, as a result of P.L. 94–142, first implemented in 1977, established the need for team conferences (IEP meetings) to discuss the needs of, and solutions for, the learning and behavior/adjustment problems of students with disabilities. Since that time, teacher assistance teams, student study teams, and a host of other formal or semiformal team arrangements have been developed and have proven their effectiveness in meeting the needs of students who require some degree of assistance to be successful in school. Indeed, it would be surprising to find a school today that did not depend on its student study team to discuss and develop interventions for students at risk of school failure. These team interactions also meet the needs of parents in their efforts to understand and encourage their children.

Beyond what takes place in team meetings, there remains a real need for everyday assistance for both special education teachers who are providing direct teaching services to students with disabilities and general educators who are charged with teaching mainstreamed or included students with disabilities, in addition to a large cadre of other at-risk students. This text is primarily devoted to helping those who assist these special and general educators to deal with the everyday, ongoing challenges presented by these students. Largely because of increased inclusion and a seemingly growing number of at-risk youth, school personnel have learned the value of collaborative work as opposed to isolated work. In a school with a collaborative work ethic, the administration supports teachers who freely seek help from others, join in groups to discuss common or individual problems, and admit that they need help. Job descriptions and expectations have changed accordingly. Special education teachers are increasingly leaving their resource rooms and special day classes and are spending part, if not all, of their school days in general education classes. School psychologists are learning alternative ways of assessing students (which includes more time observing in the classes), are taking more time talking with teachers about their referrals, and are taking increased responsiblility for assisting in the development of appropriate interventions. School counselors are more likely to see if they can be of assistance with some referrals through consultation with teachers and parents in conjunction with individual or group counseling efforts. Mentor teachers, vice principals, and others who may have the opportunity to assist teachers and parents are also seeing their roles expand to include consultation.

UNIQUE ASPECTS OF THIS TEXT

This text differs in two major ways from others that are devoted to consultation in the schools. The first difference is the inclusion of two extended case studies, one about a student who manifests disruptive behavior problems, and one describing a student with learning (achievement) problems. There is also a briefer case example about a systems-change effort. The second difference is the inclusion of separate chapters on students' learning and behavior/adjustment problems. These problems are the main reasons for referral to a school consultant, whether that person has a primary position as a special education teacher, a school counselor, a school psychologist, a mentor teacher, or a vice principal. Thus, it is important to have fundamental information about the probable causes and possible solutions to these problems.

This text has a number of strengths: (1) It is written in a user-friendly fashion. The author is very experienced in the practice of school consultation and has utilized his experiences to keep the situations described and interventions discussed at a very practical level. There is a bit of folk wisdom permeating these pages, a kind of common sense that may be lacking in some other texts that take perhaps too much of a research-oriented perspective that doesn't translate easily into the everyday needs of teachers and parents. Practitioners know that consultation is not an easy process to implement; this text presents the rough with the smooth and, because of this, lets present and future school personnel know about the realities of consulting in the public schools. (2) Most chapters have a number of student activities embedded in the narrative. These are intended to focus readers' attention on key aspects of the material and to give them a chance to discuss the issues being presented and to interact with others regarding the critical skills that need to be learned. There are a total of 82 activities in this edition. (3) There are a number of figures and tables that serve a variety of purposes, such as models of forms, examples of commonly used paperwork, and lists of ideas and suggestions that will prove interesting and practical.

In this edition I have included a set of objectives for each chapter that serve as guides to what the chapter covers. Also, there are many more specific suggestions about interventions, especially in Chapters 5, 6, and 7. The addition of a whole chapter on ethics and advocacy (Chapter 4) is not common among texts on consultation, in spite of the importance of these issues; I hope you will find it enlightening.

ORGANIZATION

Chapter 1 presents an overview of school consultation as practiced by internal (i.e., regularly employed personnel) consultants. It defines terms and discusses the characteristics of consultation that are collaborative in nature, major focus points and questions about them, and the benefits and effectiveness of school consultation. I consider the consultee as a variable, and include a list of seven important generalizations about effective consultation. There is a discussion about consultation in culturally and linguistically diverse settings. The chapter concludes with a statement of philosophy about the educational placements of students with disabilities.

Chapter 2 presents an overview of various models and functional aspects that apply to school consultation. The behavioral and mental health models are discussed in some detail. There is also information about the roles, skills, and activities of consultants; content relating to the development and conduct of inservice training; student study team functions; and issues relating to consultation with parents and families.

Chapter 3 presents an extended discussion of the communication and interpersonal skills needed for effective consultation and reviews resistance to consultation and power dynamics in the consultative process.

Chapter 4 is devoted to issues of ethics and advocacy. In addition to a general overview of ethical issues, the chapter includes a review of the CEC ethical code and the standards of practice for special educators. Case studies are presented to show how to apply the code and standards to situations that can occur in schools. A separate discussion of advocacy indicates how this potentially sensitive area can be utilized in a collaborative manner.

Chapter 5 is the heart of this text. Here I present generic models of the consultation process along with the solutions-oriented consultation system (SOCS), a 10-step practical model designed to guide school-based consultants through the often-confusing stages that are necessary for comprehensive consultation work.

Chapter 6 reviews consultation processes and other information about students with emotional and behavioral disorders. I discuss 11 possible reasons for these problems, and also present interventions for each of them. There is also information about terminology, and about diagnostic methods including functional assessment, observation, interviews, rating scales, and charting methods. I also include general ideas grouped into five major categories for modifying classroom behavior.

Chapter 7 reviews learning/achievement problems among students. There are nine possible reasons listed, along with interventions for each reason. Also included are ideas for assessment of both the classroom and the referred students. The chapter concludes with an additional list of validated interventions.

Chapter 8 is concerned with systems-change efforts. This chapter reviews key variables that govern public school work and summarizes two different methods of organizing systems-change efforts. The chapter concludes with a case example showing how a major change in service delivery to students with disabilities can be achieved.

Chapter 9 presents two extended case studies: one having to do with a boy who manifests defiant behavior, and the other focusing on a girl who is at serious risk for academic failure. Both cases demonstrate how SOCS can be used to guide consultants' work.

ACKNOWLEDGMENTS

I would like to thank the reviewers of this third edition for their constructive comments: Jenean M. Case, Troy State University and Hampton University; Jon Lasser, Southwest Texas State University; and Stephanie Stein, Central Washington University.

Discover the Merrill Resources for Special Education Website

Technology is a constantly growing and changing aspect of our field that is creating a need for new content and resources. To address this emerging need, Merrill Education has developed an online learning environment for students, teachers, and professors alike to complement our products—the *Merrill Resources for Special Education* Website. This content-rich website provides additional resources specific to this book's topic and will help you—professors, classroom teachers, and students—augment your teaching, learning, and professional development.

Our goal is to build on and enhance what our products already offer. For this reason, the content for our user-friendly website is organized by topic and provides teachers, professors, and students with a variety of meaningful resources all in one location. With this website, we bring together the best of what Merrill has to offer: text resources, video clips, web links, tutorials, and a wide variety of information on topics of interest to general and special educators alike.

Rich content, applications, and competencies further enhance the learning process.

The *Merrill Resources for Special Education* Website includes:

Resources for the Professor—

- The **Syllabus Manager**™, an online syllabus creation and management tool, enables instructors to create and revise their syllabus with an easy, step-by-step process. Students can access your syllabus and any changes you make during the course of your class from any computer with Internet access. To access this tailored syllabus, students will just need the URL of the website and the password assigned to the syllabus. By clicking on the date, the student can see a list of activities, assignments, and readings due for that particular class.
- In addition to the **Syllabus Manager**™ and its benefits listed above, professors also have access to all of the wonderful resources that students have access to on the site.

Resources for the Student—

- Video clips specific to each topic, with questions to help you evaluate the content and make crucial theory-to-practice connections.

- Thought-provoking critical analysis questions that students can answer and turn in for evaluation or that can serve as a basis for class discussions and lectures.
- Access to a wide variety of resources related to classroom strategies and methods, including lesson planning and classroom management.
- Information on all the most current relevant topics related to special and general education, including CEC and Praxis standards, IEPs, portfolios, and professional development.
- Extensive web resources and overviews on each topic addressed on the website.
- A message board with discussion starters where students can respond to class discussion topics, post questions and responses, or ask questions about assignments.
- A search feature to help access specific information quickly.

To take advantage of these and other resources, please visit the *Collaborative Consultation in the Schools: Effective Practices for Students with Learning and Behavior Problems,* Third Edition, Website at

http://www.prenhall.com/kampwirth

Contents

CHAPTER 4

Ethics and Advocacy in School Consultation 137

CHAPTER 5

The Solutions-Oriented Consultation System 153

CHAPTER 8

Systems-Level Consultation: The Organization as the Target of Change 279

CHAPTER 9

Case Studies in Consultation: Behavior and Academic Problems in the Classroom 305

Note: Every effort has been made to provide accurate and current Internet information in this book. However, the Internet and information posted on it are constantly changing, so it is inevitable that some of the Internet addresses listed in this textbook will change.

Overview of School-Based Consultation

OBJECTIVES

1. Orient the reader to the field of consultation as it is practiced in the schools.
2. Define the terms *consultation* and *collaboration,* and then show how these two terms can be used together to describe a method of consultation that validates the concept of collaboration.
3. Indicate how collaborative consultation is becoming a significant role for many school personnel, especially special educators, school psychologists, speech and language specialists, and school counselors.
4. Highlight the central purpose of consultation, which is to develop, monitor, and evaluate interventions for students with behavior and learning problems, and how consultation fits the purposes and advances the philosophies behind the No Child Left Behind Act (NCLB) and the new Individuals With Disabilities Education Act (IDEA P.L. 108-446) amendments of 2004.
5. Explain the different forms consultation takes, as well as the relationship between the process and the content of consultation.
6. Respond to frequently asked questions regarding consultation.
7. Provide a general overview of research issues and approaches in consultation.
8. Discuss consultation in relation to issues of diversity.
9. Explicate a philosophy regarding the inclusion of students with disabilities.

You are the newly appointed resource specialist, school psychologist, or counselor at Alpha School, a K–6 school in the Alpha–Beta K–12 school district. Your job includes being a consultant to teachers, parents, and others about student learning and behavior/adjustment problems. Mrs. Jones, an experienced third-grade teacher, stops you in the hallway one day in early October and says, "You've got to do something about Johnny B. He really needs a lot of help." How would you proceed?

Ms. Nguyen, principal of Martin Luther King, Jr. High School, wants you to explain your role as a consultant to the teachers. Consider how you might prepare a 2-minute presentation at the next teacher staff meeting regarding the meaning of school-based consultation. Take your presentation from the perspective of a special education teacher, or school counselor, or school psychologist.

How you might proceed is a function of many variables, such as your personal philosophy of professional practice; the expectations of your supervisors and coworkers;

and factors such as caseload, established precedents, your reinforcement history, and your training. I believe that a consultation-based service delivery model is, for most referrals and most constituents (that is, teachers, parents, and other consultees), an appropriate and useful approach when used with other service requirements of your position as a special education teacher, school psychologist, or school counselor.

CONSULTATION AND COLLABORATION: DEFINITIONS, DISTINCTIONS, AND CHARACTERISTICS

The terms *consultation* and *collaboration* have been discussed in many different ways by various authorities. *Webster's College Dictionary* (1997) defines *consult* as seeking guidance or information, or to give professional or expert advice. A consultant is a person who gives such advice. Consultation is the act of consulting; a meeting for deliberation or discussion (p. 284). The word *collaborate* means to work, one with another; cooperate (p. 257). Four key concepts are mentioned: information seeking or giving, discussion, expert, and working together. This book discusses these four concepts, among many others.

The *Webster's* (1997) definitions of consultation and collaboration, although generic, are not precise enough for our purposes. Writers in the field of consultation have worked to refine the definitions of consultation and collaboration from the perspectives of the public schools. Figure 1.1 contains examples of definitions of consultation, collaboration, and collaborative consultation taken from the current literature. Essentially, most writers believe that the term *consultation* should be reserved for instances where one person, the consultant, develops interventions for referral problems with a consultee who is primarily, if not solely, responsible for carrying out the recommended interventions. The term *collaboration* (or *collaborative*) is reserved for those instances in which two or more people agree to take somewhat equal responsibility for the implementation of the interventions. This author's preference is to combine the essence of what is embodied in the terms *collaborative* and *consultation*. This has led to the following definition that supports the content and purpose of this book: *Collaborative consultation is a process in which a trained, school-based consultant, working in an egalitarian, nonhierarchical relationship with a consultee, assists that person in her efforts to make decisions and carry out plans that will be in the best educational interests of her students.* All the terms in this definition are found in the other definitions listed in Figure 1.1, with the exception of egalitarian and nonhierarchical. These refer to the author's belief that consultees, who are usually teachers or parents, are much more likely to engage in the consultation process when they believe they have an amount of input into the planning process that is at least equal to that of the consultant (Witt & Martens, 1988).

Figure 1.1

Definitions/descriptions of *consultation, collaboration,* and *collaborative consultation*

Included below are definitions or descriptions of the words *consultation* and *collaboration* and the term *collaborative consultation.* The purpose of presenting three different sets of definitions/descriptions is to assist the reader in understanding how these terms are related and how they differ.

Definitions/descriptions of *consultation*:

School consultation is a process for providing psychological and educational services in which a specialist (consultant) works cooperatively with a staff member (consultee) to improve the learning and adjustment of a student (client) or group of students. During face-to-face interactions, the consultant helps the consultee through systematic problem solving, social influence, and professional support. In turn, the consultee helps the client(s) through selecting and implementing effective school-based interventions. In all cases, school consultation serves a remedial function and has the potential to serve a preventive function. (Erchul & Martens, 2002, pp. 13–14)

Human services consultation ... is engaged primarily for the purpose of assisting consultees to develop attitudes and skills that will enable them to function more effectively with a client which can be an individual, group or organization for which they have responsibility. (Brown, Pryzwansky, & Schulte, 2001, p. 6)

School consultation is a voluntary process in which one professional assists another to address a problem concerning a third party. (Friend & Cook, 2003, p. 151)

Definitions/descriptions of *collaboration*:

Interpersonal collaboration is a style for direct interaction between at least two coequal parties voluntarily engaged in shared decision making as they work toward a common goal. (Friend & Cook, 2003, p. 5)

Collaboration involves interaction between two or more equal parties who voluntarily share decision making in working toward a common goal. (Fishbaugh, 1997, p. 6)

Effective collaboration consists of designing and using a sequence of goal-oriented activities that result in improved working relationships between professional colleagues. (Cramer, 1998, p. 6)

Definitions/descriptions of *collaborative consultation*:

Collaborative school consultation is interaction in which school personnel and families confer, consult, and collaborate as a team to identify learning and behavioral needs, and to plan, implement, evaluate, and revise as needed the educational programs for serving those needs. (Dettmer, Dyck, & Thurston, 1999, p. 6)

Collaborative consultation is an interactive process that enables groups of people with diverse expertise to generate creative solutions to mutually defined problems. The outcome is enhanced and altered from original solutions that group members tend to produce independently. (Idol, Nevin, & Paolucci-Whitcomb, 2000, p. 1)

ACTIVITY 1.1

Speak to several people outside your field of professional interest, asking them what images or expectations come to mind when they hear the word *consultant.* What percentage of people use the word *expert?* How often do they mention the concept of collaboration? Also, ask people in public schools to define *consultation.* What is their image of what a consultant does, or should do?

ACTIVITY 1.2

After reviewing the definitions of consultation and collaboration in this chapter, identify the key activities that are common to both, and ways in which they appear to be different.

COLLABORATIVE CONSULTATION AS AN EXPANDED ROLE

Collaboration and consultation are not necessarily interchangeable because consultation is not always collaborative. Consultation is a generic term, defined, as we have previously seen, with some variations in emphasis or style but generally consistent with the *Webster's* definition.

Brown et al. (2001) suggest that it may be inappropriate to use the two terms to refer to the same process since a common meaning of collaboration includes the fact that two or more people provide direct service, whereas consultation traditionally is considered an indirect service. I believe that both terms have evolved sufficiently to allow them to be used together, with the collaborative part referring to mutual problem solving by equal partners and the consultation part referring to the fact that the central purpose of the activity is to provide improved service to a third party, the student. Whether or not the person identified as the consultant actually does some part of the direct service to the client seems moot. Pryzwansky (1977) has described a model (referred to as collaboration) wherein the consultee and the consultant assume joint responsibility for all aspects of the process, including shared implementation. Actually, in school consultation, the consultee usually does most of the in-classroom or on-the-playground implementation, and the parent as consultee does most of the at-home implementation. This reality fits the concept of collaborative consultation described herein, as well as the author's definition of collaborative consultation previously presented.

Collaboration refers to a very specific kind of consultation, one characterized by "a reciprocal arrangement between individuals with diverse expertise to define problems and develop solutions mutually" (Pugach & Johnson, 1988, p. 3), and defined as egalitarian and nonhierarchical by this author. Defined in this way, collaboration may seem very different from forms of consultation practiced in the business, medical, or military arenas because it is not necessary in collaborative consultation that any one person is the expert. This is true because collaborative consultation takes place between or among two or more people, with the role of expert shifting periodically among the participants. For example, a Student Study Team (SST) meeting might involve the regular education teacher as an expert in curriculum and teaching method, the counselor as an expert in explaining how a student's approach to tasks stems from family and cultural dynamics, the psychologist or special education teacher as an expert in suggesting a contingency reinforcement plan or a memory-enhancing system or a teaching approach that the teacher might use to increase content retention, the student's mother as an expert in reviewing how she assists and encourages the student with his academic work, and the student as an expert in reviewing his interests and preferred learning styles and reinforcers. As these participants collaborate with one another in understanding a problem and designing a program, they are sharing their expertise, with each party contributing a varying amount depending on the nature of the referral.

This philosophy also extends to plan implementation. Although the primary person carrying out the plan is usually the classroom teacher, either general or special education, the other team members contribute their expertise in ways appropriate to their training and experience. In the case just described, plan implementation might involve the counselor working with the parents in regard to family dynamics, the psychologist or special education teacher observing the general education teacher's approach in order to provide feedback, and the student contributing by self-monitoring and helping the consultee fine-tune the classroom reinforcement system. This example demonstrates how expertise and mutual assistance are the two major components of a consultation model that has come to be known as collaborative (Friend & Cook, 2003; Idol, 1990; Idol et al. 2000). Throughout this book there are many other examples of how this model can be effective with a wide variety of school referral problems.

Figure 1.2 gives a personal view of the author regarding the collaborative consultation method.

Figure 1.2

Collaborative consultation: Rationale, limitations, and suggestions—a personal view

In my way of conducting collaborative consultation, I give a lot of emphasis to the possibility that the consultee can, and should be strongly encouraged to, think through their own ideas as to how to solve the referral problems. This may not seem feasible. After all, if the consultee knew a solution to his referral question, why wouldn't he just implement it and save time and energy? Also, if the consultee's referral has been sent to you for your assistance, doesn't he have a right to expect that you will have, and impart to him, expert knowledge?

My experience has taught me that consultees, both teachers and parents, when faced with relatively difficult problems in learning and/or behavior, sometimes get confused, or stuck, in their thinking. They probably have tried some solutions, and when these haven't worked, they've experienced some level of doubt regarding their usually dependable problem-solving strategies, and they feel as though they don't know what to do next. Or, they have an idea but they just aren't sure about it, and they would like to discuss their idea with someone else. This someone else becomes their consultant. Hopefully, this person will acknowledge the consultee's experience and expertise by doing at least these two things:

1. Ask the consultee to review what she has done to improve the situation so far, and how these efforts have worked.

2. Encourage the consultee to tell the consultant what she (the consultee) wants to do next. Use such questions as "Given what you've told me, and in light of your understanding of the problem at this time, what would you like to try next?" "You've tried a number of things so far. What are you thinking of doing tomorrow?" "So far you've felt like what you've tried just hasn't been the best solution. What's next? What do you want to try now?"

I refer to this effort at intervention development by consultees as the ACCEPT method, ACCEPT being an acronym that acknowledges the consultant's philosophy about the consultee's contributions, and stands for the following behaviors, which, to me, are at the heart of collaborative consultation:

A *Acknowledging* the consultee's predominant role in carrying out the planned interventions, usually in his classroom (or home), in the context of that setting, and in his style.

C *Commenting* positively on the efforts the consultee has made to date in trying to solve the problem, and the effort he is expending now on behalf of the student.

C *Convincing* the consultee that he has good ideas to offer, and that you, the consultant, would like to hear them.

E *Expecting* that the consultee will take the lead in the development of ideas if encouraged to do so, and expecting that the consultee will give equal weight to the consultant's ideas.

P *Pointing* out possibilities for effective interventions based on the consultee's ideas. This involves taking his ideas and helping him think through the pros and cons of these ideas and the details of implementation. In this way, you provide your content expertise in the context of his ideas. When collaborative consultation is working well, the consultant's role is that of *facilitator* of the consultee's ideas.

Figure 1.2 *continued*

T *Treating* him as an equal. One of the hallmarks of a collaborative model is that it brings adults together in an atmosphere of mutual respect. Both are equally expert, both need help from the other, and both give ideas and contribute to the final solutions.

LIMITS TO A COLLABORATIVE CONSULTATION MODEL:
This model does not always work as planned. Some consultees seem bereft of ideas, or appear to be too irritated by the problem to be able to think clearly. Some get in a punishment mode, particularly in regard to serious behavior problems, and they are not able to think positively. Some think only of ways of reacting to a referred student rather than more systemically. Some always prefer to think that someone else (e.g., special education, or a more restrictive setting) should take over the student and solve his problem that way. Others are simply deferential to the consultant; they cannot get over the "consultant-as-expert" idea. They assume it's easier to get you to solve the problem, to determine the interventions and their implementation. That way, if it doesn't work, guess who's to blame? Lastly, some are too inexperienced, or at least act that way, and they simply need more direct help.

SUGGESTIONS:
Collaborative consultation sometimes seems to break down because the ideas from the consultee are inappropriate in some way. Some teachers and parents have only a limited number of ideas for intervention. When you sense that this is true, the collaboratively oriented consultant most certainly can suggest interventions. My opinion is that it is best to come up with two or three viable interventions, based on "best practices," and to ask the consultee what s/he thinks of each of them. Which of the ideas is s/he attracted to? Which does s/he seem able and willing to do? The interventions you suggest should meet at least the following criteria:

1. *Treatment acceptability:* If the consultee doesn't accept an intervention as something she is willing to do, you either have to be a good salesperson and convince her of its merits through the use of social influence (Erchul & Martens, 2002), or try to modify it. The teacher may agree to try the intervention (possibly under duress), give it a half-hearted try, claim it didn't work (it probably didn't), and require you to come up with another idea. You never know what interventions meet the criteria of treatment acceptability until you suggest them. What you do know is that if the intervention is not acceptable to the person who is to implement it, it is not likely that it will ever be implemented as intended.
2. *Treatment validity:* Is there research support for the idea? "Best practices" are those that have at least some degree of support, either from the literature or from your own experience or knowledge base.

3. *Treatment ethics:* The concern here is about the appropriateness of an intervention from the standpoint of the students' best interests; their dignity as people; probable benefits versus risks; and an orientation toward replacement of, rather than suppression of, challenging behaviors.
4. *Treatment integrity (fidelity):* Was the treatment implemented correctly? This, of course, won't be known until the treatment is tried.
5. *Treatment effectiveness:* Is the treatment working? By what standards? Does it need to be changed? Again, these answers aren't known until the treatment has been tried for sufficient time to determine its effectiveness.

It is also important to stick to the referral and not to wander off in other directions. It may be tempting to think that a given consultee needs help in many areas of which s/he may not be aware. Except in serious cases (abusive behavior toward students; chaotic, dangerous classroom management practices; personal problems that are impacting the classroom), it is best to establish well-defined goals relative to the referral problem and work toward solving them and let other issues emerge as the consultee feels the necessity for dealing with them. Remember that change is difficult; overwhelming a consultee with your ideas about how to make the classroom or home perfect may be regarded as intrusive and perhaps overwhelming. No one wants assistance from an intrusive person who wants to tell other people what to do. Do a good job helping the consultee with his current concerns and he will get back to you later about other things, or you can bring them up at some later point.

Last, but nonetheless important, consider the role of family and culture. Interventions that are selected need to be sensitive to the student's cultural background. This issue is discussed in more depth later in this chapter.

RECENT CHANGES IN EDUCATION AFFECTING SCHOOL CONSULTATION

During the 1990s and into the 21st century it has become clear that a team approach to assisting all students to become better learners has become part of a national effort known as *reform* or *restructuring*. National leaders have formulated three major reform statements: *America 2000, Goals 2000,* and the *No Child Left Behind* Act. The first of these was proposed by the first Bush administration (1991) and consisted of six goals:

1. By the year 2000, every child in the United States will begin school ready to learn.
2. High school graduation rates in the United States will increase to at least 90% by the year 2000.
3. All students in 4th, 8th, and 12th grades will be tested for progress in key subjects.
4. U.S. students will rank first in the world in science and mathematics achievement.

5. Every adult will be a skilled, literate worker and citizen.
6. Every school will be drug-free and will provide a climate in which learning can occur.

Many people welcomed these goals from our national leaders but were concerned that they might prove to be only rhetoric because the terms used in them were not specifically defined (e.g., "...will begin school ready to learn"), no explicit promise for funding was attached to them, nor did they address specifics about how to overcome the daunting problems still in existence when they were written (Halpern, 1992; Howe, 1991).

In 1994 President Clinton signed a federal school reform package (*Goals 2000*) that consisted of the same six goals plus two others:

1. The teaching force will have access to programs for continued self-improvement of professional skills.
2. Every school will promote partnerships that increase parent involvement and participation.

This more-inclusive version of national standards is monitored by the National Educational Goals Panel and the National Council on Education Standards and Testing. The panel consists of government officials, both federal and state; the council is composed of government officials as well as leaders from business, education, and other arenas. Title III of the 1994 legislation provides funding in the form of federal grants to the states for reform efforts designed to meet the eight goals (Shriner, Ysseldyke, & Thurlow, 1996).

In January 2002, President George W. Bush signed into law the No Child Left Behind (NCLB) Act, another far-reaching piece of federal legislation (U.S. Department of Education, 2002). It is essentially a reauthorization of the Elementary and Secondary Education Act of 1965. Its requirements include annual testing in reading and math of all students in grades 3 through 8, and the provision of additional funds to support schools that are underachieving in a consistent pattern. It has particular relevance for students with disabilities because of its requirements that these students participate in the "high-stakes" testing that is required by this Act.

All this federal interest in our public schools stems from the fact that many Americans, both in and out of government, are concerned about problems that seem to be increasing: declining SAT scores, lowered international opinion about our graduates and their ability to compete in a global marketplace, increased drug use, gang activity, violence invading the schools, and an increase in students who are at risk for school failure and lifelong economic and personal–social problems (California Department of Justice, 1993; Chicago Public Schools, 1994). Educators know that lofty goals from the federal level do not necessarily lead to meaningful change at the local school level. It is still up to the local level to provide the planning that will earn the federal money and the implementation that will result in an effective use of the money.

In addition to this federal concern with reform in general education, there has also been a steady stream of interest in strengthening legislation specific to special education. In November, 2004, a bipartisan House-Senate committee gave approval to revisions to the Individual with Disabilities Education Act of 1997 (P.L. 105-17). Although most provisions of P.L. 105-17 will remain intact, there have been some important changes that are of specific interest to school consultants, such as the following:

- Districts will no longer be required to establish a discrepancy between ability and achievement for the determination of a specific learning disability. They will have the option of utilizing a "problem-solving" method that depends on a student's response to "...scientific, research-based intervention as part of the evaluation procedures...." This provision will prove to be very significant in the activities of school consultants who will be expected to know about these interventions and how to implement them in general education settings.
- In regard to each student's IEP, it is no longer required to establish short-term objectives, unless the student is severely disabled. It is anticipated that many districts will continue to use some form of short-term objectives on students' IEPs. The goals and objectives help give direction to the ways that consultants can be of assistance to teachers in terms of methods, curriculum, reinforcement systems, parental support, and classroom management issues.
- The new IDEA makes a very clear statement about the role of consultation, especially as it applies to working with teachers who have students who are at risk for learning or behavior-social-interpersonal problems. In section 602 the new IDEA states: "...the term 'consultative services' means services that adjust the learning environment, modify instructional methods, adapt curricula, use positive behavioral supports and interventions, and select and implement appropriate accommodations to meet the needs of individual children."

Whatever the specific area of concern (curriculum, behavior problems, cultural diversity, physical-plant use, expertise sharing, decision-making systems, materials sharing, and so on), all can be discussed in an atmosphere that encourages shared problem solving. The older top-down, hierarchical, authoritarian administrative models are mostly passé. The challenge now is for educators, including teachers, ancillary staff, and administration, to realize that the newer models of shared governance, site-based, community-organized, and collaborative schools are not easy to develop or implement; it takes a new degree of commitment and collaboration to make these models work.

DEFINING CHARACTERISTICS AND GOALS OF COLLABORATIVE CONSULTATION

The following assumptions about the nature and characteristics of collaborative consultation follow from the definition previously offered:

1. The consultant is a trained professional. Generally this includes such people as special education teachers, mentor teachers, school counselors, psychologists, and other nonschool personnel. It may of course refer to any person, including general education teachers, who perform the services indicated by the definition. Such individuals can appropriately serve as consultants in matters in which they have expertise, such as curriculum, teaching methods, and behavior management.

2. Authentic, honest communication is essential for successful consultation.

3. The nature of the referral problem influences the roles of the consultant and the consultee, and thus the process in which they engage. Chapter 2 lists consultants' roles and activities; it is common for practitioners to shift among them.

4. The consultant and the consultee both must make a valid effort to engage in the process if consultation is to occur. The ultimate power in the consultation process rests with the consultee since she is primarily responsible for carrying out the jointly agreed-on interventions. The consultant's power is the ability to provide an objective analysis of the dynamics of the referral; to provide information useful in intervention design, monitoring, and evaluation; and in the utilization of interpersonal tactics designed to ensure consultee compliance with agreed-on interventions.

5. Task-content variables and the process of consultation interact and must be considered simultaneously. This is especially true in a collaborative consultation approach in which nonhierarchical, egalitarian positions are occupied by both the consultee and the consultant, who are both involved in idea generation within a problem-solving context.

6. Systemic variables impinge on the consultant, consultee, and student and must be considered as integral parts of the process. School consultants and consultees always operate within a larger set of variables, including not only legal and ethical codes but also societal expectations, cultural norms, district and school-level guidelines, and family concerns. Further, the interventions discussed, particularly at group meetings (SST, etc.), need to gain at least tacit approval from all constituents.

7. Consultation is governed by certain ethical guidelines that influence consultant roles as well as the process of consultation. Chapter 4 discusses ethical and advocacy issues in consultation. Practical examples demonstrating the influence of these factors appear in the case studies in Chapter 9.

8. There is an emphasis on observation and interview as assessment methods.

9. Collaborative consultation seeks solutions, not labels. While realizing that some students may benefit from special education and related services in specialized settings, most students who manifest learning and/or behavior or adjustment problems may benefit more in the long run from being maintained in the regular track with tailored and specified instruction and behavior management strategies that can be delivered by general educators with consultative help of those able to provide those services.

10. School consultants must be experts in process (the "how" of consultation; see Chapter 5), but not necessarily in all possible content (the actual interventions that are discussed and selected). This means that the collaboratively minded consultant must be adept at encouraging teachers and parents to develop plans and interventions that make sense in the context of the referral problem, and in light of the possibilities and constraints of their classrooms or homes. The consultant's job is to facilitate the thinking of these "primary care providers" (i.e., parents and teachers serving as consultees) so these individuals can feel empowered to carry out their ideas about how to best assist the student, under the guidance and encouragement of the consultant.

11. Occasionally consultees may bring information into the discussion that is more closely related to their personal lives and problems than to the learning or behavior problems of the referred student. The consultant has to be careful not to confuse the consultative relationship by taking on the role of a counselor to the consultee. Decisions about the relevance of any particular piece of information are not always easy to make, but it is usually best to gently steer the conversation back to the appropriate work-related problem. Of course, if the consultant perceives that the consultee does have a personal problem that should be dealt with, whether it is affecting the referral problem or not, she may refer the consultee to a resource where he can get whatever help is needed. Because it is possible for a consultee to have personal issues that interfere with his ability to view the referral problem objectively, the consultant may need to mention any concerns he has to the consultee in a helpful and positive way (Caplan & Caplan, 1993).

12. One goal of collaborative consultation is to improve the functioning of the student while enhancing the functioning of the consultee.

13. Another goal is to find ways to ensure student success in the general education classroom as often as possible.

14. Problem solving is the primary goal of consultation. Consultants are employed for the express purpose of solving the learning and behavior problems exhibited by schoolchildren. Generically, problem solving refers to a structured set of steps or procedures intended to assist the consultee in dealing with referred students (Dougherty, 2000). This process may take many forms or styles, depending on the nature of the problem, the philosophical beliefs of both consultant and consultee, the constraints or limitations of the setting, and so on. The steps in problem solving are discussed in detail in Chapter 5.

ACTIVITY 1.3

Discuss the characteristics and goals presented above in small groups. Do the groups believe these are essential characteristics and goals? What others might they add?

CONSULTATION AT DIFFERENT LEVELS OF PROBLEM SEVERITY

Caplan (1964) described three levels of intervention: primary (prevention), secondary (corrective), and tertiary (remedial). In the primary stage steps are taken to ensure that students are unlikely to develop learning or behavioral difficulties. Standards, appropriate curriculum and teaching methods, and interventions as common as classroom rules are all part of primary prevention. Examples of interventions at this level include Success for All (Slavin, Madden, Dolan, & Wasik, 1996), Project ACHIEVE (Knoff & Batsche, 1995), and First Step to Success (Walker, Kavanagh, Stiller, Golly, Severson, & Feil, 1997). Greenberg, Domitrovich, and Bumbarger (1999) have reviewed a number of primary mental health model programs.

Secondary refers to actions taken when a student appears to be having difficulties adapting to behavioral or academic expectations. Student Study Team (SST) meetings, parent conferences, in-class modifications, social skills training, specialized tutoring, and other mild forms of intervention are common during this stage. Referral to special education services may also occur here, but this should be suggested only after the full range of services possible in the general education classroom have been attempted and found insufficient.

In the tertiary level the referral problems are very serious; major steps need to be taken (e.g., special education eligibility, possible service delivery in settings other than general education, suspensions). Those concerned with the student's welfare need to consult with each other and collaboratively develop plans that are in the best educational interest of the student. Wraparound services (Eber, Nelson, & Miles, 1997) that involve out-of-school agencies such as community mental health, respite services, and social services are an example of collaborative efforts at the tertiary level.

In a school setting, most referrals for consultant assistance are either secondary or tertiary, which is unfortunate. More emphasis on preventive programs, especially for students who are at risk, has been recommended in the human services field for decades (Meyers & Nastasi, 1999). However, pressures to deal with currently severe problems, combined with inadequate staffing ratios, have slowed the impetus to a prevention-oriented service delivery approach. Bergan (1995) comments that this may be true partly because no specific funding exists for consultation (or primary prevention) services while funds do exist for placing and supporting students in special education services.

Once plans for any of the three levels have been developed and are being implemented, the role of the collaborative consultant becomes largely one of monitor and evaluator. The teacher or parent consultee will need some assistance in the area of treatment integrity (Gresham, 1989; Witt, 1990), and possibly treatment ethics. Ongoing evaluations of the effectiveness of the interventions are also necessary.

ACTIVITY 1.4

Reflect on your experiences in the school. How were interventions for students with disabilities and other at-risk students developed? Who monitored their implementation? How were they evaluated? Did these processes seem well-structured or rather casual?

THE TRIADIC NATURE OF CONSULTATION

The most common form of consultation in schools consists of interactions among a consultant, the consultee(s), and a student. As Figure 1.3 shows, the consultant and the consultee freely interact in a nonhierarchical, reciprocal relationship. To some extent this reciprocity can also occur between the consultee and the student, although a teacher–student relationship usually is more constrained than the one that should exist between the consultant and the consultee. However, the consultant may

Figure 1.3
The triadic nature of consultation

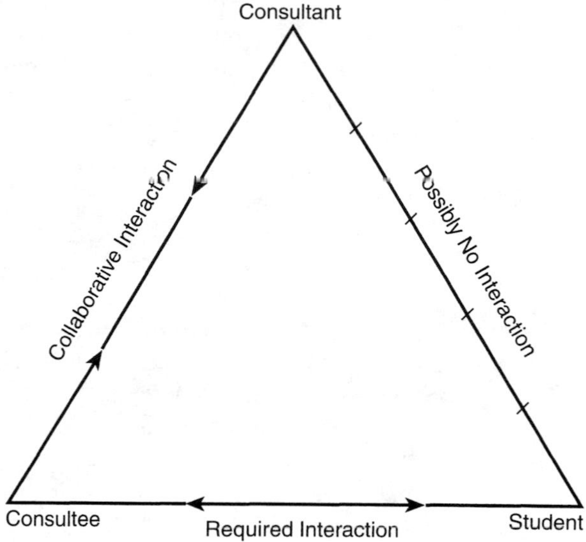

never have any direct interaction with the student. Because of this, consultation is usually considered an indirect service. It may occur, however, that in collaborative planning between the consultee and the consultant, some type or degree of direct interaction between the consultant and the student may occur, such as co-teaching, tutoring, or counseling. In the vignette in the beginning of the chapter, Mrs. Jones asks the consultant for help in dealing with a student. Because the teacher has presented a poorly defined problem, the consultant may spend considerable time talking with Mrs. Jones but may never talk with or observe the student. It is certainly possible, and in most cases desirable, for the consultant to have some degree of relationship with the student, if only to observe her in the classroom or on the playground. It is not, however, necessary.

THE ROLE OF PROCESS AND CONTENT EXPERTISE IN CONSULTATION

People in general usually relate the concept or practice of consultation to activities carried out by skilled businesspeople, engineers, and medical professionals, and the public tends to think of consultation in terms of expertness. In the business world, a consultant may be hired to solve a particularly tricky problem in production, merchandising, or taxes. The hiring firm expects that the consultant will have expertise in the area and will come up with a solution that has a good chance of working well. For this level of "expert consultation," business executives expect to pay well (Lippitt & Lippitt, 1986).

One might expect that successful consultants working in the schools with teachers and parents should also adopt a stance of expertise. I take the position that expertness should be expected in the area of *process* and that it is highly desirable but not sufficient in the area of *content*. By process, I mean the interactions that occur between the consultant and the consultees through which a behavior or a learning problem is approached and solved; it is concerned with *how one acts* as a consultant. Content refers to the actual ideas that the consultees will implement, such as a contract method, cooperative learning, a parent conference, or the use of stickers or stars as reinforcers; it represents *what people will do* as a result of consultation. Collaborative consultation requires expertise in process; without such expertise, the process disintegrates, resistance increases, and consultees become dissatisfied with the consultative approach for dealing with their needs as teachers. As indicated by the definitions and discussion previously presented, the collaborative approach depends on a degree of mutual expertise in problem solving, resulting in content decisions that are jointly generated and approved by both the consultant and the consultee(s) within a nonhierarchical, reciprocal relationship (Friend & Cook, 2003; Idol et al., 2000).

Among human services personnel, particularly in the schools, there is a general consensus that the expert model, defined as one in which a consultant, sometimes from outside the local school or district, unilaterally decides which interventions would be most appropriate for a teacher or parent to use, has limitations that make it less than ideal. For example, an outsider (unlike a business consultant) cannot always indicate the best way to solve a problem because the outsider may not understand the interpersonal, ecological, and other dynamics that exist in a school or a school district. Further, in both schools and the business world, people tend to be more likely to implement changes that they have been involved in discussing and creating (Comer, 1993; Heron & Harris, 2001; Rappaport, 1981; Weiss, 1993).

ACTIVITY 1.5

Discuss the role of process versus content. Do you think a school consultant needs to have a set of interventions for every problem or issue a teacher or parent can describe? How might you deal with a consultee who insists on your having answers for every problem?

FREQUENTLY ASKED QUESTIONS ABOUT SCHOOL CONSULTATION

What Direct and/or Indirect Benefits Can Be Expected from the Consultation Model Discussed in This Text?

A number of benefits can accrue from a consultation-based service delivery program. Direct benefits include the following:

- The development of closer working relationships between general and special educators and others who serve in a collaborative consultant mode.
- The assistance given to consultees in their efforts to deal with the learning and behavior difficulties that some students present.
- The generation of ideas that more readily occurs when two or more people are involved in problem solving.

- The improved services given to referred students that derives from the increased attention to academic and social needs, rather than placement-driven labels or categories.
- The likelihood that important underlying (often systemic) issues will be raised through the discussion of individual student problems.

Indirect benefits include the following:

- The learning that goes on while dealing with the needs of a referred student (which can often be used with other students).
- The information traded among consultees based on their experiences with the consultant.
- The development of teachers' beliefs that they are part of a communicating team of professionals, which alleviates one of the more common causes of teacher stress—the feeling that teaching is an isolated profession.
- Potential spin-offs, such as the generation of ideas for inservice meetings or for development and implementation of school- or district-wide programs, or extra-district collaboratives (see Chapter 9).

Equivalent benefits can be observed when parents are involved as consultees. Directly, they can learn new ways of dealing with their child, have a chance to be heard by a professional from the school, and get to understand and contribute to the school's perspective on their child's problems and progress. Indirect benefits include less tension about child rearing, a feeling that the parents are considered part of the solution instead of part of the problem, and a chance to build their repertoire of child-rearing skills (Bennett & Gibbons, 2000; Christenson, 1995; Turnbull & Turnbull, 1997).

Why Is Collaborative Consultation Replacing Expert Models of Consultation?

During the past 20 years there has been an increase in the use of collaborative consultation in the schools. Idol et al. (2000) indicate that the term *collaborative consultation* was first used by them (Idol, Poalucci-Whitcomb, & Nevin, 1986) to refer to a model of consultative interactions that are not so much dependent on the superior knowledge base of the consultant as they are on shared expertise, a confluence of ideas generated in an atmosphere of nonhierarchical cooperation. As such they were utilizing the concept of empowerment (Dunst & Trivette, 1987; Rappaport, 1981), which posits that change is most likely to occur when it comes from the ideas and experiences of those closest to the problem and those most likely to implement whatever changes (i.e., interventions) are proposed. Erchul and Martens (2002) point out that a philosophy of empowerment "...relates to the belief that consultees already possess many basic strengths and eventually will solve their own problems if the consultant helps them develop those strengths by alerting consultees to existing resources and how they may be used" (pp. 26–27).

This is not to imply that the collaboratively oriented school consultant does not need knowledge about teaching methods, curriculum, behavior management, disabilities, culture, and a host of other areas that interact in the process of teaching. What it does imply is that the consultant does not need to act like the "expert" who is there to tell a teacher or parent what to do, without considering the opinions and ideas of these individuals. As the information in Figure 1.2 indicates, there are exceptions to this general rule of practice, especially occurring with new teachers or those who are unable to think of interventions that are likely to be successful. In these instances the collaborative consultant adopts more of the expert stance and suggests possible interventions.

What Is the Present Status of Collaborative Consultation in the Schools?

One of the reasons consultation is emerging slowly is the usual reason for the slowness of change in schools and other large-scale bureaucratic organizations: habit strength. In regard to an approach to responding to the needs of students referred for learning and/or behavior problems, there are many who continue to prefer the long-established model of refer-test-place, which has dominated the special education–general education partnership for many years (Ysseldyke, 1986). In the refer-test-place model, a student is referred, and some degree of effort is made to resolve the problem through suggestions generated by the Student Study Team. A period of time goes by, during which the problem doesn't resolve easily, and the team decides to generate an assessment plan to determine if the student is eligible for services as a student with a disability. The most likely category the student will be eligible for is learning disabilities, simply because it comprises 50% of those eligible for special education services (U.S. Department of Education, 2002), and the odds are about three out of four that if an assessment plan is generated and the assessment takes place the student will be found eligible for such services (Ysseldyke, 1986; Ysseldyke, Vanderwood, & Shriner, 1997). The student will most likely be given services in a Special Education Resource Room program for one or two periods a day with unpredictable results. One of the goals of the collaborative consultation movement is to dramatically change this picture. This text, along with those of Dettmer et al. (1999), Friend and Cook (2003), Heron and Harris (2001), and Idol et al. (2000), among others, advocate for a different approach, one where the process of collaborative consultation assumes a much stronger role, with the goals being to forestall placements outside the general education track as often as possible and to increase both special and general educators' ability and willingness to accommodate to the needs of at-risk students through jointly designed interventions. In this way the practice of collaborative consultation may serve to enhance the probability of there one day being one system of education for all students instead of the two-tiered (general and special education) system that has prevailed for so long (Stainback, Stainback, & Forest, 1989; Wang, Reynolds, & Walberg, 1986; Will, 1986; Ysseldyke & Marston, 1999).

Another reason that prevents this model from being fully utilized is that it requires changing to a system that might involve relatively prolonged, intensive efforts to accommodate to students' needs with interventions at the general education classroom level. To some teachers, administrators, and parents, this seems unnecessarily burdensome and possibly futile. The fairly well-ingrained idea that special education is good for students with mild to moderate levels of disability is difficult to overcome. The relative lack of evidence for the success of pullout programs (Affleck, Madge, Adams, & Lowenbraun, 1988; Dunn, 1968; Powers, 2001; Reynolds, 1989; Wang et al., 1986) is not acknowledged; habits resist incompatible data.

Last, since there is no one way to practice consultation, it is not clear what a person means by consultation until she describes it in some detail or you see her doing it. Current practice varies across a wide range of philosophies, roles, and activities. The different models discussed in Chapter 2 indicate some of the variations currently practiced in the schools.

RESEARCH ON THE EFFECTIVENESS OF SCHOOL CONSULTATION

Another possible reason consultation is somewhat slow to emerge as a dominant model of service delivery is because of the limited amount of compelling research evidence that supports it. The problem isn't due to a paucity of research studies. Brown et al. (2001) indicate that from 1978 to 1985 about 173 data-based consultation studies were referenced in *Psychological Abstracts*. Idol et al. (2000) studied more recent articles having to do only with collaborative consultation between the years of 1994 to 1997 and found 52 studies, 26 of which were research based. Most of these studies yielded positive results. Gutkin and Curtis (1999) reviewed a number of consultation studies conducted primarily in the areas of school psychology and special education, most of which reported at least partially successful outcomes.

There is evidence that districts that have adopted a consultation-based approach to dealing with referrals, rather than a refer-test-place model, place fewer students in special education separate classroom programs (Villa, Thousand, Nevin, & Malgeri, 1996). Gutkin, Henning-Stout, and Piersel (1988), in one of the few long-term studies of the effects of consultation as an intermediate step in the referral process, found that referred children who were not evaluated for special eduation rose from 21 to 61% during the 4 years of their study. Meta-analytic studies of consultation effectiveness, aside from their effects on reducing the need for separate special education services, have been provided by Sibley (1986, reviewed in Gresham & Noell, 1993) and Busse, Kratochwill, and Elliott (1995). In both reviews students served by consultees involved in experimental (i.e., structured, data-oriented) studies improved considerably more than did control students.

Researchers and authorities agree that the research base demonstrating the effectiveness of consultation is not yet secure. Gresham and Kendell (1987), for example, point out that the amount of research is certainly not adequate and that most of it does not address real needs or practices of school-based consultants. This may be due to the fact that many practitioners do not read the literature to learn what the research demonstrates. Moreover, the abstract and sometimes artificial nature of research (e.g., analogue studies) leads consultants and consultees to doubt its practicality in determining what they should do in real cases.

Hughes (1994) summarizes her concern about the research base by noting that the question "Does consultation work?" should be replaced with a more refined question, such as "What consultation approaches result in what effects with which clients and consultees?" (Hughes, 1994, p. 82). We could add: "And do these effects hold up over time?"

Gutkin (1993a) indicates that most of the research literature is based on what graduate students, acting in a consultation role, do in contrived situations (Pryzwansky, 1986). Gutkin comments, "Consistent with Gendlin's suggestion that we create a 'bank of clearly successful cases' (1986, p. 131) as a means for improving the psychotherapy research literature, a parallel data base of successful consultation interactions would likewise be extremely useful. Case studies and small-n methodologies would seem to be the keys to reaching this modest but important goal" (Gutkin, 1993b, p. 238). As Robbins and Gutkin (1994) note, "...consultation research will have to focus intensively on the outcomes of live, field-based consultation interventions rather than analogue and laboratory studies" (p. 150).

This book includes cases for analysis that somewhat meet Gendlin's (1986) call for "a bank of ... cases." As you will find, neither of the cases presented in Chapter 9 of this text are "clearly successful." Success is an elastic term that stretches from total to partial. The cases in this book demonstrate that range of success and clarify why some cases are more successful than others.

The search for the keys to effectiveness in consultation continues. Periodicals such as *Journal of Educational and Psychological Consultation, Exceptional Children, School Psychology Review, Journal of Learning Disabilities, Professional Psychology, Journal of Special Education, Remedial and Special Education, Teaching Exceptional Children, Journal of Counseling and Development, The Professional Counselor, Journal of School Psychology,* and *School Psychology Quarterly* contain articles devoted to the scientific study of all aspects of consultation, including process and outcome studies.

ACTIVITY 1.6

How might you structure a research study to answer some questions you have about consultation? What are some unresolved issues that need more research? Why is meaningful research on consultation difficult to do?

ACTIVITY 1.7

Working in pairs, set up a data-based research study with one teacher as the consultee and one target student. Use either an academic or behavioral issue. State your goal(s), define your terms operationally, and determine your data-gathering methods.

TREATING CONSULTEES AS ADULTS

Beginning school-based consultants need to learn that consulting with adults in the schools, as well as parents of referred students, is very different from and often more challenging than working directly with students. Successful consultants learn to appreciate that adult consultees differ in learning styles, willingness to participate in the process, ability to carry out plans, and perspectives on problems. As the two vignettes in the beginning of this chapter suggest (and as the case studies in Chapter 9 show in detail), the school consultant must be ready to deal with many different types of consultees among both teachers and parents. The ability to understand the consultee in the same way that a teacher or assessor tries to understand a student may determine a consultant's degree of success. Having all the expert content knowledge in the world in the areas of curriculum, teaching methods, and behavior management is of no use if the consultant does not know how to relate it to the consultee as an adult learner–collaborator.

Adults prefer to be self-directed; they do not want or expect to be told what to do unless they directly ask for this assistance. They prefer to be active contributors to the interactive process known as consultation; they do not prefer to be passive participants mandated to accept transmitted expertise from others (Cobern, 1993). Adults prefer to believe that they are able to solve their own problems with some facilitative (collaborative) help from the consultant. Unlike students, adults have real experiences as teachers or parents and have developed a frame of reference that they bring into a consultative relationship. This experience, coupled with the nature of the student's need and the approach of the consultant, determines how consultees want to solve the problem. Installed, other-directed solutions that fail to consider a consultee's experience, position, and points of view may gain surface acquiescence and possibly admiration but may also be honored in promises rather than execution.

A consultee's ownership of a possible solution drives her desire to make it successful (Rappaport, 1981). The consultant may actually direct how the consultee sees the problem and what should be done about it. However, whether or not consultees carry out the plan may depend on the consultant's skill in getting them to believe that they have had a central voice in the problem's conceptualization and solution.

Brown et al. (1995) give an example of a statement that a collaboratively oriented consultant might make to a parent consultee as an overture for collaboration:

Consultant: It is important for you to recognize how important you are in this process. Sometimes people involved in consulting relationships look to the consultant for "answers" and when they do that, they disregard their own ability and knowledge. My view of consultation is that we are equals. As parents, you know your child far better than I can and that knowledge is far more important in the success of this process than all the things I've learned about children. But if we combine the things I've learned about working with children with what you know about your own child, then I am confident that our work together can be successful. (p. 213)

This introductory comment is designed to free the parent consultee to be an active participant in the process; it empowers them to rely on their own good sense and knowledge of their child as they collaborate in the development of interventions.

Expectations and Preferences of Consultees

Two variables that consultees bring to the process of consultation are their *expectations* and *preferences* (Brown et al., 2001). *Expectations* are what a person believes is likely to happen in a given situation. What does a consultee expect to happen in consultation? Naturally, this varies among consultees. Sources of this variation include preconceived notions, recent experiences, overheard experiences of other consultees, and basic personality factors such as openness and optimism. Hughes, Grossman, and Barker (1990) found a significant relationship between elementary teachers' outcome expectancies and their subsequent positive evaluation of consultation, suggesting the need for establishing positive expectations as a foundation for beginning the consultation process.

Preferences are what a consultee wants to happen, which may not be the same as what he believes will happen. There is some evidence that teacher consultees have preferences about how they want to be worked with in consultation. Wenger (1979) and Hughes and DeForest (1993) report that teachers prefer collaborative methods to expert-oriented consultation. Weiler (1984) has found the same result when parents are the consultees. Morrison, Walker, Wakefield, and Solberg (1994), in a study that divided teacher consultees according to experience (preservice versus experienced) and level (elementary versus secondary), found that elementary and preservice secondary teachers prefer a collaborative approach to consultation, whereas experienced secondary teachers prefer to work alone in solving classroom problems. Most of the interactions indicate a preference for collaboration or independent solution generation rather than an expert model. Further evidence in favor of a collaborative approach is provided by Erchul, Hughes, Meyers, Hickman, and Braden (1992). They found that if a consultee and consultant saw themselves as a team, consultation was perceived to be beneficial, consultees saw themselves as being more competent and effective, and they perceived better client improvement than did those consultees who did not feel they were part of an effective team.

ACTIVITY 1.8

As an adult person, how do you like to be approached regarding a work-related issue? Do you prefer that others tell you what to do, or would you rather figure out answers for yourself with or without the benefit of assistance from others? Are you more likely to implement your own ideas or those suggested to you by others?

Useful Generalizations About Working with Consultees

Experienced consultants have learned that despite differences across consultees, settings, types of referrals, and other variables than can affect consultation outcomes, there are some generalizations that should be understood and practiced by all consultants. In addition to the following seven generalizations, the reader can look to Dettmer et al. (1999) and Friend and Cook (2003) for many additional tips.

- *Make the consultee comfortable with you.* After a first consultation meeting he should be eager to participate in another. Chapter 3 delineates the communication and interpersonal skills that enhance this possibility.
- *Make it clear that you prefer to work collaboratively.* You should not tell the consultee what to do but should help him come up with practical solutions that have a high probability of success in his classroom or home. Be prepared to switch roles from time to time: Collaboration assumes that consultant and consultee may shift leadership roles in the development of interventions. Consultants need to listen to the expertise and ideas of the consultee to understand that person's point of view. When consultees believe that their ideas are important and are being considered, they are more likely to listen carefully to the consultant's ideas and are more likely to put the collaboratively developed ideas into practice. To assist in knowing whether an intervention is acceptable to a teacher–consultee, Witt and Elliott (1985) developed the Intervention Rating Profile, a 15-item scale designed to get teachers' opinions about the acceptability of proposed interventions. In order to measure the degree with which you are utilizing a collaborative approach, Erchul (1987) provided the Consultant Evaluation Form, a 12-question rating form that includes items pertaining to collaboration in the consultant–consultee interaction.

  The following is a possible way to introduce the idea of collaborative consultation to a consultee with whom you have not previously worked.

  > "Hello, Mr. Sanchez, I'm Ms. Washington. I'm the new resource teacher here at ABC School. I'm pleased to meet you. I know you want to tell me about Isaiah, and I'm eager to get going with our discussion also, but I'd like to start by mentioning two important items. The first has to do with the way I like to be of assistance as a consultant. I prefer to work in what is known as a collaborative model. By this I mean that we problem solve together and try to come up with interventions that are appropriate for your classroom. I'm not the expert, by any means; in fact, in your classroom, you're the expert. I'm here primarily to get your insights and ideas about the problems and possible solutions. Through our discussions, I'm sure we can come up with some good ideas.
  >
  > Now, the other thing I need to mention is confidentiality. When I work with consultees in the schools, I regard everything they tell me as confidential; that is, it stays between us. I don't talk to the principal or other teachers about the details of our discussions or about what I observe in your classroom. You, however, are free to tell anyone else about our work together. Naturally, in team meetings we will both be sharing information we have discussed about Isaiah and other students. There are only three exceptions to

this confidentiality: If you tell me about anyone who is being abused, is abusing others, or is threatening others, I am obligated to report it. Is this information clear? Do you have any questions? No? Okay, let's start with you telling me about Isaiah. I'll be keeping notes just to help me keep the facts straight."

- *Don't waste people's time.* Most school-based consultation sessions need to occur in 10 to 15 minutes because teachers are too busy to devote much more than that amount of time to a single consultative meeting. Brown et al. and Schulte (2001) describe the 15-minute consultation, acknowledging that school-based consultants do not have the luxury of time available to consultants in the business world. Exceptions may occur during a first meeting (when a student's background is reviewed), when the consultant is engaged in a group consultation regarding a particularly difficult situation (perhaps as part of an SST or IEP meeting), or when the consultant is doing system-improvement work. Longer sessions may also occur with parents.
- *Think constantly about solutions.* Some consultants take pleasure in "admiring the problem"—acting as if the problem is amazing, inexplicable, or even amusing. They shake their heads and make mouth noises that punctuate the seriousness of the problem while stalling for time in hopes that someone else will solve the problem or it will go away. A competent consultant categorizes the nature of the problem, gathers the necessary data, synthesizes the information, and then leads the consultee to consider strategies for intervention. These activities represent the "directive" nature of collaborative consultation, and emphasize a problem-solving and solutions-based approach.
- *Try to get inside the consultee's world.* Observation in a classroom, a playground, or a lunchroom can give the consultant a good picture of the setting of the problem and may lead to a focused discussion of practical interventions. It also shows consultees that the consultant is really interested in seeing the problem from their perspective—in other words, "walking in their shoes."
- *Make every effort to understand the current pressures on teacher and parent consultees.* Americans demand more from their public schools every day. The constant cry for accountability, tougher standards, more discipline, higher technology, and (for students with disabilities) greater opportunities for mainstreaming and inclusion can easily overwhelm even experienced teachers (Harvard School of Education, 1993; Johnson & Johnson, 1980; National Council on Education Standards and Testing, 1992; Stainback et al. 1989). Sensitivity to a teacher's burden of stress is certainly necessary.
- *Stay with the situation until it is resolved.* A competent consultant knows that problems are rarely solved after one consultation session. Often the first session is devoted to establishing rapport, discussing how to think about the problem, considering what data to gather and how to gather it, reviewing the student's history, and discussing tentative solutions. This session does not usually involve the development of substantive or final solutions to the problem. Follow-through is necessary. One of the requirements of most initial consultation sessions is that the consultant and consultee set another time to meet again for

further discussion. The exception is when the situation is finally resolved to everyone's satisfaction or when there is mutual agreement that it might be best to put the case aside for a while.

CONSULTATION IN CULTURALLY AND LINGUISTICALLY DIVERSE SETTINGS

The public schools in early 21st-century America are increasingly characterized by diversity. In many urban and some suburban areas, Caucasian students are no longer the majority they were 50 years ago. Thus, schools have had to reconsider some of the basic ideas that have sustained them throughout their history and come to grips with the new America. It has been estimated (Gonzalez, Brusca-Vega, & Yawkey, 1997) that by the year 2050, only 50% of the total population of the United States will be non-Hispanic whites. Eurocentrism, Americanization (a belief in the melting-pot idea associated with cultural homogeneity), and similar notions are giving way to a recognition of the positive values of multiculturalism, cultural pluralism, and bilingual education (Banks, 1993).

A growing literature relates consultation to multi- or crosscultural issues. Sue and Sue (1990) point out some of the ways in which people from different cultures react differently from one another—for example, in language (including paralanguage behaviors such as inflections, use of hands, loudness, and nonverbal communication), time orientation, and proxemics (personal space). Tobias (1993) warns against "Western chauvinism," a tendency for native-born Anglo-Americans to devalue or discredit the contributions, values, or abilities of those from other countries, ethnic groups, or cultures. Ingraham (2000) has developed a comprehensive conceptual framework for multicultural and crosscultural school consultation that considers cultural similarities and differences among consultants and consultees from different backgrounds. Ingraham (2004) has also presented brief case studies of consultations when consultants and consultees were from different backgrounds, demonstrating how subtle differences in cultural and/or ethnic perspectives color the process and outcomes of consultation.

Dettmer et al. (1999) discuss approaches suggested by Cross (1988), Huff and Telesford (1994), and Lynch and Hansen (1992) that consultants should use when dealing with parents from culturally diverse groups. These ideas apply equally well to situations where the consultee and consultant may be from different racial-ethnic backgrounds.

1. Acknowledge cultural differences; they can affect parent–teacher (and consultant) interactions.
2. Examine your own cultural beliefs and ways of responding.
3. Realize that group interactions and ways of responding (such as etiquette and patterns of responding) vary across cultural groups.
4. Try to understand a student's behavior as a function of her culture.

5. Find ways to validate culturally specific ideas.
6. Learn about backgrounds and beliefs regarding schooling, disability, and child rearing.
7. Realize that many families are not used to a collaborative approach.
8. Be familiar with some words and forms of greetings that are common to the families you will be dealing with.
9. Locate members of the family's background or culture who can mediate between the constituent parties (e.g., an older sibling, or a minister).
10. For students who recently arrived from a non-English-speaking country, learn important words and phrases to assist the student's very early adjustment to the classroom.

Sileo and Prater (1998) have indicated some of the major areas of differences in cultural patterns that may affect how parents approach consultative discussions. In terms of family dynamics, they may have different expectations regarding child behaviors; in the area of acceptable interactions between children and adults, they may not agree with the dominant views in the school; regarding student characteristics, there may be differences in terms of whether children should be competitive or cooperative; and in the area of discipline, parents and schools may differ in the benefits of corporal punishment. Banks (1993) indicates two of the reasons parents from diverse groups may seem reluctant to collaborate with school personnel regarding the needs of and plans for their children: (a) coping with the everyday demands of making a living puts such a degree of stress on the parent(s) that the idea of attending meetings and brainstorming with degree-laden teachers and specialists (who possibly speak in an arcane lingo) is not appealing; and (b) some parents did not have good experiences while in school, and discussing similar problems now manifested by their own children recalls those experiences they would just as soon forget.

Gibbs (1980) has written about differences between African American and Caucasian consultees, and has made three formulations: "(a) there are ethnic (e.g., black-white) differences in the initial orientation to the consultant-consultee relationship; (b) these differences are along the dimension of interpersonal versus instrumental competence; and (c) these differences have significant implications for the implementation of the consultation process and its outcome" (p. 195). Gibbs believes that African American consultees focus on "interpersonal competence," which she defines as "a measure of the ability of the individual [the consultant] to invoke positive attitudes and to obtain favorable responses to his actions" (p. 199). She believes that Caucasian consultees prefer to focus on "instrumental competence," which is "a measure of the degree of effectiveness with which a goal or task is accomplished by the individual" (p. 199). Gibbs describes five stages in the consultation process in which the consultant and consultee evaluate each other in terms of their compatibility. Most of this occurs at the entry level, although it could occur at any time in the process.

Unfortunately, Gibbs's (1980) conceptualization does not seem to have considered moderating variables such as social class, age, gender, or experience. In an effort to validate Gibbs's ideas, Duncan and Pryzwansky (1988) asked 124 experienced African American female teachers to observe African American and Caucasian consultants on a videotape and rate their effectiveness. Preferences for the race of the consultant were not observed. There was a general preference for the instrumentally oriented consultants, contrary to what Gibbs's ideas predict.

In another study, Naumann, Gutkin, and Sandoval (1996) asked college students to listen to audiotapes of consultation sessions with a school psychologist as the consultant and a kindergarten teacher as the consultee. The referral problem was a child's failure to speak in class. Information given to the raters included the race of the consultant and the race of the child, in each case either African American or EuroAmerican. After listening to the tapes, each rater responded to questionnaires that measured intervention acceptability and consultant credibility. There were no significant effects for either consultant race or child race. Although a study of this type precludes significant generalization, it does raise some doubt about generalizations concerning the effects of race in either the consultant or the client. The race of the consultee was not a variable in this study; if it had been, this variable may have interacted with either consultant or client. As previously mentioned, generalizations across racial/ethnic groups may need to be reexamined in light of the consultant's growing knowledge of individual consultees' approaches to interpersonal relationships and acceptability of interventions. Lynch and Hanson (1998) have pointed out that applying generalizations to cultural or racial groups may be dangerous since it leads to stereotyping that can reduce understanding.

Clearly, more needs to be known about a consultant and a consultee than their race or ethnicity in order to determine the likelihood of an effective consultation process or content match. Similarly, in designing interventions for students who come from culturally and linguistically diverse homes, the culturally sensitive consultant needs to be aware of possible differences that might affect intervention validity. Harris (1991) has developed a set of competencies that address this issue, including the use of appropriate assessment and instructional strategies; the need to understand one's own culture in relation to other cultures; the importance of communication, interpersonal, and problem-solving skills; and an understanding of the role and importance of collaboration.

ACTIVITY 1.9

Students from many different racial or ethnic groups might wish to comment on the content of this previous section. Which has more influence on a person's communication style, her ethnicity or her social class? How do people vary in their preferences for interpersonal relations? Are these variations a function of ethnicity, cultural expectations, or other variables?

THE EDUCATIONAL PLACEMENT OF STUDENTS WITH DISABILITIES

I believe that all children belong in the general education program until it is demonstrated that such placement is harmful to their welfare or to the welfare of others (Yell, 1995). This belief is in accord with the mandates of the courts' rulings in *Daniel R. R. v. State Board of Education* (1989), and in *Board of Education v. Holland* (1992). In *Daniel R. R.,* the court indicated a two-part test for determining compliance with the requirement for placement in a least restrictive environment (LRE):

> First, we ask whether education in the regular classroom, with the use of supplementary aids and services, can be achieved satisfactorily for a given child. If it cannot and the school intends to provide special education or to remove the child from regular education, we ask, second, whether the school has mainstreamed the child to the maximum extent appropriate. (p. 1,048)

In *Holland* the court said:

> Thus the decision as to whether any particular child should be educated in a regular classroom setting all of the time, part of the time, or none of the time, is necessarily an inquiry into the needs and abilities of one child, and does not extend to a group or category of handicapped children. (p. 878)

It follows that ancillary personnel, such as those engaged in consultative responsibilities, should not search for intrachild deficits and treat them somewhere else but should find ways of modifying and improving the general education program to enhance educational opportunities for these students.

Among the benefits of inclusion are at least the following:

1. Students with disabilities are able to feel that they are part of the normal environment. They are able to think of themselves as being "regular" rather than "special."

2. Students with disabilities who engage in behaviors regarded as detrimental to school success may benefit from other students' modeling of appropriate behaviors. Sometimes this can work the other way around: Students without identified disabilities whose behavior is inappropriate may observe prosocial behaviors exhibited by students with disabilities.

3. Students without disabilities are exposed to those with disabilities and may develop more positive images of individuals with disabilities. Instead of thinking of students with disabilities as belonging somewhere else in the educational system, they are now able to see these students as part of the general education program and to that extent as "regular" instead of otherwise.

4. Students without disabilities may be able to exercise the human tendency to help others who need it (for example, academically or socially); likewise, students with a disability may be able to contribute to the class in ways not previously considered.

5. Inclusion is becoming more efficient and less disruptive to all concerned. In pull-out programs, students often leave the class at crucial times and miss out on the regular curriculum. This results in a very scattered school day. They may also not have access to the general curriculum while in the special education setting because of the emphasis on the attainment of the goals and objectives specified on the IEP.

6. The broader community will soon include today's students. General education students exposed to inclusive classrooms will bring the idea of inclusion to their adult lives and will look for ways to ensure that those with disabilities are treated equally, as is their right.

The last two decades have been characterized by an immense increase in awareness about, and implementation of, inclusion in regular programming for students with disabilities (Fuchs & Fuchs, 1994; Heward, 2000; Johnson & Johnson, 1980; Mastropieri & Scruggs, 2000; Stainback et al., 1989). General educators have sometimes felt that the prospect of a marriage of special and general education, as envisioned by the full-inclusion movement, was exciting to the bride (special education) but somehow failed to include a serious invitation to the groom (general education). Additionally, some general educators are concerned that they are overburdened with too many issues and demands and cannot keep up with the pressures they already have. They believe that adding the time it takes to collaborate in planning for students with disabilities is neither practical nor fair (Kaufmann & Hallahan, 1995; Zigmond & Baker, 1995). Since the courts have not tended to agree or be concerned with these arguments, citing the law as having precedence over the objections of some general educators, the inclusion movement has progressed, prompting general educators to seek ways to make it work. Inservice training, workshops on curriculum modification, teaching methods, co- or team-teaching, peer tutoring, group work, and other modifications are now becoming commonplace in schools that have embraced the inclusion philosophy.

Collaborative consultation is the key to the effectiveness of the inclusion movement. The activities of school consultants in their efforts to move the inclusion agenda forward by helping general educators accommodate students with disabilities may determine the success of this movement (Dettmer et al., 1999; Friend & Cook, 2003; Idol et al., 2000; Tiegerman-Farber & Radziewicz, 1998).

Further information and ideas about the inclusion movement can be located at these web addresses:

Council on Exceptional Children—
www.cec.sped.org

National Association of State Directors of Special Education—
www.nasdse.org

ERIC Clearinghouse on Disabilities and Gifted Children—
www.ericec.org

ACTIVITY 1.10

Those familiar with full inclusion should talk about their experiences with it, and especially how they think a school consultant could be of use to a general education teacher in the cases with which they are familiar. What were the issues that could have (or did) make the inclusion difficult, and how were potentially difficult situations handled?

SUMMARY

This chapter has defined the concept of collaborative consultation and offered some background information about it. Consultation can be an effective intervention for problem solving about students' learning and behavior/adjustment problems. It provides a method for affecting system-wide change in methods of service delivery to students and bridges gaps among teachers, parents, and ancillary personnel. It also serves efforts to keep students in regular education and return those in special education to the regular track as soon as is sensible.

Merely talking about problems does not solve them. However, many educators and parents have come to the conclusion that not enough collaborative problem solving is practiced before students are referred for special education and related services or before any effort is made to return them to the general track. Special education teachers and ancillary personnel, such as psychologists and counselors, should devote more time to the collaborative consultation activities described in this book. This would represent a healthy step away from the tendency to treat a referral as permission to find something wrong with a student and to treat that problem somewhere other than the regular class.

REFERENCES

Affleck, J. Q., Madge, S., Adams, A., & Lowenbraun, S. (1988). Integrated classroom versus resource model: Academic viability and effectiveness. *Exceptional Children, 54*, 339–348.

Banks, C. A. M. (1993). Parents and teachers: Partners in school reform. In J. A. Banks & C. A. M. Banks (Eds.), *Multicultural education: Issues and perspectives* (2nd ed., pp. 332–352). Boston: Allyn & Bacon.

Bennett, D. S., & Gibbons, T. A. (2000). Efficacy of child cognitive-behavioral interventions for antisocial behavior: A meta-analysis. *Child and Family Behavior Therapy, 22* (1), 1–15.

Bergan, J. R. (1995). Evolution of a problem-solving model of consultation. *Journal of Educational and Psychological Consultation, 6*, 111–124.

Board of Education v. Holland, 786 F. Supp. 874 (E.D. Cal. 1992).

Brown, D., Pryzwansky, W., & Schulte, A. (1995). *Psychological consultation* (3rd ed.). Boston: Allyn & Bacon.

Brown, D., Pryzwansky, W., & Schulte, A. (2001). *Psychological consultation* (5th ed.). Boston: Allyn & Bacon.

Bush, G. (1991). *America 2000: An educational strategy*. Washington, DC: U.S. Department of Education.

Busse, R., Kratochwill, T., & Elliott, S. (1995). Meta-analysis for single case outcomes: Applications to research and practice. *Journal of School Psychology, 33*, 269–285.

California Department of Justice, Division of Law Enforcement. (1993). *Profile, 1992*. Sacramento, CA: Author.

Caplan, G. (1964). *Principles of preventive psychiatry*. New York: Basic Books.

Caplan, G., & Caplan, R. B. (1993). *Mental health consultation and collaboration*. San Francisco: Jossey-Bass.

Chicago Public Schools, Bureau of Safety and Security. (1994). *Annual report*. Chicago: Author.

Christenson, S. L. (1995). Supporting home-school collaboration. In A. Thomas & J. Grimes (Eds.), *Best practices in school psychology—III*. Washington, DC: NASP.

Cobern, W. (1993). Constructivism. *Journal of Educational and Psychological Consultation, 7*(1), 105–112.

Comer, J. (1993). *School power: Implications of a preventive project*. New York: Free Press.

Cramer, S. F. (1998). Collaboration. *A success strategy for special educators*. Boston: Allyn & Bacon.

Cross, T. (1988). Services to minority populations: What does it mean to be a culturally competent professional? *Focal Point, 2*, 1–3.

Daniel R. R. v. State Board of Education, 874 F. 2d. 1036 (1989).

Dettmer, P., Dyck, N., & Thurston, L. (1999). *Consultation, collaboration and teamwork* (3rd ed.). Boston: Allyn & Bacon.

Dougherty, A. (2000). *Psychological consultation and collaboration in school and community settings* (3rd ed.). Pacific Grove, CA: Brooks/Cole.

Duncan, C., & Pryzwansky, W. B. (1988). Consultation research: Trends in doctoral dissertations, 1978–1985. *Journal of School Psychology, 26,* 107–119.

Dunn, L. (1968). Special education for the mildly handicapped: Is much of it justifiable? *Exceptional Children, 35,* 5–22.

Dunst, C. J., & Trivette, C. M. (1987). Enabling and empowering families: Conceptual and intervention issues. *School Psychology Review, 16,* 443–456.

Eber, L., Nelson, C. M., & Miles, P. (1997). School-based wraparound for students with emotional and behavioral challenges. *Exceptional Children, 63*(4), 539–555.

Erchul, W. P. (1987). A relational communication analysis of control in school consultation. *Professional School Psychology, 2,* 113–124.

Erchul, W. P., Hughes, J. N., Meyers, J., Hickman, J. A., & Braden, J. P. (1992). Dyadic agreement concerning the consultation process and its relationship to outcome. *Journal of Educational and Psychological Consultation, 3,* 119–132.

Erchul, W. P., & Martens, B. K. (2002). *School consultation: Conceptual and empirical bases of practice* (2nd ed.). New York: Kluwer Academic/Plenum Publishers.

Fishbaugh, M. S. (1997). *Models of Collaboration.* Boston: Allyn & Bacon.

Friend, M., & Cook, L. (2003). *Interactions: Collaboration skills for school professionals* (4th ed.). Boston: Allyn & Bacon.

Fuchs, D., & Fuchs, L. S. (1994). Inclusive schools movement and the radicalization of special education reform. *Exceptional Children, 60*(4), 294–309.

Gendlin, E. T. (1986). What comes after traditional psychotherapy research? *American Psychologist, 41,* 131–136.

Gibbs, J. T. (1980). The interpersonal orientation in mental health consultation: Toward a model of ethnic variations in consultation. *Journal of Community Psychology, 8,* 195–207.

Gonzalez, V., Brusca-Vega, R., & Yawkey, T. (1997). *Assessment and instruction of culturally and linguistically diverse students with or at risk of learning problems: From research to practice.* Needham Heights, MA: Allyn & Bacon.

Greenberg, M. T., Domitrovich, C., & Bumbarger, B. (1999). *Preventing mental disorders in school-age children: A review of the effectiveness of prevention programs.* Available from the Prevention Research Center for the Promotion of Human Development, College of Health and Human Development, Pennsylvania State University, State College, PA.

Gresham, F. M. (1989). Assessment of treatment integrity in school consultation and prereferral intervention. *School Psychology Review, 18,* 37–50.

Gresham, F. M., & Kendell, G. K. (1987). School consultation research: Methodological critique and future research directions. *School Psychology Review, 16,* 306–316.

Gresham, F., & Noell, G. (1993). Methods for documenting the effectiveness of consultation: A critical analysis. In J. Zins, T. Kratochwill, & S. Elliott (Eds.), *The handbook of consultation services for children* (pp. 249–273). San Francisco: Jossey-Bass.

Gutkin, T. B. (1993a). Conducting consultation research. In J. E. Zins, T. R. Kratochwill, & S. N. Elliott (Eds.), *Handbook of consultation services for children* (pp. 227–248). San Francisco: Jossey-Bass.

Gutkin, T. B. (1993b). Moving from behavioral to ecobehavioral consultation: What's in a name? *Journal of Educational and Psychological Consultation, 4,* 95–99.

Gutkin, T. B., & Curtis, M. J. (1999). School-based consultation theory and practice: The art and science of indirect service delivery. In C. R. Reynolds & T. B. Gutkin (Eds.), *The handbook of school psychology* (3rd ed., pp. 598–637). New York: Wiley.

Gutkin, T. B., Henning-Stout, M., & Piersel, W. C. (1988). Impact of a district-wide behavioral consultation prereferral intervention service on patterns of school psychological service delivery. *Professional School Psychology, 3,* 301–308.

Halpern, A. (1992). Transition: Old wine in new bottles. *Exceptional Children, 58*(3), 202–211.

Harris, K. C. (1991). An expanded view on consultation competencies for educators serving culturally and linguistically diverse exceptional students. *Teacher Education and Special Education, 14*(1), 25–29.

Harvard School of Education. (1993). The push for new standards provokes hype and fear—and both are justified. *Harvard Education Letter, 9*(5), 1–5.

Heron, T., & Harris, K. (2001). *The educational consultant* (4th ed.). Austin, TX: Pro-Ed.

Heward, W. L. (2000). *Exceptional children: An introduction to special education*. Upper Saddle River, NJ: Merrill/Prentice Hall.

Howe, H. (1991). America 2000: Bumpy ride on four trains. *Phi Delta Kappan, 73*(3), 192–203.

Huff, B., & Telesford, M. C. (1994). Outreach efforts to involve families of color. In the Federation of Families for Children's Mental Health. *Focal Point, 10,* 180–184.

Hughes, J. (1994). Back to basics: Does consultation work? *Journal of Educational and Psychological Consultation, 5*(1), 77–84.

Hughes, J., & DeForest, P. (1993). Consultant directiveness and support as predictors of consultation outcomes. *Journal of School Psychology, 31,* 355–373.

Hughes, J., Grossman, P., & Barker, D. (1990). Teacher expectancies, participation in consultation, and perceptions of consultant helpfulness. *School Psychology Quarterly, 5,* 167–179.

Idol, L. (1990). The scientific art of classroom consultation. *Journal of Educational and Psychological Consultation, 1*(1), 3–22.

Idol, L., Nevin, A., & Paolucci-Whitcomb, P. (2000). *Collaborative consultation* (3rd ed.). Austin, TX: Pro-Ed.

Idol, L., Paolucci-Whitcomb, P., & Nevin, A. (1986). *Collaborative consultation.* Austin, TX: Pro-Ed.

Ingraham, C. (2000). Consultation through a multicultural lens: Multicultural and cross-cultural consultation in schools. *School Psychology Review, 29*(3), 320–344.

Ingraham, C. (2004). Multicultural consultee-centered consultation: When novice consultants explore cultural hypotheses with experienced teacher consultees. *Journal of Educational and Psychological Consultation, 14*(3 & 4), 329–362.

Johnson, D. W., & Johnson, R. T. (1980). Integrating handicapped students into the mainstream. *Exceptional Children, 47,* 90–98.

Kaufmann, J., & Hallahan, D. (1995). *The illusion of full inclusion.* Austin, TX: Pro-Ed.

Knoff, H., & Batsche, G. (1995). Project ACHIEVE: Analysing a school reform process for at-risk and underachieving students. *School Psychology Review, 24,* 579–603.

Lippitt, G., & Lippitt, R. (1986). *The consulting process in action* (2nd ed.). San Diego, CA: University Associates.

Lynch, E. W., & Hanson, M. J. (1998). *Developing cross-cultural competence: A guide for working with young children and their families* (2nd ed.). Baltimore: Paul H. Brookes.

Mastropieri, M. A., & Scruggs, T. E. (2000). *The inclusive classroom: Strategies for effective instruction.* Upper Saddle River, NJ: Merrill/Prentice Hall.

Meyers, J., & Nastasi, B. K. (1999). Primary prevention in school settings. In C. Reynolds & T. Gutkin (Eds.), *Handbook of school psychology* (3rd ed., pp. 764–799). New York: Wiley.

Morrison, G. M., Walker, D., Wakefield, P., & Solberg, S. (1994). Teacher preferences for collaborative relationships: Relationship to efficacy for teaching in prevention-related domains. *Psychology in the Schools, 31,* 221–231.

National Council on Education Standards and Testing. (1992). *Raising standards for American education.* Washington, DC: U.S. Government Printing Office.

Naumann, W. C., Gutkin, T. B., & Sandoval, S. R. (1996). The impact of consultant race and student race on perceptions of consultant effectiveness and intervention acceptability. *Journal of Educational and Psychological Consultation, 7*(1), 151–160.

Powers, K. (2001). Problem solving student support teams. *The California School Psychologist, 6,* 19–30.

Pryzwansky, W. B. (1977). Collaboration or consultation: Is there a difference? *Journal of Special Education, 1,* 179–182.

Pryzwansky, W. B. (1986). Indirect service delivery: Considerations for future research in consultation. *School Psychology Review, 15,* 479–488.

Pugach, M. C., & Johnson, L. J. (1988). Rethinking the relationship between consultation and collaborative problem solving. *Focus on Exceptional Children, 21*(4), 1–8.

Rappaport, J. (1981). In praise of paradox: A social policy of empowerment over prevention. *American Journal of Community Psychology, 9,* 1–25.

Reynolds, M. C. (1989). An historical perspective: The delivery of special education to mildly disabled and at-risk students. *Remedial and Special Education, 10*(6) 7–11.

Robbins, J. R., & Gutkin, T. B. (1994). Consultee and client remedial and preventive outcomes following consultation: Some mixed empirical results and directions for future researchers. *Journal of Educational and Psychological Consultation, 5*(2), 149–167.

Shriner, J., Ysseldyke, J., & Thurlow, M. (1996). Standards for all American students. In E. Mayen, G. Vergason, & R. Whelan (Eds.), *Strategies for teaching exceptional children in inclusive settings* (pp. 53–80). Denver: Love Publishing.

Sibley, S. (1986). A meta-analysis of school consultation research. Unpublished doctoral dissertation, Texas Women's University, Denton.

Sileo, T., & Prater, M. (1998). Creating classroom environments that address the linguistic and cultural backgrounds of students with disabilities. *Remedial and Special Education, 19*(6), 323–337.

Slavin, R. E., Madden, N. A., Dolan, L., & Wasik, B. A. (1996). *Every child, every school: Success for all.* Thousand Oaks, CA: Corwin Press.

Stainback, S., Stainback, W., & Forest, M. (Eds.). (1989). *Educating all students in the mainstream of education.* Baltimore: Paul H. Brookes.

Sue, D. W., & Sue, D. (1990). *Counseling the culturally different: Theory and practice* (2nd ed.). New York: Wiley.

Tiegerman-Farber, E., & Radziewicz, C. (1998). *Collaborative decision making: The pathway to inclusion.* Upper Saddle River, NJ: Merrill/Prentice Hall.

Tobias, R. (1993). Underlying cultural issues that affect sound consultant/school collaboratives in developing multicultural programs. *Journal of Educational and Psychological Consultation, 4*(3), 237–251.

Turnbull, A. P., & Turnbull, H. R. (1997). *Families, professionals, and exceptionality: A special partnership* (3rd ed.). Upper Saddle River, NJ: Merrill/Prentice Hall.

United States Department of Education. (2002). No child left behind. Washington, DC: Author. Retrieved [August 16, 2002] from *http//:www.nochildleftbehind.gov.*

Villa, R., Thousand, J., Nevin, A., & Malgeri, C. (1996). Installing collaboration for inclusive schooling as a way of doing business in public schools. *Remedial and Special Education, 17,* 169–181.

Walker, H. M., Kavanagh, K., Stiller, B., Golly, A., Severson, H., & Feil, E. (1997). *First step to success: Helping young children overcome antisocial behavior.* Longmont, CO: Sopris West.

Wang, M. C., Reynolds, M. C., & Walberg, H. J. (1986). Rethinking special education. *Educational Leadership, 44,* 26–31.

Webster's college dictionary (2nd ed.). (1997). New York: Random House.

Weiler, M. B. (1984). *The influence of contact and setting on the ratings of parents for models of consultation.* Unpublished master's thesis, North Carolina State University, Raleigh.

Weiss. C. (1993). Shared decision making about what? A comparison of schools with and without teacher participation. *Teachers College Record, 95,* 69–92.

Wenger, R. D. (1979). Teacher response to collaborative consultation. *Psychology in the Schools, 16,* 127–131.

Will, M. (1986). Educating children with learning problems: A shared responsibility. *Exceptional Children, 51,* 411–415.

Witt, J. C. (1990). Face-to-face verbal interaction in school-based consultation: A review of the literature. *School Psychology Quarterly, 5,* 199–210.

Witt, J. C., & Elliott, S. N. (1985). Acceptability of classroom management strategies. In T. R. Kratochwill (Ed.), *Advances in school psychology* (Vol. 4, pp. 251–288). Hillsdale, NJ: Lawrence Erlbaum Associates.

Witt, J. C., & Martens, B. (1988). Problems with problem-solving consultation: A re-analysis of assumptions, methods, and goals. *School Psychology Review, 17,* 211–226.

Yell, M. L. (1995). Least restrictive environment, inclusion, and students with disabilities: A legal analysis. *Journal of Special Education, 28,* 389–404.

Ysseldyke, J. (1986). Current practice in school psychology. In S. Elliott & J. Witt (Eds.), *The delivery of psychological services in the schools.* Hillsdale, NJ: Lawrence Erlbaum Associates.

Ysseldyke, J. E., & Marston, D. (1999). Origins of categorical special education services in the schools and a rationale for changing them. In D. J. Reschly, W. D. Tilly, & J. P. Grimes (Eds.), *Special education in transition* (pp. 1–18). Longmont, CO: Sopris West.

Ysseldyke, J. E., Vanderwood, M., & Shriner, J. (1997). Changes over the past decade in special education referral to placement probability: An incredibly reliable practice. *Diagnostique, 23*(1), 193–202.

Zigmond, N., & Baker, J. M. (1995). Current and future practices in inclusive schooling. *Journal of Special Education, 29,* 245–250.

Models and Functional Aspects of Consultation

OBJECTIVES

1. Present information on two theoretical models of consultation: behavioral and mental health.
2. Review a sampling of functional models of consultation.
3. Specify what consultants do: their roles, skills needed, and activities performed.
4. Indicate the similarities and differences between individual and team-based consultation.
5. Present ideas about consulting with parents and families.
6. Give a framework for the development and implementation of staff development activities.

José is a junior in a comprehensive high school. He has been referred to the counselor numerous times over the past 2 years because of his academic apathy, poor academic productivity, and general disinterest in school. José has been identified as a student with academic promise. You (the school counselor) would like to heighten the awareness of the teachers and José's parents and develop a plan for dealing with José's situation. How could you do this collaboratively?

Elise, a ninth grader with a learning disability in reading and writing, is in danger of failing her general education classes in English and social studies. Her teachers are having her use only the regular texts (which she has a difficult time reading) because she has insisted that she does not want to appear "retarded" in front of her friends. You are the special education teacher consultant in this school. What are some ways of assisting Elise and her general education teachers with this situation?

A RATIONALE FOR A MODEL

A model is a way of conceptualizing or approaching a problem. A consultant is always, if only unwittingly, following a model. Some consultants follow a particular model very closely because they believe it is the most appropriate way of thinking about and solving the referral problem. Others may have only a vague notion of what the various models are; these consultants tend to follow a generalized problem-solving scheme: identifying the problem, brainstorming reasons for and solutions to the problem, deciding on possible interventions to take, encouraging the consultee to follow-through, and monitoring progress as the interventions are put into practice. This process is then recycled until the problem is solved (Gutkin & Curtis, 1999).

Kurpius, Fuqua, and Rozecki (1993) encourage consultants to strive toward some conceptual understanding of the meaning and purpose of consultation by asking questions that define the parameters of their beliefs. Such questions might include the following:

- What model(s) of consultation do I prefer?
- How do I define consultation to myself and others?

- How do I determine what approach would be most efficient and effective in any given situation?
- How will I reconcile my beliefs with those of the consultee if we differ?
- What recommendations for common problems arise from my theoretical position?
- How does my view of inclusive education influence my recommendations?

These are difficult questions, and certainly this list is not exhaustive. In every consultation case that arises in the schools these questions can be answered, if only implicitly, through a study of the actual behaviors of the consultant and consultee. Generally, however, consultants rarely verbalize them in any depth.

This chapter reviews two models, behavioral and mental health, that are regarded as theoretical because they derive from well-established theories of human behavior. Also reviewed are some of the practical, nontheoretical models discussed by West and Idol (1987), among others. Organizational consultation is presented in Chapter 8 because it relates most closely to system change issues. Collaboration as a model of consultative functioning was discussed in Chapter 1.

TWO THEORETICAL MODELS

Behavioral Model

The behavioral model is built on the theories of learning that have been adapted by behaviorists such as Skinner, Bandura, and Meichenbaum (Conoley & Conoley, 1992), and made specific in the area of consultation by Bergan (1977) and Kratochwill and Bergan (1990). Essentially, a behaviorist believes that behaviors are a function of the contingencies that control them (i.e., their antecedents and consequences), and the functional relationships between behaviors and their environmental and cognitive (i.e., self-talk) contexts. Specific to classroom applications of a behavioral model, one would look to classroom environmental stimuli and children's cognitions when trying to understand why behaviors exist and how they can be altered.

Behaviorism has progressed in many ways over the 70 years of its existence. During the 1980s and 1990s, for example, there was an increasing interest in what is known as cognitive behavior modification, which differs from more traditional thinking in its emphasis on internal, cognitive events. Traditional behaviorism was not concerned with internal events primarily because they could not be observed and counted. Now, however, it is widely recognized that ignoring internal mediating events leaves a gap in behaviorists' ability to understand the wellsprings of human behavior (Alberto & Troutman, 1999; Kaplan, 1995, 2000; Meichenbaum, 1977; Schloss & Smith, 1998).

Another major change has been formulated by Bandura (1977), who believes that social learning, or learning by observing models, is a major force in one's learning history. Using role models or rehearsing specific behaviors under conditions of positive reinforcement are some of the behavior change techniques suggested by Bandura's work.

It is clear that behavioral consultation is moving forward to embrace newer conceptualizations and applications. Kratochwill, Sladeczek, and Plunge (1995) provide a brief review of the evolution of behavioral consultation, and Noell (1996) has provided an updating of philosophy and procedures in the behavioral model.

Basic Concepts in Behavioral Consultation Dougherty (2000) suggests the following definition of behavioral consultation: "a relationship whereby services consistent with a behavioral orientation are provided either indirectly to a client or a system, [or] directly by training consultees to enhance their skills with clients or systems" (p. 279).

In traditional behavior modification, social learning, and the newer cognitive emphasis, the basic paradigm one uses to analyze behaviors consists of antecedents, behaviors, and consequences. This ABC model has been expanded by some writers (Kanfer & Saslow, 1969) but is still useful in its original format as developed by Skinner (1969).

Antecedents are events that precede, and are believed to be functionally connected to, the behavior that follows the antecedents' occurrence. Antecedents can be either external or internal. Examples of external antecedents are a teacher's direction to a student to do something, the behavior of the child sitting next to a target student, or a fire-drill alarm. Internal antecedents may include hunger, one's emotional state, or self-talk.

These examples of external and internal antecedents are what Herbert (1978) refers to as proximal rather than distal. According to Herbert, "Proximal antecedents are close in time to the actual behavior" while distal refers "to the more distant (historical) events in the client's life" (p. 56). As with most variables that exist on a continuum, it is not always easy or practical to make the distinction between identifying any given antecedent as distal or proximal. In spite of this, the distinction is valuable because it reminds observers that any behavior may be a function of antecedents that occurred years earlier rather than simply those events that are currently happening. Distal antecedents include child-rearing practices, a history of gang-related activity in a child's family, events seen on television, habit strength, memories of a situation similar to a current situation, and so on. In fact, what often appears to be the immediate (proximal antecedent) cause of a child's misbehavior may not be the main reason for the observed behavior. By knowing a child's history and, when possible, something of the child's inner life through counseling or reflective listening techniques, one may come to understand the distal antecedents of that child's behavior. Gutkin has emphasized this point, suggesting that behavioral consultation needs to attend more seriously to distal antecedents by becoming "ecobehavioral," by looking at the larger picture of a student's life and history rather than just at immediate prompting events (Gutkin, 1993; Gutkin & Curtis, 1999).

ACTIVITY 2.1

List, either by yourself or in a class group, all the antecedent reasons you can think of for classroom misbehavior (however defined). In other words, what prompts misbehavior in school? Determine which antecedents are distal and which are proximal.

ACTIVITY 2.2

Repeat Activity 2.1, this time focusing on academic learning problems. What are some reasons for poor academic performance? Which seem to be biological and which are environmental?

Consequences (defined here as the effects of a behavior on the student) are ordinarily regarded as the events that follow a behavior. These can be positive, neutral, or negative (or aversive). It is the effect on a student that determines whether a consequence is positive, neutral, or negative, not the intention of the person who delivers the consequence. The student determines the effect, which might be the opposite of that designed or caused by the person or environmental event that delivers the consequence to the student. For example, teachers (and parents) often warn children not to tip their chairs back because they might fall. If they do fall, the effect may be positive from the point of view of the adult since it validates the adult's ability to predict events. Or it may be negative, if the child is hurt and the adult feels sorry for him. From a child's point of view, the effect may be negative if he gets hurt, or it may be positive if he obtains some sort of pleasure from disrupting the classroom or obtaining approval from his peers, even if he does get hurt.

Walker and Shea (1999) discuss four kinds of consequences: positive reinforcement, negative reinforcement, extinction, and punishment. They point out, as I have mentioned, that the consequence intended by the "contingency manager" (parent, teacher, and so on) may not be the one that actually occurs in the mind of the student since the positive or negative value of a consequence is always determined by the student, as the example of chair tilting indicates.

Another possibility is an unwitting consequence: one that occurs without our planning for it or wanting it. For instance, a teacher who believes that he is positively reinforcing students by verbally praising them may find that some of his students don't seem to want or like this praise. From their perspective, which may arise from sociocultural norms, praise from a teacher, at least in public, is aversive and therefore a punishment instead of a positive reinforcement.

Given these examples, how does one know whether an adult or peer response to a targeted behavior is reinforcing or punishing? The answer lies only in a careful study of the data. Is the targeted behavior decreasing as a function of the consequences it elicits? If so, then these consequences are probably best interpreted as aversive or punishing. Are behaviors increasing as a result of the responses that follow these behaviors? If so, then you are probably providing the appropriate consequences (i.e., positively reinforcing contingencies).

Basic Beliefs Underlying a Behavioral Approach to Consultation Dougherty (2000) indicates that a behavioral approach to consultation differs from a clinical-diagnostic approach in that the focus should be on behaviors that are either observable to the teacher or parent or reportable by the student. Hypothetical constructs and pseudo-explanatory concepts and labels, such as attention deficit/hyperactivity disorder (ADHD) or conduct disorder or others listed in the *Diagnostic and Statistical Manual of Mental Disorders* (DSM-IV) (American Psychiatric Association, 1994), are not regarded as constructive except for purposes of communication among professional staff and parents. It is not valuable to state that a student acts in a certain way because he has a mental illness or disease, as popular and seductive as that approach may be, unless the purported mental illness or disease has a definite biological cause. The behaviorist does not say that a student is out of her seat and running around the room because she has ADHD. Rather, the behaviorist is inclined to say that the student engages in an excessive amount of out-of-seat behavior (operationally defined and usually determined in relation to a norm for a given classroom or other setting), which you can call ADHD if you want. ADHD cannot be treated, but out-of-seat behavior may be treatable, either by a contingency change procedure or through medication. If medication is used, the behaviorist believes that the prescribing physician must also be a behaviorist because the physician is treating the behaviors (out-of-seat and possibly others). To learn if drug therapy has been successful, a behaviorist counts the occurrence and duration of out-of-seat behavior or some other targeted behavior. The behaviorist (and the physician-behaviorist) share the same goal: to reduce the frequency of symptoms because, as the behaviorist believes, the symptom is the disease (Ullmann & Krasner, 1965).

ACTIVITY 2.3

A teacher tells you that she is concerned about a student who is anxious. What else do you, as a behaviorally oriented consultant, want to know about the child? What are the behaviors of anxiety? Which can be treated, the anxiety or the behaviors? How might a traditional behaviorist differ from a cognitively oriented behaviorist in his approach to this problem?

Stages in the Behavioral Consultation Model Bergan (1977) and Bergan and Kratochwill (1990) have delineated four stages that form the structure of the behavioral consultation model: problem identification, problem analysis, plan implementation, and problem evaluation. The following is a description of the activities carried on during these stages and an indication of some of the objectives that underlie each stage (Gutkin & Curtis, 1999; Martens, 1993).

In *problem identification,* the consultant receives and discusses a referral with the consultee and attempts to clarify its nature. Is it primarily a behavior/adjustment problem or a learning problem? What do the terms used by the consultee to describe the problem mean operationally? The objectives of this stage are to assess the nature of the consultee's concerns; prioritize problems; select target behavior(s); make an initial estimate of the problem's seriousness; decide on tentative goals; discuss the antecedents, sequences (i.e., how the behavior unfolds in time), and consequences; discuss possible data-collection ideas; and set a next meeting date. Gutkin and Curtis (1999) indicate that a consultee's description of a complex of problems may seem initially overwhelming and confusing, particularly if the consultee's descriptions are clouded by anger, frustration, or the intermixing of facts and opinions.

In *problem analysis,* the consultant delves further into the nature of the problem, usually by observing it directly, conducting a functional assessment if appropriate, (see Chapter 6), clarifying issues with the consultee, and brainstorming possible interventions. Other activities at this stage are to analyze the data; solidify goals; verify antecedents, behavioral sequences, and consequences; determine strengths and assets of the student and the school that can be incorporated into the planning; and design and get agreement about the intervention plan. If the behavioral consultation is being conducted in the collaborative mode, the consultee makes the final determination about what to implement and how to do it, with the expert guidance and facilitation of the consultant. Both parties discuss ongoing data-collection methods, and schedule the next interview and/or observation.

In *plan implementation,* the consultee proceeds with the appropriate interventions. The consultant's main objectives in this stage are to monitor what the consultee is doing (to ensure treatment integrity), suggest modifications as appropriate, and reinforce the consultee for their efforts.

For *problem evaluation,* Bergan (1977) suggests three steps: evaluating goal attainment, evaluating plan effectiveness, and planning postimplementation. The goals should have been established during the problem identification stage and should have flowed naturally from the nature of the problem. The primary objective of this stage is to determine how well the goals have been met. The collected and analyzed data form the scientific basis for determination of goal attainment. Continuation, modification, or termination of the plan are determined in this stage. A plan may look elegant and may have worked elsewhere, but the consultant and the consultee have to determine how well it has worked in the present case, which is always different in important, if subtle, ways from all other instances of similar problems.

Postimplementation planning refers to a discussion of how to proceed after the current consultative relationship is terminated. What steps should be taken to ensure that the problem won't recur? Should data continue to be kept? In school consultation, consultants should learn to expect recurrence of problems from certain students and from certain teachers. Some cases continually resurface due to students' home conditions; serious learning disabilities; or other biophysical, psychodynamic, or classroom ecological influences. Sometimes postimplementation simply means putting a partially successful case on the back burner, sometimes because a "tincture of time" is useful, sometimes because the pressure of other cases forces you into this situation.

Kratochwill and Bergan (1990) elaborate on the steps a consultant should take to implement the four stages I have described. Their set of suggested interview procedures and objectives is the most detailed of any model and certainly should be studied by all school-based consultants.

ACTIVITY 2.4

Form teams of two (dyads). Member A thinks of a social relationship problem she has observed in a student. Member B acts as a consultant and tries to get functional information about the problem from the consultee. The consultant asks for a behavioral definition of the social relationship problem and gets information about the antecedents and consequences, frequency of occurrence, durations, intensities, and so on. Then reverse roles, seeking a behavioral definition concerning academic underachievement.

ACTIVITY 2.5

In dyads, the consultee lists five behavior or learning problems of a student. The consultant helps the consultee prioritize these concerns, and together they agree about what concerns to address first. They select one of the behavior or learning problems and do a functional assessment, obtaining as much information as they can about the problem, using only the interview process.

ACTIVITY 2.6

As a class, define behavioral objectives for the following: excessive talking out, gum chewing in class, and low academic productivity. Define these activities more accurately by inventing baseline data before establishing behavioral objectives. Add a timeline to your plan.

Current Thinking About the Behavioral Model Bergan (1995) has updated the behavioral model of consultation since its inception about 25 years ago. He points to a wide literature that supports this highly structured approach and indicates how it has assisted consultants and consultees in defining problems that can be operationalized and solved. He specifically indicates a problem-centered approach, which is not always evident in approaches taken by consultants who follow other theoretical or functional models. This approach avoids the focus on a referred student's negative behavior and instead asks questions that focus on a program of possible skill development. For example, instead of asking "What's wrong with Johnny?" the consultant asks "What would you like to see Johnny accomplish in the area of skill development this year?" While it is likely that referral questions may contain some explication of what a student is doing wrong (such as variations on "He won't behave or do his work"), this is not necessarily the problem the consultant should work on. Rather, it is more appropriate to stress the teaching goal for the student (such as "What social or academic skills does the student need to work on, and how can we arrange the environment, broadly defined, to see that this happens?").

The behavioral approach has considerable surface appeal in addition to a solid track record of empirical validation. Nevertheless, many teachers do not use behavioral approaches. Indeed, some teachers and administrators want nothing to do with them. Axelrod, Moyer, and Berry (1990) point to a number of reasons why this is so. Some teachers balk at this approach because data have to be kept, a teacher may have to change her own behavior, and programs need to be individualized. Also, reinforcement is often misinterpreted as bribery. Some teachers believe in the "Protestant ethic," by which they mean that students should do work because they are told to; thus, "bribing" them is unnecessary, even immoral. Such teachers believe that this behavioral approach may be all right for rats and pigeons but not for people.

Finally, most teachers have not been trained in behavioral techniques, and a "behavior mod" zealot may turn them off by conveying a superior attitude. Given the rich database that supports the behavioral approach, it is not surprising that those who have studied and applied it successfully might be evangelistic in their efforts to get others to use behavioristic methods. Astute behaviorally oriented school consultants need to guard against this attitude or impression. They need to remember that teachers usually don't read the *Journal of Applied Behavioral Analysis,* may not be at all impressed with studies done under controlled conditions (which classrooms are not), and are primarily concerned with the students in their classrooms, not others who seem to live in laboratories somewhere else.

Bergan (1995) has pointed to an area of development in behavioral consultation that currently receives increased emphasis: family involvement. Recognition of the central role of family-centered contingencies in the lives of children has prompted current behaviorists, such as Kramer (1990) and Sheridan and Kratochwill (1992), to expand their ideas about behavioral applications with families. This aspect of the behavioral model is referred to as conjoint behavioral consultation (Sheridan & Colton, 1994; Sheridan, Kratochwill, & Bergan, 1996). In this system, both parents and teachers serve as consultees, thus increasing the complexity of the consultant's data-gathering and communication efforts. Colton and Sheridan (1998) report on a conjoint project utilizing the efforts of both parents and teachers in a collaborative effort to modify the play behaviors of three boys diagnosed with ADHD. By utilizing a 15-day social-skills training program with four components (coaching and role, playing, self-monitoring, home-school communications, and positive reinforcement), which was individually tailored for each student, they were able to demonstrate a marked reduction in the negative behaviors associated with ADHD and an increase in positive behaviors displayed by all three boys that held up at follow-up for two of the three boys. Perhaps future research will provide more evidence for methods characterized by conjoint efforts between school personnel and parents and will have more broadly applicable results than interventions designed to touch only on the student's hours in school.

Summary of the Behavioral Model This brief overview of the behavioral model presents a foundation for understanding and appreciating the contributions of this model to the consultation process. You may detect considerable overlap between what has been presented here as the behavioral model and what is presented later in Chapter 5 as an ecobehavioral model (Gutkin & Curtis, 1999). The ecobehavioral model is a blend of the behavioral model and a more generic problem-solving model presented earlier by Gutkin (1993) and Gutkin and Curtis (1982). Readers intending to pursue the behavioral approach to consultation should review the primary sources of information to obtain a more thorough understanding of the methods used by behaviorally oriented consultants (Alberto & Troutman, 1999; Bergan, 1977; Bergan & Kratochwill, 1990; Crone & Horner, 2003; Elliott & Busse, 1993; Gresham & Davis, 1988; Gutkin & Curtis, 1999; Kazdin, 1984; Kratochwill & Bergan, 1990; Kratochwill, Elliott, & Rotto, 1995; Martens, 1993; Meichenbaum, 1977; Sheridan et al., 1996; Sugai & Tindal, 1993; Watson & Steege, 2003; Witt & Elliott, 1983; Zirpoli & Melloy, 2001).

Mental Health Model

The mental health model is based on psychodynamic theories of human interaction (Conoley & Conoley, 1992; Erchul, 1993). It was primarily developed by Gerald Caplan, M.D. His seminal text, *The Theory and Practice of Mental Health Consultation* (Caplan, 1970), reviews the many intricacies of this complex model. In 1993 and again in 1999, Dr. Caplan and Ruth Caplan authored an updated text on the mental health model, which added the word *collaboration* to the title: *Mental Health Consultation and Collaboration* (Caplan & Caplan, 1993/1999).

In strong contrast to the behavioral model, which emphasizes contingencies of reinforcement, modeling, and self-reinforcement, the mental health model stresses intrapsychic feelings and shows how they affect interpersonal relationships. Although the primary distinguishing factor in mental health consultation is its emphasis on intra- and interpersonal variables, it does not ignore environmental influences. Caplan makes many references to the importance of the ecological context in which behavior unfolds, such as communication patterns between the client and the consultee and organizational and community influences on the behavior of both clients and caregiver-consultees.

Every school-based consultant needs to be sensitive to one of Caplan's discoveries: when outsiders (consultants) enter the world of insiders (consultees), they need to understand that they are entering a world different from their own, one that has its own norms, beliefs, habits, and ways of doing things. No matter how expert a consultant may be, the consultee is largely responsible for the way in which an intervention is finally put into effect. Therefore, Caplan and Caplan (1993) stress the need for a collaborative approach to consultation. They discuss the problems that arise when the consultant attempts to take over a case and assume the expert role. This may reduce the consultee's involvement in the case and his subsequent willingness to generate or follow-through on solutions to the referral problems.

Key Concepts of the Mental Health Model Caplan and Caplan (1993, pp. 21–23) list 14 basic characteristics of their mental health model. The following list adapts five of these characteristics as they apply to school consultation:

1. *The relationship between the consultant and the consultee is coordinate and nonhierarchical.* Throughout this book I emphasize this basic tenet of the collaborative model. Even though the consultee has referred the problem to the consultant and

might therefore be thought of as the dependent person in the dyad, the working relationship established in the collaborative model soon clarifies an "equal-partners" dyad.

2. *Consultation is usually conducted as a short series of interviews.* In public schools there is no time for many lengthy sessions between a consultant and a consultee. While it may be true in extreme cases that weekly meetings occur for some months, the usual case involves between two and five meetings, some of which may be brief phone conversations. Because of the large number of students needing the services of those staff who deliver consultative services, there is necessarily a premium on time efficiency. It follows that there is little inclination to develop any sort of dependency relationship between a consultant and a consultee.

3. *The consultant does not get involved in the personal problems of the consultee.* If it is clear that the consultee is undergoing some sort of emotional conflict that impedes her ability to carry out a consultation plan, the consultant should make an appropriate referral to another source for counseling.

4. *A long-term goal of all consultation is to improve the on-the-job functioning of the consultee.* Toward that goal, the consultant attempts to give the consultee skills, knowledge, confidence, and a sense of objectivity that the consultee may be lacking and that will be useful in future cases that the consultee might have to deal with.

5. *Caplan intends his model to be used primarily for mental health problems.* However, the ideas discussed in his work can apply to any behavior or learning problem a student is experiencing.

Types of Mental Health Consultation Caplan and Caplan (1993) discuss four types of consultation: client-centered case, consultee-centered case, program-centered administrative, and consultee-centered administrative. The first two types concern individual client (or small-group) issues, and the latter two are system-oriented. Another way to divide the four types is in terms of focus: on the consultee or on the client (or the program in the case of the program-centered administrative type).

In *client-centered case consultation* the consultant deals directly with a client (student) in order to provide some service (such as assessment or treatment) or to develop ideas that a consultee can use when working with the client. The consultant has little direct interaction with the consultee. This seems to be the least pure form of collaborative consultation.

School-based example: A teacher refers a student to the resource specialist or school psychologist because of learning problems. This specialist takes the student from the general education classroom, does some assessment work, and writes a report for the teacher telling him what he should do to help the student.

In *consultee-centered case consultation* the consultant deals directly with the consultee in order to assist the consultee in formulating a plan for dealing with the client. The consultant has little or no direct interaction with the client. This is the model described by the triangle pictured in Figure 1.3, and is the most common model used in school-based collaborative consultation.

School-based example: The resource teacher meets with the general education teacher, assists her in making a plan for helping a student, and monitors the plan as it unfolds. In this situation the consultant may never meet directly with the student; a meeting is optional, depending on the situation.

In *program-centered administrative consultation* the consultant evaluates a policy or program and develops a plan for improving it.

School-based example: A reading expert, possibly from outside the district, is brought in to evaluate a district's reading program and to develop a set of guidelines for improving it.

In *consultee-centered administrative consultation* the consultant works with a group of consultees to help them develop better ways of managing their program.

School-based example: The consultant meets with elementary school principals (consultees) to review their schoolwide behavior management methods and to help them develop better plans that will meet their needs as well as those of their students.

Each of these four types are commonly used in the schools. The first two, which focus on individual student cases, are by far the most common, especially for internal, school-based consultants such as school counselors, special education teachers, and school psychologists. The last two tend to be relegated to external consultants or to administrators within the district, if only because of tradition. There is no reason why school-based consultants cannot perform these administrative (i.e., system improvement) consultation functions. Most of this text is devoted to individual or small-group consultation work; Chapter 8 focuses on the last two (administrative) types of consultation.

The Four "Lacks" of Consultees Caplan and Caplan (1993) point out four "lacks" that may explain why a consultee has difficulty dealing with a client: *knowledge, skill, confidence,* and *objectivity*. In a situation in which *knowledge* is lacking, the consultee simply needs to know more about a targeted student or about techniques that can be used to assist the student. In school-based consultation, this lack occurs with some frequency. Some teachers do not know much about a student's background or about cultural factors that may be influential. Some teachers take pride in never reading the cumulative folders of their new students; others have not read psychological or medical reports that are already in the file. The consultee may not have a good grounding in various ways to teach reading or other academic subjects or how to question students in order to develop their critical thinking skills. As Sandoval (1996) indicates, "Some consultees are a tabula rasa and need to be helped to gain knowledge" (p. 93). To whatever extent is necessary, the school consultant needs to impart information to the consultee in order to help her deal more effectively with the student, hoping that these facts or insights will be used with other students as appropriate. Many topics designed to increase the knowledge base of consultees can be delivered in staff development forums, which are discussed later in this chapter.

A lack of *skill* is diagnosed when the consultee has the requisite knowledge but doesn't seem to know how to apply it successfully. The best way to diagnose this condition is to watch the consultee apply his knowledge to solve a particular problem. The consultant may observe that the consultee knows what to do but not how to do it. An example might be the use of contingency contracts. The consultee has written a good contract but does not enforce it consistently or tries to demand more than the contract calls for before delivering the specified reinforcer.

The third lack is *confidence.* Some teachers and parents simply lack confidence to try things they know how to do or could easily learn. They may have tried specific tactics in the past and believed they were not successful, or they may be currently dealing with what appears to be a more difficult or threatening situation and are fearful of trying something and possibly failing. Consider a successful teacher who takes on a new challenge of teaching a class for emotionally disturbed students. The behaviors of these students frighten the teacher. During the first few weeks, the teacher seems reluctant to implement the behavior management techniques that have always worked in the past and were part of the reason he was nominated for this position. He would benefit from having someone observe the interactions in the class and assist him in gaining more confidence in his ability to redirect these students.

According to Caplan and Caplan (1993), the fourth lack, *objectivity,* is the most common "in a well-organized institution or agency" (p. 107). If consultees have the knowledge, skill, and confidence it takes to deal with their work-related problems but are still having difficulty, they may be letting subjective perceptions and judgments impair their ability to deal with issues involving students who present with difficult problems. The consultant's role in these situations is to help the teacher (or parent or administrator) to see the case in more objective terms, to reassess the behaviors of concern, and to point out that the student does not represent some class of people or perhaps some type of disability that shares common potential difficulties for the consultee.

ACTIVITY 2.7

A teacher consultee tells you that he expects the student to be loud and sarcastic because he has seen many children from similar home backgrounds "and they all act like that." Assume that you understand this to be a lack of objectivity. How would you, as a consultant, get this consultee to understand that this line of reasoning may be coloring his expectations? How might you get the consultee to be more objective in dealing with the client? Do you think it may be a simple case of a lack of knowledge, as suggested by Sandoval (1996)?

ACTIVITY 2.8

Select one of Caplan's four lacks. Specify the way in which that lack manifests itself among a group of teacher consultees. Design an inservice or staff development meeting to assist consultees with this lack. For example, if you select skill, develop a workshop to teach the deficit skill (such as communicating with teenage girls who use an abrasive communication style).

It is interesting to note that Caplan refers to objectivity as a possible lack on the part of consultees. However, though Caplan doesn't address it, it certainly may be a lack on the part of a school consultant, as could any of the other three lacks. All consultants need to continually look at their own behavior and question themselves about the possibility that the plans they suggest are a result of their own lack of objectivity. There is no doubt that each of us has his or her own personal baggage, beliefs that may not be appropriate, specific ideas that we like even though they may not be the most appropriate for any given situation, and so on. Sometimes we learn about this from our consultees, who question our ideas based on the objective facts. Self-reflection can go a long way toward guarding against this possibility, as can review of your work with other competent practitioners in the schools.

ACTIVITY 2.9

Caplan talks about objectivity as a lack on the part of the consultee. However, consultants may also allow this lack to affect their work. List some common themes among school-based consultants that may interfere with their abilities to have objective, compassionate dealings with students or consultees.

Three lacks—skills, knowledge, and confidence—are a reality in the schools (as they are in most settings related to human services work, including parenting), but the fourth lack—objectivity—which the Caplans once believed was the most common, does not seem to be as insidious as they thought. Gutkin (1981) has found that loss of objectivity is actually the least common of the problems that teachers manifest compared to possible lacks of skill, knowledge, or confidence. Sandoval (1996) gives examples of how a consultant worked with teachers of students with physical disabilities to help them to reconceptualize their "themes" about the abilities and limitations of students with these disabilities. The "themes" these teachers held were reconceptualized as lacks in the area of knowledge.

Current Approaches to the Mental Health Model Caplan, Caplan, and Erchul (1995) have presented their views on the importance of the shift to a collaborative model for school consultants who want to use a mental health approach. The Caplans continue to believe that the term *consultant* should refer to an outside expert who has psychological distance from the consultee and the situation in the school. Schools, however, have embraced the idea that internal staff (counselors, special education teachers, psychologists, mentor teachers) should do consultation. I am convinced that this school consultation should be collaborative consultation since it is an indirect service delivered in a nonhierarchical atmosphere of collaboration among experts from diverse fields. The two terms (*consultation* and *collaboration*), although they define specialized purposes (see definitions in Chapter 1, Figure 1.1), fit together well when the interaction among school personnel fits the description previously presented.

As an indication of the enduring significance of the mental health model, two entire issues of the *Journal of Educational and Psychological Consultation* (volume 14, issues 3 and 4; Lopez; 2004) were devoted to issues regarding consultee-centered consultation.

Summary of the Mental Health Model The mental health model espoused by Caplan (1970) and Caplan and Caplan (1993/1999) is not as commonly used in the schools as is the behavioral model. The mental health model is important because it serves to emphasize aspects of interpersonal and intrapersonal relationship factors that are not regarded as important in the behavioral model. The four lacks, especially the first three (knowledge, skill, and confidence), need to be addressed. The fourth lack, objectivity, seems (fortunately) not as common as Caplan suggests. The variations of Hodges and Cooper (1983); Parsons and Meyers (1984); Marks (1995); and Meyers, Brent, Faherty, and Modafferi (1993) seem to have more appeal and practical utility. Caplan et al. (1995) have provided some contemporary views of mental health consultation. Brown, Pryzwansky, and Schulte et al. (2001) provide an extensive review of the current modifications of the mental health model.

ACTIVITY 2.10

Can a consultant use ideas from behaviorism and the Caplan model in the same case? Can a person be both a psychodynamicist and a behaviorist? Discuss these questions in regard to a sample case, such as that of a student referred for acting-out behavior. See Maital (1996) for a discussion of this possibility.

FUNCTIONAL ASPECTS OF CONSULTATION

Functional Models of School Consultation

The process of consultation in the schools is continually evolving. Current beliefs have prompted individuals to develop working models of service delivery for consultation that vary depending on the philosophies, policies, practices, and goals of those charged with implementing services. Some of these models are based on theories of human behavior and derive their operations from these theories (see previous sections, Behavioral Model and Mental Health Model), while many others borrow from theoretical positions but also depend on notions of human behavior, influence, and, to some extent, values that are not specifically tied to well-developed theoretical positions. They may be more appropriately thought of as functional or eclectic in their formulations and derivations.

Following are brief descriptions of four models that are currently being used in the schools.

1. *Resource/consulting teacher (R/ct) program model.* For many years the special education resource specialist in the public schools was expected to set up a classroom designed to provide special education services on a "pull-out" basis. Students

would leave their general education classrooms for part of their school day to be given special assistance in these resource rooms. Over the past 15 years or so, this model has changed from an emphasis on "pull-out" to one that emphasizes mainstreaming and inclusion. Currently, resource teachers are more likely to be in the general education classrooms, providing specialized assistance to students and consulting with general education teachers about modifications and accommodations for students with disabilities, as well as others. The R/ct model, developed by Idol, Paolucci-Whitcomb, and Nevin (1986), works as a bridge between these two models: The resource consultant offers direct service to referred students through tutoring and small-group instruction (similar to that in most special education resource rooms) but also offers indirect service through the consultation process to teachers who have mainstreamed or included students in their classrooms. This is one of the most common ways in which resource specialists and special day-class teachers are moving toward a consultation-based mainstreaming-emphasis model of service delivery for students identified as having disabilities. Its strengths include flexibility of programming and opportunities for close communication between general educators and special educator–consultants. Possible problems are attributable to excessive case loads, insufficient time to plan, and role confusion. West and Idol (1990) have made suggestions for finding time for general and special educators to plan for collaboration using this R/ct model, including the following:

- Specifying times to meet outside of classroom time.
- Having someone else teach the class for 1 hour a week, which is then devoted to planning time.
- Meeting during regularly scheduled whole school hours.
- Periodically providing substitute teachers.

2. *School consultation committee model.* In this model most of the work is done through a committee. In many schools this committee (student study team, student guidance team, teacher assistance team, school-based intervention team, and so on) is a general education function designed to provide a forum for the discussion of referrals for assistance in dealing with student learning and behavior/social adjustment issues. This team should make recommendations for interventions and (it is hoped) provide consultative help for teachers and parents. Knopf and Batsche (1997) found a 67% drop in special education placements through their Project ACHIEVE, which relied somewhat on a team consultation model among other components. McDougal, Clonan, and Martens (2000), based on their school-based intervention team mode, found, among other positive results, that most of the objectives established for students were met, and there was a 36% drop in referrals to special education. Rosenfield (1992) implemented the school-based consultation teams project over a multiyear period and found that during the first year, 73% of the students referred to the teams were placed in special education, but by the fourth year of the project only 6% of the referred students were placed.

These committee models have to be implemented carefully. Dettmer, Dyke and Thurston (1999) point out that when the process is a committee function, responsibilities sometimes get diffused, confidentiality is harder to ensure, and the process is very time consuming. Ironically, in order to deal with the problem of time limitations, committees sometimes operate on strict time frames such as those suggested by Sprick, Sprick, and Garrison (1994), restricting the easy flow of ideas that is helpful to the problem-solving process. More information about the team model is presented later in this chapter.

3. *The problem solving model.* Over the past 10 years a number of states have developed a set of decision-making alternatives for placing students in special education services. Through a variety of waivers obtained from government agencies, personnel in at least five states have implemented what is generally known as a problem-solving model, which is to be distinguished from a model heavily dependent on formal, norm-based psychometry, particularly the aptitude–achievement discrepancy model for the determination of eligibility for special education and related services in the category of learning disabilities. In the problem-solving model, a team attempts to help a general education teacher in devising interventions that are closely monitored by a school-based consultant and evaluated primarily through curriculum-based measures. A student becomes eligible for special education only if interventions at the general education level prove insufficient. One of the strengths of this model is its emphasis on evaluating ecological variables such as school and class environment, curriculum, and instructional methodology. Ysseldyke and Marston (1999) and Powers (2001) review the generally positive results emanating from this alternative model.

4. *Collaborative consultation model.* This is the most widely known of the functional models. Since 1990, it has been emphasized throughout the educational and psychological literature as the model of choice (Aldinger, Warger, & Eavy, 1992; Brown et al., 2001; Cole & Siegal, 1990; Conoley & Conoley, 1992; Dougherty, 2000; Friend & Cook, 2003; Pugach & Johnson, 1995; Reyes & Jason, 1993; West & Idol, 1990). Its leading spokespeople are Idol et al. and Nevin (1986); Idol, Nevin, and Paolucci-Whitcomb (2000); Pugach and Johnson (1995); and Thomas, Correa, and Morsink (1995). The key components of this model are shared decision making and an emphasis on mutuality in all stages of the process. A definition of collaborative consultation given by Idol et al. (2000) is contained in Chapter 1, as is this author's definition. Here is a brief overview of the components that form the model's requisite skills, knowledge base, and attitudes:

a. *Interpersonal, communicative, interactive, and problem-solving skills.* Effective consultants need to demonstrate interpersonal intelligence (Armstrong, 1994; Gardner, 1983): the ability to be sensitive to verbal and nonverbal behavior, to interpret subtle behavioral cues, and to respond effectively to feelings as well as words. Also included in this area are interpersonal attitudes. Idol et al. (2000) have listed 11 attitudes, including (3) behave with integrity, (5) take risks, and (9) respond proactively. The ability to work with others in groups, where many decisions about school-based problems are discussed (such as SSTs and IEPs), as well as in informal chats, is also necessary. Skills in communication interact strongly with interpersonal skills. Finally, the effective collaborative consultant needs to have a firm problem-solving structure from which to operate. This ensures a steady progression toward goals based on a continuing accumulation of data. In this way, the collaborative consultation model subsumes the problem-solving model. A further explication of these skills is spelled out in Chapter 3 (Interpersonal and Communication Skills). Problem solving is reviewed further in the next section of this chapter on "roles." Steps and procedures to be followed in problem solving are reviewed in detail in Chapter 5.

b. *The knowledge base.* Idol and West (1993) suggest 12 modules, or essential components of an underlying knowledge base, including (1) knowledge of the elements of effective instruction, (5) ability to observe and interpret instructional environments, (7) curriculum adaptation, (8) instructional adaptation, and (10) knowledge of effective classroom management and discipline.

These skills, knowledge, and attitudes make up what Idol (1990) referred to as the "artful base" of school-based collaborative consultation.

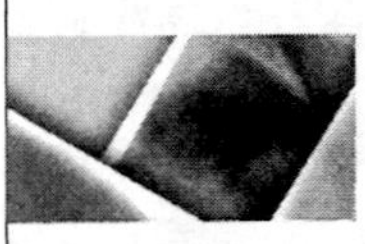

ACTIVITY 2.11

Evaluate various models of SST that are being used in local districts or that are described in the literature. Have teams of five to seven people act out the ways in which these meetings are held. Discuss the merits of each system.

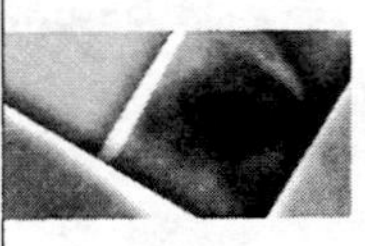

ACTIVITY 2.12

Some people can understand models better if they are pictured rather than defined with words only. Select one of the numerous models discussed in this chapter and draw a picture to help explain how the model works. You may wish to go to some of the original sources to get more specifics about each model before you try to represent it with a drawing.

Roles, Skills, and Activities of School-Based Consultants

Professionals engaging in school-based consultation have as their primary role the responsibility of providing assistance to other school personnel and parents regarding issues involving students' learning and behavior/adjustment problems. As previously indicated, this primary role requires skills in communication, interpersonal effectiveness, and problem solving (Dougherty, 2000; Heron & Harris, 2001), which are manifested in a wide range of activities. This section delineates additional roles of school-based consultants, the skills they need to be effective in these roles, and some of the numerous activities they engage in while carrying out these roles.

Roles The word *roles* refers to the perceived purposes or reasons for the existence of an activity. People are employed, generally, to engage in role-specific behavior, which is often spelled out in a job description provided to a prospective employee. Increasingly, job descriptions for special education teachers, school counselors, and school psychologists refer to consultation as an expected role. In some states, this expectation is spelled out in laws or regulations. For example, in its Education Code, the state of California defines the role of resource teachers in part as the "Provision of consultation, resource information, and material regarding individuals with exceptional needs to their parents and to regular staff members" (Hinkle, 2004, pp. 4–22 (3)). That same document also spells out an expectation that school psychologists will provide "consultative services to parents, pupils, teachers, and other school personnel" (p. A–28 [b]). Additionally, school counselors are expected to offer "counseling and consultation with parents and staff members on learning problems and guidance programs for pupils (p. A–27 [4]). Most other states have established similar legislative bases for the roles of school-based consultants.

The following are some of the roles that have been found appropriate for school-based consultation:

1. *Information delivery*. The consultant gives consultees information, ideas, facts, opinions, and food for thought about students' learning and behavior/adjustment problems. For example, consultants may provide an explanation, in practical terms, of the meaning of an information-processing deficit manifested by a student identified as having a learning disability, or they may review methods of teaching sight vocabulary to students who are not profiting from whatever methods are currently being used, or they may assist a teacher in the development of a contingency contract.

2. *Coordination/facilitation/teaching*. The consultant develops collaborative ways of facilitating planning for targeted students. An example is organizing a structured meeting of the regular education teachers of a targeted student to discuss ways of accommodating learning tasks to the student's abilities. Consultants need to think of themselves as "habit-change coordinators"—persons who recognize that, to change the behavior of targeted students, the adults who control antecedents, contingencies, and activities need to change the way they respond to these students. This involves changing the behaviors (habits) of the adults who provide direct services (teaching, parenting) to students. Another way of fulfilling this role would be to provide demonstration lessons in general or special education classrooms in an effort to show, for example, how to provide accommodations and modifications for students with disabilities and other at-risk students. Pugach and Johnson (1995) point out that the facilitative problem-solving role differs substantially from the way in which an expert may give advice because facilitation specifically focuses on helping consultees develop their own ideas and skills. Being facilitative, rather than taking over problems for consultees, is one of the most challenging tasks for beginning consultants to learn. This is what a somewhat experienced consultant says about learning to be facilitative:

> In my early perception of consulting I viewed myself as the expert. Experience has taught me I am not. Expert language is usually understood by very

> few. Knowing how to frame good questions is an invaluable tool. I used to think I knew what was best for the child. Experience again has shown me that this is not so—we must all get our respective "what's bests" on the table and mediate. I felt that I needed to have all the workable solutions to the problem at hand, but this was assuming too much. I thought everyone likes and respects the "expert" and wants his or her help. I now perceive my task as one of earning the right to become part of the planning for any child. This means that I must be as knowledgeable as possible, not only in my own field, but about the total environment (physical and mental) of each child. I am still learning that effective intervention takes time and careful planning. (unknown author, cited in Dettmer, Thurston, & Dyck, 1993, p. 12)

Facilitation requires the ability to get people with different perspectives to work together. Being able to sit in on a teacher–parent conference and keep the conversation issue-oriented and directed toward solutions can make an immense difference in a student's life.

Ellis and Fisher (1994) indicate four general principles that are designed to aid in facilitation of the consultation process:

a. *Clarification of issues.* What really is the problem/issue? From whose perspective? There may be multiple problems/issues; each constituent may see these primarily from his or her point of view. Try to stay objective through the processes of problem identification and problem analysis (Bergan & Kratochwill 1990), realizing that there may be multiple problems/issues with potentially multiple solutions.

b. *Promotion of a positive climate.* One of the enduring concerns of school-based consultants is the necessity of keeping consultees and other involved constituents in a positive, problem-oriented (i.e., solutions-oriented; see Chapter 5) frame of mind. When problems are difficult and complicated, or when consultees think that key individuals may not be carrying through with appropriate interventions, they may become discouraged and even negative. Reframing is one of the techniques that may be used to put a more positive spin on events, so that people may be more encouraged to keep trying in the face of discouraging events.

c. *Allowing group members to save face.* In the case of group consultations (i.e., SST), it sometimes occurs that individuals will say something that is potentially destructive of the consultative process. Others in the group may question what they heard and may react negatively to it. The consultant needs to put these issues on the table and have members explain themselves, even at the risk of temporarily increasing tension. It is hoped that through this process and the use of the following conflict reduction techniques, parties to the conflict can come to a closer agreement about how to proceed:
   - Name the conflict or its source.
   - Have parties to the conflict explain their positions.
   - Stick to facts, not opinions or personalities.
   - Brainstorm possible solutions.

- Seek mutual agreement.
- Be hard on ideas, but soft on people.

Littlejohn and Domenici (2001) and Barsky (2000) have written valuable resources for dealing with conflict.

d. *Promote integration of knowledge.* The school-based consultant has to develop a system for putting together the facts, opinions, desires, goals, and realities of the constituent consultees. Then she will need to forge mutually agreed-on interventions, a set of steps to be followed, and answers to the questions of who will do what, where, when, and how. Hard answers to some of these questions may not be possible at the preliminary stages, but need to be addressed before intervention implementation can progess.

3. *Indirect service provision.* The school-based consultant acts indirectly in the service of students by working directly with teachers and parents, who in turn (for the most part) are the direct service providers to the students. The vignettes at the beginning of this chapter show the need for this type of service. Although some part of the program developed for a student may involve direct services on the part of the consultant (such as counseling or specific skill development, or co-teaching activities), it is generally understood that the primary service providers are the general education or special day-class teacher, the parents, or an outside agency.

The development of this indirect service role marks a watershed in the conceptualization of the work of many people who service students in the schools. Most people now being asked to engage in this role were originally trained to give direct service to students through teaching, counseling, assessment, or therapy (speech and language, occupational or physical, and so on). Their role has expanded to include the indirect service of consultation, which is usually carried out in the triadic model discussed in Chapter 1. Because of this shift from direct to indirect service, there may be some role confusion within schools and in the thinking of these newly ordained consultants. For example, consultants need to realize that they probably will have considerably less direct contact with the referred students compared to what they used to have. Their primary interaction with the student will now be through observation, usually in the consultee's classroom or on the playground.

Skills/Knowledge To carry out the roles I have described, the school consultant needs to be skillful in a number of areas. Bradley (1994) has listed some of the essential skills and necessary components of the knowledge base for school consultants. These include the ability to examine the personal characteristics of consultees (including preferences and expectations) and to understand how the values and attitudes of consultees interact to affect the collaborative process; knowledge about communication dynamics, including the interactive process, problem-solving skills, and interpersonal skills; knowledge of stages in the consultative process as well as teaching and behavior management strategies and methodologies that may be valuable to consultees; and awareness of various models of consultation service delivery. Here is a sample of the skills identified by Bradley and others as crucial to the practice of school-based consultation:

1. *Communication.* Consultants spend much of their time simply talking and listening. Teachers, parents, bus drivers, administrators, and others need someone to talk to when they are unable to solve the puzzles created by students who aren't being successful in school. Because this is such a key role for the consultant, there is an expanded discussion of communication skills in Chapter 3.

2. *Problem solving.* The consultant engages consultees in the process of problem definition, analysis, and solution seeking. He interprets and breaks down barriers, encourages participation in the collaborative problem-solving process, facilitates the development of plans, and monitors implementation of these activities. An expanded look at the process of solutions-oriented problem solving is contained in Chapter 5.

3. *Plan development and implementation and progress evaluation.* Closely related to facilitative problem solving is the expectation that the consultant will be able to assist with the actual development of an intervention plan, follow-through with some degree of implementation monitoring, and assist with ongoing evaluation of the intervention. Dougherty (2000) has indicated that school consultants need to have these skills:

- Convincing people to accept them in the consultative role.
- Clarifying and defining the problem.
- Evaluating factors contributing to the problem.
- Interpreting data.
- Analyzing the forces that are related to nonproductive behaviors of students and teachers.
- Developing plans with consultees through a collaborative process.
- Monitoring the implementation of these plans.
- Evaluating the success of these plans.

4. *Interpersonal effectiveness.* A basic question that should be asked following an initial consultation session is "If I have met once with a consultee, will he or she want to meet with me again?" A large part of this answer will be determined by the degree to which the consultant manifested the skills previously listed in addition to their interpersonal skills. Because this set of skills is so important, I have given detailed attention to it in Chapter 3.

Activities What does a school consultant do to operationalize the roles and skills we have just discussed? What are the actual, observable behaviors of school consultants? Here is a sample of the major activities of consultants, many of which have been alluded to in the discussion of roles and skills.

Conducting interviews or facilitating discussions. This is the primary activity of consultants, and Chapter 3 devotes considerable space to it. Group-oriented interview procedures, such as those found in SST and IEP meetings, are discussed later in this chapter and in Chapter 5.

Observing interactions. It is quite common for a consultant to provide a fresh perspective by observing a student or the interactions of a number of students, or classroom or playground dynamics. These activities are discussed in Chapters 5 and 6 (for behavior-related issues) and 7 (for teaching-learning issues).

Reviewing records. Taking time to review a student's records to determine what others have said and done about her is essential. If you are able to do this before meeting with a consultee, they will be favorably impressed by your diligence.

Coordinating services. Although not a consultation activity per se, coordinating services may assist the case carrier (for students identified as exceptional) in processing the steps needed to provide services for these students or to direct the implementation of interventions for other at-risk students. Whenever there are more than two people involved in an intervention, someone must take charge of the process to see that all parties are fulfilling their roles. Otherwise, plans can go awry and confusion can develop. A consultant may be involved in face-to-face interactions, phone calls, faxes, e-mail, in-house memos, and so on.

Keeping accurate records. When a consultant meets with a teacher, a parent, or an administrator about a student, he should keep a written record of that interaction and provide a copy of it to the person with whom he met or place it in a central information location where others can see it, such as a running log of events that may be housed in the student's school records or special education file. Records of consultative interactions provide evidence of what has been discussed and planned and keep participants aware of progress toward their goals. In complex cases especially, it is important to leave a paper trail attesting to everyone's efforts. Special education due process hearings, mediations, and court cases are sometimes won or lost on the strength of a district's documentation of its efforts (Prasse, 1986, 2002). Forms for this purpose are presented in Chapters 3 and 5.

Coordinating or presenting inservice/staff development activities. Because this activity is so important and involves so much detail, the next section of this chapter is devoted to it.

INSERVICE/STAFF DEVELOPMENT ACTIVITIES OF CONSULTANTS

How do teachers and other school staff members improve their teaching or other services to students? Once their formal, credential-earning training is behind them and they are becoming more experienced in their work, what can they or their district do to maintain and enhance their skills? Keeping teachers current and continuously motivated is one of the challenges that districts need to accept. One common response to this challenge is to provide some varied types of Inservice/Staff Development (ISD) activities that are relevant, practical, timely, and cost-efficient.

ISD is here considered to be any effort ranging from personally developed and conducted to district-wide, week-long trainings, and can consist of any formally established approach that has an agenda, a structured set of goals and activities, and a method of evaluation. The time period can vary considerably. For example, ISD can be a brief half-hour, one-time meeting of a team or a larger staff group in which the consultant presents some new information, or it can be a semester-long, 3-hour-per-week seminar devoted to a thorough explication of enduring issues relevant to public education. It may occur in the teacher's lounge or in a separate facility rented specifically for the purpose. It is not devoted to clinical (that is, one-child) issues as are most individual consultation meetings or team meetings such as SSTs or IEPs. Its value has been noted by many researchers, including Darling-Hammond (1997, 1999), who recently demonstrated the connection between training in effective teaching tactics and improved student achievement.

Sparks and Loucks-Horsley (1989) indicate five different, though overlapping, forms of ISD:

- Individually guided, where a teacher (individually or with advice from another) may decide on a goal, set steps to achieve it, and then monitor the success in doing so.
- Observation/assessment, which occurs with the assistance of another professional (peer, supervisor) who observes the teacher work and together with the teacher sets goals for improvement (as appropriate) and monitors progress toward the goals.
- Development/implementation process, which is similar to the observation/assessment method, except that here the target is larger groups (departments, grade levels, etc.), who are given information, tools, materials, and so forth that are designed to improve the classroom skills of the whole group.
- Training, which is the most common of the five methods presented here, is what most people think of when the idea of ISD is discussed. It usually involves a whole school or district and often involves a featured speaker and break-out sessions.
- Inquiry, which is similar to the individually guided model (see above), except that here there is a more formal emphasis on research-based approaches to solving the problem, the development of a research question that requires a data-based approach, and an analysis of the data. This approach is sometimes referred to as "action research." It may be done in conjunction with a collaborative model between a district and a research-oriented institution, such as a university.

Which of these models or combinations of them would be best for any given situation depends on at least the following factors:

Teacher level of experience and competence.
Teacher self-motivation.
Felt needs of local teachers, community, and administration.
Need to develop new skills for shifting roles.
Value of hearing about others' ways of perceiving problems and solving them.
Financial considerations.

School consultants are increasingly being asked to become involved in staff and professional development among personnel in a school, a district, or a larger administrative unit. Such training includes providing information about students' learning and behavior/adjustment difficulties, laws relating to special education, teaching techniques, the development of behavior support systems, parent conferencing, mediation and due process procedures, strategies and tactics for inclusion, assessment, and other topics of particular interest regarding students who are disabled or at risk. A school district may use both school-based and external consultants to provide training in skills or in team building. A school consultant may be giving a workshop one week and attending one from someone else the next week; collaborative models of team functioning often lead to this sort of parity among team members.

The purpose of ISD is to provide activities that will enhance the skill and knowledge base of team members who collaborate for the educational welfare of students. Dettmer and Landrum (1997) indicate five purposes for ISD:

1. Job maintainance
2. Professional development
3. Role modification
4. Personal growth
5. Inspirational

Identify Needs

An essential first step in planning ISD is to determine what training needs exist. Generally, there are two sources of needs: those determined by the service providers and those determined by their supervisors. For example, teachers who are service providers might feel a need for more approaches to teaching reading. Their principals might think there is a greater need for these teachers to learn curriculum-based assessment methods. Whose needs shall be met? Probably the best answer is "both." Each group in the school may believe that others have a need for learning certain information or skills; this belief may not be shared by those others. Negotiating the content of ISD can be a delicate matter.

The best approach to determining needs is to conduct both formal needs assessments and informal discussions among the staff. Formats for needs determination include questionnaires, surveys, checklists, interviews, and other sources of input, such as supervisors' formal evaluations of teachers. Figure 2.1 is an example of a combined checklist/open-ended survey of regular education teachers' needs in mainstreaming/inclusion.

ACTIVITY 2.13

Working in teams of three to five people, develop ISD programs to meet a mutually agreed-on need of teachers, such as those suggested in this chapter. Go through the steps indicated and lay out ideas about how you could develop an effective ISD program.

Figure 2.1
Needs/interests for staff development

Teachers: Please indicate your interest in each of the listed topics by ranking them in order of importance to you. Then at the bottom of the sheet, tell us what specific information you would like to gain in the course of our ISD services this year. Please return these forms by Friday, September 6, to Dr. Kampwirth's box. Thanks.

________ Teaching phonics-within-literacy skills to slower learners.

________ Effective positive discipline tactics for students who are disruptive.

________ Teaching to different learning styles (such as "frames of mind").

________ Alternative assessment methods (such as CBM, authentic, portfolio, etc.).

________ Different methods for development of cooperative groups.

________ Preparing students for state-wide tests.

________ Utilizing our No Child Left Behind funds.

Please indicate your ideas about what you would like to have presented during our ISD this year:

Setting Goals and Expectations

Based on the information gathered in needs determination, the ISD planning team generates a set of goals/expectations that are both skill- and knowledge-based. They may determine that teachers need/want more information about classroom management, varied ways of teaching reading, parent conferencing, and math games and activities. They decide that they can meet these needs in the context of the four teacher/staff development days that are allocated for the year in addition to some follow-up activities designed to reinforce the material presented at the all-day workshops. They specify the order in which these topics will be presented. For example, in the Appleton Elementary District (K–8) the teachers seem most concerned about behavior management, so the ISD planning team has scheduled that topic for the first day. The team then goes back to the Appleton teachers with another needs survey instrument asking for more specific needs in this area. Based on this refined set of ideas, the team decides what it will plan to offer. These are the goals and activities for this first workshop:

- Increase knowledge about reasons for poor behavior (guest speaker).
- Generate ideas about proximal and distal causes for behavioral challenges.
- Teach the basics of two different approaches to behavior management, a communication-based approach and a contingency-based approach (guest speaker).
- By grade levels, discuss the possible use of these two methods, using case examples provided by the teachers.
- In small groups (three to five people), discuss approaches to dealing with common behavioral challenges experienced by each group member.

Determining expectations involves setting goals for measurable outcomes. When a decision is made to present an ISD on a topic, it should be accompanied by a statement delineating an objective that is data-based. Therefore, these objectives will need to be operationally defined and observable. Additionally, there will need to be a method established for recording and analyzing the data. Except for inspirational purposes, ISD should result in some observable change in behavior, at least on the part of the recipients of the ISD, and preferably on the behavior/achievement of the students.

Presenting the ISD

Joyce and Showers (1980) discuss six methods for presenting the ISD. These are:

1. *Verbal description of an idea or approach.* This is largely the lecture approach that has dominated the ISD world for many years. Though now considered to be of limited value in and of itself, it still has its place and purpose when integrated with the next five methods.
2. *Modeling.* Here a technique, method, approach, or style is shown, either live or through prerecorded material. Although presenters may show both a "wrong" way and a "right" way to do something, it is appropriate that much more emphasis be put on the correct or recommended method one is trying to teach.
3. *Practice.* Here the ISD presenter allows time for the participants to practice the modeled activity, usually with a peer or in a small-group setting. They should be given guidelines in the form of an outline as to how to perform the new activity.
4. *Structured feedback.* After ISD participants have engaged in practice of the method being taught, the presenter reviews their practice of it and answers questions regarding technique, applicability in diverse settings, and possible pitfalls that could occur when using the method. The presenter may remodel the method if appropriate in order to emphasize certain aspects of it, or he may ask individuals from the audience to model it. Certainly he will want to use volunteers for this activity, since participants who aren't confident may not want to risk looking incompetent when asked to demonstrate something with which they are not yet comfortable.

5. *Unstructured (open-ended) feedback.* Small groups of ISD participants may get together to discuss the role, use, applicability, and merits of the new methods or technique they have practiced. If a recorder keeps notes of these discussions, the presenter may wish to get further feedback from the small groups regarding their responses to the methods or techniques that were practiced.
6. *Coaching.* This term has moved from the athletic field to all aspects of help-giving or assistance. In the context of ISD, it may refer to either work with an individual teacher or a small group. Its purpose is to refine skills that are already in evidence, but would benefit from slight modifications. It has been used in a series of experiments conducted by Noell and his colleagues (see, for example, Noell, Witt, LaFleur, Mortenson, Ranier, & LaVelle, 2000) who provided in-class coaching and performance (i.e., structured) feedback of teachers in their efforts to implement interventions. These experiments indicated that more performance feedback and monitoring of progress by consultants resulted in greater maintainance of the consultees' efforts over time. Showers (1990) conducted a controlled study in which teachers coached each other in the use of teaching strategies they had learned in staff development activities. After 1 year, 80% of the teachers who had used the peer coaching services were using the new strategies, while only 10% of those who had not used the peer coaching methods had integrated the new strategies.

Idol (1998) has shown how these six methods can be used at different levels of training a staff in the philosophy and methods of a collaborative approach to the integration of special and general education services.

Follow-Up, Monitoring, and Long-Term Evaluation of Effects of ISD

One of the criticisms of the standard lecture/demonstration form of ISD is that it too often consists of a one-shot burst of interest and energy that quickly fades because nothing is done to ensure its maintenance. Follow-up and monitoring of its effects need to be part of the total ISD package. This is a valuable role for the school consultant. How and to what extent this is done is a function of time, accessibility, and interest, issues that usually can be worked out to some degree. Like so many things, following-up by using some of the techniques previously described (structured feedback, coaching, etc.) is a question of values: If the need to follow-up is considered important, people find time to do it. Classroom visits to observe a new skill that has been modeled and practiced, meetings with small groups of teachers to discuss their use of the skill, brief refresher seminars, and reports of successes at weekly staff meetings are some of the ways in which districts monitor skills applications. Whatever can be done to reduce isolation in teachers' efforts to learn new skills can be effective. Learners, either children or adults, like to know that they are sharing the experience of learning with others. The support they give each other has ramifications for staff morale and for the collaborative team-building efforts so necessary in this era of school reform. Whatever administrators can do to encourage the use of new skills will be noticed by the staff. Release time for planning and consultation, public recognition of efforts, private conferences for reinforcement, and so on are all ways in which administrators can show their acknowledgment of efforts at service delivery improvement.

Is ISD effective? The answer depends on a number of factors, especially your definition of effective. There may be many reactions to and effects of ISD, some directly related to its purposes, some indirect but by no means less important. Perhaps the Appleton district's 1-day inservice on behavior management was not well received for a variety of reasons, but the discussions it generated led to a different format for approaching discipline, quite unexpectedly, and this new format is proving to be successful. Because individuals disagreed so much about the proposed "return to phonics" workshop, the subsequent series of small-group discussions about methods of teaching reading have resulted in a modified phonics-with-whole-language approach that most people are happy with and that data show is being effective (i.e., reading scores are improving). These spin-off benefits, including the fact that teachers can find a forum for discussion among themselves about how to solve their problems and issues, are possible only in systems that are open to collaborative approaches to decision making. Administrative nay-saying about these spin-off effects are certain to put a chill on the creative interests and commitments of teachers who manifest interest in change at the task and impact concerns levels.

Figure 2.2 is a modification and summary of the steps presented by King, Hayes, and Newman (1977) that are needed for planning, programming, presenting, and evaluating ISD activities.

Figure 2.2

Planning, programming, presenting, and evaluating inservice staff development activities

1. Establish a planning committee for the delivery of ISD. Constituents should include teachers, ancillary staff, and administrators.

2. Identify needs and desires.

   Whose are they? Administration? Those of the presenter? Staff? Recipients of the ISD need input into its contents. To get this input use surveys, questionnaires, and so on.

   Know your audience: What do they want and need?

3. Examine feasibility and assign priorities.

   Review requests for content. This should be done by the planning committee.

   Consider the goals of the school and financial possibilities, especially if outside presenters will be used.

4. Obtain commitment from administration and others.

   Does the administration support it, philosophically and financially?

   Do the staff who will be involved in presenting the ISD support it?

Figure 2.2 *continued*

5. Planning and programming. Have the committee discuss at least these issues:

   Purpose and desired outcomes.

   Dates, times, and locations.

   Review expectations with presenters.

   Will the participants need information about the topic prior to the meeting?

   Detail expenses.

   Prepare announcements: What, who, where, when? Make the announcements attractive.

   Arrangements for outside presenters (hotel, transportation, and so on).

   Preparations for "The Day":

   Furniture arranged.

   Procedure for signing in participants (name tags? group assignments?).

   Refreshments: What are they and who is responsible?

   Materials needed: Audio-visual aids, handouts, activity materials.

   Develop a final check-off sheet specifying activities, timing, responsible persons, and so on.

6. Presenting the ISD.

   Who will give the opening remarks: Administration? Bargaining agent representative? Principal? Planning committee chair?

   Presenters utilize a blend of different teaching approaches (little lecture with visual backup; activities such as demonstrations, role-playing, small-group discussion; aim for maximal audience involvement).

   Be alert to audience reactions; set breaks.

7. Evaluation.

   Prepare materials in advance; perhaps distribute them in advance.

   Keep them simple; blend check marks with open-ended questions.

   Design it so it will tell you what you want to know.

8. Follow-up.

   How can you be sure there will be some retention of material or behavior change on the part of the participants as a result of the ISD?

   Send letters to presenters thanking them and informing them of the participants' evaluations.

ACTIVITY 2.14

Discuss class members' experiences with ISD. What types have they participated in? What formats have they observed? Who decided the content? What input did students have concerning goals/objectives, presenters, purposes, and so on? What were the strengths and weaknesses of the activities?

TWO SETTINGS FOR CONSULTATION: INDIVIDUAL AND TEAM-BASED

School consultants work with individual consultees and with teams of other consultants and consultees. Many chapters in this book present information about individual consultee work, in which the consultant accepts a referral from the consultee, meets individually with him, and together they work out a plan for understanding and dealing with the referral. Although there are variations in this scenario (such as two consultants or consultees, more than one client, and so on), generally this one-on-one model remains the most common form of school consultation (Brown et al., 2001; Dougherty, 2000; Friend & Cook, 2003; Thomas et al., 1995). It is popular and practical mainly because it involves the least number of individuals. Excessive reliance on team-based meetings is often regarded as impractical and/or frustrating in schools because of the conflicting demands and time limits of team members.

However, it is widely recognized that individual consultation by itself has serious limitations (Dettmer et al., 1999; Evans, 1990; Friend & Cook, 2003; Rosenfield, 1987; Rosenfield & Gravois, 1996; Thomas et al., 1995). Recently, school consultants have been emerging from this one-on-one micro level, recognizing that they should be working in and through teams more than they may have in the past. This change in emphasis has come about for a variety of reasons, including the following:

- If more people collaborate on a problem, it may result in a wider diversity of ideas about how to solve the problem (Cramer, 1998; DeBoer, 1995).
- Special education regulations require prereferral interventions, which are often, though not necessarily, developed in the context of a team meeting and are referred to variously as student study teams, teacher assistance teams, school guidance teams, school consultation teams, instructional consultation teams, intervention teams, mainstream assistance teams, and so on (Allen & Graden, 2002; Basham, Appleton, & Dykeman, 2000; Bay, Bryan, & O'Connor, 1994; Friend & Cook, 2003; Fuchs, Fuchs, & Bahr, 1990; Idol et al., 2000; Kovaleski, 2002; Rosenfield & Gravois, 1996; Ross, 1995; Safran & Safran, 1996; Thomas et al., 1995).
- There is a current emphasis on school reform and restructuring, which depends on teamwork. Teams provide possibilities for change within a context of ownership and empowerment that is not available to individuals (Basham et al., 2000; Maeroff, 1993; Sarason, 1990).

- Ideas generated in a team spread throughout the team and often beyond in a ripple effect that has a potential impact on the larger environment of the school or district (Dettmer et al., 1999; Thomas et al., 1995). Chapter 8 is devoted to issues of system-level improvement through consultation with teams of constituents at the local school or district level.

Given the potential of team approaches and the necessity for consultants to understand their role in these team meetings, we will discuss next the role and activities of the team that is primarily designed to deal with students referred for learning and behavior/adjustment problems, which is called the Student Study Team (SST) throughout this book.

Student Study Teams

The SST is essentially a general education procedure designed to assist teachers (and parents) in working out ways to more effectively meet their teaching and behavior management responsibilities to students (Friend & Cook, 2003; Fuchs et al., 1989; Huebner & Hahn, 1990; Safran & Safran, 1996). Buck, Fad, Patton, and Polloway (2003) point out that the SST process has never been required by federal law; it is entirely up to districts to decide if and how they will conduct SST meetings.

The membership of an SST usually reflects constituencies beyond that of general education, such as special education and ancillary services. The SST ordinarily consists of a facilitator or leader (who may or may not be a school administrator), a recorder (someone assigned to keep notes on the procedures), the referring teacher(s), another teacher or two from the general education staff, a special education teacher, possibly some ancillary staff (such as the school counselor, speech and language specialist, or the school psychologist), and the parents of the referred student who should be invited and encouraged to attend. Preferably, staff members with interest or expertise in the problems being discussed are asked to participate when appropriate. Students may also be invited if the group believes that their presence will be helpful to the student concerned and the process.

SSTs mean various things throughout the country. There is no one format or approach that defines the activities of these teams. Indeed, they can have different approaches and styles in different schools within a district. What they do share is a common philosophy or purpose: to work together to solve learning and behavior/adjustment problems of students, and to try to solve these problems within the context of general education. According to Meyers, Valentino, Meyers, Boretti, and Brent (1996), educators believe that SSTs should have at least the following goals:

1. Help at-risk students and their teachers by providing alternatives in terms of teaching and behavior management strategies.
2. Prevent learning problems and unnecessary placement in special education.
3. Delineate and clarify suggestions for teachers.

4. Approach school problems by using teamwork and brainstorming.
5. From an administrative standpoint, provide a method for tracking cases and coordinating services.

To meet these goals, the SST usually meets on a weekly basis for varying amounts of time per student (depending on the complexity of the problem), and varying numbers of times concerning any given student. Examples of variations on this basic theme were presented earlier in this chapter in Functional Models of School Consultation.

Students referred to SST, either prior to or following referral to a school-based consultant, are considered to have achievement or social-personal-behavioral issues that are serious enough to prompt the teacher to seek assistance from others. The purpose of the SST is to review the teacher's or parent's concerns about a student, to study the classroom or wider school issues associated with the student's difficulties, and to recommend specific interventions designed to ameliorate the difficulties. Only after a serious effort is made to deal with the problems at the general education classroom level (i.e., if the student demonstrates "resistance to intervention" [Gresham, 1991] by not responding favorably to the various interventions) should the SST consider a referral for assessment for possible special education consideration. SSTs are general education functions that are primarily intended to be sources of assistance for general education teachers.

The makeup of an SST varies considerably across districts, as do the power relationships of members. Designated school consultants need to study the dynamics of these teams (as well as IEP teams) to be as effective as possible. As I have indicated, these teams exist in order to help teachers deal with students in the mainstream. Although not required by reauthorized IDEA (P.L. 108-446), most states have adopted the stance that before a student can be referred for assessment to help determine if he is a child with exceptional needs, a multidisciplinary team must determine that the student's needs cannot be met with a modification of the regular education program. The various states have taken on the task of designing a means to ensure that this requirement is met. For example, Chapter 4 of Part 30 of the California Education Code (Hinkle, 2004) states, "A pupil shall be referred for special educational instruction and services only after the resources of the regular education program have been considered and, where appropriate, utilized" (California Department of Education, 2004, sec. 56303). Given this requirement and other concerns in the special education field (such as an ever-increasing number of students being labeled "disabled," especially "learning disabled"), states have increased their emphasis on the role of the SST as a monitoring device designed to make every effort to keep students in the mainstream while assuring that students who definitely need special education or related services are not denied them (Buck et al., 2003; Reschly, 1988; Reschly & Tilly, 1999).

School consultants need to be aware of the dynamics of multidisciplinary teams in the schools. Most teams take their job seriously and try to develop interventions that are appropriate for the general education setting. Sometimes team members have agendas that, for various reasons, may not be in the best interest of the referred student. Part of the consultant's job is to keep the meeting focused on the relevant facts and the available data. In some schools there may be a feeling that if the teacher has referred a student, that is reason enough to go immediately to the assessment phase, which prompts a formal referral and subsequent federal guideline controls. If the parent agrees with this step, this establishes a legal agreement that an assessment will be conducted and an IEP scheduled within 50 days of the signing of the assessment plan. Once this step is taken, the case takes on a whole new perspective: Does the student have a disability that meets federal and state criteria? Unfortunately, this new emphasis may detract from the efforts of general educators who continue to assist the student in the regular track. Since students who are assessed for special education and related services are usually found to be eligible for such services (Ysseldyke, Vanderwood, & Shriner, 1997), some teachers may begin to divest interest in general education interventions once a referral for assessment is made, assuming the student will soon be receiving special education services.

Although there are situations in which the development of an assessment plan may be the most appropriate thing to do, the team is still legally required (i.e., according to state guidelines, where applicable) to document the fact that modifications to the regular program have been made and that these modifications have not had a sufficiently positive effect. A common situation is the one in which the teacher has tried her preferred methods for dealing with behavior or learning problems but the student continues to present with difficulties. Most teachers want to keep their students; they develop a bond with them and only reluctantly want to discuss the possibility of considering the student for special education, especially in a self-contained class. What the teacher and usually the parent really want is assistance so that they can keep the student in the general education program. This is the situation where consultation assistance, either through individual efforts of consultants or through the SST, is most valuable (Deno, 2002; Tilly, 2002).

The essential purpose of an SST is to do group problem solving. This implies that the group agrees, at least to some extent, on the nature of the problem, the kinds of data that are needed to understand the problem, and how to develop appropriate interventions. Just how any SST goes about this is a function of the style of the formal or informal group leader. The formal leader is often an administrator or a designee. An informal leader may be appointed or may simply emerge based on a variety of factors. Sometimes the student's parent may emerge as the informal SST leader by virtue of her forceful personality. Although school personnel are always nominally in charge, a parent may be the person who most strongly influences whatever decisions are made. In any event, the group leader may find that the process bogs down for a variety of reasons, such as disagreement about the nature of the problem, what should be done about it, or the role of the regular educator in the intervention process.

Meyers et al. (1996) present data indicating that SSTs vary considerably in their approach to group problem solving. Since there are no federal government requirements or guidelines for the conduct of these meetings, each state is allowed to implement their use as it sees fit. Some states have no regulations or guidelines; hence, implementation becomes a local district or area issue. Obviously this leads to diversity in processes, goals, and outcomes. Three potential areas of difference across teams are their varied perspectives about seeing problems from student-deficit (focus on presumed intrachild weaknesses) or student-asset (focus on student strengths), teacher-skill (focus on how the teacher can bring his skills to bear on concerns about a referred student) or teacher-deficit (focus on subtle or serious mistakes the teacher is making), or student-need (focus on one student at a time) or system-need (focus on how a whole school or district can change its approaches).

Dettmer et al. (1999) suggest a number of strategies that can be used in group problem solving. All are used extensively in the business world but may be underused in the education field. *Brainstorming* allows the free development and expression of ideas with a view toward loosening the thinking of participants to develop more creative solutions. Some school personnel may be uncomfortable with brainstorming if it seems to be taking participants too far afield or consuming precious time.

For those wishing to try brainstorming, Parsons and Meyers (1984) suggest some explicit steps to follow to ensure that the process does not deteriorate into chaos. First, clarify and agree on the general topic. Second, establish a time limit; they recommend 5 minutes. Third, try a warm-up activity, possibly brainstorming about an irrelevant topic or deliberately coming up with ridiculous ideas. Fourth, have the consultant act as recorder. Fifth, have participants list ideas: censor nothing; record them all. Sixth, after the time limit has elapsed, evaluate, clarify, and elaborate on ideas. If a group seems reluctant to participate in "out loud" brainstorming, they may feel more comfortable in writing their ideas on cards, not signing the cards, and then having all the ideas read and recorded without reference to the ideas' originators. People who haven't tried brainstorming are often amazed at the results and are often eager to try it again.

Lateral thinking can be contrasted with vertical thinking, which is the logic-oriented method favored by most people. In lateral thinking the group is asked to think of the problem from a different angle. According to Dettmer et al. (1999), a group using this approach might come up with the idea of having a student provide reinforcing comments for teachers who engage in more effective teaching practices rather than offering the ordinary recommendation that the teacher should provide all the reinforcement.

Concept mapping is now commonly used by some teachers as an alternative to outlining. With this method individuals express ideas about the problem and its solution. These are drawn on sheets of paper with lines connecting them as appropriate. Ordinarily, major concepts emerge, and each will have connected themes, impressions, or facts. This helps sort out ideas and allows major concepts to dominate subordinate ones.

Idea checklists consist of premade lists of intervention ideas or sources of assistance that may come in handy when people are feeling stuck. For behavior and learning problems, the lists of ideas (that is, possible interventions) offered by Choate (1993), Cummins (1988), McCarney and Cummings (1988), McCarney and McCain (1995), McIntyre (1989), Rathvon (1999), and Sprick and Howard (1995) have proven to be quite useful to some SSTs. It must be emphasized that just because intervention ideas appear in these sources, or any other sources, it is important to try to determine the degree of empirically based support for these interventions prior to using them with students. Chapters 6 and 7 give many possible interventions that could be discussed at SST meetings.

Districts and local educational agencies have developed myriad forms for SSTs to use to keep track of the referrals, proceedings, data, and plans that the teams discuss or develop. Figure 2.3 gives an example of a form that often accompanies a referral to SST, in which the teacher delineates her concerns.

Figure 2.3

SST referral—checklist of concerns

Student Name ____________________

Date ____________

Reading:

__________ Reads (moderately; significantly) below grade level
__________ Limited ability to sound out words
__________ Poor reading comprehension
__________ Limited recall of material read
__________ Other ______________________________

Written Language:

__________ Printing (cursive) writing is poor
__________ Spelling is (somewhat; considerably) impaired
__________ (Punctuation; capitalization; grammar) is below grade expectations
__________ Produces minimal work in written assignments
__________ Other ______________________________

Mathematics:

__________ Deficient in basic processes
  __________ addition; __________ subtraction; __________ multiplication
__________ Poor conceptual grasp of mathematics; poor number sense
__________ Needs manipulatives
__________ Doesn't transfer skills
__________ Cannot tell time
__________ Poor money concepts
__________ Poor measurement concepts
__________ Deficient in advanced processes
  __________ fractions; __________ decimals; __________ percentages;
  __________ pre-algebra
__________ Other ______________________________

Information Processing Skills:

__________ Appears not to understand spoken instructions

__________ (If bilingual, indicate here)

__________ Seems confused by visual-spatial concepts (e.g., up-down; right-left)

__________ Difficulty copying

__________ Poor fine-motor coordination

__________ Poor gross-motor coordination

__________ Poorly organized; often seems confused

__________ Doesn't attend well; attention/concentration wander; poorly focused

__________ Other ______________________________

Speech and Language Skills:

__________ Poor articulation (indicate deficient sounds: __________)

__________ Stuttering

__________ Confused syntax

__________ Reluctant to speak

__________ Limited vocabulary

__________ Language usage is immature

__________ Voice is hoarse or harsh

__________ Other ______________________________

Work Habits:

__________ Limited work production

__________ Starts well, but never finishes on time

__________ Usually doesn't have appropriate materials (paper; pencils)

__________ Often off task

__________ Often needs to re-do assignments

__________ Needs to be continually prompted to continue working

__________ Limited homework completion

__________ Difficulty organizing work/materials

__________ Poor use of time

__________ Poor study skills

__________ Seems uninvolved/disinterested in academic productivity

__________ Other ______________________________

Figure 2.3 *continued*

Social Skills:

__________ Difficulty getting along with other students
__________ Rude; inconsiderate
__________ Defiant toward authority; nonconforming
__________ Projects blame onto others; denies responsibility for actions
__________ Has few friends; friends make equally poor choices
__________ Disturbs work of others
__________ Aggressive (verbally; physically)
__________ Makes inappropriate noises; talks out inappropriately
__________ Hyperactive; impulsive
__________ Destructive of property
__________ Steals
__________ Needs to be constantly monitored
__________ Other ____

Emotional Behavior:

__________ Seems chronically depressed, sad, unhappy, or preoccupied
__________ Complains about other students bothering him
__________ Intrusive; irritating
__________ Shy; withdrawn; uninvolved with others
__________ Needy; clinging; timid
__________ Expresses poor self-concept
__________ Overreacts; gets angry easily
__________ Shows extreme mood shifts
__________ Needs to be center of attention; class clown
__________ Other ____

Figure 2.4 is a form used for organizing an initial SST meeting. It delineates the major areas to be discussed by the team.

After the team meets and discusses the areas listed in Figures 2.3, and 2.4, action is taken as specified on the form (Figure 2.4) for the period indicated, and the team meets again on the date listed as "next meeting date" unless some contingency suggests the need for an earlier meeting. At the next and subsequent meetings the team again discusses the target student, this time possibly using a slightly altered form designed for the second and all further meetings regarding this student. An example of a follow-up meeting form is shown in Figure 2.5.

Figure 2.4
SST information and planning form: Initial referral

Student:	**Date:**	**Referring teacher:**
Age:	**Grade:**	**Parent(s):**

Reason for referral:

Brief history (family, health, school):

Student assets or strengths:

Interventions tried, with results to date:

Questions to be answered:

Possible solutions (include resources needed, personnel involved, time commitment, locations of services, timelines):

Today's plan (include who, what, when, where, how):

Next meeting date:

Participants:

Figure 2.5
SST information and planning form: Follow-up meeting

Student:	**Date:**	**Referring teacher:**

Follow-up meeting # __________

Results of interventions:

Current status/continuing concerns:

Today's plan:

Next meeting date:

Participants:

A copy of each form containing the information gathered and decisions made should be sent to each participant and all others mentioned on the forms, always including the student's parents. In the interests of economy, a single copy of the forms intended for use by all involved school personnel may be kept in a confidential place within the school. School personnel will be informed of this procedure. Obviously, whoever is the recorder will need to be given time to put his notes in good order for appropriate distribution.

The Importance of Structure

Schools have generally come to understand the need for providing a good deal of structure in these team meetings. Poorly organized meetings tend to be inefficient and unproductive; busy teachers and others resent having to attend them. Elements of structure include having a set schedule for when the team will be meeting and who will be on it, with at least a week's notice given to expected attendees, along with the names of the students to be discussed. At least a week is needed to inform parents so that they can make arrangements if they plan to attend. In addition, the referring teacher and others who have information to contribute need time to prepare themselves and gather relevant data. Consideration needs to be given to time constraints: How long will the team meet and how much time will be devoted to each student? Although it is possible to spend one full hour on one student, this is rarely necessary. A more typical structure is to set the meeting for 1 hour, to discuss three or four students, and to select time allotments based on the leader's estimate of the amount of time needed at this meeting for each student. Usually the team leader will prepare an agenda for the following week at the end of each weekly meeting. Figure 2.6 is an example of an agenda announcing an SST meeting for an elementary school.

The amount of time devoted to a given student (in Figure 2.6, 15 or 30 minutes) may not seem like enough to allow the team to fully discuss the status and needs of the student and those interacting with him. The choice is either to have a structured time limit or to run the risk of talking excessively and thereby ruining any chance for other students to be discussed. There had been a tendency in the past to allow participants to say their piece, no matter the time cost. Currently, however, this is not common practice. As Rosenfield and Gravois (1996) point out, time is a most precious resource. In their efforts to introduce instructional consultation teams (IC-teams) to schools, they have had to confront this problem. They provide suggestions for facilitators to use to keep members of IC-teams on track.

Each SST needs to decide on its parameters based on the needs and norms of the school culture. However, all team members should be informed that, whatever structure is decided on, it should be taught in a staff development format, and parents should be informed of the structure when they attend their first SST. It is possible to put time limits on each of the separate elements of the SST meeting (see Figure 2.4), such as 1 minute for a statement of the reason for referral; 3 minutes for the family, health, and school history; and so forth.

Figure 2.6
SST meeting agenda

Memo to School Staff
October 5, 2004
SST Agenda for October 12, 2004—Smith School

7:45—Sammy Wilson (initial meeting). Teacher: Persill; Ancillary to attend: Falama, Kampwirth, Jackson

8:00—Shawna Cutrell (follow-up #4). Teacher: Zill; Ancillary to attend: Kampwirth, Peterson; parent invited

8:15—Bill Loftus (follow-up #1). Teacher: Simpson; Ancillary to attend: none; Student Bill Loftus will attend; parent invited

8:45—Adjourn

In selected cases, however, it may be unduly rigid to impose an arbitrary set of limits; some students have a much more involved history and present with many more challenges than do others. Different teachers may have tried many interesting interventions before coming to SST, and these take time to be discussed. The development of plans in some cases is more involved than it is in others. All of these reasons, in addition to not wanting to rush parents who probably are not used to such a structured situation, argue against the predetermination of rigid timelines for any given segment of the SST plan. A total time limit, however, is recommended; your agenda is useless without it.

Meyers et al. (1996) point out that, in spite of the many real and potential advantages of an SST system, not all educators who participate are convinced that it is a useful expenditure of their time and effort. In their study, prereferral intervention team members indicated the following potential weaknesses of this teaming effort:

1. Insufficient teacher involvement/participation in the process.
2. Lack of respect for the teachers by some team members.
3. Meetings not held with sufficient frequency or consistency.
4. Inconsistent attendance by some team members.
5. Insufficient follow-up.
6. Process too slow and possibly delaying the provision of needed services (such as special education).
7. No solutions to problems.
8. Reluctance to refer to special education.
9. Problem with group process.

10. Consultation not provided sufficiently.
11. Consultation ideas difficult to implement.

Meyers et al. indicate that some respondents saw the strengths of the teams in the opposite of several of these problems. Obviously, the list contains a depressing reality: Not all efforts at team problem solving are effective. The variation across schools and districts can be immense. It is important to remember that the potential for team collaboration is positive, but poorly conducted team meetings, an inability or unwillingness to deal with predictable sources of resistance, and a lack of regard for some of the issues raised in this list will negate that positive potential and cause dissension and discouragement among the team members.

ACTIVITY 2.15

In small groups, select 2 or more of the 11 potential problems just listed above and discuss ways of preventing or dealing with these problems.

Additional information about SSTs can be found in Rosenfield and Gravois (1996), as well as Buck et al. (2003). Further comments about SSTs appear in Chapter 5 of this text in the description of how the SST can be used as part of the solutions-oriented consultation system (SOCS).

CONSULTING WITH PARENTS AND FAMILIES

Consultation with parents is increasingly recognized as a valuable, indeed essential, responsibility of the school-based consultant (Brown et al., 2001; Dettmer et al., 1999; Friend & Cook, 2003; Marks, 1995; O'Shea, O'Shea, Algozzine, & Hammitte, 2001; Sheridan, 1993; Sheridan et al., 1996; Turnbull & Turnbull, 1997). It is a truism that students identified as disabled and others at risk for school failure need to be served from a base broader than the one that occurs during the 6 hours of the school day. Aside from 8 hours for sleep, there are another 10 hours in a schoolchild's life. What goes on during those 10 hours can make a significant difference in how well students achieve and behave in school (Booth & Dunn, 1996; Children's Defense Fund, 1999; Epstein, 1995; Hanson & Carta, 1996).

Schools have traditionally believed in the value of school-home links; for students with disabilities, these links are required by the Individuals with Disabilities Education Act (IDEA P.L. 108-446). For other at-risk students, more schools are reaching out with a variety of approaches and philosophies to embrace the family as a critical component in dealing with the challenges associated with the needs of these students (Berger, 1995; Buzzell, 1996; Swap, 1987). The benefits of parent consultation and/or collaboration include at least the following (Christenson & Cleary, 1990):

- For students, improved grades, attitudes, and school attendance.
- For teachers, improved attitudes and better parent and principal ratings.

- For parents, more interaction with children in a more productive way.
- More parental cooperation with school personnel in solving children's learning and behavior/adjustment problems.

The question for the school-based consultant is rarely as simple as "Should we contact the parents about this problem?" More likely questions center around issues of when the parents should be contacted, by whom, how often, and with what agenda, goals, or offers to assist.

When. In the solutions-oriented consultation system (SOCS) process discussed in Chapter 5, there are suggested specific entry points for interaction with parents. However, the process also allows this interaction to be continuous, preferably starting with a teacher who contacts the parents of a targeted student and continuing throughout the entire SOCS process, with the contact made by the consultant, the teacher, or both. Any observation of a targeted student in a school by a person acting in a consultative fashion should be conducted only with the knowledge and permission of the student's parents.

By whom. There are no formal rules as to who is the best person to be in contact with parents about their children. Traditionally, the classroom teacher has been the primary contact person, and this remains generally true when students have been identified as disabled and are being served primarily by a special education teacher. In today's more collaborative methods of serving the needs of identified students with disabilities, parent contact may be shared equally by either the regular or the special education teacher. Circumstances and need can determine the pattern (Dettmer et al., 1999; Thomas et al., 1995).

How often. Again, the answer depends largely on circumstances. School personnel try to balance the need to communicate with the parent's right to privacy; certainly it doesn't help to intrude into family life when it isn't appreciated. The sensitive consultant will determine the amount of parent contact necessary (beyond initial permission) and the parents' willingness to engage in these contacts. Of course, the parents can take the lead by contacting school personnel whenever they want. Most parents do not abuse this privilege.

An agenda for parent consultation. The school-based consultant or teacher who contacts the parents needs to have a predetermined, specific agenda to govern her consultative interactions. Here are some topics to think about before contacting the parents:

- What exactly do I want to convey? What is the problem or issue? How can I frame it in an objective manner so as to ensure a cooperative relationship and not generate parent defensiveness? A main purpose of the first contact is information trading. What information do I want to give, and what do I want to get?
- Just who is this parent? Do I know her? What is the family structure? Who lives at home? What are their resources?
- How can I frame my concern as an invitation for the parent to work with me? What positive things can I say about his child? How can I express my concerns in language he can understand? For most parents, use the language of laypeople; avoid jargon and technical terms.

- Assuming a positive, or at least neutral, response from the parent, what can I suggest as a next step? What do I want her to do? Shall I invite her in for a conference? Shall I give her a specific task? How can I suggest we collaborate? Depending on school policy and other factors, this meeting may actually be an SST meeting. If so, inform the parents of this fact, or have the person who usually sets up SST meetings inform the parents about the nature of that team process.
- In the case of a family in which a language other than mine is spoken, who can translate for me? What implications does this have for the nature of the phone contact?

The consultant also needs to consider this information:

1. Each family constructs its own reality; members may not see the problem as you do.
2. Many families do not have the amount or type of education you have; be careful not to talk down to people.
3. Some families are not forthcoming about themselves or their customs, values, or beliefs. Be alert for their unwillingness to share much about themselves or their child while you try to remain objective about the facts and the need to take some action.
4. Some families accept problems as a part of life and may not share your desire to do something about it. While recognizing this value difference, try to indicate why their assistance would be helpful and show or tell them specific things they can do to assist in problem remediation.
5. Parents generally appreciate being asked to collaborate in problem solving (Illsley & Sladeczek, 2001; Sheridan, 1993; Thomas et al., 1995; Turnbull & Turnbull, 1997). They may respond positively and with many good ideas if asked for their advice about the referral problem. Others express a belief that you as the educator know best what to do. Many parents put the same amount of faith in educators that they do in physicians. While I am not advocating a doctor-patient expert model, I believe that the sensitive consultant needs to understand that not all parents are able or willing to collaborate beyond a willingness to listen and participate as doers rather than planners.
6. Establish goals and explain what is needed, who will do it, when it needs to be done, where it will be done, and how we will know if it has been successful.
7. Assume, until evidence indicates otherwise, that all families want to be an integral part of the problem-solving process, and be ready to join with them in this spirit. Think of the family as the best possible case manager for the child, and respect members' desire to have that distinction.
8. Last but not least, remember that consultation, whether with teachers or parents, is not about winning arguments or gaining some tactical advantage as in a debate. It is also not about blaming or a search for intrachild (or intrafamily) deficits. It is about problem solving. Seeley (1985) reminds us that learning is not produced by schools but is obtained by students who have supportive assistance from their schools, parents, and communities. This is a positive and constructive frame of mind to bring to parent consultation work.

In a first meeting with parents, the nature of the discussion varies according to the referral problem, the needs of the participants, time constraints, and other factors. Leadership of the school-based team, at least for the purposes of this meeting, needs to be determined in advance, as do the goals and agenda for the meeting. The following are suggested steps for the conduct of the meeting whether it is in the SST format or otherwise:

1. Secure a comfortable, attractive room for the meeting. It should reflect the seriousness and importance of the meeting and should be free from distractions. Refreshments, though optional, are always appreciated. A recorder of important information should be assigned, especially when the information relates to plan development.

2. The person conducting the meeting should be alerted to the arrival of the parents by the secretary at the front office and should come out to greet the parents, lead them to the meeting room, offer them seats, and conduct the introductions of all team members. Having name cards in front of all participants may be a good idea, especially in large meetings. Remember, parents may be overwhelmed by a crowd of strangers. Whether or not the student attends the conference depends on factors such as the student's age, his ability to attend to the content of the meeting, the parents' wishes, and so on. One factor to consider is the sensitive nature of the information to be delivered. If the committee believes that the student may not be able to comfortably integrate the complexity or personal nature of the information, it is better to inform the student about the essential substance of the meeting in a private setting with the parent and a faculty or staff member well-known to the student.

3. Some small talk designed to establish rapport and help the parents to relax may be useful. Then the team leader should announce the purpose and goals of the meeting, asking the parents to give their input regarding these issues.

4. The problem should be stated in behavioral terms, avoiding jargon and disease-oriented terminology. For example, it is better to say "We are concerned about Billy's high level of activity and his difficulty in approaching his assignments in a calm and task-oriented way" rather than "Observation of Billy suggests ADHD, probably stemming from some form of cerebral deficit or other constitutional dysfunction. Do others in Billy's family find it hard to concentrate? Have you taken Billy to the doctor about this problem?" Frame the issues in a way that suggests an educational approach will be useful, even if you believe and ultimately suggest that some medical advice may also be helpful. Again, get the parents' opinions about the nature of the problem. Do they see it at home? How does it manifest itself there? Have they tried specific approaches to deal with it? How have these approaches worked? What are they doing about it now? Some of this information may be expanded on later through the use of a questionnaire or rating scale that the parent will fill out with the assistance of the school staff, usually a school psychologist.

5. Analyze the problem to the depth necessary to develop a set of goals and interventions. Keep the parent input coming, being sure to add their comments to whatever written documentation is being developed. Develop only as many goals as are necessary and possible to attain, at least in the foreseeable future. These goals

must be stated in language that describes specific behaviors. "Billy will increase the amount of time he is seated in his desk and actively working on his assignments" is preferable to "Billy will improve his behavior and reduce his hyperactivity." Each goal should be accompanied by one or more interventions that may be implemented by a variety of team members, including the parents, and Billy himself. The who, what, when, where, and how questions mentioned previously need to be answered here. Loose ends need to be tied, or people will get frustrated later when the plan unravels due to poor planning.

It is best in a group meeting when the parents are in attendance for the consultant and other team members to be ready to suggest a variety of interventions that may be useful. This is done because parents ordinarily do not know enough about school or classroom procedures to make practical suggestions. Additionally, most parents expect the school team to know what to do; they would find it odd to be asked by the team what the team should do in school. Again, however, I am not implying that the school representatives will decide the goals and interventions; some parents have strong and often valuable ideas in regard to both these issues, especially goals. Encourage parental participation and input, being ready to indicate when their suggestions are useful and offering modifications as needed.

6. Assuming that the parents (or the student) will have a role in the implementation of the selected interventions, you must be sure that they are able to do their part in carrying them out. At the point of assigning responsibilities to the parents, remember that you may be asking them to engage in behaviors or undertake activities with which they are unfamiliar or uncomfortable. Christenson (1995) suggests that the school team should ask the parents "What resources or support would you like to have as you try this idea?" Sometimes parents don't know how to answer because they haven't experienced this sort of question before. It may be good to suggest ways in which the school can help, at least informing the parents of the school team's intention of following-up on plan implementation. Do this in a way that suggests that you are there to help, not to spy on or pressure the parents. Black (1998) discusses the following six kinds of family involvement that should be encouraged:

a. *Effective parenting.* Meeting students' basic needs for food, safety, and physical and emotional well-being.

b. *Consistent communication between families and school.* Phone calls are returned, report cards are evaluated, and conferences are attended. It is not uncommon in special education for there to be a daily log sent back and forth between parents and families.

c. *Volunteer service.* Many parents are eager to help out at school; they only need to be asked. Others can't because of other commitments. It is sometimes refreshing and illuminating to see how families can be of direct or indirect help at school if their help is solicited in a positive—"We need you"—manner.

d. *Support via home learning.* Homework assistance and trips to the library and other sources of cultural enrichment are examples of ways families can support the school's efforts and can provide an enjoyable outing for parents and their children, which oftentimes are relatively inexpensive. Heron and Harris (2001, p. 403) provide a thorough list of guidelines regarding homework.

e. *Decision-making efforts by family members and school personnel.* It is increasingly common for parents to belong to PTAs, site-based management teams, and other avenues of increased collaboration between home and school.

f. *Collaboration efforts.* Beyond those between home and school, the family may become involved with other community agencies, both professional/legal and voluntary, that may be of assistance to the educational needs of their students.

7. It is now time to bring the meeting to a close. It is a good idea to briefly summarize the purpose, the goals and interventions developed, and the team members' responsibilities. If a written document is ready at this time, copies can be given to relevant personnel. The parents are thanked for their participation, and a plan for the next follow-up procedure is established.

The plan is then implemented, problems are worked out according to the steps in the SOCS (see Chapter 5), and ongoing evaluation indicates what activities, including future meetings, are needed.

Further discussion of issues relating to parents and families in the consultation process can be found throughout this book. Chapter 1 presents information about treating consultees as adults. Certainly the information presented there applies to parents as consultees. Resistance to consultative efforts by parents and families is discussed in Chapter 3. Consultation with families is discussed throughout Chapter 5, especially in step 4 of the SOCS; and the participation of families is a major part of each of the case studies (see Chapter 9).

ACTIVITY 2.16

Effective parent-school consultant teams depend on a framework such as the one I have just mentioned and considerable practice. Working in teams of varying sizes, with different members taking turns at various roles and using the following problems, rehearse (role-play) consultation meetings. After each rehearsal, discuss your adherence to the steps and considerations just listed. In addition to other topics of your choosing, deal with the following situations:

1. Third-grade boy, poor reader, starting to act aggressively toward others. Intact family.
2. Fifth-grade girl, very poor academically, little parent contact over the past 2 years. Single mother, works full time.
3. High-school sophomore, refuses to go to his resource class anymore. Says he's "sick of being one of those geeks." Parents cooperative but seem to be losing control of their son at home.
4. Twelve-year-old with severe developmental disabilities. Parents want him fully included in the regular sixth-grade class, preferably without an aide, since none of the general education students have aides.
5. Seventh-grade girl, long history of antisocial and withdrawn behavior, has told her friends of her suicide ideation. Parents to date have denied any problem.

ACTIVITY 2.17

Review why consultation as a service-delivery model has been slow to develop. Dettmer et al. (1999) suggest four reasons for this: lack of understanding about roles, lack of framework for consultation, lack of assessment and support for consultation, and lack of preparation for the roles. Which of these reasons stands out in the local school districts with which you are familiar?

SUMMARY

This chapter has summarized two theoretical models of consultation that are relatively well-known and well-respected (behavioral and mental health), as well as other functional models, roles, skills, and activities used by consultants; inservice/staff development activities of school-based consultants; information about SST goals and processes; and suggestions for integrating parents into the consultative process. The behavioral model is the more common of the two theoretical models and has a much stronger research base. I make numerous references to this model in the chapters that follow, particularly in Chapter 6, which is about students who present with behavior disorders. Although the behavioral model is currently dominant, the Caplans' ideas, contained in the mental health model, especially about consultee lacks, adds another dimension to the dynamics of the consultation process.

Roles, skills, and activities of school-based consultants that are applicable to both individual consultation (that is, consultant and consultee alone) or consultation conducted in larger groups or teams (e.g., SST) were reviewed. This chapter also examined a number of functional models of consultation, which are characterized by their ready applicability in the schools and their generally favorable research support. Inservice and staff development techniques were presented as valuable activities for both internal and external consultants. SST policies and practices were discussed, and issues and opportunities for consulting with families were reviewed.

REFERENCES

Alberto, P. A., & Troutman, A. C. (1999). *Applied behavioral analysis for teachers*. Upper Saddle River, NJ: Merrill/Prentice Hall.

Aldinger, L., Warger, C., & Eavy, P. (1992). *Strategies for teacher collaboration*. Ann Arbor, MI: Exceptional Innovations.

Allen, S. J., & Graden, J. L. (2002). Best practices in collaborative problem solving for intervention design. In A. Thomas & J. Grimes (Eds.), *Best practices in school psychology—IV* (pp. 565–582). Bethesda, MD: NASP.

American Psychiatric Association. (1994). DSM-IV: *Diagnostic and Statistical Manual of Mental Disorders*. Washington, DC: Author.

Armstrong, T. (1994). *Multiple intelligences in the classroom*. Alexandria, VA: Association for Supervision and Curriculum Development.

Axelrod, S., Moyer, L., & Berry, B. (1990). Why teachers do not use behavior modification procedures. *Journal of Educational and Psychological Consultation, 1*(4), 309–320.

Bandura, A. (1977). *Social learning theory.* Upper Saddle River, NJ: Prentice Hall.

Barsky, A. (2000). *Conflict resolution for the helping professions.* Belmont, CA: Brooks/Cole.

Basham, A., Appleton, V., & Dykeman, C. (2000). *Team building in education: A how-to guidebook.* Denver: Love Publishing.

Bay, M., Bryan, T., & O'Connor, R. (1994). Teachers assisting teachers: A prereferral model for urban educators. *Teacher Education and Special Education, 17,* 10–21.

Bergan, J. R. (1977). *Behavioral consultation.* Upper Saddle River, NJ: Merrill/Prentice Hall.

Bergan, J. R. (1995). Evolution of a problem-solving model of consultation. *Journal of Educational and Psychological Consultation, 6*(2), 11–124.

Bergan, J. R., & Kratochwill, T. R. (1990). *Behavioral consultation and therapy.* New York: Plenum.

Berger, E. H. (1995). *Parents as partners: Families and schools working together.* Upper Saddle River, NJ: Merrill/Prentice Hall.

Black, S. (1998). Parent support. *The American School Board Journal, 185*(4), 50–52.

Booth, A., & Dunn, J. F. (Eds.). (1996). *Family-school links: How do they affect educational outcomes?* Mahwah, NJ: Lawrence Erlbaum Associates.

Bradley, D. F. (1994). A framework for the acquisition of collaborative consultation skills. *Journal of Educational and Psychological Consultation, 5,* 51–68.

Brown, D., Pryzwansky, W., & Schulte, A. (2001). *Psychological consultation* (5th ed.). Boston: Allyn & Bacon.

Buck, G. H., Fad, K., Patton, J. R., & Polloway, E. A. (2003). *Prereferral intervention resource guide.* Austin, TX: Pro-Ed.

Buzzell, J. B. (1996). *School and family partnerships.* Albany, NY: Delmar.

Caplan, G. (1970). *The theory and practice of mental health consultation.* New York: Basic Books.

Caplan, G., & Caplan, R. (1993/1999). *Mental health consultation and collaboration.* San Francisco: Jossey-Bass.

Caplan, G., Caplan, R., & Erchul, W. (1995). A contemporary view of mental health consultation: Comments on "Types of Mental Health Consultation" by Gerald Caplan (1963). *Journal of Educational and Psychological Consultation, 6*(1), 23–30.

Children's Defense Fund. (1999). *The state of America's schoolchildren yearbook.* Washington, DC: Author.

Choate, J. C. (1993). *Successful mainstreaming.* Boston: Allyn & Bacon.

Christenson, S. L. (1995). Best practices in supporting home-school collaboration. In A. Thomas & J. Grimes (Eds.), *Best practices in school psychology—III* (pp. 253–268). Washington, DC: NASP.

Christenson, S. L., & Cleary, M. (1990). Consultation and the parent-educator partnership: A perspective. *Journal of Educational and Psychological Consultation, 1*(3), 219–241.

Cole, E., & Siegal, J. (1990). *Effective consultation in school psychology.* Toronto: Hogrefe & Huber.

Colton, D. L., & Sheridan, S. M. (1998). Conjoint behavioral consultation and social skills training: Enhancing the play behavior of boys with attention deficit hyperactivity disorder. *Journal of Educational and Psychological Consultation, 9*(1), 3–28.

Conoley, J. C., & Conoley, C. W. (1992). *School consultation: A guide to practice and training* (2nd ed.). Upper Saddle River, NJ: Merrill/Prentice Hall.

Cramer, S. F. (1998). *Collaboration.* Boston: Allyn & Bacon.

Crone, D., & Horner, R. (2003). *Building positive support systems in schools.* New York: Guilford press.

Cummins, K. (1988). *The teacher's guide to behavioral interventions.* Columbia, MO: Hawthorne Educational Services.

Darling-Hammond, L. (1997). Principals and teachers must devise new structures to meet the challenges of education in the 21st century. *Principal, 77*(1), 5–11.

Darling-Hammond, L. (1999). Target time towards teachers. *Journal of Staff Development, 20*(2), 31–41.

DeBoer, A. (1995). *Working together.* Longmont, CO: Sopris West.

Deno, S. (2002). Problem solving as "best practice." In A. Thomas & J. Grimes (Eds.), *Best practices in school psychology—IV* (pp. 37–56). Bethesda, MD: NASP

Dettmer, P., & Landrum, M. (1997). *Staff development: The key to effective gifted programs.* Waco, TX: Profrock.

Dettmer, P., Dyck, N., & Thurston, L. P. (1999). *Consultation, collaboration, and teamwork.* Boston: Allyn & Bacon.

Dettmer, P., Thurston, L. P., & Dyck, N. (1993). *Consultation, collaboration, and teamwork for students with special needs.* Boston: Allyn & Boston.

Dougherty, A. (2000). *Consultation: Practice and perspectives* (3rd ed.). Pacific Grove, CA: Brooks/Cole.

Elliott, S. N., & Busse, R. T. (1993). Effective treatments with behavioral consultation. In J. E. Zins, T. R. Kratochwill, & S. N. Elliott (Eds.), *Handbook of consultation services for children* (pp. 179–203). San Francisco: Jossey-Bass.

Ellis, D. G., & Fisher, B. A. (1994). *Small group decision making: Communication and the group process* (4th ed.). New York: McGraw-Hill.

Epstein, J. L. (1995). School/family/community partnerships: Caring for the children we share. *Phi Delta Kappan, 76*(9), 701–712.

Erchul, W. P. (1993). *Consultation in community, school, and organizational practice: Gerald Caplan's contributions to professional psychology*. Washington, DC: Taylor & Francis.

Evans, R. (1990). Making mainstreaming work through prereferral consultation. *Educational Leadership, 47,* 73–77.

Friend, M., & Cook, L. (2003). *Interactions: Collaboration skills for school professionals* (4th ed.). New York: Allyn & Bacon.

Fuchs, D., Fuchs, L., & Bahr, M. (1990). Mainstream assistance teams: A scientific basis for the art of consultation. *Exceptional Children, 57,* 128–139.

Fuchs, D., Fuchs, L., Reeder, P., Gilman, S., Fernstrom, P., Bahr, M., & Moore, P. (1989). *Mainstream assistance teams: A handbook on prereferral intervention*. Nashville, TN: Peabody College of Vanderbilt University.

Gardner, H. (1983). *Frames of mind: The theory of multiple intelligences*. New York: Basic Books.

Gresham, F. M. (1991). Conceptualizing behavior disorders in terms of resistance to intervention. *School Psychology Review, 20,* 23–36.

Gresham, F. M., & Davis, C. J. (1988). Behavioral interviews with teachers and parents. In E. S. Shapiro & T. R. Kratochwill (Eds.), *Behavioral assessment in schools: Conceptual foundations and practical applications* (pp. 455–493). New York: Guilford Press.

Gutkin, T. B. (1981). Relative frequency of consultee lack of knowledge, skill, confidence, and objectivity in school settings. *Journal of School Psychology, 19,* 637–642.

Gutkin, T. B. (1993). Moving from behavioral to ecobehavioral consultation: What's in a name? *Journal of Educational and Psychological Consultation, 4*(1), 95–99.

Gutkin, T. B., & Curtis, M. J. (1982). School-based consultation: Theory and techniques—Intervention in the schools. In C. R. Reynolds & T. B. Gutkin (Eds.), *The handbook of school psychology* (pp. 796–828). New York: Wiley.

Gutkin, T. B., & Curtis, M. J. (1999). School-based consultation: Theory, techniques, and research. In T. B. Gutkin & C. R. Reynolds (Eds.), *The handbook of school psychology* (3rd ed., pp. 598–637). New York: Wiley.

Hanson, M. J., & Carta, J. J. (1996). Addressing the challenges of families with multiple risks. *Exceptional Children, 62*(3), 201–212.

Herbert, M. (1978). *Conduct disorders of children and adolescents: A behavioral approach to assessment and treatment*. New York: Wiley.

Heron, T., & Harris, K. (2001). *The educational consultant* (4th ed.). Austin, TX: Pro-Ed.

Hinkle, P. (2004). *California special education programs: A composite of laws*. Sacramento: California Department of Education.

Hodges, W. F., & Cooper, S. (1983). General introduction. In S. Cooper & W. F. Hodges (Eds.), *The mental health consultation field* (pp. 19–25). New York: Human Services Press.

Huebner, E., & Hahn, B. (1990). Best practices in coordinating multidisciplinary teams. In A. Thomas & J. Grimes (Eds.), *Best practices in school psychology—II* (pp. 325–246). Washington, DC: NASP.

Idol, L. (1990). The scientific art of classroom consultation. *Journal of Educational and Psychological Consultation, 1*(1), 3–22.

Idol, L. (1998). Collaboration in the schools: A master plan for staff development. *Journal of Educational and Psychological Consultation, 9*(2), 155–163.

Idol, L., & West, J. F. (1993). *Effective instruction for difficult-to-teach students*. Austin, TX: Pro-Ed.

Idol, L., Nevin, A., & Paolucci-Whitcomb, P. (2000). *Collaborative consultation* (3rd ed.). Austin, TX: Pro-Ed.

Idol, L., Paolucci-Whitcomb, P., & Nevin, A. (1986). *Collaborative consultation*. Rockville, MD: Aspen.

Illsley, S., & Sladeczek, I. (2001). Conjoint behavioral consultation: Outcome measures beyond the client level. *Journal of Educational and Psychological Consultation, 12*(4), 397–404.

Joyce, B., & Showers, B. (1980). Improving inservice training: The message of research. *Educational Leadership, 37*(5), 379–385.

Kanfer, F., & Saslow, G. (1969). Behavioral diagnosis. In C. M. Franks (Ed.), *Behavior therapy: Appraisal and status* (pp. 417–444). New York: McGraw-Hill.

Kaplan, J. (1995). *Beyond behavior modification: A cognitive-behavioral approach to behavior management in the schools* (3rd ed.). Austin, TX: Pro-Ed.

Kaplan, J. (2000). *Beyond functional assessment: A social-cognitive approach to the evaluation of behavior problems in children and youth.* Austin, TX: Pro-Ed.

Kazdin, A. E. (1984). *Behavior modification in applied settings* (2nd ed.). Homewood, IL: Dorsey.

King, J. C., Hayes, P. C., & Newman, I. (1977). Some Requirements for Effective Inservice. *Phi Delta Kappan, 58,* 686–687.

Knopf, H. M., & Batsche, G. M. (1997). *Project ACHIEVE: Background information.* Unpublished manuscript.

Kovaleski, J. (2002) Best practices in operating prereferral intervention teams. In A. Thomas & J. Grimes (Eds.), *Best practives in school psychology IV* (pp. 645–656). Bethesda, MD: NASP.

Kramer, J. J. (1990). Training parents as behavior change agents: Successes, failures and suggestions for school psychologists. In T. B. Gutkin & C. R. Reynolds (Eds.), *Handbook of school psychology* (2nd ed., pp. 685–702). New York: Wiley.

Kratochwill, T. R., & Bergan, J. R. (1990). *Behavioral consultation in applied settings: An individual guide.* New York: Plenum.

Kratochwill, T. R., Elliott, S. N., & Rotto, P. C. (1995). Best practices in school-based behavioral consultation. In A. Thomas & J. Grimes (Eds.), *Best practices in school psychology—III* (pp. 519–537). Washington, DC: NASP.

Kratochwill, T. R., Sladeczek, I., & Plunge, M. (1995). The evolution of behavioral consultation. *Journal of Educational and Psychological Consultation,* 6(2), 145–157.

Kurpius, D. J., Fuqua, D., & Rozecki, T. (1993). The consulting process: A multidimensional approach. *Journal of Counseling and Development, 71,* 601–606.

Littlejohn, S., & Domenici, K. (2001). *Engaging communication in conflict: Systemic practice.* Thousand Oaks, CA: Sage.

Lopez, E. (Ed.). (2004). Consultee-centered consultation. *Journal of Educational and Psychological Consultation, 14*(3 & 4) (Whole Issues.).

Maeroff, G. I. (1993). Building teams to rebuild school. *Phi Delta Kappan, 75,* 512–519.

Maital, S. L. (1996). Integration of behavioral and mental health consultation as a means of overcoming resistance. *Journal of Educational and Psychological Consultation, 7*(4), 291–303.

Marks, E. S. (1995). *Entry strategies for school consultation.* New York: Guilford Press.

Martens, B. K. (1993). A behavioral approach to consultation. In J. E. Zins, T. R. Kratochwill, & S. N. Elliott (Eds.), *Handbook of consultation services for children* (pp. 65–86). San Francisco: Jossey-Bass.

McCarney, S. B., & Cummings, K. (1988). *The prereferral intervention manual.* Columbia, MO: Hawthorne Educational Services.

McCarney, S. B., & McCain, B. R. (1995). *The behavior dimensions intervention manual.* Columbia, MO: Hawthorne Educational Services.

McDougal, J., Clonan, S., & Martens, B. (2000). Using organizational change procedures to promote the acceptability of prereferral intervention services: The school-based intervention team project. *School Psychology Quarterly, 15,* 149–171.

McIntyre, T. (1989). *A resource book for remediating common behavior and learning problems.* Boston: Allyn & Bacon.

Meichenbaum, R. (1977). *Cognitive-behavior modification: An integrative approach.* New York: Plenum.

Meyers, B., Valentino, C. T., Meyers, J., Boretti, M., & Brent, D. (1996). Implementing prereferral intervention teams as an approach to school-based consultation in an urban school system. *Journal of Educational and Psychological Consultation, 7,* 119–149.

Meyers, J., Brent, D., Faherty, E., & Modafferi, C. (1993). Caplan's contributions to the practice of psychology in the schools. In W. P. Erchul (Ed.), *Consultation in community, school, and organizational practice: Gerald Caplan's contributions to professional psychology* (pp. 99–122). Washington, DC: Taylor & Francis.

Noell, G. H. (1996). New directions in behavioral consultation. *School Psychology Quarterly, 11,* 412–418.

Noell, G. H., Witt, J., LaFleur, L., Mortenson, B., Ranier, D., & LeVelle, J. (2000). Increasing intervention implementation in general education following consultation: A comparison of two follow-up strategies. *Journal of Applied Behavior Analysis, 33,* 271–284.

O'Shea, D., O'Shea, L., Algozzine, R., & Hammitte, D. (2001). *Families and teachers of individuals with disabilities.* Boston: Allyn & Bacon.

Parsons, R. D., & Meyers, J. (1984). *Developing consultation skills.* San Francisco: Jossey-Bass.

Powers, K. (2001). Problem solving student support teams. *The California School Psychologist, 6,* 19–30.

Prasse, D. P. (Ed.). (1986). Litigation and special education. *Exceptional Children, 52,* 311–390.

Prasse, D. P. (2002). Best practices in school psychology and the law. In A. Thomas & J. Grimes (Eds.), *Best practices in school psychology—IV* (pp. 57–76). Bethesda, MD: NASP.

Pugach, M. C., & Johnson, L. J. (1995). *Collaborative practitioners, collaborative schools.* Denver: Love Publishing.

Rathvon, N. (1999). *Effective school interventions.* New York: Guilford Press.

Reschly, D. (1988). Alternative delivery systems: Legal and ethical implications. In J. Graden, J. Zins, & M. Curtis (Eds.), *Alternative educational delivery systems: Enhancing instructional options for all students* (pp. 525–552). Washington, DC: NASP.

Reschly, D., & Tilly, D. (1999). Reform trends and system design alternatives. In D. J. Reschly, W. D. Tilly, & J. P. Grimes (Eds.), *Special education in transition.* Longmont, CO: Sopris West.

Reyes, O., & Jason, L. A. (1993). Collaborating with the community. In J. E. Zins, T. R. Kratochwill, & S. N. Elliott (Eds.), *Handbook of consultation services for children* (pp. 305–316). San Francisco: Jossey-Bass.

Rosenfield, S. A. (1987). *Instructional consultation.* Hillsdale, NJ: Lawrence Erlbaum Associates.

Rosenfield, S. A. (1992). Developing school-based consultation teams: A design for organizational change. *School Psychology Quarterly, 7,* 27–46.

Rosenfield, S. A., & Gravois, T. A. (1996). *Instructional consultation teams: Collaborating for change.* New York: Guilford Press.

Ross, R. P. (1995). Implementing intervention assistance teams. In A. Thomas & J. Grimes (Eds.), *Best practices in school psychology—III* (pp. 227–238). Washington, DC: NASP.

Safran, S. P., & Safran, J. S. (1996). Intervention assistance programs and prereferral teams. *Remedial and Special Education, 17*(6), 363–369.

Sandoval, J. (1996). Constructivism, consultee-centered consultation, and conceptual change. *Journal of Educational and Psychological Consultation, 7,* 89–90.

Sarason, S. B. (1990). *The predictable failure of school reform: Can we change before it's too late?* San Francisco: Jossey-Bass.

Schloss, P., & Smith, M. (1998). *Applied behavioral analysis.* Boston: Allyn & Bacon.

Seeley, D. S. (1985). *Education through partnership.* Washington, DC: American Enterprise Institute for Public Policy Research.

Sheridan, S. M. (1993). Models for working with parents. In J. Zins, T. R. Kratochwill, & S. N. Elliott (Eds.), *Handbook of consultation services for children.* San Francisco: Jossey-Bass.

Sheridan, S. M., & Colton, D. L. (1994). Conjoint behavioral consultation: A review and case study. *Journal of Educational and Psychological Consultation, 5*(3), 211–228.

Sheridan, S. M., & Kratochwill, T. R. (1992). Behavioral parent-teacher consultation: Conceptual and research considerations. *Journal of School Psychology, 30,* 117–139.

Sheridan, S. M., Kratochwill, T. R., & Bergan, J. R. (1996). *Conjoint behavioral consultation: A procedural manual.* New York: Plenum.

Showers, J. (1990). Aiming for superior classroom instruction for all children: A comprehensive staff development model. *Remedial & Special Education, 11,* 35–39.

Skinner, B. (1969). *Contingencies of reinforcement: A theoretical analysis.* Upper Saddle River, NJ: Prentice Hall.

Sparks, D., & Loucks-Horsley, S. (1989). Five models for staff development for teachers. *Journal of Staff Development, 10*(4), 40–57.

Sprick, D., & Howard, L. (1995). *The teacher's encyclopedia of behavior management.* Longmont, CO: Sopris West.

Sprick, R., Sprick, M., & Garrison, M. (1994). *Interventions.* Longmont, CO: Sopris West.

Sugai, G., & Tindal, G. (1993). *Effective school consultation: An interactive approach*. Pacific Grove, CA: Brooks/Cole.

Swap, S. M. (1987). *Enhancing parent involvement in the schools*. New York: Teachers College Press.

Thomas, C. C., Correa, V. I., & Morsink, C. V. (1995). *Interactive teaming: Consultation and collaboration in special programs*. Upper Saddle River, NJ: Merrill/Prentice Hall.

Tilly, D. (2002). Best practices in school psychology as a problem-solving enterprise. In A. Thomas & J. Grimes (Eds.), *Best Practices in School Psychology—IV* (pp. 21–36). Bethesda, MD: NASP.

Turnbull, A. P., & Turnbull, H. R. (1997). *Families, professionals, and exceptionality: A special partnership* (3rd ed.). Upper Saddle River, NJ: Merrill/Prentice Hall.

Ullmann, L., & Krasner, L. (1965). *Case studies in behavior modification*. New York: Holt, Rinehart, & Winston.

Walker, J. E., & Shea, T. M. (1999). *Behavior management: A practical approach for educators* (7th ed.). Upper Saddle River, NJ: Merrill/Prentice Hall.

Watson, T., & Steege, M. (2003). *Conducting school-based functional behavioral assessments*. New York: Guilford Press.

West, J. F., & Idol, L. (1987). School consultation: An interdisciplinary perspective on theory, models, and research. *Journal of Learning Disabilities, 20*(7), 388–408.

West, J. F., & Idol, L. (1990). Collaborative consultation in the education of mildly handicapped and at-risk students. *RASE: Remedial and Special Education, 11*(1), 22–31.

Witt, J. C., & Elliott, S. N. (1983). Assessment in behavioral consultation: The initial interview. *School Psychology Review, 12,* 42–49.

Ysseldyke, J., & Marston, D. (1999). Origins of categorical special education services in schools and a rationale for changing them. In D. Reschly, W. D. Tilly, & J. P. Grimes (Eds.), *Special education in transition: Functional assessment and noncategorical programming*. Longmont, CO: Sopris West.

Ysseldyke, J., Vanderwood, M., & Shriner, J. (1997). Changes over the past decade in special education referral to placement probability: An incredibly reliable practice. *Diagnostique, 23*(1), 193–202.

Zirpoli, T. J., & Melloy, K. J. (2001). *Behavior management: Applications for teachers*. Upper Saddle River, NJ: Merrill/Prentice Hall.

Communication and Interpersonal Skills

OBJECTIVES

1. Review the elements of effective communication skills.
2. Provide a set of activities designed to assist the reader in developing a communication and interpersonal style that is likely to result in personal and professional acceptance by consultees and the development of effective interventions.
3. Analyze the nature of interpersonal skills as they apply to the practice of consultation.
4. Discuss the nature of power in interpersonal relationships, and how consultants can effectively develop and maintain a collaboratively oriented power base.
5. Review the nature, types, and causes of resistance to consultation and provide suggestions for dealing proactively with resistance, both individual and systemic.

Ms. Baker, a third-grade teacher, was asked to comment on her work with Mrs. Osprey, who is the resource specialist–consultant at her school. Ms. Baker said she greatly enjoyed her work with the consultant because she thought that Mrs. Osprey listened to her ideas, knew how to help her describe problems accurately, and helped out not by taking over her job but by showing her how to deal with problems more effectively. Together they clarified issues regarding a schedule for Mrs. Osprey's direct work in Ms. Baker's class. Ms. Baker would gladly welcome help from the consultant again.

Mr. Cook (a seventh-grade teacher–consultee), commenting on his work with Dr. Tilly, the school psychologist (the consultant) at Williams Junior High, said that he was not happy with his recent consultation experience. He thought that Dr. Tilly acted like he knew everything, didn't listen well, rushed to conclusions based on previous cases that he wanted to brag about, and implied that the consultee should have been able to solve the problem without having referred it to the consultant. The consultee has decided not to bother with this process in the future. The consultant was heard to comment that he had just finished successfully helping Mr. Cook with a very complicated problem.

This chapter discusses and analyzes the subcomponents of communication and interpersonal skills, as well as two related phenomena, power and resistance. As the previous vignettes indicate, these interdependent phenomena occur simultaneously as the consultant and the consultee deal with one another. In the first case, the consultant's effective and positive communication and interpersonal skills made Ms. Baker feel that consultation was a very useful experience, one that she wants to repeat. In the second case, Mr. Cook left the consultation experience with the exact-opposite feeling. Dr. Tilly needs to improve his communication and interpersonal skills, stop generating resistance, and stop abusing his power position. In both cases, the consultees were influenced by the way in which they and their consultants were communicating (verbally and nonverbally) with each other and the way in which they were relating (bonding, distancing, merging, dissolving, accepting, resisting) as the consultation sessions proceeded. As Kurpius and Rozecki (1993) have said, "...if the consultant does not have a mastery of the art of communication and an understanding of the intricacies of interpersonal interaction, the consultation process will most often appear lifeless and unlikely to be of long-lasting help" (p. 143).

When school-based consultants enter into a consultation role with consultees, they need to remember that they are playing multiple subroles and engaging in many activities that are essential to the consultative function, such as gathering and considering data, generating plans, identifying resources, teaching skills, encouraging, clarifying, modifying plans, and so on. These general activities are supported by the communication and interpersonal skills that are presented in this chapter. The third primary skill needed by school consultants, problem solving, is considered in Chapter 5.

COMMUNICATION SKILLS

Communication has been defined in a varicty of ways, all intended to indicate that the process requires a sender of a message, the message itself, and a receiver. Without these three components, plus some others, there is no communication. Communication requires an exchange of meaning where each participant recognizes and/or tries to influence the other's experience or beliefs.

The following skills are among the many needed for effective communication.

Attending

Nothing is more annoying in a conversation than having a listener who isn't paying attention. Attending skills are characterized by good facial mannerisms such as eye contact, head nods, and squinting or lifting of the eyebrows as appropriate. Consultants need to be careful not to let personal habits interfere with their communication style and detract from it. Some people squint too much, twirl their hair, look at their nails, or look at the clock or their watch every 30 seconds. All of these tell the listener that they aren't paying attention, possibly because they are bored, or because they are anxious for the consultee to stop talking so they can pass on their opinions about the situation and their remedies for it.

Effective body language is necessary for anyone who wishes to convey the idea that he really cares about what another person is saying. It is one of the nonverbal aspects of communication, which often carry a more important message than do the verbal aspects. Mehrabian (1971) estimated that the impact of a person's spoken message is only 7% verbal (the actual words used), 38% vocal (paralinguistic aspects; how you say the words), and 55% facial and body expression (what you convey nonverbally).

Beyond the surface appearance of attending, however, are the more important internal attending skills, which require a balance among listening to the words the consultee is using; translating them according to your experiences and preferred theories (your personal filter); and blocking out your urges to interrupt, pass judgment, or rush to a conclusion. Urging your consultee to cut to the chase is a good fantasy but will give him the clear impression that he and his perceptions of the problem and possible solutions are not important.

ACTIVITY 3.1

In teams of two (dyads), have one person try to speak to another who seems bored, disinterested, distant, or otherwise nonattending, perhaps behaving as others have done to you. Discuss how this makes the speaker feel. Then have one of the partners use better attending skills, modifying them until they feel comfortable both to the speaker and the listener.

Active (Reflective) Listening

Active, or reflective, listening as a communication skill has gained in popularity since the 1970s because of the works of Carkhuff (1969), Ginott (1972), and Gordon (1974). Active listening shows the speaker that you have heard both the subject content and the emotional content of her message. The active listener reflects back the speaker's words in such a way that the speaker knows that her words have been accurately heard and that the listener has understood the feelings behind the words.

Gordon (1974, pp. 48–49) has presented 12 "roadblocks" to active listening. These are methods or tactics that have the effect, wittingly or otherwise, of blocking communication. Three of these roadblocks are presented here with examples of what a consultant might say to demonstrate each one. Of course, using these roadblocks will likely spoil a consultation relationship. Imagine how you would feel if any of the following statements were made to you!

1. *Ordering, commanding, directing.* "Never mind what might happen; just ignore the student when he acts out. You have to do it; it's a 'best practice.'"
2. *Advising, offering solutions or suggestions.* "Well, be that as it may, it would be best to do it my way. I've seen it work before in other classes; it ought to work for you."
3. *Name calling, stereotyping, labeling.* "You're like a lot of beginning teachers I've seen. You're afraid that if you're firm, the kids won't like you. I call that being wishy-washy."

ACTIVITY 3.2

Review Gordon's (1974) roadblocks to active listening. Think of a comment that a child or an adult might make that has embedded feelings not directly expressed (for example, "Oh my God! My mother-in-law is coming over this weekend!"). Invent responses that would fit each of the roadblocks presented above. Do you know anyone who uses some or all of these roadblocks?

Other subskills of active listening include the use of *prompts, clarification-seeking, summarizing,* and *paraphrasing*. An example of a prompt is:

"You're feeling angry because Mrs. Brown has said some things that you don't think are fair."

Generally a response like this makes the speaker feel that you have really been attending to his message, not just to his words, and that you want to hear more about it. Here are some examples of clarification-seeking:

"I'm not sure that I understand what is happening between you two. Could you tell me more about it?"

"Tell me more about his rudeness to the other children. Just what does he say to them?"

"So what you're telling me is that only the cold-stare technique seems to be having any effect. Is that correct?"

The following are examples of summarizing:

"Now, let me summarize to be sure I'm hearing everything you've told me."

"OK, here's what I'm hearing: ______. Are those the main points?"

Paraphrasing involves restating in one's own words what another person has just said. Here are some examples of speaker A saying something, and speaker B paraphrasing it:

A: "Without a full-time aide, I don't see how I'll be able to give these inclusion kids what they need."

B: "You're concerned that the children with disabilities in your class won't get what they need without the assistance of an aide."

A: "So Ms. Jones came to see you, did she? I bet she really unloaded on you."

B: "You're feeling that since I saw Ms. Jones, I must have gotten a load of something from her."

One of the reasons for engaging in active listening, apart from the feelings of connectedness it gives a consultee, is that it keeps us close to the facts. For example, not summarizing accurately can get us into the position so well demonstrated by the "Gossip" game, where a group of people, in turn, hear whispered information from someone on their left and then whisper it to someone on their right. After about eight people have done this, it is almost certain that the information will have changed, sometimes dramatically, from the way it started.

Being Empathic

Empathy is implied by active listening, but I highlight it because it is crucial to the consultant's general style and demeanor. Teachers and parents expect professionals in the field of education to be empathic. They want educators to listen to their concerns, to understand them at a level greater than just the word meanings alone, and not to rush to preformed solutions. Indeed, empathy is one of the most important, and often one of the most difficult, skills and attitudes that school consultants need to possess.

ACTIVITY 3.3

In dyads, person A speaks to person B about some real or imagined trauma that she remembers from her childhood. Person B puts a mark on a piece of paper every time he feels like commenting instead of listening until person A has told her whole story. Reverse the roles. How did person A feel when she found that she could tell her whole story without being interrupted? How many times did person B have to mark his paper because he felt like commenting or questioning person A?

Being Assertive

The consultant often needs to be assertive in her response style. Adler and Towne (1996) indicate that there are five essential components to an assertive message: *an objective behavior description* ("The incidence of name-calling has increased."); *interpretation that adds meaning* ("This indicates that the intervention of extinction hasn't worked, at least so far."); *the inclusion of a feeling statement* ("I'm bothered by the possibility that perhaps we've let the extinction intervention go on too long."); *indication of possible consequences* ("This may not be in the student's best interests, or the best interests of the class."); and *a statement of intention, or purpose to these comments* ("We need to think about other possible interventions. Let's share some ideas.").

Dettmer, Dyck, and Thurston (1999) have discussed seven basic aspects of an assertive communication style, which are listed below with an example of each:

Use an "I" message instead of a "you" message: "I'm concerned about our lack of progress. [or] I think a change of interventions would be a good idea."

Say "and" instead of "but": "Your firmness was really needed there, and your efforts at controlling the whole group have really improved."

State behavior objectively: "What I saw when I was in your room was that Joanne twice hit other children, but not hard or with what I would call an attempt to harm them. Is this usually the way she interacts with others?"

Name your own feelings: "I just wanted to tell you how thrilled I am with the way you deal with the 'fearsome foursome.' You are providing the curriculum and methods that encourage attending and responding from them as well as the others. It's great to watch it working so well."

Say what you want to happen: "We had agreed that you would separate the 'fearsome foursome' and assign them to the same group only rarely. We know that doing this reduces the number of disruptions. I believe you ought to be implementing that intervention. What do you think?"

Express concern for others: "Bill, teaching your students is one of the toughest jobs on this campus. People aren't exactly waiting in line to take your class. It's draining; it's frustrating. I admire you for being as patient as you are when so many of your students are having a bad time of it all at once."

Use assertive body language: Consider your regard for, and willingness to work closely with, individuals who have trouble establishing and maintaining eye contact, slouch, mutter, seem very unsure of anything, and act like they would rather be somewhere else. Most people would rather spend their professional hours with people who reflect the opposite picture to the one I've just painted. Effective consultants use their assertive body language to convey the image that the referral problem will be solved, that they and the consultee can work together to solve it, and quitting is not a viable option.

As simple as these suggestions may seem, some consultants find them increasingly difficult to practice when the consultation relationship starts to falter, possibly due to uncooperative behavior from the consultee. Some consultees seem to project a passive resistance that is hard to pin down. Here the consultant needs to use an assertive style that lets the consultee recognize the consultant's concerns and perceptions without blaming or accusing. Further information about, and ideas to remedy, resistance in consultation are developed later in this chapter.

ACTIVITY 3.4

In dyads, have each person invent a two- or three-sentence message they would like to send to a consultee about a potentially conflictual situation, such as failure to join in the consultative effort, reluctance to engage in agreed-upon interventions, or being casual about data collection. Try to use as many of the seven suggestions by Dettmer et al. (1999) as possible in your assertive statement. Partners should help each other in the construction of these statements.

Questioning

This is the most important and most delicate skill in the consultative interaction because questions, by their very nature, can be both inviting and threatening. Their primary purpose, of course, is to gain information; but the manner in which they are used may often have unfortunate consequences, particularly if the consultee suspects that the point of a question is other than what its surface content implies. It is therefore incumbent on the consultant to ask questions in such a way that the consultee is not threatened by the questions and, by extension, the consultation process.

Questions serve three main purposes: to gather information and data, to seek opinions, and to detect attitudes. The first purpose is the most important and ostensibly the one that underlies most questions. The other two purposes may be more covert: The consultant gets information about the subjective realities that may be coloring the interactions between the consultee and the student but are not spoken about objectively. For example, consider a teacher–consultee who has implemented a behavior management program that he does not want to use because he believes it is either too labor-intensive or simply won't work. His responses to the consultant's questions about how it is working will give the consultant a pretty good idea that the consultee doesn't want to continue with this strategy. Consider the following interchange between a consultant and a consultee about a token-economy system:

Consultant: Bill, tell me how the point system is working for Allen.

Consultee: Yeah, well, we're doing it. I don't know. He might be getting better.

Consultant: You sound a little unsure. Is the frequency of yelling out decreasing since you started using the point system?

Consultee: Oh, I don't know. I'm too busy teaching all the other kids to be doing all this charting and whatever. He's probably better. I'm going to go back to using the sentence-writing strategy. [This is a punishment tactic in which the client writes "I must not talk out in class" 50 times for every time he talks out. It is this consultee's favorite technique; he's well known for it.] Allen needs to know that I mean business.

It seems clear that the consultee has not bought into the point system. A possible assertive response to this consultee's attitude and reluctance to implement the intervention might sound like this: "I understand that implementing this point system requires some extra effort. This reluctance to do it is of some concern to me because we're getting nowhere without it. I believe we need to review our purposes and methods here, otherwise we're back to square one. Let's find some time to review where we are and what to do next. Do you have 5 minutes now?"

Benjamin (1987) indicates that there are three format considerations in the questioning process: open/closed, direct/indirect, and single/multiple. An open question is designed to gain maximum information over a relatively broad scope. "Tell me about Jane's progress over the past 2 months" is quite open since it asks for (apparently) any kind of information over a long period of time in any area that strikes the consultee as important. A closed question, however, asks for brief answers to highly focused questions, such as "Tell me how often Bill hit others on the playground today during the morning recess" or "Tell me how many words José read correctly in this week's 1-minute assessment." Note that neither of these "questions" ends with a question mark.

A direct question is a straight request for information: "How do you like teaching students who have learning disabilities?" or "How many words did José get right on the 1-minute assessment?" An indirect question seeks information in a more subtle fashion: "I'd sure like to know how it must be to work with these kids all day long" or "It must be frustrating dealing with parents who don't respond to their children's needs." Note that these indirect questions, like those concluding the previous paragraph, do not have question marks; they seem to lie somewhere between a statement and a direct question. Consider the following "fencing match" between a consultant using a series of direct questions and a consultee who acts guarded in his response style:

Consultant:	So how's it going with Shaquelle?
Consultee:	Fine.
Consultant:	Is he getting to school more often now?
Consultee:	I guess so.
Consultant:	Has his responsiveness to you increased?
Consultee:	Hard to tell.

The consultant will sense that the consultee seems to be avoiding a meaningful discussion through the use of noncommittal and vague responses. In that case, the consultant may shift to a more indirect method of asking for information, such as the following: "I know you've been concerned with Shaquelle's apparent disinterest in school, and you've tried some interventions. Tell me how you see the picture now." This addition of a "prefatory statement" (Friend & Cook, 2003) is useful for establishing a context for the question and reminding the consultee of the steps already taken or suggested.

Single questions such as "What do you do when Omar gets into his dawdling mode?" seem to enhance the communication process much more than do multiple questions, such as "What do you do when Omar gets into his dawdling mode? Do you get after him right away or wait awhile? How do you know when to intervene? Some people react too quickly I think; what do you think?" Confronted with that barrage of multiple questions, most consultees probably, and correctly, ask you to wait until they can answer one question before you ask another.

It is generally best to focus our questions for a number of reasons. First, we get the kind of information we're after. Second, our time is usually limited, and although we might like to spend more time with each consultee, we and they usually don't have that luxury. Third, by being focused we give the consultee the impression that we are efficient and competent. Finally, it is dangerous to be casual in our choice of questions with some consultees because they take that as an excuse to ramble. There are definitely times to ask "How's it going?" but we are likely to make more specific progress if we ask "In regard to the extinction plan, can you give me an example of when it seemed to work?" When the consultee has responded to that single, direct, and closed question, then you may want to ask "And can you give me an example of when it didn't?"

ACTIVITY 3.5

Class members should list examples of poor questioning techniques that they have encountered. Discuss why these techniques were poor, why they were used, and what effect they had on the communication process. Class members should suggest ways to improve these techniques.

For example, a consultant is concerned about the appropriateness of a given curriculum for an included student. She says to the teacher, "Can't you find something more appropriate for Billy to do?" Instead of using this confrontive technique, how might she have begun the discussion of the curriculum?

ACTIVITY 3.6

In teams of three, have partner A ask a very general, broad, open question, such as "Well, how's it going?" Partner B should focus the question, such as "How does the rules-ignore-praise plan seem to be working?" Partner C should turn it into a closed question, such as "Since implementing the R.I.P. program, what has been the frequency per day of Billy's loud outbursts?" Team members should take turns practicing the different ways of asking questions and reflect on how they would feel as a consultee if they were asked questions in the various styles possible.

ACTIVITY 3.7

In teams of three, generate some realistic topics for a consultant–consultee interchange. Then have member A play the role of the consultant, member B the consultee, and member C an observer. The consultant conducts the interview for about 5 minutes, while the consultee responds. The observer then comments on the interview (mainly positive criticism) using the following criteria:

Was some degree of rapport established?

Did the interview flow well?

Was there a good balance between open and closed questions, and direct and indirect questions?

Were single questions primarily used?

Were questions posed in such a way that the consultee didn't appear to be threatened by them?

If most of the answers were positive, the consultant did a good job. Change roles until each partner has had a chance to play each role.

ACTIVITY 3.8

Videotape a simulated consultative interaction, preferably with a consultee with whom you are not familiar. When reviewing the tape, respond to the questions presented in Activity 3.7. Note your body language and nonverbal communication efforts. Were you aware of them? Do you believe they add to or detract from your interviewing skills?

The Interview

All of the communication skills we have discussed are used in an interview format, which may be informal or formal. Informal interviews are more common. They consist of those numerous occasions when the consultant and the consultee meet in the hallway or the teacher's lounge and spend a relatively unstructured (but not purposeless) 5 minutes or so talking about a student. Formal interviews are planned in advance, are held at a specified time and place, have a definite agenda and set of goals, and may occur in a group or team setting (for example, an SST).

When a consultant is informed of a consultee's concerns, it is generally best to schedule an informal meeting first, simply to find out how severe the referral problem is. Sometimes this informal meeting is all that is necessary. The consultee may leave with the information or idea that she needs in order to deal effectively with the problem without any further assistance. Usually, however, the result of this first (informal) meeting is the decision to either direct this referral to the SST or to some other ancillary consultant, or to meet again in a formal way.

When setting up a formal interview, it is important to establish a nonhierarchical, collaborative relationship at the outset. You can do this by having the consultee establish the time and place of the meeting. Since teacher–consultees have a fairly rigid daily schedule compared to that of most school consultants, this flexibility on the part of the consultant should be expected. These meetings usually take place in the consultee's classroom and, of course, at a time when the students are elsewhere.

The consultant should have at least a semistructured set of questions to ask during the formal interview. The nature of the questions depends on the nature of the referral. In the case of behavior problem referrals, the consultant will want to know about type, frequency, duration, impact, and goals of the behaviors in addition to information about antecedents, consequences, and the sequence of actions that constitute the behavior problem. Referrals focusing on academic deficiencies will address the areas of concern, assessment data, curricular materials, teaching methods, student groupings, and so on. A number of formal methods of interviewing have been developed. Shapiro (1996) has presented the Teacher Interview Form for Academic Problems, which includes very specific items pertaining to a student's functioning in the basic academic areas. Bergan and Kratchowill (1990) have developed interview formats for use in a behavioral consultation model. They include interview items for the three areas of problem identification, problem analysis, and treatment evaluation.

Taking Notes, Keeping Track

It is important for the consultant to take notes during a formal interview. Since some consultees may be disconcerted by your note keeping, it is necessary for you to explain why you will be doing so, especially if this is the first formal interview you have had with a particular consultee. Your reasons will probably include at least the following:

1. It is important that you keep information accurately since many situations are complicated.
2. You are dealing with many student–teacher–parent issues at the same time, and it is easy to get cases confused as the weeks go by if you don't keep fairly detailed notes.
3. You will probably be writing a report on this referral at some point, especially if it becomes a referral for special education eligibility consideration, and your notes are necessary for this purpose.

My experience is that teacher and parent consultees seem favorably impressed when they see that I am keeping notes; one teacher commented that she wished her physician seemed as interested in what she had to say as I did!

As the interview progresses, it usually becomes clear that additional information will be needed in order to understand and deal with the problem. Some of this information will be obtained by the consultee, and some by the consultant. Some may come from conversations with others (such as parents, last year's teacher, the counselor, outside agency personnel, and so on); and some will be obtained through observation by the consultee, the consultant, or both. When the interview moves to the plan development stage, the "wh" issues (who, what, when, where) need to be settled so that both parties know their respective responsibilities in regard to the next steps.

Figure 3.1 is an example of summary notes given to a consultee after a first consultation meeting with a consultant. These summary statements were generated from the notes the consultant took during the interview with the consultee and are a good example of solutions-oriented collaborative consultation.

Controlling the Consultative Interaction

To what extent should the consultant attempt to control the flow of conversation in consultation? Behaviorists (Bergan, 1977; Erchul, 1987; Erchul & Martens, 2002; Kratochwill & Bergan, 1990) believe that it is appropriate and necessary for the consultant to structure verbal interactions in order to gather the required information as efficiently as possible. Erchul (1987), for example, concluded that dominance (defined as the ratio between attempts to control an interaction by the consultant and consultee's yielding such control) and consultee's perceptions of consultant effectiveness were positively related and approached statistical significance ($p < .08$). Gutkin (1999) has pointed out some inconsistencies in the Erchul (1987) article, as well as other articles (Erchul & Chewning, 1990; Witt, Erchul, McKee, Pardue, & Wickstrom, 1991) purporting to demonstrate the advantages of dominance or other aspects of control on the part of consultants. DeForest and Hughes (1992); Hughes and DeForest (1993); Maitland,

Figure 3.1

Summary notes from a first consultation meeting (Billy)

Consultee (teacher): Ms. Sallie
Grade: 5 (and RSP)
Consultant: Ms. Morrison, resource specialist program, (RSP) teacher

Date: 9-26-04
School: Jefferson
Room: 14
Parent: Mrs. Appleby
Age: 10-4

Student referred: Billy Appleby
Student's birthdate: 5-20-94

Reason for referral: Billy isn't completing his work in any subjects in his mainstreamed fifth-grade class with Ms. Sallie. He dawdles, plays with toys, talks to and bothers others, and alternates between being the class clown and playing the role of the tough guy (e.g., "You can't make me"). Ms. Sallie is suggesting a self-contained class for him.

Background information: Billy is the second of three children of parents who were divorced in June 2003. His schoolwork started to fall off last year (mother's report). Mom now works full time. Father has moved to another state. Billy is doing well in his one period of special education with me.

Solutions that have been tried and results: Billy has been kept after school, made to take work home, been moved nearer the teacher, and been put on a behavior contract. His mother has also tried tutoring him at home. The contract has helped somewhat but probably needs to have stronger contingencies. Otherwise, he just seems to be getting worse.

Tentative ideas that were discussed: Review behavior contract (consultant and consultee); conference with mother; conference with Billy; counseling for Billy; use Billy as a tutor, dependent on increased productivity of work (possibly in a different special education class); get Billy a tutor from an upper grade; get Billy an in-class study-buddy; I'll assess further to determine specific skill deficiencies in the content areas; increased consultation time between Ms. Sallie and me.

Today's plan: Consultant will arrange a conference with Billy's mom and then with Billy. Consultee will review behavior contract with Billy, seeking input from him on more effective reinforcers. Consultee will review Billy's day with him at the close of every day for one week; a note will be sent home to Mom summarizing each day. I'll do an additional assessment within a week. I'll contact Mr. Pruzek (school psychologist) about possible counseling.

Next meeting date: 10-4-04 at 10:30, Ms. Sallie's room.

cc: Mr. Poplar, principal; Mrs. Appleby; Mr. Pruzek, counselor.

Fine, and Tracy (1985); and Schowengerdt, Fine, and Poggio (1976) have demonstrated the effectiveness of a collaborative approach through studies that point to the importance of interpersonal skills that have the effect of making the consultee feel supported in his efforts. Other studies (Babcock & Pryzwansky, 1983; Pryzwansky & White, 1983) have shown potential consumers of school consultation services to have a clear preference for a collaborative relationship rather than one dominated by consultant control of the process. Those who favor a more collaborative mode are comfortable with letting the consultee give direction to the conversation based on her needs and interests as long as the conversation is goal-directed (Friend & Cook, 2003; Thomas, Correa, & Morsink, 1995).

Gutkin (1999) and Erchul (1999) have provided a lively debate about issues of control in the consultative process, with Erchul citing research support in favor of strong consultant control of the process, and Gutkin showing design faults with most of that research (see previous paragraph), as well as presenting arguments that many issues in consultation are too subtle to be dealt with in most research paradigms.

Potential Difficulties in Communication

It is not uncommon in interpersonal communications for people to miscommunicate, to talk past each other, to simply disagree, and possibly to slip into an argument that may disrupt, if not destroy, the consultative process. Although consultants cannot control the reactions of consultees, they can avoid behaviors on their part that may lead to poor communication and problem-solving breakdowns. Pugach and Johnson (1995) discuss several barriers to effective communication. These are presented here, with an example statement made by a consultant using these methods:

1. *Advice.* ("So, Ms. Garcia, Willy is one of your poorest readers. He must need more work in phonemic awareness. Give him an extra half-hour whenever you get the time. That should do it.") Eventually, consultants do give advice (i.e., develop interventions collaboratively), possibly as a confirmation or facilitation of a consultee's thinking about his own problem-solving efforts. When teachers and parents are stuck for ideas, the consultant should certainly be able to suggest a number of alternative interventions, which should be based on best practices. The error is in giving your advice before the consultee has had a chance to explore his own thinking about solutions; in giving your advice too quickly, before you have a good grasp of the problem and/or before the consultee is ready for it; or because it is your favorite technique. Our "quick fixes" often do not meet the criteria of treatment acceptability or treatment validity (see Chapter 5). Sometimes we give advice because we feel pressured to do so. If the context of a consultative interaction is that the consultee has "come to you for advice," and you don't have any to give, or believe it is too soon to generate an intervention program, the consultee may feel let down, or that you are incompetent. You can avoid this situation by reviewing the nature of the collaborative model, reminding the consultee that more data should be obtained before hurrying to plan development, reviewing what the teacher is currently doing or has done in the recent past, and then agreeing on some possibly temporary tactics the consultee can use until the referral problems are understood in more depth.

2. *False reassurances.* ("Hey, not to worry. Those outbursts are probably due to something going on at home. They'll pass in a few days or weeks. Most things we get ourselves concerned about don't amount to a thing. Remember, don't sweat the small stuff.") Some consultants, in an effort to relieve the stress of a consultee, make it sound like the referral issue is really quite simple and may resolve itself, or will quickly be improved. This may serve to minimize the consultee's feelings and devalue her concerns. It may also set up a feeling within herself that she must be incompetent to be worried about something so trivial. Finally, it may set up a situation where time proves that the consultee was right about the seriousness of a problem, thus indicating a lack of competence on the part of the consultant. The false reassurance is similar to one of Gordon's (1974) roadblocks to effective communication.

3. *Misdirected questions.*

(Consultant):	So, Ms. Ortiz, tell me about Alphonso.
Ms. Ortiz (Consultee):	Well, his reading is really quite poor. He—
Consultant:	(Interrupting) Oh, like so many of those second-language boys. By the way, does he have a brother in the fourth grade? I think I know him.
Ms. Ortiz:	Well, yes he does. But Alphonso is really almost a nonreader—
Consultant:	(Interrupting again) Well, here's what we have to do. Can you get me his cumulative folder? Put it in my mailbox. Now, if he's like his brother, well, you tell me. Does he have ADHD?"

These misdirected questions happen for one of two reasons: (a) the consultant has his own agenda and seems determined to force it on the consultee, attempting to have the problem fit a predetermined notion the consultant has formed about the problem or (b) the consultant's listening skills are so poorly developed that he has no idea that he is interrupting or asking irrelevant questions. The consultant is flying off in all directions, lacking focus and sensitivity to the needs and interests of the consultee. Somehow the question of how to get help for Alphonso in reading has become a family-related problem, epidemic among English-language learners, and possibly associated with ADHD. One wonders if this consultant will ever begin to problem solve about Alphonso's reading problem.

4. *Wandering interaction.* ("Yes, Alphonso's reading problem. I thought it was math. Well, either way, I believe he has a brother who is similar. There is interesting research on familial characteristics. I had to read it once for a course I took.") This is similar to the issue of misdirected questions, but here the consultant seems to be the person with ADD. She can't remember what was told to her a few minutes ago, gets cases mixed up, and seems unable to focus on what is relevant.

5. *Interruptions.*

(Consultee):	LaTreece needs so much help. We have to review...
Consultant:	(Interrupting) Yes, I know. So many do.

Consultee: Well yes. As I was saying, LaTreece can't do any of the work at grade level...

Consultant: (Interrupting again) This business of work at grade level. Really now, how many times do I have to tell teachers...)

Just as the consultee is getting to the heart of the concern, the consultant breaks in to ask questions or to make comments that frustrate the efforts of the consultee to tell her story. This sort of consultant impulsivity breaks the flow of the interaction and suggests that trying to problem solve with this consultant is not worth the effort.

6. *Cliches.* ("Peter? Oh, yes, shady eighties, isn't he? Have you met his parents? As they say, the apple doesn't fall far from the tree.... Speaking of trees, he isn't the brightest light in your tree, is he?") The use of cliches tends to diminish the stature of the person to whom they are directed. To refer to a student as a "shady eighty," a reference to one for whom there are lowered academic expectations because his or her IQ is in the 80s, or to imply that parentage is the root of a student's problems, as in "The apple doesn't fall far from the tree," not only implies lowered expectations for the student but may cause the teacher-consultee to give up trying to implement accommodations on behalf of the student.

7. *Credibility gap.* (Consultant, to herself, upon seeing a referral from Mr. Wong: Oh, boy, another waste of time from Wong. I'll knock myself out giving suggestions, he'll nod his head, won't do any of them, and will continually remind me about how "these kids" just can't learn.) (Consultee to himself, when told at the SST meeting that the interventions discussed will be monitored by the consultant Mr. Smith: Oh, boy. Smith, as usual, won't have a clue about how I should implement these ideas. He never does.) This is the most subtle of the communication problems. It involves the usually unspoken belief on the part of one or both parties that they shouldn't take the consultation process seriously because the other party isn't (a) competent, (b) in a position to collaborate, or (c) of any real help. This can occur when a consultee has been so uncooperative in the past that the consultant enters a dyadic interaction with little hope for a positive outcome. It can also occur if a consultee has no faith that the consultant can grasp the significance of a problem or can help construct meaningful interventions. In either case, the lack of faith precludes success because collaboration cannot operate in a climate of little faith in each other.

Evaluating Your Communication Skills

Both beginning and experienced consultants will do well to occasionally have their efforts at consultation evaluated by their consultee(s). Feedback of this sort can help the consultant to understand how others perceive both the consultant personally and her effectiveness. Conoley and Conoley (1982) have provided a self-analysis form that could easily be used by others to evaluate the consultant. In their later book, Conoley and Conoley (1992) provide a consultant–trainee evaluation form that could easily be modified to suit the purposes of the experienced consultant. By engaging in this level of self-analysis, along with the more objective feedback provided by their consultees, consultants can develop the feeling of confidence that comes from the awareness that they are effective communicators.

ACTIVITY 3.9

Devise a self-analysis method that includes at least the following dimensions for evaluating your communication skills:

Listens without interrupting
Accepts consultee's point of view
Identifies important points
Summarizes, paraphrases, clarifies
Interprets nonverbal language to self and possibly to consultee
Pursues issues assertively
Reinforces consultee's efforts

One of the best methods for self-evaluation is the use of the video camera. By taping one or more real or simulated consultative interactions, it is possible to review what took place during the interactions in light of the communication skills and subskills discussed previously. Figure 3.2 shows a form that could be used for self-evaluation purposes while viewing a videotape of one's consultative interactions.

Figure 3.2
Videotape self-evaluation scale

VIDEOTAPE SELF-EVALUATION SCALE

Date: ____________ **Consultee:** ____________ **Meeting #** ____________

(Note: in these sections, write narrative evaluative comments)

Quality of initial greeting:
Establishment of rapport:
Statement of purpose of meeting:
Review of concerns:
Review of intervention techniques:
Review of progress:
Development of future plans:

(Below, score yourself in each of the areas and give examples of effective or ineffective uses of each of these areas)

Attending	1	2	3	4	5
Active (Reflective) Listening	1	2	3	4	5
Being Empathic	1	2	3	4	5
Being Assertive	1	2	3	4	5
Questioning	1	2	3	4	5
Conducting the Interview	1	2	3	4	5
Controlling the Interaction	1	2	3	4	5

INTERPERSONAL SKILLS

Consultation is essentially a problem-solving process that is dependent on effective communication and interpersonal skills. Communication skills can be successful only if delivered in the context of an interpersonal relationship that is positive and professional. This section reviews information and provides activities designed to improve a consultant's knowledge and skills in interpersonal relationships, power dynamics, and methods for understanding and dealing with resistance.

ACTIVITY 3.10

The following examples contrast positive and negative interpersonal traits and suggest comments that characterize them. The first example in each pair is a positive trait; the second is negative. After reading each pair of comments, create a different positive response that is appropriate for the trait.

Open: "I'm glad you could see me."

Closed: "You want to see me now? Well, I suppose."

Accepting: "I'm sure that you did what you felt was best."

Judgmental: "Why would you want to do it that way?"

Empathic: "It must really be difficult dealing with students who challenge us so often."

Callous: "What did you expect? That's what teaching here is all about."

Puts consultee at ease: "Tell me about your day."

Puts consultee on defensive: "Certainly there must be better ways to teach reading."

Stresses collaboration: "We can get together to mutually solve these problems."

Plays expert: "Oh, no, research clearly shows that doing it the other way is better. Trust me."

Professional approach: "Let's review to be sure I've heard you accurately."

Immature approach: "Billy? Did we discuss him already? What was our plan? Did we have one?"

Broad-minded: "Well, that's an interesting way to look at it. How might we use that idea?"

Narrow-minded: "Well, we've never tried that before. We'd better stick to the tried and true."

ACTIVITY 3.11

Think about the various kinds of relationships you have established with coworkers and supervisors over the past few years. Some, no doubt, were more positive than others. What were the interpersonal skills that some of these people manifested that made you enjoy working with and for them? What mannerisms (behaviors, traits) made you dislike or not want to work with others?

Desirable Interpersonal Characteristics and Skills

Your responses to Activity 3.10 and the list of positive traits you discussed in Activity 3.11 should make it clear that people generally respond more positively to, and are more likely to want to work with, consultants who manifest positive and professional interpersonal skills. Consultants who are open, constructive, caring, task-oriented, enthusiastic, calm, flexible, and respectful of others' points of view are more likely to have success than those who manifest the opposite traits (Harris, 1996).

Brown (1993) has presented a list of competencies needed for effective consultation that covers three main areas: knowledge base, skills, and judgmental competencies. Interpersonal competencies are found in each of Brown's three areas. For example, under *knowledge base,* he has listed conflict resolution, group dynamics, and theories of consultee resistance. Under *skills,* he includes developing collaborative relationships and synthesizing a personal model of consultation. His *judgmental* competencies list includes intervening in group process; developing an awareness of personal style and the ability to vary style based on the characteristics of the consultee; and providing successful consultation, as measured by consultee and client (student) variables, to teachers, parents, and other caregivers.

Compared to the counseling literature, which has many studies of effective interpersonal skills (Herman, 1993), research in the consultation field has not yet developed a wide base specifying the relationships among interpersonal traits and effectiveness in consultation. There has, however, been some research in this direction. For example, Schowengerdt et al. (1976) have found that consultants who exhibit warmth, understanding, and empathy are likely to have a positive and significant impact on their consultees. Bushe and Gibbs (1990) have found that a high degree of intuition and level of ego development (i.e., maturity; serious approach to tasks; desire to be helpful) are predictors of consultation success as measured by trainer and peer evaluations. Savelsbergh and Staebler (1995) have measured the interpersonal styles of 31 consultant–teachers with the Myers-Briggs Type Indicator (Briggs Myers, 1976) and found that when these consultants were both data-based and outgoing (extroverted), they were perceived by their supervisors as being more effective.

The following is a list of interpersonal skills that are important for successful interactions in the schools, with suggestions for how a school consultant can manifest these skills.

Forging Positive Relationships Although one shouldn't fall into the trap of believing that it is essential to be liked by all people at all times (Ellis, 1973), it is certainly the case that people are more willing to work with affable, outgoing, friendly people than with people who aren't.

Suggestions: Become one of the staff. Don't be aloof. Get out of your office or your own classroom. Make comments that indicate that you identify with your consultees rather than with any other group. Be the kind of person that consultees feel comfortable talking to. While maintaining your own professional identity (resource specialist, school psychologist, and so on), try to walk in your consultee's shoes. Learn the art of small talk and when to use it. For some consultees, 5 minutes of rapport building before serious talk begins is essential; for others, 10 seconds of small talk is enough.

Conveying Competence and Confidence Being friendly is essential, but consultees won't have any use for you if that's all you are. You need to be prepared to be a helper by developing a solid knowledge base in all relevant areas (e.g., curriculum, method, classroom behavior management, special education), and by developing a repertoire of evidence-based interventions that can be adapted to fit a variety of situations. Confidence comes from a feeling of being well trained and prepared for consultation and from successful experiences. Confidence bred of egotism or an inflated self-image not supported by the reality of one's competence will soon be detected by your consultees.

Suggestions: Develop as many of the skills listed in this chapter as you can. School-based consultants first have to be competent in process; content knowledge comes with experience and continued study of the literature. When a situation arises for which you can't find any answer or solution and none is forthcoming from your consultee, admit that this is the case and then go out and find helpful information. Talk to your peers, search the literature for best practices, and review your experiences in other cases to see what you can come up with for your next meeting. Challenge your consultee to do the same.

Projecting the Idea That the Situation Is Going to Improve A consultant can make a valuable contribution by being optimistic. Try to convey that the situation of concern is amenable to improvement. Don't buy into the hopelessness you often hear from some consultees; provide an antidote to the defeatism that is so common, especially in inner-city schools. Try to adopt the mantra: *No excuses: it's our job.* A good source of information about this phenomenon is Seligman's (1991) *Learned Optimism.* For ideas on ways of improving education, especially in urban areas, see Hill, Campbell, and Harvey (2000); Langer (2001); and Ready, Edley, and Snow (2002).

Suggestions: Much of the defeatism that consultants hear in the schools is a function of stress and burnout (Raschke, Dedrick, & DeVries, 1988; Sapolsky, 1994). Teaching is a very difficult profession, and when a teacher's ego needs are thwarted by students who are disruptive or failing, these stresses may begin to have an effect. By the time the referral gets to the consultant, the teacher often wants relief in the form of the removal of the student or the implementation of some punishment plan.

When you perceive this degree of stress, remember the following:

- Be a good listener. Plan to spend some time allowing the teacher to vent frustrations.
- Reflect the emotional content of the consultee's message.
- Project the possibility that, by working together, you and the consultee can improve the situation.
- Demonstrate competent problem-solving skills (e.g., getting specifics, reviewing data), seek points of agreement, and stress the possibilities.
- Ask how you can help (short of removing the student from the teacher's responsibility).
- Set a time to meet again. This will show the consultee the ongoing nature of your commitment.

Following Through with Enthusiasm One of the condemning definitions of consultants is that they "pop in, pop off, and pop out." Consultation as a service delivery method will be accepted as a viable, worthwhile model only if consultants demonstrate commitment manifested by timely follow-up, staying with the situation until it is resolved or until the consultee decides that she wants to let it develop on its own for awhile. Consultants need to follow-through without becoming a nag or a pest.

Suggestions: Always set a time for a next meeting, and be there. Come prepared with a copy of the notes you wrote after your last meeting. (An example of summary notes of consultation meetings was presented earlier in this chapter in Figure 3.1.) Be sure you have done the part of the plan assigned to you. Go beyond this if possible. Have some new ideas to discuss. Suggest some fresh perspectives. Review current goals and interventions. Be prepared to praise efforts. Validate treatment integrity (assuming you have observed it). Be thorough without being overbearing. Respect your consultee's time constraints.

Developing and Maintaining Trust Anyone who has been new to an organization knows that a period of time is necessary before trust is established. As the proverb says, it takes a lifetime to build trust but only a moment to lose it. Consultees need time to build an opinion of a new consultant, to see if that person is true to his word. Similarly, consultants need time to build trust in those with whom they work. If a consultee says he has tried an intervention, has he? If a principal says she will provide support for a program, will she?

Suggestions: Be sure that you are honest and dependable in your dealings with others. Practice being a "high-trusting" person, one who expects others to do as they say, just as you do. If you find that you cannot follow-through on some project as you said you would, be sure to inform your colleagues as soon as possible. Collaborative consultation is built on mutual trust, not just on hope.

POWER IN THE CONSULTATIVE RELATIONSHIP

One of the key concepts that underlies a collaborative approach to consultation is that of egalitarianism, or a nonhierarchical relationship between the consultant and the consultee. However, you cannot assume that the existence of this collaborative philosophy guarantees that power dynamics won't influence the relationship. It is best to understand power in interpersonal processes so that you can use it constructively.

French and Raven (1959) have discussed five forms of social power that can be influential in most types of interpersonal relationships. In the following examples, person A is usually (but not necessarily) in an authority position relative to person B.

- *Reward*, in which person A is able to bestow benefits, valued praise, or awards on person B.
- *Coercive*, in which person A can either dispense or withhold benefits from person B, or can legitimately confront person B.
- *Legitimate*, in which person B believes that person A has a legal or an authoritative ability to control person B.
- *Referent*, in which person B sees person A as similar to himself or holding like values and may therefore comply with suggestions from person A.
- *Expert*, in which person A is perceived as having knowledge or expertise not possessed by person B.

Later, Raven (1965) added a sixth source, informational power, in which the information has the power, not the person (A) who gives out the information. Martin (1978) and Harris and Cancelli (1991) point out that reward, coercive, and legitimate power should probably be reserved for supervisory or administrative personnel and that the power sources for a collaboratively inclined consultant should be referent, expert, and informational.

Referent Power

The collegial nature of consultation, its nonhierarchical foundation, its voluntary status, and the use of indirect rather than direct confrontation tactics are all hallmarks of referent power. Consultees want to feel that you are one of them, or at least that you can see their problems from their points of view. Even veteran teacher-consultees will wait to see if the consultative interaction shows that the consultant is someone who can empathize, see the problem from their perspective, join in the development of effective interventions, and be positive and professional in relationships with them. If they come to believe that the consultant has these positive characteristics, in addition to a solid knowledge base, they probably will accept him, no matter what his background is.

If, however, consultees believe that they cannot identify with the consultant, that he does not possess positive interpersonal characteristics and presumes to know more about the consultees' responsibilities than they know, consultees will reject him, and the consultant's efforts will collapse. In this case consultees will not see the consultant as having referent power and therefore may devalue his potentially useful contributions. Naturally, all of this could occur even if the consultant does have teaching experience and an extensive knowledge of curriculum, method, and behavior management, but simply doesn't know how to use this information as a source of informational power, or only wants to tell the consultee how he used to handle problems in their class, heedless of the differences between his experience and that of this consultee's current situation.

ACTIVITY 3.12

Assume that you are a special education teacher–consultant who has not taught in general education. A general education teacher–consultee subtly questions your ability to understand what teaching in general education classes is all about. How might you deal with this potential threat to your referent power base?

Expert Power

I have pointed out in Chapter 1 that the expert model is not emphasized in this text because consultees in the human services field often reject it either overtly or subtly (Caplan & Caplan, 1993; Evans, 1980; Lippitt & Lippitt, 1986; West, Idol, & Cannon, 1989). They may reject this model because they don't believe the "expert" ideas are appropriate in their classroom, because they do not feel any ownership of a solution if it is handed down to them, because they subtly reject being told what to do, or for other reasons.

This is not to say that a consultant's expertise has no value in a collaborative model; it certainly does. Expertise in the process of consultation is essential. If a school consultant is not expert in the processes of consultation, she must seek help to become expert or abandon the enterprise. She should also be expert in the content of consultation (that is, specific information about interventions for learning and behavior problems and best practices in education), because it can assist the consultee in developing his ideas about what he might be able to do about the referral problem. Collaborative consultation requires a nonhierarchical relationship between the consultant and consultee. When the consultant acts as the expert in the content area, the consultee can feel demeaned and may develop a dependency that spoils his ability to problem solve alone in future cases (Lippitt & Lippitt, 1986). Vernberg and Reppucci (1986) have commented that they see "expert" consultants as those who take over the problem-solving process, usually limiting their ideas to a few with which they are most familiar and thereby putting restrictions on the range of possible solutions. As an alternative, they suggest following the ideas generated by Rappaport (1981), which stress *empowerment,* a term conceptually related to collaboration. One empowers consultees by listening to their ideas, developing interventions compatible with these ideas, and thereby strengthening the beliefs of the consultee that he can be an effective problem solver himself.

Naturally there are exceptions to these generalizations. Beginning teachers need the knowledge they can gain from an experienced consultant, as do those with limited experience in specific settings. Insecure and passive consultees might also need to have specific ideas given to them, but these ideas should always be thought of as options that the consultee can consider and modify to suit her style and particular classroom contingencies. Generally, however, it is best to encourage the consultee to come up with his own solutions based on his background, the goals for his class, his teaching style, and so on. Imposing ideas and values is a temptation that should be resisted. The consultant's expertise in both process and content should be used to help the consultee work out the details of his plans, to suggest ways to improve his ideas, and to list alternative steps or strategies from which he selects appropriate interventions based on his ideas about what he would like to do, as well as ideas from the consultant that are compatible with the consultee's expert judgments. Martin (1978) has suggested that competent consultants will try to strike a balance between referent and expert power bases. One doesn't want to appear to "have all the answers," nor does one want to be "just like everyone else" and not bring additional insights and information to the consultative effort.

It is possible to get trapped into playing the expert and abandoning the collaborative model when under pressure from consultees to do so. The following scenario, along with the cases presented in Chapter 9, demonstrates how a collaboratively minded consultant avoids the expert trap. Note how the consultee, a general education teacher, continually tries to get the consultant, a resource teacher who has just started working with "Sammy," to solve the problem and how the consultant "out-defers" the consultee (Conoley & Conoley, 1982).

Consultant: Good morning, Mrs. H. How are you today?

Consultee: Not so good. You know Sammy, of course. He's no better. When we had the SST meeting on him, you told me to get back to you if things didn't improve. Well, I'm back.

Consultant: Sounds discouraging. Let's see if I remember the details. He's in your fourth grade, weak academically, a bit hyper, off task. Right so far? You were going to gather some data on his work completion and something else… I forgot what it was. We had also discussed using a contract. Is that right?

Consultee: Oh, you remember him all right. The "something else" was out-of-seat behavior. I tried the contract. It worked for a week or so. I really think he belongs full time in special ed. Why are we wasting time this way? Two periods of RSP aren't enough.

Consultant: Yes, the contract. I'm glad you were able to try it. Tell me about it.

Consultee: Well, you know, stay in your chair, finish some work for a change, and you can earn some free time. The usual sort of thing. He didn't know what to do with himself when he earned the free time (only twice, you know), so he seemed disinterested right away. What are you going to do about him?

Consultant: I'm not sure what we can do; it's kind of up to you. I'll be glad to help, but I really need to know more about what's been tried, what the data looks like, and where you'd like to go next with it.

Consultee: Well, the data sheets are in my room if you want to see them. They don't show any change since I started keeping track 2 weeks ago. If it is up to me, where I'd like to go next is back to SST, get a referral for assessment, and get on with full-time placement. That's what he needs. So should I put in another referral or what?

Consultant: No, that won't be necessary. We can bring it up at the next meeting for another look, if you'd like. But listen, have you got 5 minutes right now? Let's take a look at that data and then talk over some ideas about how to help Sammy.

Consultee: Well, 5 minutes, OK.

(Together they go to the consultee's room and review the data sheets.)

Consultee: Well, what should I do with him?

Consultant: Let's start with what has been tried and then see if some of those ideas are working and how we can build on what you've already tried with him.

Consultee: Well, as I say, nothing seems to work. I mean there is nothing I can do about his poor reading. If I stop to help him with every word, the group starts to moan.

Consultant: OK. Let's stay with that. The poor reading is a real problem, and we'll hope that his two periods a day in RSP with me are going to be helpful to him. After I get to know Sammy better I'd like to coordinate our programs for him. In the meantime what are some ways you can get around his inability to read the books and still ensure his learning the content?

Consultee: Well, I suppose if I could find a study-buddy for him whom he wouldn't clown around with so much...

Consultant: Good idea. Think about who your more serious students are; one of them would be a good role model for him. That's a good idea. What else have you thought about?

Consultee: We did the contract, and it was a flop. What could I do with that? How should I do it? I wish you'd write one. Maybe I don't know how.

Consultant: When you were using the contract, what ideas did you have about why it wasn't working? Why did it flop?

Consultee: Well, as I told you, he didn't know how to take advantage of the reinforcer. He just wandered around the room, bothered a few kids, and acted bored.

Consultant: So he hasn't learned how to make good use of free time, even when he's earned it. Tell me about the reinforcer. Where did the idea of free time come from? Was it his choice?

Consultee: No, it's what I always use. I took a course at the university, and that's what the teacher said: Use free time as a reinforcer because everybody likes it.

Consultant: Well, what do you think of that now, I mean for Sammy?

Consultee: Well, he's an exception. One for every rule, you know. What are you suggesting?

Consultant: You know Sammy. What do you think he'd be willing to work for?

Consultee: I don't know. But I'm not into giving away candy or anything else. Once you start doing that that's all they want.

Consultant: Have you seen the reinforcement survey some of the teachers use? It's that one-page questionnaire that gets at what kids like and are willing to work for. Many of the things listed aren't things you have at school; they're things their parents get or do with them. Do you think it might help to see how Sammy responds to this? Your contract idea might work after all if you're able to get a more specific set of reinforcers to use.

Consultee: Yeah, well, maybe. Do you have a copy of it? I've seen it but haven't used it yet. And I need you to look at the contract before I try it again. It needs something to make it jazzier.

Consultant: I'll be glad to. I'll get you some copies of the reinforcement survey, and after you've filled it out with Sammy, put it into my box and I'll come to see you about the contract wording and design. [Makes a few notes for himself.] Now, here's where we are now. I'll get you some copies of the survey, and you'll return it to me and we'll meet then to develop another contract. I'll also put Sammy's name on the SST meeting agenda if you still want me to.

Consultee: For sure.

Consultant: Meanwhile, you'll be getting Sammy a good role model as a study-buddy, and what else would you like to try with him before we go to SST again?

Consultee: I'm going to call his mom again. I had asked her to, well, you know, we talked about it at the last SST, getting him some books at his level from the library and sitting down with him every night to help him with his reading, writing, and spelling. I don't think she's done a thing about it. His homework doesn't look like anybody helped him with it.

Consultant: You may be right. Could I make a suggestion? Perhaps you might put more focus on what Sammy's mother can do. Sometimes parents get overwhelmed when asked to work on too many things. What do you think?

Consultee: Oh, I don't know. I think she can spend 20 minutes a night. They've only got one other child, and she has a husband at home. I'll feel her out about it. I gotta go. See you whenever. Get me that stuff. Say hello to your wife.

In this case, the consultee approaches the consultant feeling agitated and defeated. She has let her worst fears take over and has given up on her own ability to help the student. The consultant does not allow himself to fall into this trap of saving her by readily accepting her catastrophic reactions to what seems to be the result of a poorly designed contract, a poorly monitored study-buddy system, and a lack of follow-up on a plan that Sammy's mom was supposed to follow. In only 5 minutes or so, all of this is revealed, and steps are planned to remediate much of it. The consultant has assigned himself some tasks, and the consultee has some work to do. Since the consultee wants something official to happen, she is asking for another SST meeting. She knows that the SST is the forum where she can press her case for full-time special education for Sammy, and she may be able to talk the team into agreeing with her. The consultant hopes not, however, and he will continue to try to get all other sources of help for Sammy activated. Perhaps members of the SST will agree and make other suggestions that will further that aim.

Notice how often the consultee tries to get the consultant to do something: to take over responsibility for Sammy, or to activate a process of removing the problem from the consultee's doorstep. As you review how this consultant deflects these direct requests/demands, you should get some notion of how a collaboratively minded consultant works. It would have been very easy to do one (or both) of two things: give in and agree that full-time placement is needed, or act like the expert and tell the consultee just what she should do to deal with Sammy. When the consultee defers to the consultant's assumed expertise in solving all problems, the consultant out-defers her by getting her to think about what she has done and how she might improve it. When done well, this sort of verbal interchange between a consultee and a consultant exemplifies "the scientific art of collaborative consultation" (Idol, Nevin, & Paolucci-Whitcomb, 2000).

What forms of expert power did the consultant use? He was expert in his ability to maintain a calm demeanor, in his willingness to listen and integrate data, in his wanting to be helpful without taking over, and in setting a plan. These are all examples of process expertise. He did not tell the consultee how to manage Sammy's reading problem or how to apply contingencies to Sammy's out-of-seat behavior. He might at some point, however, if the consultee asks about these problems and makes it clear that she doesn't know how to manage them. Perhaps the revised contract they jointly develop will add specificity to these issues.

ACTIVITY 3.13

Review the previous scenario. Rewrite the consultant's lines to make them reflect an expert's approach. Then rewrite the original again, making the consultant even more collaborative, if you can.

It is important to remember in collaborative relationships that expert power works both ways; the consultees also have this power (Martin, 1978). They have expertise in teaching or classroom behavior management that a consultant may not have. They know the curriculum, their students, and their own frame of reference regarding what is possible in their classrooms, what has worked for them in the past, and so on. Their knowledge base needs to be understood, respected, and used. Ignoring it threatens the consultative relationship and alienates teachers (Pugach & Johnson, 1989). The same comments apply to parents when they are serving as consultees (Brown, Pryzwansky, & Schulte, 2001).

Informational Power

According to Raven (1965), informational power derives from the fact that information based on scientific findings, or based on the experiences of people who know about the topic, is almost always recognized as valuable. To the extent that a person has informational power we tend to think of them as expert. In any given consultant-consultee dyad, either party may have more informational knowledge than the other. The source isn't as important as is the perceived usefulness of the information. One of the roles of the consultant discussed in Chapter 2 is that of information giver. Consultees expect that school-based consultants have their positions because they have informational power in addition to some degree of expert power based on their experience, training, advanced degrees, and the ability to project themselves as experts.

Recent Thinking About Power Issues in Consultation

Raven (1992, 1993) and others (Raven, Schwarzwald, & Koslowsky, 1998) have revisited the original French and Raven (1959) ideas about social power. In these current writings Raven introduces a power/interaction model of interpersonal influence. Factors to consider in using this model are one's motivation to influence (Just why does a consultant believe she should be involved in this situation?), an assessment of the availability of the power bases previously discussed (Which ones can be accessed to advantage?), preparation of the influence attempt (How should the consultee be approached?), and the need to assess results (Just how will we know if our use of power was truly influential?). Erchul and Raven (1997) have discussed strategies for the use of this model.

O'Keefe and Medway (1997) have also taken a further look at the uses of power (which they refer to as interpersonal influence) in consultation. They believe that a major role for the school consultant is to try to influence the consultee to change his attitude and behavior toward the student without resorting to manipulative tactics. Related to this line of reasoning is the Elaboration Likelihood Model (ELM) of attitude change (Petty, Heesacker, & Hughes, 1997). This model posits the belief that intervention ideas that are developed collaboratively and that consultees consider "reflectively" are more likely to be implemented and become a permanent part of the consultee's repertoire than are those considered "nonthoughtfully." A reflective consideration involves giving thought to the underlying assumptions that support the intervention, while a nonthoughtful adoption of an intervention is based on giving in to the alleged superior knowledge or experience of the consultant. Nonthoughtful adoptions tend not to be taken seriously. Petty et al. (1997) suggest that consultants try to make the interventions personally valued by the consultee, make the consultee's role explicit, be sure the consultee has the knowledge and skill to implement the interventions, and keep a positive emotional atmosphere throughout the consultation process. They also suggest that consultees are more likely to be reflective if they have collaborated about the design of the interventions, see the interventions as valuable from their perspective, and are congruent with their thinking about the problem. This model is very similar to the one utilized by Conoley, Conoley, Ivey, and Scheel (1991) in which those researchers attempted to enhance consultation effectiveness by matching intervention recommendations to the consultee's perspective.

In a recent study designed to measure school psychologists' use of power in consultative relationships Erchul, Raven, and Ray (2001) found that these consultants preferred to use "soft" as opposed to "harsh" power bases. The soft bases included referent, expert, and informational power, while the harsh relied on impersonal coercion, personal coercion, and legitimate position sources of power. Erchul et al. suggest a cautionary note to those who may believe that power has no place in consultative relationships by pointing out that school consultants should recognize the positive influence that strategies drawn from noncoercive power bases can have.

ACTIVITY 3.14

In dyads, have partner A invent a school-relevant problem and act very deferential toward the consultant (partner B). The consultant should practice deflecting this deference and urge the consultee to apply her own problem-solving skills to the problem.

RESISTANCE

A consultee's behavior, like that of everyone else, has one of two functions: to get something or to avoid something. Those who decide that they don't want something develop behaviors designed to avoid it. If consultees or students don't want to engage in the changes intended by a consultative effort, they usually find some way to avoid that effort. We call these avoidance tactics *resistance*.

Resistance seems to occur in just about all change efforts. It appears to be a natural reaction to self-initiated change efforts as well as those we perceive as being suggested or directed by others (Carner & Alpert, 1995; Piersal & Gutkin, 1983; Resnick & Patti, 1980; Wagner, 1998; Wickstrom & Witt, 1993). It occurs when a consultee feels either threatened by proposed changes in his work environment, as would be necessary if he needed to change his behavior in order to affect a change in a student's behavior, or if he believes that his views on the issues were not given appropriate consideration.

Gallesich (1982) states, "Resistance to consultants is a natural phenomenon. The integration of any new person into an ongoing social structure unbalances it, creating reactions and forcing members to make adjustments" (p. 279). Gallesich reminds us that resistance can be healthy or unhealthy. A healthy form of resistance might occur when the changes being suggested are really counterproductive and the consultee resists on that basis. Unhealthy resistance might take the form of blocking needed changes that would benefit the student or the system but would be inconvenient for the consultee to perform or would be alien to the consultee's beliefs or accustomed ways of behaving. Another example of unhealthy resistance would be when the consultee is angry or fearful about a proposed change (innovation; intervention) and does not express this anger directly, but rather does so indirectly by subtly sabotaging or ignoring the recommended intervention. An example of sabotage is given in Activity 3.15.

ACTIVITY 3.15

Mrs. Provo, the third-grade teacher of Ahmad, agreed with the resource specialist to try a "Good Behavior Card" for Ahmad just so she could end the conference. This consists of putting a card on the corner of a student's desk that has target positive behaviors written on it, which the teacher is to check off as they occur. Mrs. Provo thought the idea added too much extra work for her, but she did it, although with a tone of voice and attitude that made Ahmad feel more like he was being punished than rewarded.

1. Analyze the dynamics behind this situation.
2. How might the consultant handle this situation once it becomes clear that Mrs. Provo is being passively resistant to the intervention?

Gross (1980) views resistance "as a normal coping behavior having as its purpose the preservation of the organism rather than the obstruction of change" (p. 1). These two effects may occur together: The organism, defective or perfect, is preserved as change is obstructed. Here, again, resistance can be seen as healthy or otherwise.

Margolis (1991) has commented that resistance is usually not malicious. The role of the consultant is to understand the factors fueling resistance (much as one would conduct a functional behavioral assessment of a student who presents with behavioral challenges), to take the specific perspective of the consultee into consideration, and to encourage "...influential participation in decision making of those responsible for implementation" (p. 7). This point of view fits the model of collaborative consultation perfectly.

Wickstrom and Witt (1993) define resistance as follows:

> Within the context of the consultant–consultee relationship, resistance includes those system, consultee, consultant, family and client (that is, student) factors that interfere with the achievement of goals established during consultative interactions. Resistance, then, is anything that impedes problem-solving or plan implementation and, ultimately, problem resolution, including both passive and active components of an ecology that functionally operate to get in the way of intervention planning, implementation, or outcome. (p. 160)

This is a broad definition of resistance that goes beyond the belief that resistance is always and only something that exists in the behavior of the consultee. I, along with Wickstrom and Witt, take the view that systemic factors, governmental regulations, well-accepted school norms, and even subtle hints from administrators can be the sources of resistance that impede the consultative process.

During an interview with a consultee, or in the context of a group meeting (i.e., SST), the consultant must be aware of resistance tactics that may be used, wittingly or otherwise, by consultees with an agenda that differs from yours. These tactics delay progress or, at worst, completely thwart the spirit and purpose of consultation. The following information will help you to understand resistance in terms of its types, causes, and ways of dealing with it.

Types of Resistance

All experienced consultants have their own lists of behaviors they have observed that demonstrate resistance. Here are some of the most common types of resistance:

The Direct Block There are some teachers who have no interest in consultation, ignore any efforts to get them to change their minds, and simply stonewall the whole process. Or they may engage in the process up to the point of implementation and then decide that they don't want to participate any longer. Fortunately, this response style is not common in today's schools.

"Yes, but...." The consultee always seems to have some reason not to try anything. Although he may agree that an idea has merit, he concludes that it is not worth trying because it might not work. He may give some of the following reasons:

"I tried it before with a different student, and it didn't work."

"Somebody else said she tried it, and it didn't work."

"The problem is too serious."

"This student has [some disability], and this needs to be treated elsewhere."

"I don't have the time."

"This sounds like a good idea, but I'm just not sure that a change would be good right now."

"If I do that for this student, it will seem unfair to the others."

All of these reasons (excuses) for not implementing a change effort may have some truth. Only an analysis of the situation can determine what part is truth and what part is an excuse or stalling tactic. As discussed in Chapter 2, those aligned with the mental health theory of consultation would suggest that any of the reasons listed previously may be due to a consultee's lack of confidence, objectivity, skill, or knowledge, or a combination of these.

"I did it, but it didn't work." The consultee has (or claims to have) tried the recommended interventions and found them wanting. You often don't find out that this has happened until you inquire about the effectiveness of the intervention. If the consultee calls you to tell you that an intervention isn't working and asks for further help, she probably isn't resisting. Resistance occurs after a plan has been developed, time has gone by, and the consultee supposedly has tried the plan and been unsuccessful but hasn't bothered to tell you about it. This sort of passive resistance may be due to a feeling of embarrassment due to the plan's not working. Of course, it is entirely possible that the recommendations haven't been successful for a variety of reasons other than resistance. When you look into the situation and see if the consultee is eager to move forward or not, you will have a better sense of whether the problem is resistance or something else. Naturally, it is necessary to investigate to determine if there was treatment integrity; that is, was the treatment carried out as intended (Gresham, 1989; Kratochwill, Sheridan, & Van Someren, 1988)?

Friend and Bauwens (1988) list other types of resistance common to school consultation: the *reverse,* in which the consultee agrees to planned interventions but does not follow-through or does them in a manner that is unlikely to work (as in the example in Activity 3.15); the *projected threat,* in which the consultee refuses to cooperate because some person (principal, parent, perhaps even the student) won't like it; *the guilt trip,* manifested by a consultee who acts as though the extra burden of the intervention is excessive; and *tradition,* in which history is invoked as an argument against trying anything new or different.

Whatever the type of resistance, it is necessary to investigate both the causes and possible ways of working with the resistance in order to reduce or eliminate it. Hoskins (1996) indicates four ways of understanding resistance:

1. Determine the perspective of the resistor. Does he believe he is too busy; does he feel "picked on"?
2. Does he fear that something bad will happen? Perhaps he feels he may fail or lose control of his classroom.
3. What does the resistor really want? What does he believe would make him more in control, or successful?

4. How can you help the resistor achieve what he wants while meeting the needs of the student(s) and other members of the collaborative group?

Detailed information about strategies for dealing with resistance are presented later in this section.

ACTIVITY 3.16

After reviewing the types of resistance, discuss strategies for dealing with them. Have one partner present with one or more of these types, and have the other partner attempt to discuss them with an attempt to answer the questions indicated by Hoskins.

Causes of Resistance

Any threat to the status quo can cause some people to put up defensive barriers and to find many reasons to resist. The following are among the most common causes for resistance.

Habit Strength Teaching and parenting are supported in part by the usefulness of habit, or consistency. Teachers and parents tend to do today what they did yesterday, last week, and last year. Even schools have as a priority the maintainence of a consistent approach to education. A consultant is usually called in because the consultee's habitual reactions to the referral situation aren't working. Thus, trying to get the consultee to try new approaches is to some extent a question of appreciating the strength of the consultee's habits and suggesting a new behavior with which the consultee has a good chance of being successful. For example, a consultee's usual reaction to the disruptive behavior of a student is a mild reprimand, a cold stare, a brief talk with the offending student after class, a punishment consequence (perhaps having the student write class rules a number of times), and then a conference with the parents, usually in that order. Imagine that your consultee tried these tactics with a student, then redid them more strongly, but to little avail. Because she has used up her habit repertoire, she refers the student to the school's SST, and you proceed with your consultative efforts. You may find that the only kinds of suggestions that she will come up with, or will accept from you, are those closely related to the five habitual ideas she has already tried. Success in this case might well depend on the consultant's ability to structure recommendations that are similar to, or compatible with, these five habitual responses yet have a better chance of working than those the consultee has already tried. It is also possible that the consultant can get the consultee to reframe the problem, to think about it differently, and on that basis to accept ideas that she may not have thought of herself.

Threat to Role Image or Security Like all professionals, teacher-consultees have an image of themselves as being generally competent. Students with moderate-to-severe learning or behavior problems may threaten this image. Having to ask someone else for assistance puts the consultee in a "one-down" position, which can lead to the types of resistance we have discussed. An example is the case of a veteran teacher (Mrs. Jones) who has a good reputation for dealing with difficult students. She now gets the most troublesome student she has ever had, one who has caused her to lose her professional demeanor in front of her class and who definitely threatens her security and comfort level as a teacher. Needing to refer this student erodes Mrs. Jones's self-image further. Defensiveness may accompany this situation as she tries to project her belief that she has tried everything, that the problem lies within the student, and that she shouldn't have to try anything else. She believes that special education (or suspension or movement to a different classroom) is needed.

Your success as a consultant in this case depends on your ability to develop a positive rapport with Mrs. Jones—to convince her that you appreciate what she has done and that it would be helpful to try some new tactic with the student, if only for the sake of your relationship, or because a reframing or variation of her own good ideas might work, or in the interest of gathering data.

Too Much Work Consultants need to be sure that the ideas they and the consultee have discussed are not really too labor-intensive. It is common to find that resistance develops after the consultee tries the suggested intervention; only then does it become clear that, as the consultee sees it, it really is too much work. Interventions that derive from the behavior modification approach seem to some consultees to be too much work when they involve cumbersome ways of data collection, awkward timing of reinforcement delivery, or dealing with the bookkeeping that seems to be part of token systems.

An example occurred with Mr. Sanchez, who seemed happy about the potential use of a behavioral contract. After a week without much progress toward the goals, he complained that it was just too much work charting the behaviors and communicating with the parents about the reinforcers they were to deliver. The consultant agreed that it may have been too much all at once, and they discussed a method for utilizing the contract for only 2 hours a day, and providing reinforcers at school. After another week, Mr. Sanchez agreed to chart the data for a half-day.

Philosophical Belief Conflicts In school-based consultation, we need to recognize that each participant in a collaborative consultation team has an implicit philosophy or set of beliefs and values that governs his practice and views regarding the needs and welfare of students. One of the sources of philosophical dispute that is currently in the schools has to do with the concept and practice of full inclusion of students with disabilities in general education classes (Halvorsen & Neary, 2001; Kavale & Forness, 2000; MacMillan, Gresham, & Forness, 1996). Others, such as the responsibilities of general education teachers for dealing with students who have mild-to-moderate disabling conditions (such as learning disabilities and behavior disorders, including ADD and ADHD), are more common sources of disputes. To what extent should a teacher–consultee vary her approach for a student? At what point does the consultee have a right to say "You're asking too much of me. The other students are suffering. A student like this is what resource rooms or special education day classes are for."?

Naturally, there is no answer without knowledge of a specific case. There is, however, recognition, shared by most school personnel, that we are in a period with a wider span of acceptance and an increased use of accommodations within the general education track for students who may well have been sent to special education, possibly for their entire educational career, only a decade ago (Heward, 2000). Although some teachers and other professionals (Hallahan & Kauffman, 1995; Kauffman, Gerber, & Semmel, 1988; MacMillan et al., 1996; Smelter, Bradley, & Yudewitz, 1994) caution against total participation in this current thinking, most special and regular educators maintain a cautiously benevolent attitude toward the inclusion movement (see Chapter 1).

Another philosophical belief that many teachers and parents apparently have is that positive reinforcement is akin to bribery. They do not believe that students ought to be given special recognition or rewards for "doing what they are supposed to be doing." They seem to maintain a puritan ethic that requires, but does not reinforce, perfection in behavior. Perhaps a gentle reminder might be helpful that the first dictionary definition of bribery implies a payment to someone in authority for something that is illegal or immoral. Using inducements (a second definition of a bribe) such as free time, stickers, or social praise for students who need an extra boost hardly seems to fit the first dictionary definition of bribery (*Webster's*, 1997).

Poor Planning/Delivery Certainly there exists the possibility that consultation is being resisted because it has been poorly designed, either at the conceptual level (that is, not well explained as a service delivery model) or at the case level (when an actual case is being poorly managed by the consultant). Some specific steps to take to ensure competent delivery of consultative services are:

1. *Establish rapport before discussing details of a case or intervention.* Getting to know the teacher or parent beyond surface appearances is not always easy in schools because of the busy schedules all professionals (and parents) have. Still, it doesn't take long to convey to people the idea that you are interested in what they have to say, that you are particularly interested in what they have done to date about the concerns they have, and that you are interested in their ideas about what to do next.

2. *Do not get caught up in the "I'm in a rush; tell me what to do" syndrome that seems to characterize many informal referrals that occur in schools.* Be firm about the process that has been established for accessing your services and, with some exceptions based on emergencies, stick to it. Your staff will regard you as more professional if you indicate that you believe their issues are important enough to set aside time for a meaningful discussion.

3. *Keep notes.* (An example of this was presented in Figure 3.1.)

Psychological Deficits Within the Consultee There are times when a consultee will not participate in the consultation process for reasons that are not clear. She may vacillate between compliance and refusal or may work very hard at the interventions for a period of time and then ignore them inexplicably. Such behavior may signal the presence of some disturbed intrapsychic activity that should be dealt with outside the consultative interactions, preferably in a therapeutic setting. Common indicators of stress that may be leading to impaired functioning are a long-term change in mood from well-modulated to depressed or angry; rapid, inexplicable mood shifts; overreaction to mild setbacks; and comments that indicate that the person is "on the edge" emotionally (Maslach, 1982; Sapolsky, 1994; Selye, 1993). Caplan and Caplan (1993) have discussed manifestations of psychological deficits under their "lack of objectivity" condition, which was discussed briefly in Chapter 2.

Lack of Skills Imagine that, in the course of discussing the disruptive behavior of a student, a consultee mentions the use of a contract. The consultant agrees that this would be a good idea and encourages the consultee to do it. The consultee, Mr. Smith, has never written a contract before; he's just heard about it. In the course of their quickly terminated conversation, the consultee doesn't tell the consultant that he needs help in designing a contract. A week goes by; nothing happens. The consultant inquires about the situation, and the consultee states that he hasn't had time to look into it. Another week goes by: same thing. By now the consultant is convinced that the consultee is resisting, for unknown reasons, so she confronts him mildly. At this point it becomes clear that the consultee doesn't know how to write or implement contracts but is shy about admitting it. This would be an example of a skill deficit, one of the four "lacks" found in some consultees (see Caplan & Caplan (1993) and Chapter 2).

The case of Mr. Smith may not really demonstrate resistance; but to the consultant, resistance appears to be involved until she learns that the problem involves a skill deficit. My point is that the consultant has to be sure that the activity called for in the intervention plan is within the skill repertoire of the consultee. Treatment integrity and acceptability (Gresham, 1989) depend on the consultee being able to do what is intended in the intervention; any deficits in skill must be clarified and remediated.

Most teachers are more skillful in areas of curriculum delivery than they are in areas of behavior management. This relative lack of skill can be attributed to at least two sources: poor teacher training in the area of behavior management (many teacher training programs devote only scant attention to this area, perhaps assuming behavior will be appropriate if the curriculum is delivered adequately); and a reluctance to be firm, perhaps due to a concern that students will rebel if held to high behavioral standards that are consistent. Because of the paramount need for consultants to be useful to teachers in this area, Chapter 6 is devoted to the causes, effects, and remedies for classroom behavior management problems.

Inadequate System Support This is related to the concepts of "threat to role image" and "poor planning/delivery," but is specific to situations in which the consultee may want to participate in the desired intervention but believes that the system (school, district) will not support it for some reason. For example, consider a case in which systematic suspension for flagrant disruptive behavior is suggested.

The teacher agrees, as does the principal, until it comes time for implementation. At this point, the principal decides to clear such a strong contingency with the assistant superintendent. Together they decide that the action is so important that the board of education had better support it before it is carried out. The board takes the suggestion under advisement and decides to consult with the county board lawyer, who promises to get back to the board with an opinion as soon as possible. Meanwhile, 2 months have gone by, and the disruptive behavior has gotten worse. Is this resistance or merely life in the bureaucracy? In any event, the scenario fits Wickstrom and Witt's (1993) conceptualization of a system factor that interferes with the achievement of goals established during consultative interactions. The moral of the story is that the consultant and the consultee should have other plans devised and ready to implement while waiting for the administration to make up its mind about policy.

The Principal's Office Parsons and Meyers (1984) describe schools as either proactive or reactive. A proactive school is led by a principal who is familiar with cutting-edge philosophies and methods and, while not embracing anything blindly, is open-minded about studying newer ideas with a view toward incorporating them into the school. In contrast, the reactive principal usually only reacts under pressure; some outside force compels this person to take action, and it is taken reluctantly, with a negative affect coloring its implementation. School desegregation, under court order, was often handled in this way, as is, to a much lesser degree, full inclusion. In reactive systems, maintenance of the status quo is more important than the desire to seek ways to improve the system. Consultants working with reactive principals need to devote more time to establishing relationships, laying the groundwork, and explaining all steps of the process than do those working in more comfortable proactive sites. The new consultant, as well as an experienced member of a staff who now wishes to change her role and behaviors, needs to bond with the school principal into a team that has as its purpose the improvement of the school, particularly improvement in the ways in which education is presented to students who have learning or behavior/adjustment problems. New or experienced consultants who find themselves working with reactive principals should pay close attention to the material presented later in this section on ways of dealing with resistance.

ACTIVITY 3.17

In small groups, review the causes for resistance previously discussed. Are there others not mentioned in that material? In settings with which you are familiar, what seem to be the major causes for resistance? Develop at least one method for dealing with each of the resistance scenarios previously discussed.

ACTIVITY 3.18

From your experiences in the schools, develop a behavioral chart like the one presented below and use it to analyze the ABCs of a resistance situation. An example is given:

Antecedents	*Behaviors*	*Consequences*
Consultant: "So we've decided to go with the nonverbal reminder when Lawanda speaks out loudly."	Teacher continues to loudly reprimand Lawanda.	Lawanda's behavior remains the same. Consultant makes a classroom observation.
Consultant: "What I observed was your reprimanding Lawanda instead of using the nonverbal reminder."	*Teacher:* "Yes, well, it's all she understands. That's the way these kids are raised." (Interfering belief)	*Consultant:* "Lawanda's behavior isn't improving. Would you be willing to implement another intervention?"

Resistance by Parent–Consultees

Most of what we have discussed about resistance applies to teachers as consultees, but, with some modification of focus, much of it could also apply to parent–consultees. Students who present with serious behavior/adjustment or learning challenges threaten the professional status and satisfaction of teachers, and these same behaviors or conditions also threaten and upset the personal lives of parents. The idea that an outsider (an individual representing the school) is asking to get involved in a family's life may have threatening connotations, especially for families that traditionally handle problems within the family rather than seek outside resources. Many families are confused about how to deal with their child's school-related problems (Cobb & Medway, 1978; O'Shea, O'Shea, Algozzine, & Hammitte, 2001). Maital (1996) has noted that parents may seek and at the same time build defenses against information and advice that they find uncomfortable.

There has been less study about the dynamics of parent resistance to consultation than about teacher resistance. Most of what is available is from the behavioral consultation school (Sheridan & Kratochwill, 1992) or has been borrowed from the family therapy literature (Chamberlain & Baldwin, 1988). In their 1988 article, Chamberlain and Baldwin give some suggestions for dealing with parental resistance, at least in a family therapy context:

- Develop a strong therapeutic alliance with the parents.
- Reframe suggestions made to parents to keep them consistent with the parents' preferred parenting style.
- Teach parents new parenting skills despite their possible disinterest.
- Develop a network of support for the therapist.

Liontos (1992) has delineated some of the sources of resistance to effective collaborations with families, including feelings of inadequacy; previous bad experiences with schools; suspicion about treatment from government institutions; limited knowledge about school policies, procedures, and ways to assist with schoolwork; and economic issues such as child care, transportation, and other daily survival constraints. Educators may resist working with some families because of their own biases, lack of objectivity, lack of knowledge of cultural differences, or language barriers.

Christenson (1995) has described a program (PEPS: Parent–Educator Problem Solving) consisting of a four-step procedure designed to include parents as integral members of a team whose purpose is to understand student adjustment and learning problems and to collaborate in solving them. Data indicate that this program has been related to improved home–school interactions and communications. Ortiz and Flanagan (2002) indicate three general principles for assuring success when consulting with families:

> *Establish rapport and build trust.* Introduce yourself and other concerned parties in a way that denotes respect for the family and their cultural heritage. Encourage full participation from family members, while understanding possible difficulties with language differences or cultural customs. Use interpreters/translators as appropriate.
>
> *Identify the presenting problem.* Presumably the problem has been discussed between the teacher and the family and has now come to your attention because it has not been satisfactorily resolved. Listen to the family's perception of the problem, what they have tried to do about it to date, and what ideas they have for solving the problem at this point. The family may deny the problem; they may be defensive; they may project the problem on to school personnel. Try to get them to help you work out interventions.
>
> *Learn the family system.* While you are discussing the situation with the family you should also be trying to get a deeper understanding of the family's composition and dynamics. Understanding these factors may be of assistance in the development and monitoring of interventions, particularly if they involve the active participation of the family.

Overcoming Resistance

The main methods for dealing with resistance from either teacher– or parent–consultees are to uncover its roots, deal realistically with them, look for ways to modify the plan or a consultee's responsibilities, provide reassurances, emphasize the rewards that may accrue if the plan is carried out, seek help from other sources of support such as a principal or a mentor teacher, and, if necessary, call a halt to the project for awhile. Given the intensity of some of the situations that call for consultation, it is sometimes necessary to take time out from plan building. When you return to it, people are sometimes more willing to progress. In any case, do not take resistance personally. The difficulty may be in the consultant's relationship with the consultee, or it may be that the plan simply isn't effective. In either case, treat resistance as an objective problem that can be worked out. Taking it personally, getting defensive, or, in the worst case, complaining to others about the consultee's lack of effort or professionalism only jeopardizes your relationship with the consultee and may tarnish your reputation in the school and the district.

Once the sources and types of resistance are delineated, the consultant needs to determine methods for dealing with them. Included here are a number of ideas from the literature as well as suggestions derived from practice.

Brown et al. (2001) suggest the following six ideas for dealing with resistance.

Reducing the Threat Resistance may be tied to a belief on the part of the consultee that engaging in consultation may generate a loss of status or feelings of incompetence. The primary way to deal with this is through the implementation of a collaborative approach in which the consultee is acknowledged as a co-equal in the consultation process. Since a collaboratively oriented consultant encourages the consultee to come up with her own solutions to problems, with the consultant serving as a facilitator for the consultee's ideas, the consultee holds a position of power in the relationship. In this approach, the strengths of the consultee are continually reinforced by the consultant. In cases in which the consultee has no ideas for intervention and feels threatened because of the expectation that he should, the consultant assists by suggesting interventions that have proven effective and waiting for the consultee to help in deciding which ones would work best in his classroom or home, or ways in which the home or classroom system might be changed in order for improvement to occur. These selected ideas are then refined by both parties, and the consultee implements them with the support and encouragement of the consultant.

Developing Positive Expectations Sometimes a consultant has to lay some groundwork designed to affect the belief system of the consultee regarding the potential value of the intervention. This can be done by citing similar cases from your experience in which the intervention worked well, by having the consultee talk to other consultees who have had similar situations that were handled successfully, or by reviewing the literature that described the intervention being used successfully.

Incentives An unfortunate reality in our culture is that teachers and parents need to seek their own reinforcers. In most states, all teachers with the same years of experience receive the same salary. There are very few other sources of reinforcement given to those who do an excellent job. For every "teacher of the year," there are hundreds of other teachers who do a wonderful job, unbeknownst to anybody except a few of their astute students and some parents and peers. Perhaps you, as the consultant, are the only one who knows what a teacher has done; therefore, you become the main source of reinforcement for that teacher. You can do this by informing the teacher that you are aware of his efforts, that his efforts are appreciated, and that through his efforts the student has a better chance for success than she would have had otherwise. In this way you are tapping into the primary sources of reinforcement for teachers and parents: personal pride; the knowledge that they have made their student or child more successful and, by extension, have made themselves successful.

Brown et al. (2001) suggest that consultees should be afforded release time to participate in consultation. When I was employed as a school psychologist, I was fortunate in one of my schools to have an elementary principal who would take teachers' classes for 15-minute periods to provide time for consultation during the regular school day. Most principals simply don't have the time or inclination to do that, especially on a consistent basis.

The willingness to participate in consultation could become part of a teacher evaluation method. Teachers who have engaged in successful behavior-change projects could be written about in a newsletter or identified positively in some other manner to give them recognition for taking part in this valued activity. Focusing on the nature of their success in ameliorating behavior or academic challenges of students could prompt others to be more hopeful and eager to engage in consultative activities.

Establish a Clear Contract In schools, the contract (agreement) between the consultant and the consultee to work together to solve a student's behavior or learning problem is almost always informal and implicit. This reality has a potential advantage in that informality leads to flexibility and an easy give-and-take that allow participants to make changes as appropriate as long as communication remains open and treatment integrity is not threatened. Elements of an agreement might include the following:

1. The consultant can offer a clear statement of her role:

> My role as a consultant is to give you assistance in your efforts to work more effectively with this student. As such, I will be gathering information about the problem through interviews with you and observations of the classroom behavior of the student. I am not here to evaluate you. My job is to help you think through some possible ways of assisting the student to perform better in the classroom or on the playground.

2. The consultant can mention some specifics about the process of consultation, such as its give-and-take nature, its emphasis on collaboration, and the need for some data gathering and analysis. Early in their interaction, the consultant might tell the consultee:

> One of the ways in which I like to work with teachers is to encourage them to come up with their own ideas about how they would like to solve a student's problem. I have found that teachers have many good ideas but sometimes just need someone to discuss them with. Two heads are often better than one, and pooling our ideas can work better than if just one of us does all the work in generating ideas. Besides, we're talking about your classroom, and the fact is that you are the one who is going to be implementing most of the changes we will be discussing. Therefore, it makes sense that we work with your ideas, approaches with which you feel comfortable, rather than those of someone like myself who isn't going to be implementing them. Also, one of the activities I believe is most worthwhile is the gathering of information or data that will help us to know just how we're doing. In other words, we need to keep track of what the student is doing as we try different approaches to modify her behavior or learning patterns. We'll try to make this data gathering as convenient as possible so as not to interfere with your teaching. Do you have any questions or comments about this approach?

ACTIVITY 3.19

Working in dyads, have one person act the role of the consultant, and the other a potential consultee. Assume that this is a first meeting between the two. Have the consultant introduce herself and explain the consultation process to the consultee. Have the consultee simply be accepting during this interchange. Repeat the process but have the consultee express doubts about the process based on the information you have learned about resistance, such as the extra amount of work, the need for data gathering, the implications of being observed, the belief that the referred student needs special education, and so on. In class, review strategies for dealing with these common forms of resistance.

Reduce the Consultee's Effort Ordinarily, when a referral for assistance is made, either directly to the school-based consultant or to the SST, the teacher is already spending more time with the target student than with most students because of the nature of the presenting problems. The teacher hopes that through the referral process he will obtain some sort of relief. If he finds out that consultation results in more work rather than less, he may show resistance in the present case and also be unwilling to use the process again.

Depending on the case and the consultee involved, it may be a good idea for the consultant to be upfront about this reality and to point out that, at least initially, the consultation process may result in somewhat more effort on behalf of the student (e.g., discussions, data keeping). If all goes well, the amount of effort will be reduced as the problem is resolved, and in the long run will be less than what would have been needed without the referral and the subsequent consultation. It is sometimes helpful to point out that the consultee is presently spending extra time with the target child and apparently isn't feeling that this expenditure of time is resolving the concerns. The new or different approaches generated through the consultation process may cost the consultee less time or trouble than do the approaches he is now using.

Another way of reducing the consultee's efforts is to give direct assistance to the teacher as time and other responsibilities of the consultant allow. Data gathering, co-teaching, preparing special materials, and monitoring other students while the teacher deals privately with a target student are some ways of providing the extra pair of hands teachers often need.

Developing Multicultural Sensitivity Understanding resistance to consultation in situations where there is a multicultural component is largely a matter of understanding facts and values. The facts one needs to consider have to do with differences in communication styles, preferred styles of interpersonal interactions, and traditional ways of dealing with problems and issues that arise in regard to dealing with children. The values may center around one's worldview, perspectives on the importance of individual achievement as compared to group cohesiveness, and the role of the family as compared to that of government institutions in decisons about students with disabilities. When a consultant and consultee come from different cultural backgrounds, it is necessary for the consultant to take the lead in negotiating the differences in opinion and approaches that may arise as a consequence of these cultural differences. Gibbs (1985), in her studies of African American consultees, concluded that consultants would do well to attend to the importance of interpersonal relationships rather than task-issues at the onset of a consultative relationship. Tarver Behring and Ingraham (1998) review issues similar to these in their call for a multicultural emphasis in consultation which, if followed, would likely reduce some of the more subtle aspects of resistance that may occur in situations where constituents from differing cultural perspectives work together toward problem solving. Ingraham (2004) has provided case examples demonstrating these possibilities. In the field of counseling, where many of the communication, interpersonal, and problem-solving skills are very similar to those of consultation, Arredondo et al. (1996) have operationalized a set of multicultural competencies that apply equally well to consultation. Additional sources of relevant information can be found in Duncan (1995); Harris, Ingraham, and Lam (1994); Harris (1996); Jackson and Hayes (1993); Miranda (1993); and Tobias (1993).

ACTIVITY 3.20

Mr. SanFillipo, the resource teacher at Grove Middle School, calls Ms. Phan, mother of a 13-year-old boy, Henry, who is having attendance, behavior, and achievement problems. Ms. Phan turns the phone over to her husband, who informs Mr. SanFillipo that they are not interested in discussing their son, and that they will take care of their own family's business. A month goes by and Henry shows no change in his behavior. What steps might a consultant take at this point?

Figure 3.3 presents a list of the important manifestations and causes of resistance in consultation, based on the acronym RESISTANCE. Also presented in Figure 3.3 is a list of some of the most useful approaches for dealing with resistance, following the acronym FACILITATE.

In summary, expect resistance, build in a plan for dealing with its most obvious causes, learn to recognize its symptoms, and realize that change is not easy for many people. Assuming that you, as either a self-selected or administratively appointed consultant, believe in the value of this approach to dealing with students' learning or behavior-adjustment problems, do what you can to sell the idea to others, especially your consultees. Proceed only with administrative support, and gain the support of the influential teachers on the staff. A year after you have begun, evaluate yourself and your efforts. You will very likely be pleased.

Figure 3.3

Manifestations and causes of resistance, and methods for dealing with them

MANIFESTATIONS AND CAUSES OF RESISTANCE IN SCHOOL-BASED CONSULTATION

There are many ways that consultees can resist the consultation process. The following list uses the acronym "RESISTANCE" to remind us of the manifestations and causes of the insidious reality of resistance to consultation.

R Refusal; active or passive

E Expectations too high

S Skill inadequacy

I "I did it; it didn't work."

S System lack of support; real or imagined

T Threat to existing ecology of the classroom

A Anxiety over being watched

N Nonreinforcement for efforts

C Confidence, lack of

E Easier to insist that someone else (e.g., special ed.) do it

DEALING WITH RESISTANCE

Understanding resistance is one thing; dealing with it is quite another. The following is a brief list of suggestions based on the acronym for the key word in resistance-busting: "FACILITATE."

F Facilitate

A Assist in their thinking and plan building

C Communicate both your support and ideas

I Interpersonally relate

L Live in their shoes

I Inquire

T Teach

A Acknowledge their efforts

T Tolerate their discrepant views, but don't allow inappropriate practices

E Evaluate your collaborative efforts

SUMMARY

The three most important skills that consultants must have are communication, interpersonal effectiveness, and problem solving. This chapter has presented information and activities pertaining to communication and interpersonal effectiveness, including power functions in interpersonal relations and resistance in consultation.

Your ability to communicate and to deal positively and effectively with others often determines the success or failure of the consultative enterprise. Certainly anybody who believes that consultation is worth doing will need to study and master the skills referred to in this chapter. Feedback from a teacher or your peers regarding your skills in communication and interpersonal effectiveness can be very useful.

REFERENCES

Adler, R., & Towne, N. (1996). *Looking out/Looking in*. Fort Worth, TX: Harcourt Brace.

Arredondo, P., Toporek, R., Brown, S. P., Jones, J., Locke, D. C., Sanchez, J., & Sadler, H. (1996). Operationalization of the multicultural counseling competencies. *Journal of Multicultural Counseling and Development, 24,* 42–78.

Babcock, N. L., & Pryzwansky, W. B. (1983). Models of consultation: Preferences of educational professionals at five stages of service delivery. *Journal of School Psychology, 21,* 359–366.

Benjamin, A. (1987). *The helping interview*. Boston: Houghton Mifflin.

Bergan, J. (1977). *Behavioral consultation*. Upper Saddle River, NJ: Merrill/Prentice Hall.

Bergan, J. R., & Kratochwill, T. R. (1990). *Behavioral consultation and therapy*. New York: Plenum Press.

Briggs Myers, I. (1976). *Myers-Briggs Type Indicator*. Palo Alto, CA: Consulting Psychologists Press.

Brown, D. (1993). Training consultants: A call to action. *Journal of Counseling and Development, 72,* 139–143.

Brown, D., Pryzwansky, W., & Schulte, A. (2001). *Psychological consultation: Introduction to theory and practice* (5th ed.). Boston: Allyn & Bacon.

Bushe, G. R., & Gibbs, B. W. (1990). Predicting organizational development consultation competence from Myers-Briggs Type Indicator and stage of ego development. *Journal of Applied Behavioral Science, 26,* 337–357.

Caplan, G., & Caplan, R. B. (1993). *Mental health consultation and collaboration*. San Francisco: Jossey-Bass.

Carkhuff, R. R. (1969). *Helping and human relations* (2 vols.). New York: Holt, Rinehart, & Winston.

Carner, L., & Alpert, J. (1995). Some guidelines for consultants revisited. *Journal of Educational and Psychological Consultation, 6,* 47–57.

Chamberlain, P., & Baldwin, D. V. (1988). Client resistance to parent training: Its therapeutic management. In T. R. Kratochwill (Ed.), *Advances in school psychology* (Vol. 6, pp. 131–171). Hillsdale, NJ: Lawrence Erlbaum Associates.

Christenson, S. L. (1995). Families and schools: What is the role of the school psychologist? *School Psychology Quarterly, 10*(2), 118–132.

Cobb, D. E., & Medway, F. J. (1978). Determinants of effectiveness in parent consultation. *Journal of Community Psychology, 6,* 229–240.

Conoley, C. W., Conoley, J. C., Ivey, D. C., & Scheel, M. J. (1991). Enhancing consultation by matching the consultee's perspectives. *Journal of Counseling and Development, 69,* 546–549.

Conoley, J. C., & Conoley, C. W. (1982). *School consultation: A guide to practice and training*. New York: Pergamon.

Conoley, J. C., & Conoley, C. W. (1992). *School consultation: Practice and training*. New York: Pergamon.

DeForest, P. A., & Hughes, J. N. (1992). Effect of teacher involvement and teacher self-efficacy on ratings of consultant effectiveness and intervention acceptability. *Journal of Educational and Psychological Consultation, 3,* 301–316.

Dettmer, P., Dyck, N., & Thurston, L. (1999). *Consultation, collaboration, and teamwork for students with special needs* (3rd ed.). Boston: Allyn & Bacon.

Duncan, C. F. (1995). Cross-cultural school consultation. In C. Lee (Ed.), *Counseling for diversity* (pp. 129–139). Boston: Allyn & Bacon.

Ellis, A. (1973). *Humanistic psychotherapy: The rational emotive approach*. New York: Julian.

Erchul, W. P. (1987). A relational communication analysis of control in school consultation. *Professional School Psychology, 2,* 113–124.

Erchul, W. P. (1999). Two steps forward, one step back: Collaboration in school-based consultation. *Journal of School Psychology, 37,* 191–203.

Erchul, W., & Chewning, T. (1990). Behavioral consultation from a request-centered relational communication perspective. *School Psychology Quarterly, 5,* 1–20.

Erchul, W., & Martens, B. (2002). *School consultation: Conceptual and empirical bases of practice*. New York: Kluwer Academic/Plenum Publishers.

Erchul, W. P., & Raven, B. H. (1997). Social power in consultation: A contemporary view of French and Raven's bases of social power. *Journal of School Psychology, 35,* 137–171.

Erchul, W., Raven, B., & Ray, A. (2001). School psychologists' perceptions of social power bases in teacher consultation. *Journal of Educational and Psychological Consultation, 12*(1), 1–24.

Evans, S. B. (1980). The consultant role of the resource teacher. *Exceptional Children, 46,* 402–404.

French, J. R. P., & Raven, B. H. (1959). The basis of social power. In D. Cartwright (Ed.), *Studies in social power* (pp. 150–167). Ann Arbor: University of Michigan, Institute of Social Research.

Friend, M., & Bauwens, J. (1988). Managing resistance: An essential consulting skill for learning disabilities teachers. *Journal of Learning Disabilities, 21,* 556–561.

Friend, M., & Cook, M. (2003). *Interactions: Collaboration skills for school professionals* (4th ed.). White Plains, NY: Longman.

Gallesich, J. (1982). *The profession and practice of consultation*. San Francisco: Jossey-Bass.

Gibbs, J. T. (1985). Can we continue to be color-blind and class-bound? *The Counseling Psychologist, 13,* 426–435.

Ginott, H. (1972). *Teacher and child*. Upper Saddle River, NJ: Prentice Hall.

Gordon, T. (1974). *T.E.T.: Teacher effectiveness training*. New York: McKay.

Gresham, F. M. (1989). Assessment of treatment integrity in school consultation and prereferral intervention. *School Psychology Review, 18,* 37–50.

Gross, S. (1980). Interpersonal threat as a basis for resistance in consultation. Paper presented at the annual meeting of the American Psychological Association, Montreal.

Gutkin, T. B. (1999). Collaborative versus directive/prescriptive/expert school-based consultation: Reviewing and resolving a false dichotomy. *Journal of School Psychology, 37,* 161–190.

Hallahan, D. P., & Kauffman, J. M. (1995). *The illusion of full inclusion*. Austin, TX: Pro-Ed.

Halvorsen, A., & Neary, T. (2001). *Building inclusive schools: Tools and strategies for change*. Boston: Allyn & Bacon.

Harris, A. M., & Cancelli, A. A. (1991). Teachers as volunteer consultees: Enthusiastic, willing, or resistant participants. *Journal of Educational and Psychological Consultation, 2,* 217–238.

Harris, A. M., Ingraham, C. L., & Lam, M. K. (1994). Teacher expectations for female and male school-based consultants. *Journal of Educational and Psychological Consultation, 5,* 115–142.

Harris, K. (1996). Collaboration within a multicultural society: Issues for consideration. *Remedial and Special Education, 17*(6), 355–362, 376.

Herman, K. C. (1993). Reassessing predictors of therapist competence. *Journal of Counseling and Development, 72,* 29–32.

Heward, W. L. (2000). *Exceptional Children* (6th ed.). Upper Saddle River, NJ: Merrill/Prentice Hall.

Hill, P. T., Campbell, C., & Harvey, J. (2000). *It takes a city: Getting serious about urban school reform*. Washington, DC: Brookings Institute.

Hoskins, B. (1996). *Developing inclusive schools: A guide*. Port Chester, NY: National Professional Resources.

Hughes, J. N., & DeForest, P. A. (1993). Consultant directiveness and support as predictors of consultation outcomes. *Journal of School Psychology, 31,* 355–373.

Idol, L., Nevin, A., & Paolucci-Whitcomb, P. (2000). *Collaborative consultation* (3rd ed.). Austin, TX: Pro-Ed.

Ingraham, C. (2004). Multicultural consultee-centered consultation: When novice consultants explore cultural hypotheses with experienced teacher consultees. *Journal of Educational and Psychological Consultation, 14*(3&4), 329–362.

Jackson, D. N., & Hayes, D. H. (1993). Multicultural issues in consultation. *Journal of Counseling and Development, 72,* 144–147.

Kauffman, J. M., Gerber, M. M., & Semmel, M. I. (1988). Arguable assumptions underlying the regular education initiative. *Journal of Learning Disabilities, 21,* 6–11.

Kavale, K., & Forness, S. (2000). History, rhetoric, and reality: Analysis of the inclusion debate. *Remedial and Special Education, 21,* 279–296.

Kratochwill, T. R., & Bergan, J. R. (1990). *Behavioral consultation in applied settings.* New York: Plenum.

Kratochwill, T. R., Sheridan, S., & Van Someren, K. (1988). Research in behavioral consultation: Current status and future directions. In J. F. West (Ed.), *School consultation: Interdisciplinary perspectives on theory, research, training, and practice* (pp. 77–102). Austin, TX: Association of Educational and Psychological Consultants.

Kurpius, D. J., & Rozecki, T. G. (1993). Strategies for improving interpersonal communication. In J. E. Zins, T. R. Kratochwill, & S. N. Elliott (Eds.), *Handbook of consultation services for children* (pp. 137–158). San Francisco: Jossey-Bass.

Langer, J. A. (2001). Beating the odds: Teaching middle and high school students to read and write well. *American Educational Research Journal, 38*(4), 837–880.

Liontos, S. B. (1992). *At-risk families and schools: Becoming partners.* Eugene: ERIC Clearinghouse on Educational Management, College of Education, University of Oregon.

Lippitt, G., & Lippitt, R. (1986). *The consulting process in action* (2nd ed.). San Diego, CA: University Associates.

MacMillan, D. R., Gresham, F. M., & Forness, S. R. (1996). Full inclusion: An empirical perspective. *Behavioral Disorders, 21,* 145–159.

Maital, S. L. (1996). Integration of behavioral and mental health consultation as a means of overcoming resistance. *Journal of Educational and Psychological Consultation, 7*(4), 291–303.

Maitland, R. E., Fine, M. J., & Tracy, D. B. (1985). The effects of an interpersonally based problem-solving process on consultation outcomes. *Journal of School Psychology, 23,* 337–345.

Margolis, H. (1991). Understanding, facing resistance to change. *NASSP Bulletin, 75*(537), 1–8.

Martin, R. (1978). Expert and referent power: A framework for understanding and maximizing consultation effectiveness. *Journal of School Psychology, 16,* 49–55.

Maslach, C. (1982). *Burnout: The cost of caring.* Upper Saddle River, NJ: Prentice Hall.

Mehrabian, A. (1971). *Silent messages.* Belmont, CA: Wadsworth.

Miranda, A. H. (1993). Consultation with culturally diverse families. *Journal of Educational and Psychological Consultation, 4,* 89–93.

O'Keefe, D. J., & Medway, F. J. (1997). The application of persuasion research to consultation in school psychology. *Journal of School Psychology, 35,* 173–193.

Ortiz, S., & Flanagan, D. (2002). Best practices in working with culturally diverse children and families. In A. Thomas & J. Grimes (Eds.), *Best practices in school psychology IV* (pp. 337–352). Bethesda, MD: NASP.

O'Shea, D., O'Shea, L., Algozzine, R., & Hammitte, D. (2001). *Families and teachers of individuals with disabilities.* Boston: Allyn & Bacon.

Parsons, R. D., & Meyers, J. (1984). *Developing consultation skills.* San Francisco: Jossey-Bass.

Petty, R., Heesacker, M., & Hughes, J. (1997). The Elaboration Likelihood Model: Implications for the practice of school psychology. *Journal of School Psychology, 35,* 107–136.

Piersal, W., & Gutkin, T. (1983). Resistance to school-based consultation: A behavioral analysis of the problem. *Psychology in the Schools, 20,* 311–320.

Pryzwansky W., & White, G. (1983). The influence of consultee characteristics on preferences for consultation approaches. *Professional Psychology: Research and Practice, 14,* 457–461.

Pugach, M. C., & Johnson, L. J. (1989). The challenge of implementing collaboration between general and special education. *Exceptional Children, 56,* 232–235.

Pugach, M. C., & Johnson, L. J. (1995). *Collaborative practitioners, collaborative schools.* Denver, CO: Love Publishing.

Rappaport, J. (1981). In praise of paradox: A social policy of empowerment over prevention. *American Journal of Community Psychology, 9,* 1–25.

Raschke, D., Dedrick, C., & DeVries, A. (1988). Coping with stress: The special educator's perspective. *Teaching Exceptional Children, 21*(1), 10–14.

Raven, B. H. (1965). Social influence and power. In I. D. Steiner & M. Fishbein (Eds.), *Current studies in social psychology* (pp. 371–382). New York: Holt, Rinehart, & Winston.

Raven, B. H. (1992). A power/interaction model of interpersonal influence: French and Raven thirty years later. *Journal of Social Behavior and Personality, 7,* 217–244.

Raven, B. H. (1993). The bases of power: Origins and recent developments. *Journal of Social Issues, 49,* 227–251.

Raven, B.H., Schwarzwald, J., & Koslowsky, M. (1998). Conceptualizing and measuring a power/interaction model of interpersonal influence. *Journal of Applied Social Psychology, 28,* 307–332.

Ready, T., Edley, C., & Snow, C. (Eds.). (2002). *Achieving high educational standards for all: Conference summary* (pp. 183–217). Washington, DC: National Academy Press.

Resnick, H., & Patti, R. (Eds.). (1980). *Change from within.* Philadelphia: Temple University Press.

Sapolsky, R. (1994). *Why zebras don't get ulcers: A guide to stress, stress-related diseases, and coping.* New York: W. H. Freeman.

Savelsbergh, M., & Staebler, B. (1995). Investigating leadership styles, personality preferences, and effective teacher consultation. *Journal of Educational and Psychological Consultation, 6,* 277–286.

Schowengerdt, R. V., Fine, M. J., & Poggio, J. P. (1976). An examination of some bases of teacher satisfaction with school psychological services. *Psychology in the Schools, 13,* 269–275.

Seligman, M. (1991). *Learned optimism.* New York: Knopf.

Selye, H. (1993). History of the stress concept. In L. Goldberger & S. Brevitz (Eds.), *Handbook of stress* (2nd ed.). New York: Free Press.

Shapiro, E. (1996). *Academic skills problems: Direct assessment and intervention* (2nd ed.). New York: Guilford.

Sheridan, S. M., & Kratochwill, T. R. (1992). Behavioral parent-teacher consultation: Conceptual and research considerations. *Journal of School Psychology, 30,* 117–139.

Smelter, R., Bradley, W. R., & Yudewitz, G. J. (1994). Thinking of inclusion for all special needs students? Better think again. *Phi Delta Kappan, 76,* 35–38.

Tarver Behring, S., & Ingraham, C. L. (1998). Culture as a central component of consultation: A call to the field. *Journal of Educational and Psychological Consultation, 9,* 57–72.

Thomas, C. C., Correa, V. I., & Morsink, C. V. (1995). *Interactive teaming: Consultation and collaboration in special programs.* Upper Saddle River, NJ: Merrill/Prentice Hall.

Tobias, R. (1993). Underlying cultural issues that effect sound consultant/school collaboratives in developing multicultural programs. *Journal of Educational and Psychological Consultation, 4,* 237–251.

Vernberg, E. M., & Reppucci, N. D. (1986). Behavioral consultation. In F. V. Mannino, E. J. Trickett, M. F. Shore, M. G. Kidder, & G. Levin (Eds.), *Handbook of mental health consultation* (DHHS Publication No. ADM 86-1466, pp. 49–80). Washington, DC: U. S. Government Printing Office.

Wagner, T. (1998). Change as collaborative inquiry: A constructivist methodology for reinventing schools. *Phi Delta Kappan, 79,* 512–517.

Webster's College Dictionary (2nd ed.). (1997). New York: Random House.

West, J., Idol, L., & Cannon, G. (1989). *Collaboration in the schools.* Austin, TX: Pro-Ed.

Wickstrom, K. F., & Witt, J. C. (1993). Resistance with school-based consultation. In J. E. Zins, T. R. Kratochwill, & S. N. Elliott (Eds.), *Handbook of consultation services for children* (pp. 159–178). San Francisco: Jossey-Bass.

Witt, J., Erchul, W., McKee, W., Pardue, M., & Wickstrom, K. (1991). Conversational control in school-based consultation: The relationship between consultant and consultee topic determination and consultation outcome. *Journal of Educational and Psychological Consultation, 2,* 101–116.

Ethics and Advocacy in School Consultation

OBJECTIVES

1. Orient the reader to the purpose, sources, and importance of ethical practice.
2. Summarize the major ethical principles that affect school consultation.
3. Indicate through the use of cases how ethical codes and standards of practice are applied in school-based consultation situations.
4. Delineate the role of the consultant in issues of advocacy for students and families.
5. Provide activities that readers can use to sensitize them to the ethical codes, standards of practice, and advocacy issues that are discussed in this chapter.

Mr. Romero is the special education teacher at Chavez Elementary School. He has been working with the general education staff to increase the amount and quality of services for students with disabilities in the general education classes. Lately he has been particularly concerned with the actions of Ms. Peterson, a second-grade teacher, who steadfastly refuses to make any accommodations for José, an 8-year-old with moderate hearing loss. Since there is no "front of the classroom" as there had been when Mr. Romero was in school, Ms. Peterson's voice seems to come from all over and at varying degrees of volume. When Mr. Romero talked to her about it, Ms. Peterson just brushed him off, stating that she can't be going over to José all day to repeat things to him in a louder voice. Mr. Romero sees this as a violation of the spirit of inclusion, in addition to a failure to provide the necessary accommodations for José. Is this a violation of ethical standards? What steps should Mr. Romero take to deal with this issue?

At Jackie Robinson High School the teacher of students with moderate-to-severe disabilities, Mr. Struck, continues to conduct his class as he did 30 years ago. He does mainstreaming reluctantly and only when he is directed to by IEPs. He seeks no collaborative relationships with general education classes. Is Mr. Struck violating any ethical principles with this attitude and behavior? What standards of practice or advocacy issues arise when a teacher acts like Mr. Struck?

THE PURPOSE, SOURCES, AND IMPORTANCE OF ETHICAL PRACTICE

Attention to ethical responsibilities is important for at least the following reasons:

1. Consultants are trying to influence activities in relation to the lives of other people, including minors who are relatively powerless to influence what happens to them in the schools.
2. In the practice of consultation one attempts to use various forms of social influence (Erchul & Martens, 2002) and some degree of power in order to convince a consultee to take certain actions. One needs to be careful not to let influence turn into secretive or noncollaborative manipulation (Lippitt, 1973).
3. Issues of confidentiality exist whenever consultants discuss students and their families.

4. These same issues exist when consultants discuss or observe teaching practices.
5. Any hint of unethical practices, whether validated or not, can destroy credibility and future efforts at consultation.

Professionals assuming the role of school consultants, whether internal or external, must be aware of and attend to ethical practices. As of this writing, there is no national association of consultants that has developed an ethical code, but fortunately other associations and organizations have. The codes provided by the Council on Exceptional Children (CEC); (1997), the American Psychological Association (APA); (1992), the American Counseling Association (ACA); (1995), the National Education Association (1975, cited in Sadker & Sadker, 2005), and the National Association of School Psychologists (2000) give direction and guidance to school consultants. Ewing (2001); Gable, Arllen, and Cook (1993); Heron, Martz, and Margolis (1996); Howe and Miramontes (1991); Hughes (1986); Jacob-Timm (1999); Newman (1993); Pryzwansky (1993); and Taylor and Adelman (1998) have also provided commentary and guidance. Howe and Miramontes (1992), Jacob-Timm and Hartshorne (1998), and Koocher and Keith-Spiegel (1998) have devoted texts to this subject, and Cook, Weintraub, and Morse (1995) have provided an interesting chapter on the ethical ramifications of restructuring in special education.

PRINCIPLES OF ETHICAL BEHAVIOR

Brown, Pryzwansky, and Schulte (2001) provide six principles that summarize the contents of the APA and ACA codes as they apply to consultation.

Principle 1: Competence. No person should extend her services as a consultant unless she is competent to do so by training and experience. Unfortunately, it is not at all clear what competence means because consistency in standards of training is not common. Just exactly what sort of training and how much experience you should have is not clearly spelled out in codes of ethics, or in standards of practice, which are guidelines established by professional groups to assist practitioners in the determination of appropriate practice. Professional responsibility often comes down to your own self-insight: If you don't feel competent to engage in a professional activity, you probably aren't and you shouldn't do it. Instead, explain your situation to your superior, and try to help the district find other persons to accomplish the task or seek additional training for yourself.

ACTIVITY 4.1

It has been mentioned in this text that the three primary competencies in consultation are communication, interpersonal skills, and problem solving. Discuss what it means to be competent in each of these three areas. What training or experience makes one competent to engage in the process of consultation? Additionally, what experience and training would be helpful in the overall area of content, such as knowledge of interventions and when to recommend them?

Principle 2: Protecting the welfare of clients. This is usually regarded as the most important ethical principle in human service work. In consultation it is necessary to regard both the consultee and the student as clients. Also, there may be multiple consultees and clients, so the welfare of all involved parties becomes significant.

A student's welfare may be threatened through the use of assessment instruments that are not appropriate for that individual, the development of policies that may be biased against certain people, the encouragement of dependency on the consultant, and the use of interventions that are not well validated by empirical measures or through the personal experiences of either the consultee or consultant.

ACTIVITY 4.2

Discuss the concept of client (student) welfare. Give examples from your experience that indicate a positive example of meeting the welfare of the student and a negative example. What steps can a school consultant take to ensure that the welfare of the student is the primary driving force behind interventions that are designed for and carried out with students?

Principle 3: Maintaining confidentiality. Whenever a consultation-based service delivery system is to be conducted in a school, confidentiality must be established at two levels: with the administration and with the individual consultees. A school principal should not ask a consultant to evaluate the performance of a teacher-consultee (unless these activities are clearly delineated in contractual arrangements), and the consultee should not have to fear that the consultant is talking to others about their conversations or the consultee's performance as a teacher.

There are limits to confidentiality, and these should also be explained to potential consultees. English (1995) comments that confidentiality protections are not absolute. There is information that *may* be disclosed (based on professional judgment), information that *must* be disclosed, and information that *may not* be disclosed. For example, abuse of other persons or threats to self or others need to be reported in all states. Individual states vary in their laws excluding certain behaviors from the ordinary right to privileged communication. For example, sexual harassment between students at all ages is forbidden by law in some states, and knowledge of its occurrence must be reported to the local authorities.

Taylor and Adelman (1998) discuss some of the fundamental dilemmas that can face a consultant when dealing with confidentiality issues in schools. There is sometimes a seemingly contradictory reality to issues of confidentiality. We want to let consultees know that we hold in confidence what they discuss with us about their teaching methods, philosophy, and ideas for intervention, as well as what we observe in the course of their teaching. You will not be welcome for long in classrooms if teacher–consultees find out that you are talking to others about what you observe that may not reflect favorably on them. However, there will be situations when you observe something that you believe is not in the best interests of students. You need to talk with the teacher about your concerns. But what if the teacher does not change the behavior of concern? What if he continues to engage in potentially detrimental behavior? Following the principle of breaking confidentiality when you become aware of behaviors that can be harmful to others, you need to tell the teacher that his continuing this behavior will result in your telling his supervisor (e.g., principal) what you have observed. In making the decision to do so, it is recommended that you follow the 10-step process described by Koocher and Keith-Spiegel (1998) that is presented on page 143.

ACTIVITY 4.3

Role-play an interview with a teacher–consultee with whom you have not consulted previously in which you explain your method of consultation and the fact of confidentiality in your proceedings, along with limitations to that confidentiality. Also, role-play giving a talk to all the teachers in the school about these same matters. How would you present your views to the principal before talking to all the teachers?

Principle 4: Responsibilities when making public statements. This usually applies to external consultants rather than to internal school-based consultants. An internal consultant needs to explain to potential employers and consultees the nature of consultation, how it will be conducted, and its limits. In the event an internal consultant has an occasion to speak to people from outside the school, especially the press, he should be careful not to disclose information obtained in confidence.

Principle 5: Social and moral responsibility. Consultants need to make sure that their behavior and statements are governed by the best interests of the constituents, not by their own needs or agendas. Backer and Glaser (1979; cited in Brown et al., 2001) have indicated numerous ways in which ethical conflicts can occur. Among them are creating unnecessary dependency on the part of the consultee, failing to recognize your own limitations, and imposing your own values on the consultee. Naturally, inappropriate physical or sexual behavior is always unethical and unprofessional.

Principle 6: Relationship with other consultants. In schools that have heavily invested in collaborative modes of problem solving and program building, numerous people may act in consultant roles from time to time. We need to respect the opinions of these individuals as well as those of external consultants while being sure to work with them in a positive manner, especially in situations when we may not agree with their approaches. It is sometimes surprising how many different people claim to speak for a given student. Each person believes she is advocating for the best interests of the student, but like the blind man and the elephant, some of them are perceiving only selected parts of the big picture. One of the roles and skills of high-functioning school-based consultants is to be able to meld these diverse ideas and personalities into a cohesive collaborative team. There is a more thorough discussion of advocacy issues at the end of this chapter.

In addition to these general principles elucidated by Brown et al. (2001), Howe and Miramontes (1992) and Jacob-Timm and Hartshorne (1998) have also contributed to this area, as has Gallesich (1982), who has developed a list of 28 guidelines for ethical behavior that she believes can serve as a code specifically designed for consultants. Among the most relevant for school consultants are these five:

1. Consultants avoid manipulating consultees. As previously mentioned, there is not a firm line between social influence tactics and manipulation. One needs to be careful to maintain the collaborative ethic and to use primarily the "soft" power bases (see Chapter 3).
2. Consultants strive to evaluate the outcomes of their services. Evaluation is the last step in the solutions-oriented consultation system discussed in Chapter 5.
3. Consultants acquire the basic body of knowledge and skills of their profession so as to meet the competence standard specified by Brown et al. (2001), mentioned previously.
4. Consultants know their professional strengths, weaknesses, and biases.
5. Consultants take active steps to maintain and increase their effectiveness.

THE COUNCIL ON EXCEPTIONAL CHILDREN CODE OF ETHICS AND STANDARDS FOR PROFESSIONAL PRACTICE

The Council on Exceptional Children (CEC; 1997) has provided a very brief code of ethics and a more elaborate set of standards for professional practice. These are available on their web site at *http://www.cec.sped.org/ps/code.html.* This code of ethics requires members to:

a. Develop the highest educational and quality of life potential of individuals with exceptionalities.
b. Promote and maintain a high level of competence and integrity in practicing their profession.
c. Engage in professional activities that benefit individuals with exceptionalities, their families, other colleagues, students, or research subjects.
d. Exercise objective professional judgment in the practice of their profession.
e. Strive to advance their knowledge and skills regarding the education of individuals with exceptionalities.
f. Work within the standards and policies of their profession.
g. Uphold and improve where necessary the laws, regulations, and policies governing the delivery of special education and related services and the practice of their profession.
h. Not condone or participate in unethical or illegal acts, nor violate professional standards adopted by the Delegate Assembly of the CEC.

A PROBLEM-SOLVING MODEL FOR DEALING WITH ETHICAL ISSUES

Koocher and Keith-Spiegel (1998) have provided a problem-solving model designed to assist consultants and others in their efforts to determine if an ethical violation exists and how to deal with it. These steps, in addition to others suggested by Corey, Corey, and Callanan (1998), are as follows:

1. Identify the problem or situation.
2. Define the parameters of the situation.
3. Define the potential ethical-legal issues involved.
4. Consult legal-ethical guidelines.
5. Consult with trusted colleagues.
6. Evaluate the rights, responsibilities, and welfare of all affected parties.
7. Generate a list of alternative decisions possible for each issue.
8. Enumerate the consequences of making each decision.
9. Conduct a risk-benefit analysis.
10. Make the decision.

TWO EXAMPLE SITUATIONS

Each of the principles in the CEC Code of Ethics, the CEC Standards for Professional Practice, and the 10 steps previously listed are used as the guidelines to help determine an appropriate course of action in each of the following two situations:

Situation 1

A special day-class teacher had referred a student with an emotional disturbance who presented with behavior-adjustment problems such as defiance toward teachers, physical assaults on other students, and inappropriate language. After a review of this situation and the development of specified interventions by the IEP team, and two individual consultations with the school psychologist, the teacher decided that what the student needed was a severe tongue-lashing in front of the class. This intervention had not been suggested by either the SST or the consultant. When the consultant followed-up with the referring teacher, this teacher admitted what she had done, and indicated that the case was closed because the student had (at least for now) stopped his inappropriate behavior.

1. *Identify the problem:* The teacher has not followed the recommended interventions and has engaged in a behavior that might be detrimental to the target student.
2. *Define the parameters:* The teacher's questionable behavior occurred in the classroom in front of all the other students in that class.

3. *Define the potential ethical-legal issues involved:* At issue is whether the teacher's behavior violates ethical or legal principles. Is it acceptable and appropriate for a teacher to berate a student, either privately or, as in this case, in front of the student's peers? What alternative behavior might the teacher have engaged in?
4. *Consult legal-ethical guidelines:* It appears that guidelines A (quality of life), B (integrity of practice), C (activities that benefit individuals with exceptionalities), D (exercise of objective professional judgment), and F (work within the standards and policies of their profession) are being violated by the teacher's behavior. The primary standard of practice that is apparently violated is in the area of "management of behavior," which stipulates that special educators are to "apply only those disciplinary methods and behavioral principles which they have been instructed to use and which do not undermine the dignity of the individual ..." (CEC Code of Ethics and Standards of Practice, 2000, Management of Behavior Section, number 1). The teacher may also be violating other aspects of this standard that are delineated in the CEC statement.
5. *Consult with trusted colleagues:* In this case the consultant had promised the teacher prior to the beginning of the consultations that he (the consultant) would hold all observations and discussions in confidence. The consultee, however, was informed that if the consultant became aware of behaviors that threatened or did harm to others, the confidentiality would be broken. The consultant decides to discuss this issue with two colleagues who, it turns out, have different views on this subject. One colleague says that the teacher did engage in behaviors that were "potentially dangerous to the student" and therefore should be informed that the consultant would be reporting this behavior to the principal. The other colleague said that the teacher's "being verbally firm with the student" was within her rights and did not constitute "probable harm."
6. *Evaluate the rights, responsibilities, and welfare of all concerned:* The teacher's right (and responsibility) is to manage her classroom and to deal with behavior challenges in a way that serves best to maintain a peaceful and productive classroom. The student's right is to be educated by individuals who have the student's welfare uppermost in their minds. As such, a student shouldn't have to endure hostile and (potentially) damaging verbalizations from his teachers. The student's parents have a right to expect that their son's teachers will maintain an atmosphere that conveys safety and concern for their child's welfare. It would appear in this case that the rights of the student and parent need to take precedence. The teacher does not seem to have acted in the best interests of the student, but rather seems to have given into frustration and (at least temporarily) lost her professional demeanor.

7. *Generate a list of alternative decisions:* The alternatives seem to be three: (a) do nothing; (b) talk to the teacher about her behavior and inform her that she is not allowed to talk to students that way and that she should desist from this behavior in the future; or (c) inform the principal, who will talk to the teacher about it and who may file an ethics violation against the teacher that, if sustained, will go into the teacher's personnel file.
8. *Enumerate the consequences of making each decision.* Choice (a) is clearly inappropriate; (b) may be acceptable, if you believe this behavior was an aberration and is not likely to happen again if you speak to the teacher about it; (c) seems to be the strongest remedy, and should probably be invoked if there is reason to think that this behavior has happened before and could happen again.
9. *Conduct a risk-benefit analysis:* The risk of utilizing choice (b) is that the teacher may not think the statement from the consultant is very meaningful, and may therefore be ignored the next time the teacher is feeling stressed by this student's, or any other student's, disruptive and disrespectful behavior. The benefit is that the teacher appreciates the faith the consultant has in her and, since she comes to think her behavior could have been damaging to the student because of what the consultant says to her about it, she vows to herself never to let it happen again. The risk involved in choice (c) is that the teacher may believe that her behavior was not out of line (she's witnessed other teachers berating their students and nothing was said to them about it) and therefore that she's being unfairly discriminated against. Since she willingly took part in the consultation process, she now believes it was a mistake because none of this would have come up otherwise. She may interpret this to mean that the consultant cannot be trusted. The benefit of choice (c) is that it announces to all who come to know about it that this sort of behavior is unethical and will not be tolerated. It sends the strongest message to the teacher and to others who come to know about it.
10. *Make the decision:* Because the consultant is the only one who knows about the teacher's behavior, it is his decision among choices (a), (b), and (c) that will decide the disposition of the case. Of course, if he chooses option (c), the principal then becomes the leading decision maker regarding further disposition of the case. The consultant decides to invoke option (b), based on his assessment of the seriousness of the offense, his knowledge of the teacher and her typical behavior, and his belief that this was likely to have been a professional lapse that will be corrected by his exercise of option (b). He talks to the teacher about it and she agrees that her behavior was excessive, certainly not typical of her, and she will not engage in that sort of behavior again.

ACTIVITY 4.4

Review the steps taken in the previous example. Comment on the reasoning process the consultant goes through in trying to decide what to do. How would you have modified the process? Do you think there could have been other options? Do you agree with the final decision?

Situation 2

Miss Sally Phillips (Ms. P) is a resource specialist-consultant in Hannibal High School. She was very pleased 3 years ago when her district decided to move toward more of a collaborative consultation mode of service delivery. She had long held the belief that her talents weren't being utilized while she was assigned the role of resource teacher and expected to teach students, primarily those with learning disabilities, all day. Because of her previous experience as both a math and science teacher at Hannibal High, she yearned to get back into the general education classrooms and assist teachers who were working with the same students with learning disabilities who were seeing her for one or two periods a day. She was convinced that she could offer many good ideas to content-area teachers if she only had the time to do consultation instead of teaching all day. Therefore, when the district decided to make the move toward a consultation-based system of service delivery for students with exceptionalities, she jumped at the chance. She's been acting as a consultant to the general education staff on a full-time basis for the past 3 years.

The problem is that she is very unpopular in her role. Specifically, general education teachers have complained to the principal that (a) she is pushy; she believes her ideas about accommodations and modifications are better than what the other teachers are doing, and she is quick to let them know that; (b) she is not a good listener; (c) when engaged in any form of cooperative teaching, she takes over as much as possible and turns lessons into what she wants them to be; and (d) her concern for the needs of the mainstreamed students seems to have fallen by the wayside in favor of her using her position to impose her ideas on other teachers. Her recommended modifications and accommodations often seem to have no empirical foundation.

ACTIVITY 4.5

The class or study group should review Situation 2 in light of the eight principles in the CEC Code of Ethics, and then follow the 10-step problem-solving method used in Situation 1. Specifically, is there an ethical issue here? Which of the eight principles seem to be violated? Based on an analysis of this situation, what decision(s) seem(s) best?

AREAS OF POTENTIAL ETHICAL CONFLICT

Snow and Gersick (1986) have discussed five areas of potential ethical conflict. The first has to do with the nature of the consultation contract itself. In schools, the central aspect of the (implicit) contract is a set of (usually) loosely understood agreements about each person's role in the consultation interaction. School consultants typically operate informally, but they certainly should be fairly explicit in explaining their role, their preferred method of interacting with the consultee, and confidentiality and its limits.

The second area concerns issues of loyalty and responsibility. In schools it often seems that consultants are serving many constituents at once: the teacher–consultee, the parent, the principal, possibly a higher-level administrator, and sometimes the sole interests of the student. Discussion of possible conflicts should occur between interested parties when it is clear that the different constituencies are at odds about how to proceed. It is sometimes not clear whose needs and interests should take precedence, although the student should be given top priority whenever possible.

The third area consists of value choices related to intervention techniques. Consultants and consultees may not agree, for a number of reasons, on what the interventions should be. Intervention choice is to some degree related to one's values, training, biases, the available empirical evidence for the interventions, and other variables that may not be made explicit. Again, discussion and compromise, hallmarks of a collaborative approach, are the best avenues to take if disputes occur. As a general rule, it is best to help the consultee develop his ideas since, for the most part, the consultee will be implementing them. Situation 2 included a good example of a consulting teacher who seemed to stand in direct violation of this ideal.

Snow and Gersick's fourth potential area of conflict is the use and limits of confidentiality. As I have previously mentioned, issues of confidentiality should be discussed and made clear before any sort of consultation work takes place. The discussion should start at the administrative level; be sure that your immediate supervisor knows your position regarding confidentiality. This should be shared with the local school principal and then with the teachers. School consultants starting a consultation service delivery system would do well to address the whole school staff to explain the process and review confidentiality issues. These should be reviewed with individual teachers the first time a consultant works with each of them. An example of how to present this to an individual consultee was presented in Chapter 1 in the material on Useful Generalizations for Dealing with Consultees.

ACTIVITY 4.6

After reviewing the material mentioned above (from Chapter 1), rehearse giving an introductory statement about your style of consulting (the implicit contract) and your position on confidentiality.

The last area of potential conflict is the degree of responsibility for outcomes to be assumed by the consultant. In a collaborative mode, responsibility is shared, and accountability is the joint responsibility of all constituent parties. If plans don't work, the implementer has the responsibility to inform the other members of the problem-solving team, who will reconvene to assess the situation. If communication processes are working well, this should not be a serious issue (Friend & Cook, 2003; Pugach & Johnson, 1995). When communication seems to be breaking down, it may be appropriate for the consultant to look for possible sources and types of resistance or barriers to consultation, which are discussed in Chapter 3.

In the final analysis, school-based consultants need to be aware that they may come across situations in which there may be some question regarding the ethical standards I have summarized. As professionals, when we believe a violation has occurred we are obligated to take some action, such as following the 10-step procedure previously described. As Jacob-Timm and Hartshorne (1998) point out, in the area of ethics, professionals have no rights, just responsibilities.

ADVOCACY AS A ROLE IN CONSULTATION PRACTICE

An advocate is a person who seeks to establish a certain condition for an individual client or group within a system. LaBorde and Seligman (1991) describe it as a process for aiding parents in their efforts to see that their children get the services and supports they need. An advocacy-oriented approach has been described by Dunst, Johanson, Rounds, Trivette, and Hamby (1992) as consisting of four categories:

1. *Beliefs* (characterized by mutual trust, being supportive, and being accepting);
2. *Attitudes* (a caring attitude, empathic and positive);
3. *Communicative style* (open, active, sharing);
4. *Behavioral actions* (problem solving, shared responsibility).

At its most elementary level, school consultation is all about advocacy; the consultant works (i.e., advocates) with the consultee(s) for the betterment of some condition for the client (student). In the most common case of a consultant working with a teacher to improve the learning of a student referred because of academic challenges, the consultant advocates for the student by assisting the teacher to take whatever steps are necessary to improve the learning environment for the student. In a more complex situation, a consultant might be working with a group of consultees (administrators, teachers, and playground aides) regarding issues of playground safety (e.g., freedom from harassment by others). They collaborate by using all the techniques described in Chapter 3 and together come up with a plan that makes good sense to the majority, has a good chance of being successful, and has the commitment of the front-line staff (probably the playground aides). In even more impactive cases, consultants advocate for systems-change efforts where relatively large-scale projects may affect teaching or behavior management methods throughout the whole school or district. In all cases a school consultant not only advocates in regard to the student, but also as a service to the student's family, helping them to understand the school issues and also helping the school to understand the family's issues, concerns, and hopes for their child. Another useful service for the school consultant is to help the families make connections with outside resources that may be of assistance to families as they thread their way through the sometimes complicated process of getting access to all sources of help for their child (Fine & Nissenbaum, 2000; Powers, 1991). Chapter 8 presents a case demonstrating how a consultant worked with school personnel to advocate for and to affect a major change in service delivery for students with mild handicaps.

Given the seemingly straightforward positive aspects of an advocacy stance, a word of caution is in order. Some school consultants interpret advocacy in a somewhat stronger sense, taking a stand for a given position and doing everything it takes to see that the position comes to be accepted or adopted by all constituents of a problem, whether or not these other individuals are in favor of this position. For example, a behaviorally oriented consultant believes that the contingencies of reinforcement are the main driving forces behind students' behaviors. She advocates solely for all teachers to adopt this point of view, perhaps blurring some teacher's (or counselor's) efforts to understand students' behavior from alternative viewpoints, such as a counseling-communications-based system, or a psychoeducational approach, or, in selected cases, a neuropsychological approach (D'Amato & Rothlisberger, 1992). Conoley and Conoley (1992) have described an advocacy model of consultation, characterized by individuals bringing ideas into an already existing structure in an effort to modify in some significant way how the structure deals with clients. Some of the more recent advocacy efforts have been in respect to acquiring permission for students to engage in prayer in schools, curriculum either for or against Darwinian evolution, the necessity for national standards, a voucher system, certain forms of bilingual education, the purging of selected books from school libraries, clubs for gay and lesbian issues, and, in an area close to the heart of the content of this text, inclusion for students with disabilities. In each case an advocacy-minded individual or group believes that they are speaking for the rights of disenfranchised or relatively powerless groups (i.e., students; perhaps parents) who cannot fight for these rights by themselves. Thus, advocacy consultation may find itself in a position of having to abandon the collaborative mode in favor of a more assertive stance, characterized by what the advocate believes is a higher value: the needs of students that may not be recognized or honored by the existing conditions of the school. Dorn and Fuchs (2004) have commented on a possible inconsistency that can arise when advocates, including lawyers, seek public payment for private education for students with disabilities, which may violate the principle of least restrictive environment. This phenomenom of a "disability voucher" program was provided for more than 1,000 students in Florida during the 2000–2001 school year, about 20 times more than the number of general education students who used the voucher system to escape failing schools (Hegarty, 2001).

An example of advocates' successful efforts to impact on a culturally accepted situation is in the area of childrens' rights. Currently most people in this culture (and all over the world) believe that it is a right of children to be safe from harm. However, it wasn't until 1833 that child labor laws were enacted in England. These stated that children between the ages of 9 and 13 could not be required to work more than 9 hours a day. In America, only 15 states had child labor laws by 1903, and it wasn't until 1938 that Congress passed the Fair Labor Standards Act, which generally set the minimum age at which children could be employed as 16. In regard to all forms of abuse, as recently as 1963 only 13 states had laws requiring the mandatory reporting of child maltreatment. We can see that it wasn't too many years ago that child labor and exploitation were common in America, as they still are in many places in the world (Sussman, 1977; see also *www.coopamerica.org*). Only through the strong advocacy efforts of reformers did those practices get abolished, either by force of law or by the slow evolution of more enlightened thinking by most citizens.

In the case of the inclusion of students with disabilities, advocates have been fighting for this right in the halls of Congress and in the halls of public schools for at least 30 years. The first major breakthrough that resulted from advocacy for the rights of individuals was P.L. 94–142, passed in 1975. This ensured students with disabilities the right to a Free Appropriate Public Education (FAPE). In the ensuing years, advocates went to the next step, that of inclusion of those with disabilities into the least restrictive environment (LRE), which was interpreted to mean the general education classroom whenever possible. Advocacy for these rights, including a clearer explication of the meaning of FAPE and LRE, continues. The role of the school consultant needs to include advocacy for students and parents, especially in situations where teachers or school administrators may be putting the interests of their classroom or the school ahead of interests of the student.

ACTIVITY 4.7

List some possible needs you believe a school consultant could advocate for. Some possibilities were mentioned earlier. Add others, such as identifying students at risk of poor reading in grades K–1, designing an assessment method for finding these students, and a remedial program to assist them. Discuss how you could convince your school to move in the direction of this project.

In the final analysis, there is a place for advocacy, but it needs to be done in a collaborative style. Getting students' rights and needs met should be the primary basis for parenting and for working in the schools. In almost all instances, the ability to work together for these rights and needs will ensure a more harmonious work environment and a greater chance to have these rights and needs met than will the taking of strong advocacy positions that may be socially, scientifically, or politically inappropriate.

SUMMARY

This chapter has presented information about issues of ethics and advocacy. Ethical guidelines developed by professional groups were reviewed, and a set of guidelines based on the Council on Exceptional Children (1997) code and standards were used to determine how decisions can be made in cases of ethical concern. Advocacy was reviewed as an essential element in the consultative interaction, and one that requires considerable sensitivity in its application.

REFERENCES

American Counseling Association. (1995). *Code of Ethics and Standards of Practice*. Alexandria, VA: Author.

American Psychological Association. (1992). *Ethical Principles of Psychologists and Code of Conduct*. Washington, DC: Author.

Backer, T. E., & Glaser, E. M. (1979). *Portraits of 17 organizational consultants*. Los Angeles: Human Interaction Research Institute.

Brown, D., Pryzwansky, W., & Schulte, A. (2001). *Psychological consultation* (5th ed.). Boston: Allyn & Bacon.

CEC Code of Ethics and Standards of Practice. Retrieved December 21, 2000, from *http://www.cec.sped.org/ps/code.html*

Conoley, J. C., & Conoley, C. W. (1992). *School consultation: A guide to practice and training*. Needham Heights, MA: Allyn & Bacon.

Cook, L. H., Weintraub, F. J., & Morse, W. C. (1995). Ethical dilemmas in the restructuring of special education. In J. L. Paul, D. Evans, & H. Rosselli (Eds.), *Integrating school restructuring and special education reform* (pp. 119–139). Fort Worth, TX: Harcourt Brace.

Corey, G., Corey, M., & Callanan, P. (1998). *Issues and ethics in the helping professions* (5th ed.). Pacific Grove, CA: Brooks/Cole Publishing Co.

Council on Exceptional Children. (1997). *CEC code of ethics and standards of practice*. Reston, VA: Author.

D'Amato, R., & Rothlisberger, B. (1992). *Psychological perspectives on intervention*. New York: Longman.

Dorn, S., & Fuchs, D. (2004). Trends in placement issues. In A. Sorrells, H. Rieth, & P. Sindelar (Eds.), *Critical Issues in Special Education* (pp. 57–72). Boston: Allyn & Bacon.

Dunst, C. J., Johanson, C., Rounds, T., Trivette, C. M., & Hamby, D. (1992). Characteristics of parent-professional partnerships. In S. L. Christenson & J. C. Conoley (Eds.), *Home-school collaboration: Enhancing children's academic and social competence* (pp. 157–174). Silver Springs, MD: NASP.

English, A. (1995). The legal framework for minor consent. Introduction. In A. English, M. Matthews, K. Extavour, C. Palamountain, & J. Lang, *State minor consent statutes: A summary* (pp. 3–7). San Francisco: National Center for Youth Law.

Erchul, W. P., & Martens, B. K. (2002). *School consultation: Conceptual and empirical bases of practice*. New York: Plenum.

Ewing, N. (2001). Teacher education: Ethics, power and privilege. *Teacher Education and Special Education, 24*(1), 13–24.

Fine, M. J., & Nissenbaum, M. S. (2000). The child with disabilities and the family: Implications for professionals. In M. J. Fine & R. L. Simpson (Eds.), *Collaboration with parents and families of children and youth with exceptionalities* (2nd ed., pp. 3–26). Austin, TX: Pro-Ed.

Friend, M., & Cook, L. (2003). *Interactions: Collaboration skills for school professionals* (4th ed.). Boston: Allyn & Bacon.

Gable, R. A., Arllen, N. L., & Cook, L. (1993). But let's not overlook the ethics of collaboration. *Preventing School Failure, 37*, 32–36.

Gallesich, J. (1982). *The profession and practice of consultation: A handbook for consultants, trainers of consultants and consumers of consultation services*. San Francisco: Jossey-Bass.

Hegarty, S. (2001, February 26). Learning disabled latch onto vouchers. *St. Petersberg Times*, 1B, 7B.

Heron, T. E., Martz, S. A., & Margolis, H. (1996). Ethical and legal issues in consultation. *Remedial and Special Education, 17*(6), 377–385, 392.

Howe, K., & Miramontes, O. (1991). A framework for ethical deliberation in special education. *Journal of Special Education, 25*(1), 7–25.

Howe, K., & Miramontes, O. (1992). *The ethics of special education*. New York: Teachers College Press.

Hughes, J. (1986). Ethical issues in school consultation. *School Psychology Review, 15*, 489–499.

Jacob-Timm, S. (1999). Ethically challenging situations encountered by school psychologists. *Psychology in the Schools, 36*(3), 205–217.

Jacob-Timm, S., & Hartshorne, T. (1998). *Law and ethics for school psychologists* (3rd ed.). Brandon, VT: CPPC.

Koocher, G. P., & Keith-Spiegel, P. (1998). *Ethics in psychology* (2nd ed.). New York: Oxford University Press.

LaBorde, P., & Seligman, M. (1991). Counseling parents with children with disabilities. In M. Seligman (Ed.), *The family with a handicapped child* (pp. 337–368). Boston: Allyn & Bacon.

Lippitt, G. L. (1973). *Visualizing change*. Fairfax, VA: NTL Learning Responses Corp.

National Association of School Psychologists. (2000). *Principles for Professional Ethics*. Bethesda, MD: Author.

National Education Association. (1975). *The Code of Ethics of the Education Profession*. Washington, DC: Author.

Newman, J. L. (1993). Ethical issues in consultation. *Journal of Counseling and Development, 72,* 148–156.

Powers, M. D. (1991). Intervening with families of young children with severe handicaps: Contributions of a family systems approach. *School Psychology Quarterly, 6,* 131–146.

Pryzwansky, W. B. (1993). Ethical consultation practice. In J. E. Zins, T. R. Kratochwill, & S. N. Elliott (Eds.), *Handbook of consultation services for children* (pp. 329–350). San Francisco: Jossey-Bass.

Pugach, M. C., & Johnson, L. J. (1995). *Collaborative practitioners, collaborative schools*. Denver: Love Publishing.

Sadker, M., & Sadker, D. (2005). *Teachers, schools and society* (7th ed.). Boston: McGraw Hill.

Snow, D. L., & Gersick, K. E. (1986). Ethical and professional issues in mental health consultation. In F. V. Mannino, E. J. Trickett, M. F. Shore, M. G. Kidder, & G. Levin (Eds.), *Handbook of mental health consultation* (DHHS Publication No. ADM 86-1446) (pp. 393–431). Washington, DC: U.S. Government Printing Office.

Sussman, A. N. (1977). *The rights of young people: The basic ACLU guide to a young person's rights*. New York: Avon Books.

Taylor, L., & Adelman, H. (1998). Confidentiality: Competing principles, inevitable dilemmas. *Journal of Educational and Psychological Consultation, 9*(3), 267–276.

The Solutions-Oriented Consultation System

OBJECTIVES

1. Review the stages of the consultation process as presented by various writers.
2. Describe in detail the solution-oriented consultation system (SOCS).
3. Provide guidance to assist consultants in developing solutions for the issues raised in each of the 10 steps of the SOCS.

You are a special education teacher who has taken a strong interest in doing more consultation with the general education staff regarding both mainstreamed and at-risk students. You have read the material in the preceding chapters but aren't yet sure what process or steps to follow. Is there a systematic way of proceeding in consultation, or should you let events dictate what steps you follow?

You have been hired to present an inservice to a district that wants to improve its consultation service delivery system. The district has increased the amount of consultation that special education teachers and ancillary staff do, but staff members seem to be consulting, as the director of special services puts it, "by the seat of their pants." The director wants you to teach them how to structure their activities. What process should they follow?

As these vignettes indicate, how you go about consulting with others may be even more important than the actual content of the consultative activities (Dougherty, 2000). In this chapter we look at some generic processes for doing school consultation. Then we examine a highly structured approach known as the solutions-oriented consultation system (SOCS), which includes all the important steps a consultant needs to consider for effective consultation to take place.

ACTIVITY 5.1

Many readers have already engaged in some form of consultation activity, either as a consultant or a consultee. Recall the steps or stages you went through in the consultation process. Did they seem purposeful or random? Did you feel they made sense in light of the problem you were trying to solve?

ACTIVITY 5.2

Recall what you have learned from other college courses or life experiences about the problem-solving process. List the steps you believe are appropriate for a generic problem-solving model.

The problem-solving process that occurs in school consultation consists of the activities engaged in by both the consultant and the consultee(s) as they work together to solve achievement or social/behavior problems or to improve teaching practices. In this chapter, we focus on how you go about being an internal consultant, someone who is employed on a (usually) full-time basis by a district or other educational entity, and whose title is not ordinarily that of "consultant," but is more likely to be a special education teacher, a school psychologist, a counselor, a mentor teacher, or a vice-principal. Almost all internal consultants have other responsibilities (e.g., to teach, to assess, to counsel, or to engage in administrative activities). Their consultation work has become an increasingly important part of what they do, particularly if they are special education teachers or school psychologists. External consultation is usually provided on a short-term basis by a professional person who is not regarded as a regular member of the school staff but who may be brought in to assist with specific cases, to direct system change efforts, or to lead staff development sessions. Activities and responsibilities of these external consultants are discussed by Brown, Pryzwansky, and Schulte (2001), Caplan and Caplan (1993), Dougherty (2000), and Erchul and Martens (2002).

STEPS TO FOLLOW IN THE CONSULTATION PROCESS

Numerous writers in the consultation field have described the consultation process. Terms such as *stages, steps, activities,* and *sequences of consultation* have been used synonymously with the more generic term *process.*

The best-known set of steps was initially presented by Bergan (1977): (1) problem identification, (2) problem analysis, (3) plan implementation, and (4) problem evaluation. Bergan (1995) reviewed his belief that these four steps constitute the core of the behavioral consultation problem-solving process. These steps were reviewed in Chapter 2.

Brown, Pryzwansky, and Schulte (2001) define eight stages of consultation: (1) entry into an organization, (2) initiation of a consulting relationship, (3) assessment, (4) problem definition and goal setting, (5) strategy selection, (6) implementation, (7) evaluation, and (8) termination. Dougherty (2000) discusses four stages—entry, diagnosis, implementation, and disengagement—with four phases embedded within each of these stages. Dettmer, Dyck, and Thurston (1999) specify 10 steps in their recommended process: (1) preparing for the consultation, (2) initiating the consultation, (3) collecting information, (4) isolating the problem, (5) identifying concerns relevant to the problem, (6) generating solutions, (7) formulating a plan, (8) evaluating progress and process, (9) following up on the consultation, and (10) repeating consultation as necessary. Marks (1995) has provided a whole text devoted solely to the issues of entry, by which he means gaining access to school- and district-level administrators, establishing relationships with teachers, and overcoming resistance to consultation.

Gutkin and Curtis (1999) have described a generic model of school consultation which they refer to as ecobehavioral consultation. It blends their previously described problem-solving and behavioral models (Gutkin & Curtis, 1982) with the phrase they preferred in 1990, ecological consultation (Gutkin & Curtis, 1990). In their ecobehavioral model they utilize the four steps of the behavioral model that were previously described (Bergan, 1995; Bergan & Kratochwill, 1990), but then go beyond those four steps to add more depth to their process. The original seven steps suggested by Gutkin and Curtis (1990) are described below in some detail because they constitute a generic, representative set of steps common to those presented by the various sources previously listed. They indicate that cycling back and forth among the seven steps should be expected because of the shifting nature of realities as the process unfolds.

Define and Clarify the Problem

One of the most frequently cited references in the consultation literature is the Bergan and Tombari (1976) study that documents the significance of the problem identification stage of consultation. It is generally agreed that if this stage is successful, a positive outcome is more likely. Their study indicated that about 60% of the variance in plan implementation was accounted for by the effectiveness of problem identification. Poor problem identification results in chaos because the consultant and the consultee are working on the wrong problem or two separate problems. This is not as unlikely as it may sound (Cleven & Gutkin, 1988; Lambert, 1976). One possible way that a problem may be poorly defined is in regard to the specification of the antecedents. A teacher may want to focus only on immediate (proximal) antecedents while the real source of a student's behavioral or learning difficulties may be the result of more distal antecedents (e.g., teacher tolerance, gang pressures, inadequate earlier schooling, a complex of risk factors arising from poverty; Walker & Shinn, 2002). Wilson, Gutkin, Hagen, and Oats (1998) have discussed the difficulties some teachers have in clarifying problems and selecting appropriate interventions. Some consultees need assistance in defining problems, and some consultants may need more training in how to elicit information from consultees to clarify problems. These are skills that subsume effective consultation and should not be taken for granted. Brown et al. (2001), in their chapter "The Consultee as a Variable," discuss the need for consultee training in problem identification. The skills discussed later in this chapter, as well as in Chapter 3, should be of assistance to consultants.

The most common mistake in this step (other than incorrect problem identification) is to rush to solutions. Inexperienced consultants may feel pressured by the consultee's desire to get a quick solution to the problem. The consultee may expect the consultant to come up with a plan for solving the problem before it has been well defined. Even though most consultees would not expect or want their physicians to come up with quick solutions to medical problems without some further degree of study of the problem, some of them will expect school-based consultants to provide such solutions on the basis of minimal information. As is clear in the cases described in Chapter 9, consultants have to guard against this problem of premature strategy selection.

Analyze the Forces Impinging on the Problem

Here the consultant looks at the ecology of the student's life and the classroom to gather information about the problem, its possible sources, and their interrelationships within the context of classroom expectations. Following the reciprocal determinism ideas of Bandura (1978), which consist of an analysis of the relationships among the person, the behaviors of concern, and the environment, the consultant looks at the referred student's history and behavior as well as that of the behavior of the teacher, the possible influence of the student's parents, the classroom situation, the curriculum, sociocultural phenomena, and any other sources of influence that could be related to the behavior(s) of concern. Evans, Evans, and Gable (1989) have provided an interview format for conducting an ecological survey consisting of questions about the general background of the student, his or her educational history and present performance, and home/community information.

Brainstorm Alternative Strategies

Once the problem and its ecology are defined and understood, at least for the present, the consultant and the consultee should discuss some possible strategies to implement. Brainstorming as a method of freeing the mind to think of diverse possibilities is recommended, with the caution that this process has to be governed to some extent so that the participants don't waste time with ideas of no practical value. Pfeiffer and Jones (1974) include the following as three basic rules for the process of brainstorming:

- Do not evaluate strategies as they are being generated.
- Generate as many interventions as possible.
- Creativity and novelty are at a premium when generating a list of possible interventions.

If there is concern that some participants may be reluctant to publicly share their ideas, all participants may be asked to write their ideas on 5" × 7" cards without attaching their names to their ideas. When this is done, the ideas have a better chance of being evaluated on their merits, rather than on the basis of who generated the ideas.

After the ideas have been discussed, modified as appropriate, and agreed upon, the group will have a collection of ideas, collaboratively derived, that will form the basis for the next step.

Evaluate and Choose Among Alternative Strategies

It is common at this point for the consultee to ask the consultant to choose which strategy to use, once again deferring to the presumed expertise of the consultant. It is important to remember that the consultee should be the final judge of which strategy to select among those that seem most promising since the consultee will do most of the implementation. In doing this, the consultant is hoping to capitalize treatment acceptability, a necessary characteristic of effective consultation. Without the teacher's (or parent's) acceptance of the intervention, it may very well not be implemented with the rigor required.

In complex problems a number of strategies may be selected at once, either for simultaneous implementation or to use as a quick substitute for the first strategy in the event of its obvious failure (for example, a plan to use extinction that results in an intolerable increase in the target behavior).

Strategy selection should be based on a mini-max principle: Select the strategy that will have the maximum impact for the minimal effort or intrusion into other classroom or family dynamics. Selecting a "can't miss" strategy that results in a chaotic classroom or turmoil among the client's siblings at home is self-defeating and should be avoided in favor of a more conservative strategy. Remember that one always has to be mindful of the ecological reality of a classroom or home. Any change in one aspect of that reality may have an unwanted influence on other aspects. The strategy of rewarding a deviant child with a preferred activity for short bursts of appropriate behavior may cause a revolt among your ordinarily well-behaved students who want equal preferred activity rewards for their ordinary good behavior. It also might be teaching the deviant student that he can be reinforced for only brief bits of good behavior. Sarason (1982) warns against the possibility of unintended negative consequences that may result from what seems to be a beneficial change for one aspect of the ecological whole. For example, a change in a method of presenting information may be beneficial to some students but have the reverse effect on others. In terms of a very large-scale intervention, the introduction of "whole-language" reading methods in California, Texas, and other states proved to be a boon to some adept readers, but much less so to many who needed structured instruction in phonetic analysis and synthesis (Stanovich, 2000).

Specify Consultant and Consultee Responsibilities

The "wh" questions—who, what, when, where (and how)—come into play here. Consultation is much more likely to be successful when the consultant and the consultee settle these questions at the outset of the process of strategy implementation or shortly thereafter. The partners have to agree on responsibilities, or chaos may ensue. In an expert model it is likely that the consultant decides these issues, but in a collaborative model the consultant and the consultee need to work together and agree on details. For example, will the general education teacher or the consultant call the parent to discuss the current plan? What data-gathering system will be used, the more comprehensive one suggested by the consultant or the simpler one preferred by the consultee? What are realistic goals for any given situation? Figures 3.1 in Chapter 3 gives an example of how this information is specified in the "Today's Plan" section of these summary notes. The cases in Chapter 9 give examples of how this process works and what a consultant should do if it begins to falter.

Implement the Chosen Strategy

If the process has worked well up to this point, the consultee should be eager to begin implementing the intervention(s). If it were always as simple as that, we could skip to the next step. Unfortunately, it doesn't always work that way for a number of possible reasons: (1) the problem itself shifts in focus somehow, and a revision is needed before the plan gets off the ground; (2) the consultee finds he doesn't have some material he will need to implement the plan, and you're both embarrassed that you didn't think of it earlier; (3) the consultee finds that he either doesn't want to do or can't really do the new behavior expected of him; or (4) the student reacts in some unanticipated way, and the consultee needs to return to an earlier step in the process.

Implementation is the moment of truth in consultation. Here any previous weaknesses in the process come to light, and the strength of the consultant–consultee relationship is tested. Some of the types of resistance discussed in Chapter 3 (e.g., habit strength, "too much work," lack of skills) are also most likely to surface at this step.

Evaluate the Effectiveness of the Interventions and Recycle if Necessary

It is possible that the chosen and implemented strategy has worked very well and that the problem has been solved with no modifications needed. This, however, is unlikely. More likely is the possibility that modifications—mild, moderate, or extreme—will be needed. The consultant's role at this point is mainly twofold: monitoring the consultee's actions and the student's reactions, and assisting in collecting data that will serve as the basis for possible program changes. Progress monitoring (Deno, Espin, & Fuchs, 2002) is the process that enables all parties to have up-to-date information about the success of the interventions. The consultant will also need to reinforce the consultee for efforts that often do not produce the hoped-for rapid results.

Eventually, one of the following or a variation will occur: (1) the project is a success, and you will present it as a triumph at your next staff meeting; (2) the project has some positive outcomes but still needs further work before both the consultant and the consultee are satisfied; (3) the project is minimally successful and requires a complete recycling through the sequence just described; or (4) the project is unsuccessful, and both the consultant and the consultee need to think about why.

If consultants follow the steps outlined by Gutkin and Curtis (1990) or those presented in the next section of this chapter (SOCS), it is probable that outcomes 1 and 2 will be the most likely scenarios.

SOLUTIONS-ORIENTED CONSULTATION SYSTEM (SOCS)

This section presents a format for school-based consultants to use when asked to consult about the behavior and learning problems of school-age children. It is called the solutions-oriented consultation system (SOCS) because it emphasizes finding solutions to problems that may be implemented in general education classrooms rather than merely studying the problems for classification or placement purposes.

Following the discussion of each of the 10 steps there is a list of possible questions to ask, next steps to take, or solutions that may be appropriate. As you learn about this 10-step sequential process, you will also read about the many ways in which consultants can vary from these steps when necessary and appropriate. As I have indicated, consultation is rarely conducted in a lockstep, linear fashion. It may be better to describe the consultation process as linear-circular since consultants often find themselves moving through these steps in creative ways, going back and forth among them as the process evolves. For those not yet experienced in consultation, it would be a good idea to follow these steps as presented because they constitute a comprehensive and orderly way to go about the consultation process. However, remember that deviations may be appropriate, based on the characteristics of the consultee and the situation.

The steps described in this section will be illustrated in the extensive case studies in Chapter 9, which demonstrate how the SOCS process can be used in a collaborative consultation program of assistance to parents and teachers.

1. Receipt of a Referral and Initial Thoughts About It

The process ordinarily starts with a teacher who perceives a need for assistance with educational planning for one or more of her students. She follows whatever steps are prescribed by the policies of her school. These usually include filling out and sending in a referral to a school consultant or the coordinator of the SST (see Figure 5.1). Most districts also require that the referring teacher have contacted the student's parents to

Figure 5.1

Consultation request information form

Teacher's name: ______________________________ Date: __________

Student's name: ______________________________ Grade: __________

Student's age: ________

Parents: ____

Referral concern: ____

History and/or other information about the problem: ____________________

____

____

Best time(s) to see me: ____________________________________

discuss the teacher's concerns and, if possible, remediate the referral problem through a collaborative process with the parents.

The consultant or SST coordinator reads the referral and forms an immediate impression based on at least the following:

- Is this regarding a student with a behavior or a learning problem, or both?
- Do I know this student or her family? If so, what does my prior knowledge tell me about this referral?
- Who is the teacher, and what does my knowledge of the teacher tell me about this referral?
- What should I do with this referral first: send it forward to SST, review with the teacher, or call the parents?

Depending on the nature of the case, any of these questions might be answered or dealt with first. Other initial thoughts involve priority (for example, responding immediately to suspected child abuse, hints of suicidal behavior, or behavior that threatens the safety of others); history of this student, if known; curricular and other classroom ecology factors; and, realistically, other time pressures.

Some practitioners may find Figure 5.1 too brief. Districts vary considerably in their approach to form complexity. An example of a more extensive referral form is available in Salvia and Ysseldyke (2004), and in Figure 2.3 of this text, modified as appropriate.

Additional Areas of Inquiry, Next Steps to Take, or Possible Solutions: At this time it is too soon to be generating specific solutions. However, the following should be considered, just based on the nature of the referral:

- Given this teacher, this grade level, and other general considerations about the ecology of the situation, what general or specific ideas come to mind?
- Should we take the time of the whole SST to discuss this referral, or would it be better to send it to an individual consultant to see if she can resolve it with the teacher and parent alone?
- Has this student been referred previously? If so, what file information do we have? What interventions were tried, and with what degree of success? Perhaps one of these successful interventions should be tried again, if the current situation is compatible with that intervention.

2. Initial Discussion with the Teacher(s)

In the event your school sends initial referrals directly to the SST, you may want to skip to step 5 of the SOCS, which deals directly with SST activities, and then return to steps 2, 3, and 4, perhaps as an SST-designated consultant. Generally, it is best to visit with the referring teacher first for a number of reasons: (1) to verify receipt of the referral; (2) to acknowledge your concern about it; (3) to inform the teacher (in case he is someone with whom you have not previously worked) about your collaborative style of doing consultation and to discuss matters of confidentiality; (4) to get more information about the referral that will be helpful in determining your next steps; and (5) to begin or reestablish the rapport process.

This initial meeting, as well as subsequent meetings, should take place during the referring teacher's natural break times rather than during an instructional period. With few exceptions, usually due to time pressures, it is best not to interrupt the teaching process to confer with teachers since teaching is the most important thing that happens in schools. You want to spend an uninterrupted 10 minutes or so to gather information that will help you understand the problem and plan your strategy.

In the case of behavior problems, you will want to get some basics such as antecedents, severity, form, frequency, timing, and consequences of the behaviors of concern. In the case of academic learning problems, you will determine the areas of strength and weakness. For either type of referral, you will want to know what the consultee has done up to this point. Also, you will be forming a tentative hypothesis about the causes and possible solutions to the referral and, again, what steps you and the consultee should take next. It is important at this point to avoid the rush to solutions that is so tempting and that some consultees will want you to do. Although the SOCS is "solutions-oriented," that does not mean you should be impulsive about intervention selection.

The consultant should take notes during the initial and subsequent meetings. This has a number of purposes: (1) it indicates to the consultee that what he says is important enough to record accurately; (2) it helps you remember details (Given the large number of cases with which the average consultant is concerned, you will find it best to keep accurate data and to record it as soon as possible after it becomes known to you. Consultees don't like to have to repeat facts every time you consult with them. Your reference to accurate notes tells them that you are well organized and efficient.); and (3) it helps both the consultant and consultee keep track of what was discussed, both the facts of the case and the plans that you have made during each consultation.

Figure 3.1 is an example of a form that a consultant completes after discussing the student with the consultee. The consultant uses the outline contained in this form and fills it out based on the information provided by the consultee. The consultant gives a copy of this form to the teacher, and to the principal if appropriate. This serves as a reminder of what was discussed and serves as a starting point for future meetings. Because teachers have a limited amount of time available, 10 to 15 minutes is ideal for this meeting, although sometimes it takes longer, particularly the first meeting (Brown et al., Dougherty, 2000). Two sessions may be necessary just to cover the information listed in Figure 3.1. Busse and Beaver (2000) have presented a very detailed outline to follow for gathering information about the specifics of a behavioral problem referral. Using an outline of this complexity will ordinarily require at least two 15-minute sessions with the teacher. Given teachers' myriad activities, the consultant has to learn to be efficient. She has to come to a meeting prepared with a structured set of questions and must not give the impression that she's wasting or filling time. A good rule to follow is that the consultant should not ask any questions that are not related in some form to solutions or intervention development.

Gutkin (1993a) has provided a problem-solving worksheet designed to give structure to the initial and subsequent interactions with the consultee. The steps in his problem-solving method are very similar to those in the SOCS formulation. Bergan and Kratochwill (1990) have also provided standardized consultation protocols designed to organize your approach to teacher or parent interviewing.

Additional Areas of Inquiry, Next Steps to Take, or Possible Solutions:

- Having gained a good idea of the teacher's perceptions of the referral, you can refine your thinking about the primary needs and concerns. This should give more focus to your beginning conceptualizations about the nature of the problems, possibilities for interventions, and probabilities for the success of some of these interventions.
- The most general type of solution at this time is to be supportive to the teacher or parent. They have come to you because the targeted student presents with challenges that are beyond their usual scope of interactions. They need to be helped through their feelings of discomfort, stress, and possibly even anger. The communication and interpersonal skills discussed in Chapter 3 will prove most useful to you at these early stages of the SOCS process.
- What types and degrees of support will this student and this teacher need? Is this a situation you can deal with between yourself and the consultee and parents, or should it go to SST at this time?
- Begin to think about the most general categories of interventions that may be appropriate here. Suggestions for behavior problem interventions are contained in Chapter 6, while academic learning problem interventions are presented in Chapter 7.

3. Classroom (Ecological) Observation

Best practice is to visit the class regarding every referral, if time permits. The purposes of observing are to verify the referral, to get an impression of the ecological dynamics that may be contributing to the referral, to study the teacher's style and methods, and to try to determine points of leverage where interventions may be useful. Ecological assessment does not deal directly with the student but focuses more on classroom and playground dynamics: what these environments look like, what teachers do, what the expectations are, what the formal and unwritten rules are, and how all of these factors influence behavior and learning. How students act is in some part attributable to how others around them act. The consultant needs to be aware that a classroom (ecological) observation is just that: an observation of what is going on in the classroom as a whole that could be affecting the behavior of the targeted student(s).

In the case of learning problem referrals, a classroom observation may be considered optional, especially if you know how the teacher works and what the curriculum expectations and teaching methods are. When observing, do so at a time when the teacher believes you would have the best view of the academic referral problem. If an academic learning referral is accompanied by a behavior problem (for example, distractibility or noncompliance), an observation should always be done.

You have to be very careful to be supportive of the teacher. You must avoid giving the impression that you don't believe or trust the teacher or that you are going into his classroom with some hidden agenda. You must show the teachers in your schools that you are functioning like any scientist: You need to observe firsthand the nature of the problem or situation. Most teachers have no objection; in fact, they may be surprised if you don't ask to observe. In my experience, nearly all teachers ask when I'm coming in to observe, particularly if the referral is regarding a student with a behavior problem.

It may turn out that the referral may be best resolved by having the teacher deal with the referred student in a different way by using different methods, materials, or general classroom management tactics. You'll have a better sense of this after an observation.

Barkley (1988) believes that direct observation of the referred student in the natural environment (the classroom and the playground) should be an important part of student assessment, along with the use of checklists and teacher interviews. The picture the consultant gets of the referred student from teacher interviews or checklists may not be objective or accurate. Because the consultee is part of the ecology of the referral problem (the primary responder to the student's behaviors), it is easy to understand how nonobjectivity can creep into ratings or comments to the consultant during an interview or on a checklist.

The consultant has a choice of a wide variety of formal or informal observation methods, which are selected based on the particular classroom, teacher, type of referral problem, and time availability. At a minimum, the following questions need to be considered before starting an observation:

1. What time should the observation be done and for how long?
2. Exactly what information will be gathered and in what form?
3. While observing, should the consultant interact with the other students, the teacher, or neither? Because you are a guest in the teacher's classroom, ask the teacher for her preferences in this regard.
4. What should the teacher tell the students about the consultant and the reason for his being in the room?
5. In addition to the targeted behaviors, should the consultant also record more general pieces of information, such as on-task versus off-task time?
6. To what extent should the teacher's behavior be noted?
7. Should the behavior of other students also be noted, for purposes of contrast with the targeted student?

Many of these questions and issues should have been mentioned and clarified during the initial discussion with the teacher.

Chapter 6 contains a more detailed treatment of classroom observation and recording methods for behavior problem referrals, and Chapter 7 does the same for learning/achievement problem referrals.

Additional Areas of Inquiry, Next Steps to Take, or Possible Solutions:

- What have you learned about this classroom (or playground) that can help you in building interventions? It is best practice to talk to the teacher after every observation. In this interview, discuss at least the following points:
  1. Indicate something positive about what you observed. Without being unduly flattering, point out some strengths the teacher exhibited. In planning to do this, you will be expanding on your ability to observe an individual's strengths, which is an excellent characteristic of effective collaborative consultants.
  2. Report facts and possible needs rather than diagnoses and deficits. Rather than saying: "Well, Arturo's ADD was really in full flower, wasn't it?", try this: "Arturo seemed not to be attending as well as most of the others I observed. What might be helpful in getting a better level of attending from him?"
  3. Verify that what you observed is the same as what the teacher observed. It is important that you and the teacher can find some level of agreement about what is happening in the classroom. Recall from Chapter 2, in the discussion of the mental health model, that there was mention of a lack of objectivity as being one of the four consultee "lacks" discussed by Caplan and Caplan (1993). This postobservation discussion can give you an estimate of the teacher's objectivity in interpretation of classroom events. Be sure, of course, that you are also objective in your interpretation of the events you observed!
  4. Assuming you have observed the targeted behavior(s), you will also have observed the antecedents and consequences of these behaviors. Review these with the teacher. Again, verify with the teacher to see if his observations of these events is similar to yours.
- In the continued refinement of your knowledge base, developed as a result of the classroom observation, you may want to think in terms of supports needed by both the referred student and the teacher. Possible supports for the teacher would include simply taking time to talk to someone like yourself who can reinforce his efforts, lower his stress level about the situation, review what he has done up to this time about the problem, discuss the results of the classroom observation(s), and, of course, begin the process of developing interventions.
- Possible supports for the student include interventions based on the student's levels of academic or social behavior, such as altered expectations, peer assistance, different instructional groupings, tutorial services, and so on. Generating interventions is discussed further in steps 5 and 7 of the SOCS, as well as in Chapters 6 and 7. We may also want to consider assessment of the student, which is discussed in step 6 and in Chapters 6 and 7.

4. Using Parents as Allies in the Consultation Process

The previous discussion regarding the first three SOCS steps has centered around referrals from teachers. Obviously referrals can also come directly from parents. In either event, the consultant will want to get parental input regarding the nature of the referral and the parents' perception of it. The consultant has some choices to make about when a conference with the student's parents (or guardians) should take place, but there is no choice about whether or not such conferences should occur. They must. Remember that the parent is usually the person who is most concerned with the referred student. Indeed, the parent may be considered the primary client in consultative services, depending on the situation and one's philosophical approach to service delivery (Stewart, 1986).

A positive home–school partnership is almost always the basis for improvement in behavior and learning problems, and this is true from preschool through adolescence (Aeby, Manning, Thyer, & Carpenter-Aeby, 1999; Brown et al., 2001; Christenson & Cleary, 1990; Christenson & Conoley, 1992; Dettmer, Dyck, & Thurston, 1999; Dougherty, 2000; Esler, Godber, & Christenson, 2002; Friend & Cook, 2003; O'Shea, O'Shea, Algozzine, & Hammitte, 2001; Sheridan, Kratochwill, & Bergan, 1996). In addition to this common-sense reason, the 2004 revisions to IDEA (P.L. 108-446) mandate parent involvement in all situations involving students with disabilities and those suspected of having disabilities.

In regard to when parents should be contacted, most school districts have adopted policies about the steps that must be taken before a teacher fills out a referral form. These steps often require the teacher to contact the parent to see if intervention at the parent–teacher level might be sufficient. Assuming the need for intervention beyond this level, the parent should also be told that the teacher is planning to ask for the assistance of the school-based consultant. In this way, the parent is already informed about the process and should be expecting some contact with the consultant in a timely manner.

In general, the consultant should have a fairly good understanding of the problem and some of the classroom dynamics before talking to the parent. Parents expect consultants to have a clear idea about what is going on at school and in the classroom in addition to having a plan for studying the problem. The detailed outline for conducting a teacher interview about a student who presents with a behavioral problem, presented by Busse and Beaver (2000), will give the consultant a very thorough knowledge of the dynamics of the problem. The Busse and Beaver outline would also be useful to follow if conducting an interview with a parent who is sensitive to the details surrounding his or her child's behavioral adjustment challenges. Brown et al. (2001) have provided an assessment outline useful for gathering information from parents, and Sonstegard (1964, quoted in Brown et al., 2001) presents an outline for interviewing parents who are concerned about the behavior problems of their children. Additional suggestions for conducting parent interviews are also available in Sattler (1998).

It is important to remember that some parents are not going to welcome a phone call from the referring teacher or from the consultant. Nobody likes bad news. Even though we try to develop the idea that our intervention with parents and their child is intended to be helpful, it may not be interpreted as such. Dettmer et al. (1999) indicate that potential barriers in the early phases of help-offering interactions may include teacher factors; lack of organizational and cultural competence; and family perceptual, attitudinal, and historical factors. Teacher factors include a range of approaches to parents from positive valuing to hostile disregard. How each person perceives the problem often determines her reaction to it. If the parent believes her child is innocent of wrongdoing or would learn very well if the school would just treat him fairly, then her perception of this offer to help will probably be negative. Similarly, if the parent believes that the school is generally a hostile place, possibly because of her own remembered experiences of schools and teachers, she may project blame for the problem onto the school. An older sibling may have also had difficulty that the parent believes was due to a faulty approach by the school, so the parent greets this present referral as a likely repetition of that bad experience. This recollection of an historical event may need to be worked through with some parents before they are willing to join the school staff in a collaborative approach to the present problem.

In addition to problems of perception, there may be other issues based on realities that may be difficult to overcome. Dettmer et al. (1999) list 24 of these reasons, of which the following are not uncommon: parent is ill; parent works, perhaps two jobs; parents are intimidated by the process; parent cannot read or write; parent has no transportation; parent is emotionally unable to deal with perceived stress; and parent believes the school should deal with the problem with no assistance from the home.

One of the areas of difficulty between some homes and some school personnel concerns values. When people believe that they are talking to someone who holds values different from their own, they tend to become uncomfortable (Conoley & Conoley, 1992; Tarver Behring & Ingraham, 1998). For example, a parent may believe that corporal punishment is acceptable in child rearing, while the school (generally) does not. A teacher may state the opinion that each student should be held accountable for having her homework done every day, preferably proofed and signed by the parent. A single mother working a late shift may not have the time or energy to do this every day, and she may question the necessity of this value-driven requirement. Even more serious value issues, such as Afrocentrism, deserve to be heard and valued, although most public schools generally adhere to American or Euro-American ideas (Asante, 1987). A teacher may believe that democracy is a fine value for adults to live by, but he may practice strict autocracy in the classroom. The referred student, however, is being raised by parents who believe in a permissive style of child rearing, or, conversely, take the biblical injunction regarding rod sparing and child spoiling literally. School-based consultants often find themselves in the middle of value contrasts among the school staff and parents.

What about the consultant's own values? Especially when dealing with parents, the consultant has to recognize value differences for what they are, try not to let them interfere with a collaborative working relationship, and remember that winning agreements is more important than winning arguments.

Dettmer et al. (1999) have provided two self-rating questionnaires, one concerning your values as a consultant (1999, p. 109), the other concerning parents' attitudes, perceptions, and involvement in collaborative efforts (1999, p. 110). Consultants who complete these forms may find that they need to take a closer look at themselves if they expect to be successful in building productive relationships between home and school.

Numerous sources are available for detailed information about parent conferences (Breen & Altepeter, 1990; Conroy & Mayer, 1994; Nicoll, 1992; O'Shea et al., 2001;

Sattler, 1998; Turnbull & Turnbull, 1997). Christenson and Conoley (1992) and Christenson and Sheridan (2001) have provided texts that detail methods and implications of home–school collaboration. Sheridan et al. (1996) have described a conjoint behavioral consultation (CBC) model in which both parents and teachers are jointly the consultees in a collaborative approach to mutual problem solving that emphasizes the interconnectedness between home and school systems. When following this model, the consultant often meets with the teacher and parent(s) conjointly, expanding the contextual basis of the consultation while discussing cross-setting influences and the reciprocity within and between systems.

Additional Areas of Inquiry, Next Steps to Take, or Possible Solutions:

- Now that you have talked with the parents and obtained their perspectives on the referral issues, it's a good time to put together the material gathered so far from the referral itself, the teacher interview, the classroom observation, and the parent interview to develop a fairly well-rounded picture of how relevant adults see the issues. The remaining piece of the puzzle may come from assessments of the student (Chapters 6 and 7). Try these questions to help you structure your knowledge up to this point:

  What are the behaviors of concern?

  What have people tried?

  How has the student responded to these interventions?

  What do the teacher and parent(s) believe would be the best intervention(s) to try at this point?

  What are your impressions of the situation, and about the interventions that have been suggested by the parent(s) and/or teacher?

  What supports and strategies for all constituents are emerging from these discussions?

  What ecological effects will any of these possible interventions have?

  What barriers or resistance may occur if any of these proposed interventions are tried?

  How can you increase the degree of cooperation and effort from teachers and parents in the development and implementation of interventions?

- Assume that parents will need more support and guidance in their efforts to implement interventions than will teachers. Parents typically know less about how to deal with children's difficulties than do teachers, so you will need to think about ways of supporting parents in their efforts to be cooperative in a conjoint program.
- The previously listed references contain many specific ideas for working with parents, including ideas that are practical and not difficult to implement. Two additional sources for specific assistance for parents are the book *Solve Your Child's School-Related Problems,* edited by Martin and Waltman-Greenwood (1995), and *The Special Education Yellow Pages,* a list of Internet resources developed by Pierangelo and Crane (2000).

5. Getting Teachers and Parents Together: The SST Meeting

At this point you need to make a choice. Are you ready for, or do you need, an SST meeting? Does your system (local school or district) require an SST meeting, or does it leave that decision up to the individual to whom the referral was made? If your district's policy is to have the SST meeting early in the process, that meeting may occur before the consultant has observed in the classroom or talked with the teacher or the parent.

The structure, purposes, and methods of SSTs were discussed in Chapter 2. The information presented in this fifth step of the SOCS is designed to show how the SST process aligns with the other SOCS steps, and to elucidate some specifics about how the SST contributes to case management for the consultant.

As indicated in Chapter 2, SST philosophies and activities vary considerably across the nation. In 1988, the state of California (Radius & Lesniak, 1988) produced a document, followed by staff development training across the state, designed to give structure to the SST process. In this document they suggest eight steps that the SST leader or a designee can use to structure meetings held to discuss individual students referred for learning or behavioral adjustment problems. First, the student's strengths are listed. This puts the group in a positive frame of mind about the student. Second, known information about the student's school background, family composition, health, and current performance levels is reviewed. Third, modifications that have been tried are noted. Fourth, the team's concerns are prioritized. Typically, these may include academics, behavior, physical issues, attendance, family concerns, and so on. Fifth, the group lists questions for which the answers are not yet known, such as the student's cognitive abilities or what will happen if a certain intervention is tried. Sixth, the group brainstorms ideas for action. In steps seven and eight, the best of these are selected, and assignments are made in terms of who will do what and when it will be done. At subsequent meetings, usually within 2 to 4 weeks, this information is reviewed and modified as appropriate.

The general purposes of the meeting are to generate hypotheses about why a problem exists, what should be done about it, and who will do it within the general education program, which may include resources other than special education (e.g., remedial reading programs). It may also include a referral for assessment that may or may not be for purposes of determining eligibility for special education and related services. Given the tight timelines often followed by SSTs, it is common for a consultant to want to ask for more details but to feel constrained by those time limits. These questions should be asked either before or after the SST meeting, sometimes privately to the parent in person or over the phone, and sometimes to the teacher at the next convenient time.

Additional sources of information about the conduct of SSTs can be found in Iverson (2002), Powers (2001), Rosenfield (1992), and Zins, Curtis, Graden, and Ponti (1988).

Additional Areas of Inquiry, Next Steps to Take, or Possible Solutions:

- Having (possibly) held the SST, in which the team has agreed on possible interventions, the consultee should now feel that the referral issue has been given serious consideration and that viable interventions that can be utilized in the general education setting have been developed. The consultant will want to review these possibilities with the consultee as soon as possible after the SST meeting to ensure the following:

Has the consultee understood the proposed interventions?

Does he agree with them?

Is he able to implement them?

What will be needed (training, materials, supports) to ensure treatment acceptability and fidelity?

What are some possible implications for the ecology of the classroom?

- Following the SST meeting there is often a feeling of elation or relief since the team, including the consultee(s), has come to believe that progress has been made, if only at the conceptual (i.e., practical ideas, not yet implemented) level. If this initial enthusiasm is not followed-up by personal consultation with the consultee, a number of things can occur:

  The consultee immediately gets busy with the ordinary rigors of teaching (or parenting) and does not quickly utilize the interventions.

  Habit strength operates as a barrier to rapid change of a teacher's or parent's response style.

  The consultee finds that he really did not understand the full requirements or implications of the proposed interventions and, unless someone (consultant) follows up with him, he puts off implementing them.

  The consultee starts to have second thoughts (buyer's remorse) about the proposed interventions, and may decide not to implement them, or to do so in a fashion with somewhat less treatment validity than the SST had in mind.

  Some combination of the various types of resistance discussed in Chapter 3 begins to appear.

- All of these possibilities point to the necessity of close monitoring of the intervention program that has been established. Therefore, the primary activities to which the consultant should be oriented at this time are support and monitoring. As previously mentioned, the time for the consultee to implement the interventions is the moment of truth in consultation. Either the consultant will be available and helpful at this stage, or the whole process may disintegrate.

6. Assessment of the Student

The consultant is always engaged in some degree of assessment while engaging in all the previous steps, especially ecological assessment while doing the classroom observation, previously discussed in step 3. In this sixth step, I spell out some more aspects of assessment that may occur in individual assessment sessions conducted by school personnel or outside agencies, or that occur in the classroom or playground. More detailed discussion of the assessment process is contained in Chapter 6 (for behavior/social/interpersonal issues) and in Chapter 7 (for learning/achievement problems).

Psychological Assessment Psychological assessment is conducted primarily by school psychologists or through referral to outside agencies or practitioners who are usually clinical psychologists or psychiatrists. School counselors may also have a role in psychological assessment based on their counseling experiences with some students and through their use of rating scales and interview techniques. The two major components of this form of assessment are cognitive (intelligence and information processing) testing and personality assessment. Information from intelligence tests is helpful in alerting us to the present levels of a student's cognitive (i.e., reasoning, problem solving, memory, perception, and other systems for processing information) strengths and relative weaknesses. If the nature of the referral indicates that knowledge of how a student functions in these areas may be important in the development of interventions, then such testing should be done. Consultants who do tests of cognitive ability are aware of the controversies surrounding the use of these instruments. Thorough explication of these issues and descriptions of the instruments can be found in the following references: Flanagan, Genshaft, and Harrison (1997); Salvia and Ysseldyke (2004); and Sattler (1998).

Learning/Achievement Assessment This assessment can be provided by the teacher, based on her observations and records of the student's class performance, or it can come from formal or informal assessments conducted by ancillary staff or a resource teacher. The depth of this evaluation depends on the severity of the problem and whether or not there is a referral for formal assessment for possible special education eligibility determination. In any event, the following outline of areas to be considered should be used to structure the assessment.

Academic area needs:

Reading	Phonological processing skills
	Word recognition skills
	Comprehension skills
Math	Number facts
	Basic computation
	Advanced computation (fractions and beyond)
	Word problems
Written expression	Printing or cursive letter formation
	Punctuation, capitalization, and spelling
	Grammar
	Connected discourse
Content areas	Appropriate study skills and habits
	Content review

Behavioral/social needs:

Acquisition and performance skills	Social skills training
	Anger management
	Conflict reduction skills
	Contingency plans
Personal counseling	Individual or small group
	Family based

Biophysical Problems This area of assessment is best monitored by the school nurse, with referral to medical practitioners as appropriate. Issues include poor health, inadequate vision and hearing, poor nutrition, or any of a host of other internal physical factors that could be causing a child to behave or learn in a less-than-expected manner.

Functional Behavioral Assessment/Analysis These activities, which are of central importance in the assessment of behavior/social/interpersonal adjustment referrals, will be discussed at length in Chapter 6.

Additional Areas of Inquiry, Next Steps to Take, or Possible Solutions:

- Now that we have added the student assessment piece of the puzzle, we should be able to focus on the most important features of the referral problem. Certainly if the assessment has detected learning difficulties that indicate possible eligibility for special education and related services, the SST will discuss this issue with the parent and, most likely, develop a formal assessment plan that meets federal and state guidelines. Once the parent has signed approval of this assessment plan, the district has 50 days to conduct the assessment and hold an Individualized Education Plan (IEP) meeting to discuss the results and prepare a plan for the special education of the student, if the student is found eligible for such services.
- If, however, it does not seem appropriate to refer the student for a formal assessment, the consultant and consultee, usually along with the parent, should review all the data and determine the areas of intervention needed.

7. Planning or Modifying Interventions

At this point the consultant has reviewed the referral, studied the pertinent records, talked with the consultees (teachers and the parents), probably observed the client and the classroom (including current interventions, if any), possibly engaged in discussion about the client at an SST meeting, done a functional assessment or a diagnosis/analysis of the learning problem, and has considered causes of the problem and possible steps to take toward a solution.

Given the emphasis on collaborative approaches that this text has emphasized, just how does the consultant work with the consultee to develop an effective plan? The consultant's job is to elicit from the consultee what he has done, is currently doing, and wants to do, given the situation, and then to encourage and facilitate these plans. The consultant will probably need to help the consultee think through the possible consequences of whatever approach he has implemented or suggested and to add refinements. This is the collaborative part, which defines the consultant as an expert in the process of consultation but not necessarily in the content. Between the two of them (or three or more, depending on parental or SST involvement), they will probably come up with a better plan than either of them would have alone.

Further information about, and rationale for, the collaborative approach to consultation can be found in Chapter 1.

As the cases presented in Chapter 9 will demonstrate, the collaborative approach is a challenging and rewarding activity for school-based consultants. The challenge comes primarily from having to rein in your own tendencies to tell other professionals and parents what to do before listening to their ideas. The rewards come when the students start to improve their learning or behavior and the consultees have a feeling of pride and empowerment because they made such a significant contribution to both the design and implementation of the interventions.

Factors to Consider in Designing or Modifying Interventions The plan that the consultant and the consultee agree on should meet at least the following criteria:

1. It makes sense in light of the referral.
2. It is designed with a specific objective in mind.
3. It is not labor intensive; the consultee should not feel that he has been given an undue burden to carry.
4. All stakeholders are involved in and supportive of the plan.
5. It has some form of evaluation built in with checkpoints established.
6. It meets the KISS standard: keep it simple and sensible.
7. It meets the five standards for treatments mentioned in Chapter 1: *acceptability, validity,* and *ethics* need to be considered in design of the interventions; *integrity* (fidelity) needs to be considered in the carrying out of the intervention; and *effectiveness,* which will be determined as the interventions are carried out, becomes the final standard to be met.

Given the singular significance of the choice of interventions, it would be comforting to know that there is a research base to direct us in matters of intervention selection. Although there is now a developing foundation for the determination of evidence-based interventions (EBIs), also known as evidence-based practice, empirically validated treatments, or empirically supported interventions (Gutkin, 2002; Wampold, 2002), there is not yet a strong research base that makes it easy to go from referral problem to assessment to intervention selection for all possible referral problems (Elliott, Witt, Kratochwill, & Stoiber, 2002; Kratochwill & Stoiber, 2000). At least four reasons (factors) account for this situation, which Elliott (1988) has identified as consultant, consultee, treatment, and client (student). Consultant factors include consultant communication as well as interpersonal and problem-solving skills, such as how the consultant conceptualizes problems and explains his ideas to the consultees. Consultee factors include the amount of experience (with more experienced consultees tending to be more critical of others' treatment plans; Witt, 1986), their knowledge of remedial or behavioral techniques, and their degree of self-confidence. Treatment variables include the amount of time required to implement the intervention and the type of treatment. For example, interventions that take little time and are positive tend to be preferred. Client (student) variables include type of problem (acting out versus acting in) and severity of problem.

Reimers, Wacker, and Koeppl (1987) discuss a model in which high treatment acceptability (that is, a treatment favored by the consultee) should be related to high treatment effectiveness. Indeed, acceptability may have much to do with effectiveness. More research on this relationship is needed. Conoley, Conoley, Ivey, and Scheel (1991) have also contributed information about the importance of interventions matching the consultee's perspectives. They found that if rationales for engaging in a treatment matched the consultee's point of view about a referral problem, the treatment would be considered more acceptable by the consultees.

In lieu of a strong and easily accessible literature for matching treatments with Elliott's (1988) four variables, consultants have to rely on their experience with people; with learning and behavior problems; and with the norms and expectancies of schools, teachers, and parents. They must also have a firm grasp of what is available in the research literature (Mastropieri & Scruggs, 2000; Morrow & Woo, 2001; Slavin & Madden, 1989; Stanovich, 2000; Wang, Haertel, & Walberg, 1993) and learn interventions that are practical, time-efficient, evidence-based, and positive.

Brown et al. (2001) suggest the following four consultant skills that are necessary in the area of intervention selection:

1. Assessing consultee's values and worldview to determine which types of intervention are likely to be most acceptable.
2. Having a working knowledge of numerous interventions related to the problems that the consultant is likely to encounter.
3. Being able to communicate the nature of an intervention as it relates to the consultee's/(student's) problems and, if necessary, teaching the intervention to the consultee.
4. With the consultee, monitoring the efficacy of the intervention and redesigning it as necessary. (p. 177)

Acceptance of an intervention can be seen as passive or active. Passive acceptance may occur in the expert model of consultation, in which the consultant more or less tells the consultee what to do and the consultee believes she is supposed to do it. Whether she does or not or how well she does it is often questionable. Active acceptance refers to the consultee's belief that the intervention is really worth doing, that it at least partly is derived from her perspective, that it meets the standards just discussed, and that she can't wait to try it. Witt and Elliott (1985) have developed an Intervention Rating Profile (IRP) that can be used to assess treatment acceptability. Four of the 15 items on the IRP measure the suitability of intervention, willingness to use it in the classroom, appropriateness, and reasonability. In a study utilizing the IRP, Wilkinson (1997) found teachers highly accepting of a standard contingency management program, which was generally successful with primary-grade students.

Another form for rating treatment acceptability and intervention effectiveness is the Behavior Intervention Rating Scale (BIRS; Van Brock & Elliott, 1987). This scale has three factors: acceptability (which is the same as the 15-item IRP previously mentioned), effectiveness (an additional 7 items), and rate of effect (2 items). The BIRS and an additional Children's Intervention Rating Scale (CIRP) are available in Elliott, Witt, and Kratochwill (1991, pp. 108–109). A treatment integrity scale is also available in the same source (p. 127).

Elliott and Busse (1993) predated the generalizations of Brown et al. (2001) by pointing out the crucial role of consultee acceptance of the treatment plan. The research they review suggests the following:

1. Professional jargon is not appreciated, and may serve as a detriment to treatment acceptability.
2. Teachers prefer treatments that require minimal consultant involvement.
3. Positive treatments are considered more acceptable than are negative treatments.
4. What a teacher will accept depends on the severity of the problem. The more severe the problem, the greater the latitude of acceptance.
5. The more teachers know about behavioral principles, the greater their latitude in accepting behavioral plans.
6. There is an inverse relationship between teacher experience and acceptance of behavioral plans.

Pugach and Johnson (1987, 1995) have demonstrated that peer collaboration seems to have a powerful positive effect on treatment acceptability. In an effort to determine the functional utility of recommendations delivered in a peer collaborative method, Johnson and Pugach (1996) used the following 15 categories of interventions in actual classroom situations:

1. *Academic adjustment.* Teacher changes methods, expectations, materials, and so on.
2. *Charting/self-monitoring.* Teacher, aide, or student keeps track of behavior frequencies.
3. *Seat change.* Teacher moves the target student or others for specified periods.
4. *Management adjustment.* Teacher changes his methods of classroom behavior management.
5. *Positive reinforcement.* Teacher uses social, activity, or material reinforcers.
6. *Assignment clarification.* Teacher emphasizes homework clarification and follow-through.
7. *Immediate assistance.* Teacher works with a targeted student to prepare her for a new assignment and to ensure that she proceeds appropriately after getting a direction or assignment.
8. *Curtail negative teacher response.* Teacher is prepared for negative student behavior and plans a positive or neutral communication style.

9. *Increase communication with parents.* Teacher believes that the parents can be influential and plans to support them in their efforts.
10. *Daily notes.* This is related to item 9 as a specific tactic.
11. *Restructure peer interaction.* This is related to items 1, 3, and 4; the teacher uses grouping to capitalize on modeling effects.
12. *Peer tutoring.* Teacher uses peer tutoring within or between classes.
13. *Contracts.* Teacher makes goals explicit, usually in writing.
14. *Clarification of tasks and expectations.* Teacher uses task analysis: breaking down difficult assignments into manageable parts.
15. *Other.* Teacher uses specialized techniques such as time-out, suspension, referral to others, and so on.

Using these relatively standard interventions in a process in which teachers assisted each other in thinking through referral problems, Johnson and Pugach (1996) found that 86% of 70 problems discussed by their peer-collaborative teams were reported to be either much improved or improved. It is difficult to know whether the apparent simplicity of these interventions rendered them acceptable and successful or whether the influence of a peer collaborator was the primary determinant in their successful use. In any event, this study demonstrates that relatively common, uncomplicated interventions can result in a high success rate. It also points to a potentially valuable model of consultation service delivery: peer collaboration (Bay, Bryan, & O'Connor, 1994). Chapters 6 and 7 present other lists of interventions that are widely known, generally have strong treatment acceptability, and are evidence-based.

Erchul and Martens (2002) point out that acceptability of an intervention by teacher consultees is desirable but not always necessary, nor does it guarantee treatment implementation or effectiveness. After all, a consultee may accept an intervention mainly because of its ease of implementation, even though it may not be powerful enough to result in a meaningful improvement in the student's behavior. One of the roles of the consultant is to help the consultee understand the importance of using interventions that have a good probability of being effective, rather than merely being easy to implement.

Gresham (1989) suggested the following conclusions regarding intervention selection based on his review of the research literature:

1. Simpler suggestions (interventions) tend to be more faithfully followed than do more complex interventions.
2. Interventions that take more time, materials, and resources tend not to be as carefully implemented as briefer or less-involved interventions.
3. The more people involved in the intervention, the less faithfully it will be implemented.
4. The consultee's belief in the validity of the treatment enhances treatment integrity.
5. The higher the motivation of the consultee, the more likely the treatment will be carried out accurately.

Zins and Erchul (1995) have provided six additional and valuable guidelines for selecting interventions:

1. In general, implement positive interventions before resorting to behavioral suppression or reduction techniques. Never introduce a suppression technique without an accompanying positive skill-building intervention.
2. Choose the least complex and intrusive interventions possible. Modifying existing practices rather than learning new skills is generally easier for consultees.
3. When a new skill must be learned by a consultee, design it to fit into current organizational (classroom) structure and routines as much as possible.
4. Promote interventions that require less time, are not ecologically intrusive, and are seen by consultees as (likely to be) effective.
5. As a long-term strategy, help consultees access existing resources or develop new ones in their own organizations.
6. Focus intervention efforts on promoting change at the highest organizational level possible.

As the cases in Chapter 9 demonstrate, our ability to understand and intervene effectively with referral problems may lie in our understanding of the psychological nature of the student, ecological influences, or biophysical factors. Also, our own philosophical beliefs influence how we approach referrals. Some people look to psychodynamics almost exclusively. Others are wedded to curriculum-based measurement to the exclusion of other assessment considerations. Others prefer rational–emotive behavior therapy (Ellis, 1995) or behavior modification or process training. I hope that consultants will keep an open mind regarding causes and assistive strategies and will not become overly restrictive in their views, and will learn to seek and use evidence-based interventions rather than popular but possibly unfounded treatments. To show how different techniques may be used to understand and deal with school learning and behavior problems, D'Amato and Rothlisberg (1992) have provided an extensive case study of a student, followed by explanations of how this student's case would be handled by practitioners representing eight different approaches.

Additional Areas of Inquiry, Next Steps to Take, or Possible Solutions:

One way of organizing your thinking about interventions is to put them in large categories and then develop specific interventions within each of these categories. The categories you choose to use in any given case depend on the referral issues. Following are five large categories with numerous specific ideas contained in each of these categories. It is possible to utilize interventions from all of these categories in any given referred student.

- Prevention

  Rearrange the classroom so the students find it easier to get around. This may reduce noise, confusion, and the accidental bumping of each other as they move about the classroom.

  Set up class rules and consequences that may serve to forestall possible conflicts or confusion in procedures. State these rules positively.

Separate students who may not be able to resist the temptation to be unproductively sociable or provocative toward each other.

At the classroom level, plan a meaningful curriculum, student-centered methods, positive motivations, and a diversity of evaluation techniques.

Develop schoolwide programs that are designed to forestall or prevent predictable problems. Strengthening programming in phonological processing can be very helpful in schools characterized by poor reading achievement (Baker, Kame'enui, Simmons, & Stahl, 1994). Programs in social skills training can serve to teach students better ways of dealing with interpersonal conflicts that may be all too common in certain schools (Gresham, 2002).

- Communication

  Simplify verbal instructions for English language learners. Develop a habit and system of talking with students about their behaviors of concern, as well as behaviors you wish to reinforce.

  Organize times in the classroom for students to talk about the classroom arrangements, curriculum, methods, and behavioral standards (Glasser, 1969; Nelson, Lott, & Glenn, 1997; Thorson, 2003).

  Utilize the services of the school counselor to talk with students with whom you find it difficult to communicate.

  Arrange times to talk with students' parents about their child's academic or social needs. Home–school communication can forestall many problems and strengthen a crucial alliance (O'Shea et al., 2001).

- Contingencies

  Establish a reinforcement menu of activities, tangibles, and other reinforcers you are willing to dispense, contingent on students reaching predetermined positive goals. These reinforcers may be earned by individual students for themselves, or you can use whole-class contingencies. Develop ways for parents to be the providers of reinforcers whenever practical.

  Develop contracts to specify the relationships between behaviors and reinforcers or other contingencies. All contracts should be written in a positive fashion (Allen, Howard, Sweeney, & McLaughlin, 1993; Miller & Kelley, 1994). School–home notes may be used as part of a contingency contract system (Pelham & Waschbusch, 1999).

- Competency Training

  Academic:

  Determine the student's levels of achievement in relevant areas; try to arrange classroom situations where the student is able to get assistance when materials are too difficult.

  Also, arrange for remedial help through whatever resources are available.

  (Note: Many more interventions for academic problems are contained in Chapter 7.)

Behavioral/Social:

Assist the student to recognize the behaviors that are not acceptable and teach alternative behaviors. Use contingency plans as previously discussed.

Arrange for out-of-classroom assistance with a counselor in school, or through an outside agency.

(Note: Many more interventions for behavior problems are contained in Chapter 6.)

Biochemical:

Arrange for a health evaluation by the school nurse or an outside agency.

Encourage parents to consult with a medical practitioner regarding medical approaches to behavioral/adjustment difficulties or for health/hygiene instruction for the family.

8. Issues in the Implementation of Interventions

Once the plan is agreed on, the consultee is ready to start the implementation process. At this point the actions and reactions of the consultee and the student are of major importance. Ordinarily the consultee does most of the implementation while the consultant monitors and advises as the implementation unfolds. Exceptions might occur in the case of a collaborative arrangement between the consultant and consultee when the consultant carries a noticeable share of the responsibility for direct intervention implementation. Co-teaching is an example of this (Dettmer et al., 1999; Friend & Cook, 2003), and would be a fairly common activity for resource teachers to engage in. Harris (1998) lists numerous ways of implementing co-teaching strategies.

Implementation may involve multiple students and consultees. Other children in the class, parents, additional teachers, and counselors all may have a part to play. The more people that are involved, the more important it is that each person understand what his or her roles are. Equally important is the consultant's concern about the skill levels of all of these people. The primary roles of the consultant in plan development and implementation are to ensure that each of the participants has the skills to carry out the plan, and that they are carrying out the interventions faithfully (with integrity, or fidelity). Neither of these criteria can be taken for granted. Consultants often find that what they thought was a simple plan to implement (for example, smile at or otherwise acknowledge the student when he gives you eye contact) may be something the consultee is not used to doing or doesn't do easily. The best way to know if the skill levels are in place is to ask the consultees (and students, when appropriate) if they feel comfortable doing what the plan requires of them, and then watch them doing it. In this way, the consultant works to ensure both treatment acceptability and integrity, which are essential if a plan is to be successful (Allen & Graden, 2002; Lentz, Allen, & Erhardt, 1996; Noell & Gresham, 1993; Witt, 1990).

The necessity of ensuring integrity derives from the common observation that interventions are not always carried out in the way in which they were intended.

Public school classrooms, playgrounds, and family–home realities often constrain the valid implementation of consultation plans. Difficulties in providing the timely provision of reinforcement; the impracticality of shifting activities when needed; and the control of variables such as mood, behavior of other students, fire drills, students coming and going (sometimes to receive needed ancillary services), and hunger are examples of problems that can affect treatment integrity.

The probability of treatment integrity increases as a function of continuing consultant involvement. One of the realities of excessive consultant–consultee caseloads is the inability of the consultant to carefully monitor each case. Be sure, when acting as a consultant, that you have reviewed the facts about each case before seeing the consultee for a follow-up session or before making a classroom observation so that you can remember the details of the background and of the treatment plan. Providing a written summary of your consultation sessions (see Figure 3.1) will assist you in this process. This inspires the consultee's confidence in you and in the process, and it enables you to determine if the treatment is being carried out with integrity.

Skills the classroom teacher-consultees typically may not have are data keeping, operationally defining behaviors, skill in reacting in certain specified ways (for example, extinction), contingency contract development, instructional modifications, and listening and reflecting skills. The role of the consultant is to assist the consultee (and students, when appropriate) in the development of the skills necessary for the treatment to be successful. Numerous sources designed to help the consultant teach these skills to consultees are available (Alberto & Troutman, 1999; Benjamin, 1987; Kanfer & Goldstein, 1986; Mastropieri & Scruggs, 2000; Morrow & Woo, 2001; Shapiro & Kratochwill, 1988, 2000a, 2000b; Walker & Shea, 1999; Zins, 1993; Zirpoli & Melloy, 2001).

Sometimes a plan cannot be implemented without materials that need to be readily at hand, such as material reinforcers, computer-assisted instructional programs, event counters, curricular materials, award certificates, and so on. The consultant should try to obtain them quickly. Plans that involve cumbersome apparatus or curricular materials that are not easily available or are too costly should probably be avoided except in the most extreme circumstances.

Monitoring a plan as it begins and progresses is the most important role of the consultant in the plan implementation phase. The consultee's efforts to carry out the plan and the student's reactions to the plan are of equal importance. It is very common, for several reasons, to modify plans after they are implemented. Perhaps the consultee isn't willing or able to carry out the plan as prescribed. The student may change his behavior in an unanticipated way, which may be either positive or negative. Events from inside or outside may have an unwanted influence on the plan. Positive or negative changes in the student's behavior or learning patterns may also occur so rapidly that a major change in the program seems warranted. It is necessary for the consultant to have sufficient time to monitor these possible events in order to talk with the various consultees involved and to make changes when needed.

Some consultants have such a heavy caseload that they find it very difficult to carry out this monitoring function. In these cases it is even more important that the consultee be well trained in what to look for and what to do, given various changes in the data. The collaborative philosophy is especially appropriate for this kind of situation because the consultee will have been included as an equal partner since the onset of the consultation, and therefore should feel competent in the area of program modification.

If the plan the consultant and the consultee(s) have decided on requires specified student actions, which is common in a cognitively oriented behavior modification or skill-learning program, the consultant and the consultee need to be sure that the student is willing and able to play his role. For example, not all students are able to keep their own data or provide their own reinforcement in the manner intended by the plan. Again, the consultant needs to think of these planned-for student actions as skills that may need to be taught, rehearsed, and monitored (Hughes, 1988).

Additional Areas of Inquiry, Next Steps to Take, and Possible Solutions:

- The interventions ("solutions") are underway. The primary needs of consultees at this point are to be supported and to know that if there are problems in the implementation of the interventions they can get fairly rapid assistance from the consultant. To that end, in an ideal world the consultant would be able to monitor the initial steps of the plan, possibly by being in the classroom in the earliest phases of the intervention. Due to the many other responsibilities of an internal school consultant, this is rarely the case. A second, more realistic option is for the consultant to make contact with the consultee shortly after the plan's implementation to discuss treatment integrity and continued acceptance of the plan.
- Some consultees expect quick results from well-planned interventions. Assuming the referral was for a fairly significant problem, it is unrealistic to expect a rapid turnaround of a student's performance, either academic or behavioral. An experienced consultant will help the consultee understand the nature of habit strength in the perpetuation of behaviors. Long-standing habits cause people to persist in, or return to, behaviors that may have been inefficient or self-defeating. Students' approaches to their schoolwork, to their social interactions, and to their negative self-talk may be ingrained because these behaviors have been to some extent reinforced for these students. Asking or expecting students to give up inefficient or inappropriate behaviors very quickly, possibly to engage in behaviors with which they are not comfortable, is asking a lot. Equally so, expecting consultees to change some of their teaching or parenting habits in short order and to maintain these changes in the face of (sometimes) slow progess in the referred students may be challenging without explicit support from the consultant.

9. Monitoring Interventions

As I have mentioned, consultation usually does not follow steps in a linear fashion as they are presented here. The process is much more circular: One may need to go back at any time to earlier steps, repeat some steps a number of times, and sometimes take leaps forward. The number of variables affecting this circularity is infinite and includes at least the following: (1) the skill levels of the participants, (2) the complexity of the situation, (3) hidden agendas that may not seem evident at the onset of the consultative relationship, and (4) naturally occuring changes in classroom ecology or in the targeted student's life that necessitate changes in the interventions.

One step that is always included, sometimes repeatedly, is ongoing consultation with the consultee(s) throughout the process. In some cases the consultant may have to meet with the consultee(s) a number of times before rapport is established; in other cases, it takes a long time before the consultee(s) has established the confidence it takes to implement a new program. At other times, a program may be started the day after the first meeting between the consultant and consultee only to end abruptly the following day and not start again until more meetings have taken place. Suffice it to say that effective consultation rarely occurs as a result of one brief visit between a consultee and consultant.

During the ongoing discussions the consultant will be involved in answering questions, dealing with resistance, gathering data, suggesting modifications, dealing with consultees' feelings of vulnerability, and trying to reassure consultees in order to ensure a successful project.

Questions that come up vary from the profound to the mundane. For example, in behavior-change programs there are questions of children's rights, bribery, long-term consequences of treatments, and the relative importance of all aspects of the program, among others. In academic learning problem cases, there will be concerns about allowing poor achievers easier assignments, grading on effort rather than achievement, and the time necessary for instructional modifications. It is easy to get sidetracked by some of these questions, and the consultant needs to weigh each one in light of the goals of the project that have been mutually decided on. This is another argument in favor of the collaborative approach to consultation. If the consultant and the consultee have been working as a team throughout the project, the mutual respect developed between them will ensure goal-directed questions and concerns rather than those that often develop when people are not in sync with each other (Friend & Cook, 2003). Excessive questioning of every aspect of the program plan and its implementation is a good sign that the consultant and the consultee have not reached that level of rapport or trust that mutuality requires. It may be necessary at times to "call the game": to back away from the content of the questions to find out about the relationship itself. Reassurance may be all that is needed, especially with consultees with whom you are working for the first time, but you may also find that you are dealing with some of the more serious forms of resistance discussed in Chapter 3.

Another function of ongoing consultation is data gathering and sharing. Data-driven decisions should be the hallmark of intervention modification. In addition to gathering baseline data before starting your intervention, you and the consultee must come up with a plan for how further data will be gathered. Will the consultee do it? How? Will the consultant have sufficient time to observe and gather data or provide other progress-monitoring strategies? This is usually not the case in the schools; time does not permit it, at least on an ongoing basis. If the responsibility will primarily be the consultee's, she is going to have to be trained well and, of course, willing to do it.

Further information on progress monitoring can be found in Deno et al. (2002), Fuchs and Deno (1991), Fuchs and Fuchs (1994), Stoiber and Kratochwill (2000), and Witt and Beck (1999). Chapter 6 has information about methods of data recording.

Consultees, particularly those for whom the consultation process is new, often feel vulnerable. This needs to be considered throughout the consultation process. Since teaching is such an isolated profession, with most teachers working by themselves behind closed doors (very little cooperative teaching among general education teachers occurs in most districts), it is not surprising that not all teachers welcome the collaborative efforts of an outsider. The idea of being observed on a regular basis, the possibility that the consultant may be talking to others about what he sees in classrooms (which, of course, is an egregious violation of ethical standards), and the fact that teachers may have to change their own behavior according to some plan, no matter how collaboratively designed, can easily make some consultees feel very vulnerable and possibly defensive. Again, the consultant needs to be sensitive to this possibility, put herself in the consultee's shoes, and make sure that she gives all the support she can to the consultee in this difficult process.

Additional Areas of Inquiry, Next Steps to Take, or Possible Solutions:

- Sometimes teachers need to have a strong foundation laid regarding the importance of and methods for recording data on a fairly continuous basis. This is not an activity many of them, particularly general education teachers, are used to doing. Since no intervention can be effectively monitored without a formative evaluation of the data, it may be that the consultant will need to train teachers in these skills and may also need to model data-keeping. Barrios (1993) indicates five steps in this process:
    1. Orienting consultees to the nature and importance of observation and data collection.
    2. Teaching the recording methods to be used.
    3. Evaluating their skills by doing reliability checks in simulated conditions.
    4. Providing experiences in real-life situations.
    5. Providing ongoing monitoring of their accuracy and reliability.
- If the interventions are going according to plan and they seem to be effective, no further solutions are needed; stay the course. By all means, don't disturb interventions that are working well just to appease your own curiosity. Informed modifications are appropriate; frivolous tinkering is not.
- If, however, any of the possible reasons for plan failure are occurring (e.g., the plan itself is ineffective; proposed reinforcers are not available or do not have an impact on targeted behaviors; resistance; inability to monitor the plan because of too many other commitments), review these with the consultee and work out solutions. Poorly conducted interventions lead to failure and increased resistance to further consultative assistance. Be proactive, or all your preliminary work is for naught.

10. Evaluation and Closure

The process of evaluation is an effort to find or determine the value of something. Patton (1986) describes it as a systematic method of collecting information about activities and outcomes in consultation that inform the evaluator about how consultation is proceeding and its effects.

Evaluation should be both ongoing (formative) and cumulative (summative). It is primarily based on an effort to determine if the goals of the consultation project are being met. Therefore, the consultant and the consultees must agree at the outset what the goals of the consultation project are. Though this seems to be obvious, it sometimes isn't done. The consultee may believe, for example, that the goal of a behavior-change project is simply to give the consultant enough data so that the consultant can refer the student back to the SST for special education consideration. The consultant, however, is convinced that if the consultee would carry out the plan effectively, the student would never have to be considered for special education. In another case, the consultant may believe that if a student who uses foul language could reduce his swearing by half, the project would be successful; the student's mother, however, believes that nothing less than a complete stop to all swearing is an appropriate goal. If these questions aren't resolved at the outset or shortly thereafter, there may be some angry participants at the conclusion of these consultative efforts.

Establishing the goals of the consultation gives direction to the evaluation and to the types of data to be gathered. Depending on the focus of the project, you may want to use objective data, such as that obtained by counting frequencies or durations of behaviors or by using questionnaires, rating scales, or checksheets. You may also gather anecdotal impressions (possibly using narrative recording procedures [Skinner, Rhymer, & McDaniel, 2000]) which you may have utilized in step 3 of the SOCS) or summarize interviews with the consultees. Another source of data might be to make pre- and postconsultation videotapes of the student engaging in the targeted behaviors.

The goal of ongoing evaluation is to provide data that can be used to modify the program. The purpose of the final evaluation is to summarize what took place and to determine its effectiveness. Dougherty (2000, p. 126) suggests the following questions to guide the evaluation process:

To what degree has behavior in the student (or system) changed in the desired direction? A response to this question requires clearly stated goals and some method for measuring intervention effects as they are occurring.

To what degree was the consultant able to enter the system psychologically? Dougherty refers here to the process in which a consultant goes beyond merely entering a situation physically; psychological entry occurs when the consultee accepts the consultant and has a positive regard for the consultative process.

In what ways has the organization changed as a result of consultation? Successful consultative efforts get people, especially administrators, talking about the possibility of applying lessons learned from the consultation to other settings. Herein lies the real power of the consultative model: If the consultant can show school- or district-level personnel that a different way of approaching problems can be successful and can get the local teacher (consultee) and the principal to talk about it outside of its local confines, the change process is facilitated.

To what degree have the goals established in the contract been met? By "contract," Dougherty refers to either the formal contract that an outside consultant might establish with the employing district or to the informal or implicit contract established when an internally based consultant and consultee agree to work together. To the extent that the goal of the contract is a change in the student's behavior, this question is similar to the question about the degree of behavior change in the student. If the goal was behavior change in a specified direction, and it has been achieved, then the contract has been fulfilled. Some degree of behavioral change on the part of the consultee is ordinarily undiscussed but clearly necessary in some behavior-change programs. As indicated in the SOCS and in Chapter 2, changes in antecedents and consequences may require specific changes in consultee behaviors. These changes can be documented along with the changes observed in the student's behavior.

To what degree have established timetables been met? School consultants rarely set firm timetables when the focus of the consultative project is a student with a behavior or learning problem. Because of the complexity of some of these problems, it is unrealistic to state at the outset that the project will be completed or successful in a given amount of time. Sometimes the consultant is pleasantly surprised when his initial consultation with a teacher results in some dramatic change in the target behavior. More common, however, is the reality that many different tactics have to be tried before the successful combination is found. In some cases, success has been achieved when the consultee simply learns to accept a troublesome behavior, even though it still exists. In this case, although the goals of the contract may not have been met, the consultee may still feel that it was successful simply because his comfort level is now higher.

How successfully has a given intervention been carried out? One of the fascinating aspects of doing consultation is that one is always learning something new about human interactions. What sometimes occurs is that the consultee implements an intervention "incorrectly" only to have it work splendidly. Given the complexity of the dynamics involved in students' behavior and learning problems, it should not be surprising (except to consultants with rigidly held theoretical positions) that our best-laid plans sometimes don't work while some curious misapplication of our plans or our theoretical positions does the job very well. We can rationalize all we want, but a better stance is to acknowledge the success we've observed and learn from it. Experience indicates that true collaboration occurs when the consultee feels free to apply treatments in a way that makes sense to her without violating treatment integrity (Caplan & Caplan, 1993; Petty, Heesacker, & Hughes, 1997). What is most important is that the consultant knows how the consultee is applying the treatment so that the results can be attributed to the actual treatment instead of what was planned on paper but never really done.

How effectively has the consultant established an effective working relationship with the consultee? I have emphasized throughout this text that consultation depends on effective relationships. This is especially true if you follow a collaborative mode of functioning. It is possible that a successful consultation can occur without a positive relationship; after all, it isn't necessary that people working together like each other. It is not likely, however, that success will occur if the relationship isn't effective. Effectiveness implies mutual respect—the willingness to work cooperatively, communicate honestly, and know when to give in and when to be firm. Sometimes the consultant and the consultee may disagree on the diagnosis or treatment. How they work out these conflicts determines if the project will be successful.

To what degree has consultation been worth the cost in time, effort, and money? The criteria of time, money, and effort are subjective. It depends on how much of these three criteria has been expended, what the results are, and how people value them. To the parent of a student who has a severe disability, a year's effort to get the student to comply with requests is well worth it. An outsider who is unfamiliar with the problem might consider this expenditure too costly in terms of staff involvement. Throughout recent years there has been an increase in tolerance for dealing with students who exhibit extreme behaviors, which was unheard of in public school classrooms only a few decades ago. The current trend toward full inclusion of all students in the regular track may mean that a disproportionate amount of resources is funneled in this direction. Whether it is worth it or not is a value question that a broad array of individuals need to consider.

Related to the value questions raised by Dougherty (2000), Phillips and McCullough (1990) add these additional considerations regarding the ecology of the classroom: Did the interventions disrupt classroom or school procedures? Were there side effects of the interventions (e.g., increased tolerance for disruptive behaviors; use of material reinforcer systems) that might have changed important dimensions of classroom instruction? How much increase in support services was needed? Were people's philosophical biases being threatened? Could the same effects be obtained with a less intrusive set of interventions? Could a successful treatment be transported to other classrooms? One could add to this list the question of whether a successful intervention could suggest a valuable system-change project.

Brown et al. (2001) have provided many examples of forms and questionnaires that can be used for evaluating the consultation process throughout its various stages, as well as the preferences and actions of consultees. Conoley and Conoley (1992) have presented a similar array of forms that could easily be adapted for one's own specific purposes. Parsons and Meyers (1984) have developed a consultee satisfaction form that asks the consultee to rate the consultant and the process of consultation in five different areas: efficacy of consultation, consultant expertise, consultant's administrative abilities, interpersonal style, and general comments. Gallesich (1982) offers a consultation evaluation survey designed to determine the consultee's perceptions of the skill and the efficacy of the consultant. Thirty-four items cover the areas of interpersonal, communication, and problem-solving skills, asking the consultee to rate the consultant on a seven-point Likert scale.

Although it is not necessary to use any of these forms or variations of them in every case, it is useful and professionally appropriate for the consultant to seek information about his efforts from his consumers—the teacher- or parent-consultees with whom he works.

Another effective way of evaluating individual consultation cases is through the writing of a case study. Pryzwansky and Noblit (1990) have presented a rationale for this activity; Merriam (1988) provides guidelines for writing case studies, many of which appear in the *Journal of Educational and Psychological Consultation*. A most recent example of a thorough case study is by Denton, Hasbrough, and Sekaquaptewa (2004).

You can find further in-depth discussions of the evaluation process as applied to consultative services in Attkisson, Hargreaves, Horowitz, and Sorensen (1978); Bell and Nadler (1979); Bergan and Kratochwill (1990); Galloway and Sheridan (1994); Gresham and Noell (1993); Gutkin (1993b); and Suchman (1967).

Closure occurs when the consultant and the consultee agree that the consultative effort ought to be terminated, at least for the present. It is also possible that a case may be closed because the relationship between the consultant and the consultee has deteriorated. In this case one or the other party simply provides his own closure even though the case is not resolved. Fortunately, this is not common. A more common observation is that some consultation cases never seem to end; certain students need assistance throughout their school careers. Most cases, however, do reach at least a tentative conclusion, although the time it takes to do so is not easily predictable. Probably the best rule of thumb is to say that consultation ends when the consultee feels it should, assuming the student's needs are being met. Since the consultee has referred the student, she is in the best position to know when the consultation should end. We hope this coincides with the project's success.

Dougherty, Tack, Fullam, and Hammer (1996) have discussed the closure process, preferring to use the term *disengagement*. They point out that this is probably the most neglected aspect of the consultation process, at least in the consultation literature. Dougherty (2000) discusses this issue at some length in Chapter 6 of his text.

SUMMARY

In this chapter I have reviewed both generic problem-solving processes suitable for school-based consultants and SOCS, a 10-step method for conducting an individual student consultation. The steps are logically and sequentially organized. As I have mentioned, however, consultation rarely evolves in the linear fashion suggested by these steps. Variations will occur, and the competent consultant will learn when and how to allow for, or encourage, deviations. Trying to keep a complex human enterprise such as consultation flowing in a lockstep fashion is like trying to herd cats. Relax and enjoy the deviations.

REFERENCES

Aeby, V., Manning, B., Thyer, B., & Carpenter-Aeby, T. (1999). Comparing outcomes of an alternative school program offered with and without intensive family involvement. *The School Community Journal, 9*(1), 17–32.

Alberto, P. A., & Troutman, A. C. (1999). *Applied behavioral analysis for teachers* (5th ed.). Upper Saddle River, NJ: Merrill/Prentice Hall.

Allen, L. J., Howard, V. F., Sweeney, W. J., & McLaughlin, T. F. (1993). Use of contingency contracting to increase on-task behavior with primary students. *Psychological Reports, 72,* 905–906.

Allen, S., & Graden, J. (2002). Best practices in collaborative problem solving for intervention design. In A. Thomas & J. Grimes (Eds.), *Best practices in school psychology IV* (pp. 565–582). Bethesda, MD: NASP.

Asante, M. K. (1987). *The Afrocentric idea.* Philadelphia: Temple University Press.

Attkisson, C. C., Hargreaves, W. A., Horowitz, M. J., & Sorensen, J. E. (Eds.). (1978). *Evaluation of human service programs.* New York: Academic Press.

Baker, S. K., Kame'envi, E. J., Simmons, D. C., & Stahl, S. A. (1994). Beginning reading: educational tools for diverse learners. *School Psychology Review, 23,* 372–391.

Bandura, A. (1978). The self-system in reciprocal determinism. *American Psychologist, 33,* 344–358.

Barkley, R. A. (1988). Child behavior rating scales and checklists. In M. Rutter, A. H. Tuma, & I. S. Lann (Eds.), *Assessment and diagnosis in child psychopathology* (pp. 113–155). New York: Guilford Press.

Barrios, B. (1993). Direct observation. In T. Ollendick & M. Herson (Eds.), *Handbook of child and adolescent assessment.* Boston: Allyn & Bacon.

Bay, M., Bryan, T., & O'Connor, R. (1994). Teachers assisting teachers: A prereferral model for urban educators. *Teacher Education and Special Education, 17,* 10–21.

Bell, C. R., & Nadler, L. (Eds.). (1979). *The client-consultant handbook.* Houston: Gulf.

Benjamin, A. (1987). *The helping interview.* Boston: Houghton Mifflin.

Bergan, J. R. (1977). *Behavioral consultation.* Columbus, OH: Merrill.

Bergan, J. R. (1995). Evolution of a problem-solving model of consultation. *Journal of Educational and Psychological Consultation, 6,* 111–124.

Bergan, J. R., & Kratochwill, T. R. (1990). *Behavioral consultation and therapy.* New York: Plenum.

Bergan, J. R., & Tombari, M. L. (1976). Consultant skill and efficiency and the implementation and outcomes of consultation. *Journal of School Psychology, 14,* 3–14.

Breen, M., & Altepeter, T. (1990). *Disruptive behavior disorders in children.* New York: Guilford Press.

Brown, D., Pryzwansky, W. B., & Schulte, A. (2001). *Psychological consultation: Introduction to theory and practice* (5th ed.). Boston: Allyn & Bacon.

Busse, R. T., & Beaver, B. R. (2000). Informant report: Parent and teacher interviews. In E. S. Shapiro & T. R. Kratochwill (Eds.), *Conducting school-based assessments of child and adolescent behavior* (pp. 235–273). New York: Guilford Press.

Caplan, G., & Caplan, R. (1993). *Mental health consultation and collaboration.* San Francisco: Jossey-Bass.

Christenson, S. L., & Cleary, M. (1990). Consultation and the parent-educator partnership: A perspective. *Journal of Educational and Psychological Consultation, 1*(3), 219–241.

Christenson, S. L., & Conoley, J. C. (1992). *Home-school collaboration: Enhancing children's academic and social competence.* Silver Springs, MD: NASP.

Christenson, S., & Sheridan, S. (2001). *Schools and families: Creating essential connections for children's learning.* New York: Guilford Press.

Cleven, C. A., & Gutkin, T. B. (1988). Cognitive modeling of consultation processes: A means for improving consultees' problem definition skills. *Journal of School Psychology, 26,* 379–389.

Conoley, C., Conoley, J., Ivey, D., & Scheel, M. (1991). Enhancing consultation by matching the consultees' perspective. *Journal of Counseling and Development, 69,* 546–549.

Conoley, J., & Conoley, C. (1992). *School consultation: Practice and training* (2nd ed.). Boston: Allyn & Bacon.

Conroy, E., & Mayer, S. (1994). Strategies for consulting with parents. *Elementary School Guidance and Counseling, 29,* 60–66.

D'Amato, R. C., & Rothlisberg, B. A. (1992). *Psychological perspectives on intervention.* New York: Longman.

Deno, S., Espin, C., & Fuchs, L. (2002). Evaluation strategies for preventing and remediating basic skill deficits. In M. Shinn, H. Walker, & G. Stoner (Eds.), *Interventions for academic and behavior problems II* (pp. 213–242). Bethesda, MD: NASP.

Denton, C., Hasbrouch, J., & Sekaquaptewa, S. (2004). The consulting teacher: A descriptive case study in responsive systems consultation. *Journal of Educational and Psychological Consultation, 14*(1), 41–73.

Dettmer, P., Dyck, N., & Thurston, L. P. (1999). *Consultation, collaboration and teamwork for students with special needs* (3rd ed.). Boston: Allyn & Bacon.

Dougherty, A. M. (2000). *Consultation: Practice and perspectives* (3rd ed.). Belmont, CA: Brooks/Cole.

Dougherty, A. M., Tack, F. E., Fullam, C. B., & Hammer, L. A. (1996). Disengagement: A neglected aspect of the consultation process. *Journal of Educational and Psychological Consultation, 7*(3), 259–274.

Elliott, S. N. (1988). Acceptability of behavioral treatments: Review of variables that influence treatment selection. *Professional Psychology, 19,* 68–80.

Elliott, S. N., & Busse, R. T. (1993). Effective treatments with behavioral consultation. In J. E. Zins, T. R. Kratochwill, & S. N. Elliott (Eds.), *Handbook of consultation services for children* (pp. 179–203). San Francisco: Jossey-Bass.

Elliott, S. N., Witt, J. C., & Kratochwill, T. R. (1991). Selecting, Implementing, and Evaluating classroom interventions. In G. Stoner, M. Shinn, & H. Walker (Eds.), *Interventions for achievement and behavior problems.* Silver Springs, MD: NASP.

Elliott, S. N., Witt, J. C., Kratochwill, T. R., & Stoiber, K. C. (2002). Selecting and evaluating classroom interventions. In M. Shinn, H. Walker, & G. Stoner (Eds.), *Interventions for academic and behavior problems II* (pp. 243–294). Bethesda, MD: NASP.

Ellis, A. (1995). Changing rational-emotive therapy to rational-emotive behavior therapy. *Journal of Rational-Emotive and Cognitive-Behavior Therapy, 13,* 85–90.

Erchul, W. P., & Martens, B. K. (2002). *School consultation: Conceptual and empirical bases of practice* (2nd ed.). New York: Plenum.

Esler, A., Godber, Y., & Christenson, S. (2002). Best practices in supporting home-school collaboration. In A. Thomas & J. Grimes (Eds.), *Best practices in school psychology IV* (pp. 389–412). Bethesda, MD: NASP.

Evans, S. S., Evans, W. H., & Gable, R. A. (1989). An ecological survey of student behavior. *Teaching Exceptional Children, 21*(4), 12–15.

Flanagan, D., Genshaft, J., & Harrison, P. (Eds.). (1997). *Contemporary intellectual assessment: Theories, tests, and issues.* New York: Guilford Press.

Friend, M., & Cook, L. (2003). *Interactions: Collaboration skills for school professionals* (4th ed.). New York: Longman.

Fuchs, D., & Fuchs, L. (1994). Classwide curriculum-based measurement: Helping general educators meet the challenge of student diversity. *Exceptional Children, 60,* 518–537.

Fuchs, L., & Deno, S. (1991). Paradigmatic distinctions between instructionally relevant measurement models. *Exceptional Children, 57,* 488–501.

Gallesich, J. H. (1982). *The profession and practice of consultation.* New York: Jossey-Bass.

Galloway, J., & Sheridan, S. M. (1994). Scientific practitioner: Implementing scientific practices through case studies: Examples using home-school interventions and consultation. *Journal of School Psychology, 32*(4), 385–410.

Glasser, W. (1969). *Schools without failure.* New York: Harper & Row.

Gresham, F. M. (1989). Assessment of treatment integrity in school consultation and prereferral intervention. *School Psychology Review, 18,* 37–50.

Gresham, F. M. (2002). Best practices in social skills training. In A. Thomas & J. Grimes (Eds.), *Best practices in school psychology IV* (pp. 1029–1040). Bethesda, MD: NASP.

Gresham, F. M., & Noell, G. H. (1993). Documenting the effectiveness of consultation outcomes. In J. Zins, T. Kratochwill, & S. Elliott (Eds.), *Handbook of consultation services for children* (pp. 249–276). San Francisco: Jossey-Bass.

Gutkin, T. B. (1993a). Cognitive modeling: A means for achieving prevention in school-based consultation. *Journal of Educational and Psychological Consultation, 4*(2), 179–183.

Gutkin, T. B. (1993b). Conducting consultation research. In J. Zins, T. Kratochwill, & S. Elliott (Eds.), *Handbook of consultation services for children* (pp. 227–248). San Francisco: Jossey-Bass.

Gutkin, T. B. (2002). Evidence-based interventions in school psychology: State of the art and directions for the future. *School Psychology Quarterly, 17*(4), 339–340.

Gutkin, T. B., & Curtis, M. (1982). School-based consultation: Theory and techniques. In C. R. Reynolds & T. B. Gutkin (Eds.), *The handbook of school psychology* (pp. 796–828). New York: Wiley.

Gutkin, T. B., & Curtis, M. (1990). School-based consultation: Theory, techniques, and research. In C. R. Reynolds & T. B. Gutkin (Eds.), *The handbook of school psychology* (2nd ed., pp. 577–611). New York: Wiley.

Gutkin, T. B., & Curtis, M. (1999). School-based consultation theory and practice: The art and science of indirect service delivery. In C. R. Reynolds & T. B. Gutkin (Eds.), *The handbook of school psychology* (3rd ed., pp. 598–637). New York: Wiley.

Harris, K. C. (1998). *Collaborative teaching casebooks: Facilitator's guide.* Austin, TX: Pro-Ed.

Hughes, J. (1988). *Cognitive behavior therapy with children in schools.* New York: Pergamon.

Iverson, A. (2002). Best practices in problem-solving team structure and process. In A. Thomas & J. Grimes (Eds.), *Best practices in school psychology IV* (pp. 657–670). Bethesda, MD. NASP.

Johnson, L. J., & Pugach, M. C. (1996). Role of collaborative dialogue in teachers' conceptions of appropriate practice for students at risk. *Journal of Educational and Psychological Consultation, 7*(1), 9–24.

Kanfer, F. H., & Goldstein, A. P. (Eds.). (1986). *Helping people change.* New York: Pergamon.

Kratochwill, T., & Stoiber, K. (2000). Empirically supported interventions and school psychology: Conceptual and practice issues—Part II. *School Psychology Quarterly, 15*(2), 233–253.

Lambert, N. M. (1976). Children's problems and classroom interventions from the perspective of classroom teachers. *Professional Psychology, 7,* 507–517.

Lentz, F. E., Allen, S. J., & Erhardt, K. E. (1996). The conceptual elements of strong interventions in school settings. *School Psychology Quarterly, 11*(2), 118–136.

Marks, E. S. (1995). *Entry strategies for school consultation.* New York: Guilford Press.

Martin, M., & Waltman-Greenwood, C. (Eds.). (1995). *Solve your child's school-related problems.* New York: HarperPerennial/NASP.

Mastropieri, M. A., & Scruggs, T. E. (2000). *The inclusive classroom: Strategies for effective instruction.* Upper Saddle River, NJ: Merrill/Prentice Hall.

Merriam, S. (1988). *Case study research in education: A qualitative approach.* San Francisco: Jossey-Bass.

Miller, D. L., & Kelley, M. L. (1994). The use of goal setting and contingency contracting for improving children's homework performance. *Journal of Applied Behavioral Analysis, 27,* 73–84.

Morrow, L. M., & Woo, D. G. (Eds.). (2001). *Tutoring programs for struggling readers.* New York: Guilford Press.

Nelson, J. R., Lott, L., & Glenn, H. (1997). *Positive discipline in the classroom* (2nd ed.), Rocklin, CA: Prima.

Nicoll, W. (1992). A family counseling and consultation model for school counselors. *School Counselor, 39,* 351–361.

Noell, G. H., & Gresham, F. M. (1993). Functional outcome analysis: Do the benefits of consultation and prereferral intervention justify the costs? *School Psychology Quarterly, 8,* 200–226.

O'Shea, D., O'Shea, L., Algozzine, R., & Hammitte, D. (2001). *Families and teachers of individuals with disabilities.* Boston: Allyn & Bacon.

Parsons, R. D., & Meyers, J. (1984). *Developing consultation skills: A guide to training, development and assessment for human services professionals.* San Francisco: Jossey-Bass.

Patton, M. Q. (1986). *Utilization-focused evaluation.* Beverly Hills, CA: Sage.

Pelham, W. E., & Waschbusch, D. A. (1999). Behavioral intervention in attention-deficit hyper activity disorder. In H. C. Quay & A. E. Hogan (Eds.), *Handbook of disruptive behavior disorders* (pp. 255–278). New York: Kluner Academic/Plenum.

Petty, R., Heesacker, M., & Hughes, J. (1997). The elaboration likelihood model: Implications for the practice of school psychology. *Journal of School Psychology, 35,* 107–136.

Pfeiffer, J. W., & Jones, J. E. (Eds.). (1974). *A handbook for structured human relations training* (Vol. 3). La Jolla, CA: University Associates.

Phillips, V., & McCullough, L. (1990). Consultation-based programming: Instituting the collaborative ethic in schools. *Exceptional Children, 56*(4), 291–304.

Pierangelo, R., & Crane, R. (2000). *The special education yellow pages.* Upper Saddle River, NJ: Merrill/Prentice Hall.

Powers, K. (2001). Problem solving student support teams. *The California School Psychologist, 6,* 19–30.

Pryzwansky, W., & Noblit, G. (1990). Understanding and improving consultation practice: The qualitative case study approach. *Journal of Educational and Psychological Consultation, 1*(4), 293–307.

Pugach, M. C., & Johnson, L. J. (1987). Peer collaboration. *Teaching Exceptional Children, 20,* 75–77.

Pugach, M. C., & Johnson, L. J. (1995). Unlocking the expertise among classroom teachers through structured dialogue: Extending the research on peer collaboration. *Exceptional Children, 62,* 101–110.

Radius, M., & Lesniak, P. (1988). *Student study teams: A resource manual.* Sacramento, CA: Rise.

Reimers, T. M., Wacker, D. P., & Koeppl, G. (1987). Acceptability of behavioral treatments: A review of the literature. *School Psychology Review, 16,* 212–227.

Rosenfield, S. (1992). Developing school-based consultation teams: A design for organizational change. *School Psychology Quarterly, 7,* 27–46.

Salvia, J., & Ysseldyke, J. (2004). *Assessment* (9th ed.). Boston: Houghton-Mifflin.

Sarason, S. B. (1982). *The culture of the school and the problem of change* (2nd ed.). Boston: Allyn & Bacon.

Sattler, J. M. (1998). *Clinical and forensic interviewing of children and families: Guidelines for the mental health, education, pediatric, and child maltreatment fields.* San Diego, CA: Author.

Shapiro, E. S., & Kratochwill, T. R. (Eds.). (1988). *Behavioral assessment in schools.* New York: Guilford Press.

Shapiro, E. S., & Kratochwill, T. R. (2000a). *Conducting school-based assessments of children and adolescent behavior.* New York: Guilford Press.

Shapiro, E. S., & Kratochwill, T. R. (2000b). *Behavioral assessment in schools: Theory, research and clinical foundations* (2nd ed.). New York: Guilford Press.

Sheridan, S. M., Kratochwill, T. R., & Bergan, J. R. (1996). *Conjoint behavioral consultation: A procedural manual.* New York: Plenum.

Skinner, C. H., Rhymer, K. N., & McDaniel, E. C. (2000). Naturalistic direct observation in educational settings. In E. S. Shapiro & T. R. Kratochwill (Eds.), *Conducting school-based assessment of children and adolescent behavior* (pp. 21–54). New York: Guilford Press.

Slavin, R. E., & Madden, N. A. (1989). What works for students at risk?: A research synthesis. *Educational Leadership, 46,* 1–8.

Stanovich, K. E. (2000). *Progress in understanding reading: Scientific foundations and new frontiers.* New York: Guilford Press.

Stewart, K. (1986). Disentangling the complexities of clientage. In S. Elliott & J. Witt, (Eds.), *The delivery of psychological services in the schools: Concepts, processes, and issues.* Hillsdale, NJ: Lawrence Erlbaum.

Stoiber, K., & Kratochwill, T. (2000). Empirically supported interventions and school psychology: Rationale and methodological issues—Part I. *School Psychology Quarterly, 15*(1), 75–105.

Suchman, E. A. (1967). *Evaluative research: Principles and practices in public service and social action programs.* New York: Sage.

Tarver Behring, S. T., & Ingraham, C. L. (1998). Culture as a central component to consultation: A call to the field. *Journal of Educational and Psychological Consultation, 9*(1), 57–72.

Thorson, S. A. (2003). *Listening to students.* Boston: Allyn & Bacon.

Turnbull, A. P., & Turnbull, H. R. (1997). *Families, professionals, and exceptionality: A special partnership* (3rd ed.). Upper Saddle River, NJ: Merrill/Prentice Hall.

Van Brock, M., & Elliott, S. (1987). The influence of treatment effectiveness information on the acceptability of classroom interventions. *Journal of School Psychology, 25,* 131–144.

Walker, H., & Shinn, M. (2002). Structuring school-based interventions to achieve integrated primary, secondary, and tertiary prevention goals for safe and effective schools. In M. Shinn, H. Walker, & G. Stoner (Eds.), *Interventions for academic and behavior problems II.* Bethesda, MD: NASP.

Walker, J. E., & Shea, T. M. (1999). *Behavior management: A practical approach for educators* (7th ed.). Upper Saddle River, NJ: Merrill/Prentice Hall.

Wampold, B. (2002). An examination of the bases of evidence-based interventions. *School Psychology Quarterly, 17*(4), 500–507.

Wang, M. C., Haertel, G. D., & Walberg, H. J. (1993). Toward a knowledge base for school learning. *Review of Educational Research, 63,* 249–294.

Wilkinson, L. A. (1997). School-based behavioral consultation: Delivering treatment for children's externalizing behavior in the classroom. *Journal of Educational and Psychological Consultation, 8*(3), 255–276.

Wilson, C. P., Gutkin, T. B., Hagen, K. M., & Oats, R. G. (1998). General education teachers' knowledge and self-reported use of classroom interventions for working with difficult-to-teach students: Implications for consultation, prereferral intervention and inclusive services. *School Psychology Quarterly, 13,* 45–62.

Witt, J. (1986). Teachers' resistance to the use of school-based interventions. *Journal of School Psychology, 24,* 37–44.

Witt, J. (1990). Collaboration in school-based consultation: Myth in need of data. *Journal of Educational and Psychological Consultation, 1,* 367–368.

Witt, J., & Beck, R. (1999). *One minute academic functional assessment and interventions: "Can't" do it…or "won't" do it?* Longmont, CO: Sopris West.

Witt, J. C., & Elliott, S. N. (1985). Acceptability of classroom management strategies. In T. R. Kratochwill (Ed.), *Advances in school psychology* (Vol. 4, pp. 251–288). Hillsdale, NJ: Lawrence Erlbaum Associates, Inc.

Zins, J. E. (1993). Enhancing consultee problem-solving skills in consultative interactions. *Journal of Counseling and Development, 72,* 185–190.

Zins, J., Curtis, M., Graden, J., & Ponti, C. (1988). *Helping students succeed in the regular classroom.* San Francisco: Jossey-Bass.

Zins, J. E., & Erchul, W. P. (1995). Best practices in school consultation. In A. Thomas & J. Grimes (Eds.), *Best practices in school psychology III* (pp. 609–623). Washington, DC: National Association of School Psychologists.

Zirpoli, T., & Melloy, K. (2001). *Behavior management applications for teachers.* Upper Saddle River, NJ: Merrill/Prentice Hall.

Consulting About Students with Emotional or Behavioral Disorders

OBJECTIVES

1. Present a list of general reasons for emotional or behavioral disorders.
2. Review systems for categorizing emotional or behavioral disorders.
3. Present information about diagnostic methods useful to consultants that are in accord with IDEA provisions.
4. Provide numerous evidence-based interventions for meeting the needs of students with emotional or behavioral disorders.

Mr. Jacobs is an English teacher. In his opinion, his 10th-grade class is his worst class of the day because of the presence of three boys who always seem to be doing something to irritate him. They are mildly defiant, just enough to get a small laugh from some of the others, and they always seem to be talking to somebody. Their work is careless and sometimes contains suggestive comments. He has separated them and once sent one of them to the vice-principal's office, but he is reluctant to do more, hoping they will soon see that their behavior is self-defeating and leading to poor grades. He sees you, the school-based consultant, in the teacher's lounge in November and asks you for some advice. How might you respond to Mr. Jacobs' request?

Miss Peterson, an experienced primary-grade teacher, has been assigned a student in her third-grade regular education class who presents with severe handicaps (Down syndrome and acting-out behaviors). She is not pleased with this placement, which she feels was forced on her by a too-compliant administrator. During the first week in her class, this student has caused major disruptions. She has sent you an SOS requesting your immediate consultation. How might you, the RSP/consulting teacher, respond to this request?

Mrs. Gonzalez, a ninth-grade English teacher, has sent a referral to the SST regarding a new girl in her class who is a social isolate, cries for no apparent reason, and often seems to be daydreaming. Conversation with the girl's mother indicates that she too is concerned about her daughter, but doesn't know what to do about it, and was not forthcoming in regard to possible reasons for the girl's behavior.

AN ORIENTATION TO THE NATURE OF EMOTIONAL OR BEHAVIORAL DISORDERS (EBD)

School-based consultants will undoubtedly be asked to assist consultees with problems related to EBD in the classroom, such as those described in the three previously presented vignettes. In this chapter, I use the term EBD very broadly to refer to any student action that either manifests an emotional adjustment problem and/or is intended to disturb, or has the effect of disturbing, the learning process of the student or other students.

In the case of a classroom EBD, it is not always easy to determine whether the student is trying to get something (such as teacher attention, peer attention, power, or revenge), avoid something (such as completing work, being harassed by others, personal discomfort, or boredom), or both (perhaps peer attention as an alternative to boredom, or disruptively seeking the attention of the teacher as a means of avoiding having to think and work independently). Evans and Meyer (1985) frame the issue of purposes in terms of three functions that a behavior may serve: (1) *social communicative*, where a student, either verbally or nonverbally, indicates a communicative intent, such as saying or implying "Leave me alone!"; (2) *self-regulatory*, where a student responds to a physical state such as hunger or overstimulation and her behavior is an effort to deal with or alter this physical state; and (3) *self-entertainment (play)*, where a student believes that school is a place for social interaction and he seeks it out at every opportunity, even when others may be bothered by it.

ACTIVITY 6.1

Recall situations from your own childhood or your school-based professional experience in which similar behaviors were regarded as, or treated as, problems depending on the teacher or on another aspect of the classroom ecology, such as class size, type of class, presence of an aide, or philosophy of the school administration. What caused the same behaviors to be treated as a problem in one situation but not in another?

Most EBD have multiple determinants. It is rare that a student has only one reason for her poor classroom behavior (Kazdin, 1985). This is important since the treatment you apply needs to be tailored to the many causes that may operate in a case. Typically, causes are both external (for example, gang influences) and internal (such as a desire for power; physical conditions such as health, hunger, or neurological impairment; emotional reactivity to stressors; or self-defeating self-talk). Cause may be related to a distal antecedent: anything that has happened in the student's past to have predisposed him to a given pattern of behavior or responding, such as child-rearing practices; or it may be related to a proximal antecedent, which occurs close to the target behavior and is presumed to have been the most immediate prompt to that behavior, such as one student calling another a derogatory name. However, it may be multifaceted, influenced by two or more reasons. If a student tells herself that others want to hurt her, and someone looks at her in a way that she perceives to be threatening, she may react to this stimulus by yelling at or hitting the other student. External antecedents are easier to detect: one child provokes another; the teacher raises her voice; the principal appears on the playground; or the building shakes violently from an earthquake, causing some students (and teachers) to panic.

Legal Basis for Consultations Regarding Students with EBD

IDEA (P.L. 108-446) defines emotional disturbance as a category of eligibility for services in the following way:

(i) The term means a condition exhibiting one or more of the following characteristics over a long period of time and to a marked degree, which adversely affects educational performance:
   a. an inability to learn that cannot be explained by intellectual, sensory, or other health factors;
   b. an inability to build or maintain satisfactory interpersonal relationships with peers and teachers;
   c. inappropriate types of behavior or feelings under normal circumstances;
   d. a general pervasive mood of unhappiness or depression;
   e. a tendency to develop physical symptoms or fears associated with personal or school problems.

(ii) The term includes children who are schizophrenic. The term does not include children who are socially maladjusted unless it is determined that they have an emotional disturbance.

This definition has been criticized since its inception over 20 years ago, primarily because it is vague (Kauffman, 2000). For example, one of the five possible characteristics previously listed, "An inability to learn which cannot be explained by intellectual, sensory, or other health factors," makes it possible that a student with a learning disability might be construed to be emotionally disturbed.

IDEA does not have a category for students who manifest behavior disorders. If those disorders are considered symptoms of emotional disturbance in a student, then they are addressed in the development of the IEP for that student. An alternative definition inclusive of both emotional and behavioral disorders has been proposed by the National Mental Health and Special Education Coalition (Forness & Knitzer, 1992) and reads as follows:

(i) The term Emotional or Behavioral Disorder (EBD) means a disability characterized by behavioral or emotional responses in school so different from appropriate age, cultural, or ethnic norms that they adversely affect educational performance. Educational performance includes academic, social, vocational, and personal skills. Such a disability
   a. is more than a temporary, expected response to stressful events in the environment;
   b. is consistently exhibited in two different settings, at least one of which is school-related; and
   c. is unresponsive to direct intervention in general education or the child's condition is such that general interventions would be insufficient.

(ii) Emotional and behavioral disorders can coexist with other disabilities.

(iii) The category may include children or youth with schizophrenic disorders, affective disorders, anxiety disorders, or other sustained disturbances of conduct or adjustment when they adversely affect educational performance in accordance with section (i).

IDEA does discuss provisons for dealing with students who manifest behavior disorders, as long as those students are otherwise determined to have a disabling condition. In the language of IDEA, any student who is identified as disabled under the provisions of that legislation, and whose behavior "...impedes the child's learning or that of others" (IDEA), section 614, [d] [3] [B] [i]) must have a functional behavioral assessment conducted and a behavior intervention plan written for him. There are technical and legal difficulties surrounding the implementation of this regulation, partly because IDEA gives so few guidelines as to how the regulation should be implemented, and also because of the subjective nature of interpretation of a student's behavior as intending to disturb, or having the effect of disturbing her learning or the learning of others. Details about the legal aspects of these IDEA provisions can be found in Drasgow and Yell (2001), and Watson and Steege (2003).

Another source of legal guidelines for dealing with EBD is contained in Section 504 of the Vocational Rehabilitation Act of 1973 (Rehabilitation Act of 1973, P.L. 93–112). Section 504 is a civil rights act and as such is unfunded. It requires that schools protect the rights of students whether or not they have been identified as having disabilities if they have difficulty in a major life activity such as school learning. Accommodation plans for students who are determined to fit these regulations are intended to be carried out in general education settings (Conderman & Katsiyannis, 1995). For example, children with ADHD who are not otherwise disabled are given accommodations designed to assist them with behavior or learning problems in the general education classroom.

GENERAL REASONS FOR BEHAVIOR PROBLEMS

Eleven reasons are presented for the presence of both emotional and behavioral disorders. This list is not intended to be exhaustive, but it does contain those general reasons that should be considered by consultants when students manifesting behavioral challenges are referred to them. Additional perspectives on causes for EBD are given by Charles (2002) and Alberto and Troutman (1999).

Attention from Others

According to Dreikurs and Gray (1995), the student who seeks attention does so because he believes he is not getting enough attention, or at least the attention he desires. Getting positive attention from others is a powerful human need and shouldn't be denied in the proper context. Unfortunately, students identified as having behavior problems mainly seek attention in disruptive or obtrusive ways, so the attention they get is very often negative rather than positive. Oddly, for some students, any attention, positive or negative, is better than the feeling of being ignored.

ACTIVITY 6.2

Give some examples of attention-seeking behaviors that are disruptive to the learning process. In groups of three, analyze these behaviors and develop some tentative plans for dealing with them.

Child-Rearing Practices; Home and Community Influences

This may be both a distal antecedent to EBD (i.e., these practices may have occurred years ago but still have an influence) or a proximal antecedent (as in the case of a student who comes from a home where he sees conflict, confusion, and negativity every morning before leaving for school). There are many ways in which parents can fail to provide the kind of emotional and physical stability needed for a student's feeling of well-being and emotional security, including divorce (or the threat of it), laxness, inconsistency, harshness, demeaning comments, coercive control, and so on. In the matter of divorce, the national Vital Statistics Report (2001, reported in Jones & Jones, 2004) indicated that only 11% of children born in the 1950s saw their parents divorced or separated, whereas almost 55% of children born in the 1990s are coming to school from homes broken by divorce or separation. In regard to violence, some students have experienced this tragedy as a relatively common occurrence in their neighborhoods. O'Neil (1991), in a study conducted in Chicago's south side, reported that 26% of elementary school children reported that they had seen someone shot, and 29% had witnessed a stabbing. Feldhusen, Thurston, and Benning (1973) provided data from a longitudinal study of elementary and middle school students that showed a strong correlation between home environment and school behavior. They demonstrated that many students who were persistently disruptive came from families characterized by the following four factors:

1. Parents were inconsistent in their discipline, or were too lax or too strict.
2. Parents were indifferent or hostile to their children. They belittled their children and utilized many physical punishments.
3. Their marriages were characterized by a lack of closeness, and the family did not operate as a unit.
4. The parent projected the blame for their childrens' misbehavior on to peers.

A 1994 publication by the American Psychiatric Association, titled *Violence and Youth,* noted essentially the same results as did Feldhusen et al. (1973).

Patterson, Chamberlain, and Reid (1982) have identified five positive parenting practices that are important in this regard: (1) fair, timely, and consistent discipline; (2) close monitoring of the activities, whereabouts, and affiliations of their children; (3) positive behavior management techniques that show children that they are valued, encouraged, and supported; (4) involvement in a child's activities, such as Scouts, sports, and entertainment; and (5) problem-solving and crisis-management skills that help the child resolve conflicts. Patterson et al. (1982) have taught these skills to parents with very positive results. Olds, Hill, Mihalic, and O'Brien (1998) report on a successful program designed to prevent EBD among the children of high-risk (i.e., young, single, impoverished) mothers. Webster-Stratton (1998), working with families of children enrolled in Head Start programs, has demonstrated a method for teaching positive reinforcement, discipline, monitoring, and play behavior that has resulted in improvement in parenting skills, and decreases in child aggression and other EBD. Reid, Eddy, Fetrow, and Stoolmiller (1999) have tested their LIFT (Linking the Interests of Families and Teachers) program (which consists of three elements: child social skills training, the playground Good Behavior Game, and parent management training) with elementary-grade students. This program has shown decreases in child aggression and parent-aversive behavior, and increases in the teacher's opinion of students' social skills with peers.

ACTIVITY 6.3

Have class members role-play some ineffective parental practices and discuss how a consultant might approach parents in an effort to have them change these practices. For example, two students could role-play a coercive interaction (Patterson, Reid, Jones, & Conger, 1975) characterized by the parental figure giving a command, the child whining or demanding her way out of it, and the parent either escalating or giving in. Review how this interaction might be improved. Do this also for ineffective teacher practices.

Classroom Management Practices

Even to casual observers, including parents, it seems clear that some teachers need more training in classroom behavior management. They lack either the will or the skill to take behavior management seriously. Their classes are marked by disorganization, disruptive noise, and a general lack of evidence that they are in control. Students in these classes are often more hyperactive, louder, more disrespectful, and more unproductive than are students in other classrooms. Often, students who misbehave in these classrooms do not do so in classes under better management. Kampwirth (1988) has developed a list of questions that consultants can use to assist them in evaluating classrooms marked by many behavior problems in order to determine teacher behaviors or classroom arrangement variables that may contribute to these problems. Some of these questions are related to preventive aspects, such as the quality of the classroom's physical appearance (neat, attractive, functional), whether rules are clearly displayed or otherwise conveyed, whether students have knowledge of the consequences for both appropriate and inappropriate behavior, and evidence of an organized plan for teaching. Ysseldyke and Christenson (2002) have developed the Functional Assessment of Academic Behavior (FAAB), an observation and interview system designed to yield information about many components of teacher behavior and student responses.

There are a number of excellent texts that provide a wide range of ideas about, and methods for, dealing with issues of classroom behavior management (Alberto & Troutman, 1999; Bauer & Sapona, 1991; Charles, 2002; Emmer, Evertson, Clements, & Worsham, 1994; Evertson, Emmer, Clements, & Worsham, 1997; Jones & Jones, 2004; Walker & Shea, 1999; Zirpoli & Melloy, 2001).

ACTIVITY 6.4

Students should interview teachers they know in order to get ideas about their behavior management techniques. What do teachers who are skilled at behavior management do about relatively common behavior management problems such as talking out, bothering one's neighbor, engaging in off-task behavior, and so on?

Conflict with Authority

Many Americans are ambivalent about authority figures. On the one hand, most of us respect people in these positions (such as police officers and teachers) because we recognize that someone must be in control so that the needs and rights of all people will be respected equally. On the other hand, an increasing number of people are recognizing that authority figures are not always right, fair, or honest, and that ordinary citizens have a right and a duty to monitor the behavior of authority figures even as they monitor ours. This ambivalence extends to the classroom. Teachers and researchers report that students today are considerably less impressed with the authority of teachers than they were a few decades ago (Charles, 2002). Teachers report that they currently spend more time just trying to get their classes under control so that they can teach. Teachers need to prove that they can control the class and that they have the authority to do so. In some inner-city urban areas, teachers are paid an extra stipend for teaching in some schools because the stress of unruly classes drives teachers away from these areas. In many other urban districts, the opposite picture has emerged (Kuykendall, 2003; Ladson-Billings, 2003; Smith, 1993).

For some students, the desire for power in interpersonal relationships extends to their relationships with the teacher. They overtly or subtly test teachers to see who will win a power struggle. For others, revenge against past hurts that are real, imagined, or projected onto the schools from their home situations is a primary, though often unverbalized, reason for misbehavior. Dreikurs (1968) has discussed the phenomena of power and revenge along with attention and withdrawal, the four behaviors or activities that he has identified as the mistaken goals of misbehavior. Levin and Shanken-Kaye (2002) have pointed out that when discipline problems increase, some teachers' motivation to teach becomes diminished and may be replaced by a "get-even" mentality that invariably increases power struggles, which some students feed on and which places the teacher in a no-win situation.

The general heading of disrespect for authority includes the influence of gangs, ethnic conflict, and the sense of alienation from the schools that are realities for some students. Gangs reject schools and influence their members to avoid school or to be disruptive when there (Stoff, Breiling, & Maser, 1997; Walker, Colvin, & Ramsey, 1995). Other students, who may or may not be under gang influence, sense that they are not accepted by school personnel. As a result, they become alienated from the school's educative and socializing influence, often in the same way that they feel alienated from their own parents. Glasser (1992) believes that schools have traditionally practiced coercive practices with students, especially those who feel alienated from these institutions. Instead of having the effect of drawing these students toward the goals of the school, these practices usually have the opposite effect. In his book he lists many examples of how schools can become less characterized by "boss-management" and more characterized by "lead-management."

If a student is also caught up in conflicts between social or ethnic groups in school, this distracts him from academic efforts. His ability to focus psychic energy on learning is disrupted in favor of self-protective or revenge efforts that sometimes involve the use of weapons. This was the tragic consequence that played out in Columbine High School in Littleton, Colorado, as well as in Paducah, Kentucky, and Jonesboro, Arkansas, among other places where student alienation flared into fatal violence (Poland, Pitcher, & Lazarus, 2002).

ACTIVITY 6.5

Discuss gang-influenced or other sources of anti-authoritarian behaviors class members have observed in the schools. What are schools doing about these behaviors? What ideas do students have about different approaches to these behaviors? Mathews (1992) discusses a "pro-youth" strategy for confronting and dealing with gang issues in the schools.

Media Influence

The modeling influence of current media, particularly movies, video games, and television, is related to aggressive behavior in youth. Widom (1989), in a literature review of the topic, found that TV violence was clearly related to aggressive behavior in children. The American Psychological Association report *Violence and Youth* (1994) reports similar conclusions, as does the American Psychiatric Association in the 2002 document *Psychiatric Effects of Media Violence*. American schoolchildren spend more time watching television during the week (23 to 28 hours) than they spend in school (American Psychological Association, 1994). Lieberman (1994) believes that primarily the visual media, but also recorded music geared toward teens, has desensitized our culture to violence and created a disrespect for authority to the point where violence and hostility are portrayed as culturally normative.

Predictably, media representatives tend to deny any causative relationship between portrayed violence and its increase in our society, claiming that their portrayals merely reflect society, not govern it, in spite of considerable evidence to the contrary (Lieberman, 1994). Video games commonly display aggressive behaviors that often result in severe injury or death to numerous characters; killing is casual and results in no grief, mortification, or apparent long-term effects on any of the remaining game characters. The player who kills more of the games' characters is the winner. Hughes and Hasbrouck (1996) review the scientific data available on this issue and point out that the effects of violence portrayed on TV and other media are conditioned by other factors but that, in general, TV violence does contribute to the level of aggression and subsequent violence and criminality among children and teens.

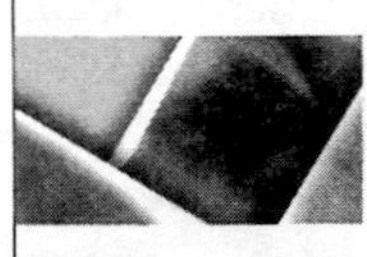

ACTIVITY 6.6

Stage a debate between students acting as educators and others acting as media representatives on the topic: "Does media violence influence the behavior of schoolchildren?"

Wanting to Have Fun, Alleviate Boredom, or Deal with Frustration

"Kids just wanna have fun!" For some students, the desire to enjoy themselves is more important than any other agenda the teacher may have. Glasser (1992) believes that having fun is a student need that schools ignore or try to repress at great cost. He states that this need is as important as three others he discusses: belonging, power, and freedom. Often, students' efforts to have fun are benign and tolerable, but sometimes they seriously intrude on the teacher's efforts to keep all students productive and on task, after which the teacher has to intervene. Jones (1987, 2001) points out that most misbehavior simply consists of students' efforts to be sociable with each other, usually in a positive, fun-oriented way. This socializing is done for two reasons: people are gregarious, and schoolwork is often not very interesting. Jones's observations of classrooms led him to conclude that most behavior problems are simply massive time wasting, consisting of students chatting with each other, passing notes, moving about the room socializing, and generally goofing off. Some of the teachers he observed lost almost 50% of their teaching time to correcting these minor but real irritants.

Frustration because of not being successful at school tasks can be a major source of classroom behavior problems, particularly among EBD students. By definition, about 25% of students in any class are subject to feelings of frustration because they are behind in their achievement compared to the remaining 75% of the peers.

ACTIVITY 6.7

In small groups, discuss the role of "fun" in learning. What can teachers do to meet students' needs (or desires) to have fun while learning?

Psychiatric Diagnoses of Disruptive Behaviors

Attention deficit (hyperactivity) disorder (ADHD), conduct disorder (CD), and oppositional defiant disorder (ODD) are three diagnostic categories in the *Diagnostic and Statistical Manual* (DSM-IV) of the American Psychiatric Association (1994). They constitute three of the most common labels given to children who exhibit a wide variety of behaviors considered inimical to the learning process. Although behaviorally oriented consultants probably consider these terms to have communicative rather than explanatory value, we often hear them used as causative entities—for example, "Of course she can't sit still; she has ADHD." (The next section of this chapter discusses this issue further.) In addition to these three disruptive behaviors, the DSM-IV lists anxiety, depression, somatization, schizophrenia, and other internalizing disorders, all of which may be used to label children and to give a putative cause for the behaviors of concern.

An issue of the *School Psychology Review* (National Association of School Psychologists, 1996) was devoted to the DSM-IV and its utility in the practice of school psychology and counseling, including issues concerning diagnoses and special education decision making. The authors of the various articles indicated some of the strengths of the DSM-IV (for example, a fairly comprehensive list of the commonly accepted symptoms that constitute clinical diagnoses, guidelines regarding behaviors that may predict future adjustment problems, and suggested explanations for behavioral syndromes). They also mentioned some concerns, such as a lack of specification about how behaviors are to be measured or who constitutes a valid informant, a similar lack of specification regarding the degree of symptom strength needed for inclusion in a child's protocol, failure to account for situational specificity of syndromes, no gender or age differences in criteria, and diagnosed conditions being either present or absent based on an absolute number of minimum behaviors needed. Gresham and Gansle (1992) have also commented that the DSM-IV, along with other classification systems, is not linked directly to interventions and does not lead to treatment plans that are useful. They, along with most others who view behaviors from a school-based behavioral intervention standpoint, regard functional assessment and functional analysis to be the approach of choice for dealing with the social/behavioral/emotional problems of children (Chandler & Dahlquist, 2002; Shapiro & Kratochwill, 2000). This approach will be discussed further later in this chapter.

ACTIVITY 6.8

Class members should review the DSM-IV criteria for the various diagnoses related to childrens' behavior disorders. These criteria should be compared to the criteria established in IDEA (P.L. 108-446) for the determination of the categories of "Emotional Disturbance" and "ADHD."

Health and Safety Issues

Some students have allergies that affect their ability to concentrate on schoolwork. Others may have a poor diet that leads to hypoglycemic-type behavior marked by irritability and uncooperativeness. Some students may have other undetected medical conditions (such as poor vision or hearing, Tourette's disorder, and so on) that can influence their behavior. Hill (1999) provides a more detailed discussion of health issues that can influence behavior.

In regard to safety issues, it is now well accepted that many students do not feel safe at school. Violence, the threat of weapons, bullying, and a sense of being emotionally abandoned in large, impersonal high schools seriously affects the mental health of many of our most vulnerable students. DeVoe et al. (2002) report that between 1993 and 2001 the number of children who reported being bullied at school went from 5% to 8%. Snell, MacKenzie, and Frey (2002) have reviewed multifaceted approaches to the problem of bullying in our schools. Olweus and Limber (1999) have found substantial reductions in bullying and victimization by using The Bullying Prevention Program in numerous settings around the globe.

ACTIVITY 6.9

Have students discuss the nature and incidence of bullying in schools with which they are familiar. What programs of bullying prevention or intervention are they familiar with? How might they, as school-based consultants, deal with the issue of bullying?

Communication Skill Difficulties

Teachers often report that students with behavior disorders often don't seem to understand the class rules, expectations, or consequences. Sometimes the reasons for this possibility are obvious: English language learners and students with hearing impairments may not fully understand what teachers or other students are saying. More subtle, though, is the possibility that a student may have an information processing dysfunction that impairs her ability to understand some or all of what is being conveyed to her, either verbally or through nonverbal cues that most students understand easily. Receptive language problems may appear to be simple inattention or distractibility, but may be due to a slowness or insecurity in processing language symbols. Students with this kind of disorder often have learning disabilities, especially in the language arts areas (Lerner, 2000). Referral to a speech and language specialist may be appropriate in these cases.

ACTIVITY 6.10

From their experience, have students discuss symptoms and causes for apparent communication problems that may be related to either behavior or learning problems.

Differences in Temperamental Traits

Some students seem inherently more impulsive and irritable than others. Inborn differences in activity levels, adaptability, and mood may be strongly interacting with environmental variables to produce the behaviors we observe. Chess and Thomas (1996) have discussed nine different dimensions of behavioral style: activity level, adaptability, approach/withdrawal, attention span and persistence, distractibility, intensity of reaction, rhythm, threshold of responsiveness, and quality of mood. They have grouped children into three clusters ("slow to warm up," "difficult," and "easy") based on the apparently inherent behavioral styles that these students exhibit at an early age. Buss and Plomin (1984) conceptualize temperament as a set of genetically determined personality traits or dispositions: activity (tempo and vigor), emotionality (emotional and behavioral arousal), and sociability (preference for others). There is little doubt that these inborn traits, which are manifested well before preschool, can have powerful effects on how students respond to stimuli. Understanding them can provide useful approaches to the analysis of some forms of problem behavior in students. In an attempt to measure the presence and strength of these temperamental differences, Martin (1996) has developed the Temperament Assessment Battery for Children (TABC). Carey and Jablow (1997) have provided some valuable suggestions for methods of approaching students who manifest different temperamental traits. Carey (1998) provides an interesting perspective on the diagnosis of ADHD, which may be an incorrect diagnosis if temperamental traits have not been taken into consideration.

ACTIVITY 6.11

Class members can consider and describe their own temperamental traits or those of someone they know well. They might also indicate how these traits were useful or detrimental in their own educational or vocational experiences.

Events as Antecedents in Specific Settings

The potential for disruptive behavior exists in any situation in which students are gathered. Some students will look for opportunities to irritate their peers, and they usually know who will react. Some "accidentally" bump into others, knock things off tables, make unacceptable noises, bully others, or simply exist, which in itself irritates others and leads to problems. Sometimes teachers give confusing instructions that lead to murmuring, loss of concentration, and escape behaviors.

Some teachers need to be helped to understand that these seemingly random antecedents inevitably occur among students, with certain students apparently destined to contribute more spice to the behavioral stew of a classroom than others, often for a number of the reasons previously cited. Consultants who have a firm grasp of the causes of behavior problems can help teachers understand these causes and possible solutions. At the end of this chapter, the section "General and Specific

Ideas for Managing Classroom Behavior" offers numerous suggestions that can be modified to suit different situations and teacher styles.

ACTIVITY 6.12

Class members should observe a class of students and look for the "little things" that often make a difference, such as those suggested earlier. What seemingly innocuous behaviors of some students, or the teacher, resulted in an escalation of maladaptive behavior in the classroom or playground?

CATEGORICAL SYSTEMS FOR EBD

There are essentially three different systems used for the classification of EBD students: DSM-IV (American Psychiatric Association, 1994); a set of categorical systems that are empirically derived by sophisticated statistical methods (factor analysis, etc.); and that provided by IDEA (P.L. 108-446), which was discussed earlier in this chapter.

DSM-IV

The most well-known system for organizing clusters of behaviors (symptoms) into discrete categories is that provided by the DSM-IV (American Psychiatric Association, 1994). This is the classification system used by psychiatrists, clinical psychologists, and other mental health practitioners in nonschool environments. Some school psychologists and counselors may also use this system, which relies on a rating-scale approach. For example, in order for a student to be diagnosed as having a *conduct disorder* the student would need to manifest at least 3 of the 15 behaviors listed under this category (e.g., Often bullies, threatens, or intimidates others; Has deliberately destroyed others' property [other than by fire setting]; Is often truant from school, beginning before age 13 years; American Psychiatric Association, 1994).

Empirically Derived Systems

Achenbach and McConaughy (1997) have reviewed empirically based assessment systems for delineating types of emotional/behavioral disorders. They have categorized behavior problems along the continuum of internalizing–externalizing. Externalizing is some combination of three disruptive behaviors: attention deficit (hyperactivity) disorder, conduct disorder, and oppositional defiant disorder. Internalizing is characterized by depression, anxiety, obsessive-compulsive tendencies, overcontrolled behavior, suicidal ideation or attempts, and somatization. Students who manifest these internalizing problems are characterized as being overcontrolled. Their symptoms can easily go unnoticed since these students do not act out, intrude on others, or defy classroom rules as do those students whose behaviors are classified as externalizing. One author has referred to internalizing disorders as *secret illnesses* (Reynolds, 1992). It is important to understand that these internalizing conditions are potentially more serious for the long-term mental health of students than are the externalizing behaviors that more readily command our attention. An edition of *School Psychology Review* (National Association of School Psychologists, 1990) was devoted to internalizing problems in school-age students. Merrill (2003) has presented a chapter on the assessment of these disorders.

Quay and Peterson (1996) have identified six major categories of behavior problems: conduct disorders, anxious/withdrawn, immaturity, psychotic behavior, motor excess, and socialized aggressive.

These various categorization systems have been described and researched at length (Merrill, 2003; Reynolds & Kamphaus, 1990; Shapiro & Kratochwill, 2000), and each is favored by some theorists and school personnel. Some of these systems have been operationalized through rating scales or interview formats, most of which are commercially available (Achenbach & McConaughy, 1996, 1997; Connors, 1997; McConaughy & Ritter, 2002; Quay & Peterson, 1996; Reynolds & Kamphaus, 2004).

BEHAVIORAL DIAGNOSTIC METHODS

The primary use for the categorical systems previously described is in eligibility/placement decisions. Most school-based consultants usually do not emphasize or rely on these traditional category systems of diagnosis. They believe a behavioral or functional approach to assessment to be more practical. Hartmann, Roper, and Bradford (1979) have listed the differences between the traditional and behavioral approaches, which demonstrate why the behavioral approach is more appropriate for school purposes. Table 6.1 presents important elements of those differences.

As Table 6.1 indicates, the behavioral approach differs in significant ways from the traditional, or categorization, approach. The behavioral approach looks at the function of behavior, while the traditional approach regards behavior as symptomatic of an underlying condition that produces the behavior. For example, if a student is

Table 6.1

Selected differences between behavioral and traditional approaches to assessment

Behavioral	Traditional
Current contingencies maintain behavior.	Behavior is a function of intrapsychic determinants.
Behavior must be carefully delineated since it will constitute the main focus of change.	Behavior is a symptom of underlying conflict.
Antecedents and consequences are important maintaining variables.	Behavior is used to determine diagnostic labels.
Direct observations of behavior are most important.	Interviews, projective tests, and self-reports yield important diagnostic data.

disruptive, defiant, and uncooperative toward a teacher, the behaviorist looks at the student's learning history and the contingencies currently operative in the classroom. Personality constructs such as "oppositional" are merely used as descriptors for communication purposes, or perhaps can be used to define a "trait" if the behavior is consistent across many settings, but not as explanatory constructs. The traditionalist probably would diagnose the disruptive, defiant student as having a conduct disorder since the student's behaviors match those listed in DSM-IV under that category. Such a diagnosis runs the risk of confusing the cause with the symptom, so that one might be led to believe that the condition "conduct disorder" causes the described behaviors. This belief in the process of reification, or giving categories a life of their own, along with the subsequent power to produce symptoms, has been a major stumbling block in any rapprochement between behaviorists and traditionalists (Deitz, 1982).

Thus, while both behaviorists and traditionalists are interested in the causes of behavior, they look at different sources for those causes. The behaviorist looks at current functions that the behavior is attempting to serve and the contingencies that support the behavior, while the traditionalist looks at past history or internal events that have led to the disease or disability (that is, the category), which in turn leads to the observed behaviors.

It is interesting to note that behaviorists are forced by the current legal bases for special education (and, in the case of hospital or clinic treatment, by the insurance industry) to use a category system based on fairly traditional nosological systems (such as the DSM-IV) in order to provide the settings or resources for their treatment approaches. Thus, a student has to be labeled something before treatment can be provided. In spite of two decades of argument against a categorical system of funding special education and related services in the schools (Hunt & Marshall, 1999; Prasse & Schrag, 1999; Ysseldyke & Marston, 1999), the system is still being used, and even more categories are being developed every few years. ADHD and traumatic brain injury (TBI) are among the latest to be added: ADHD under Section 504 of the Vocational Rehabilitation Act of 1973 and TBI under IDEA (P.L. 108-441), which currently lists 13 eligibility categories.

DIAGNOSING BEHAVIOR PROBLEMS BEHAVIORALLY

No matter their theoretical predilections, all authorities agree that some systematic method of diagnosis is necessary prior to the instigation of interventions (Alberto & Troutman, 1999; Reynolds & Kamphaus, 1990). Behaviorists, in their emphasis on behavioral referents, utilize behavioral assessment, which has been defined as "the identification of meaningful response units and their controlling variables for the purposes of understanding and altering behavior" (Hayes, Nelson, & Jarrett, 1986, p. 464). Currently there is an emphasis on the use of functional assessment, a method now required by IDEA for understanding the purposes of behaviors that impede learning.

Functional Assessment of Behavior

Functional assessment is a process of "gathering information on the events and other variables associated with the occurrence of a targeted behavior" (McComas, Hoch, & Mace, 2000, p. 80). Watson and Steege (2003) indicate that functional behavioral assessment is an "...amalgamation of techniques that have the same purpose: identifying the variables that control a behavior and using that knowledge to design individualized interventions" (p. 5).

This process is primarily used with students referred because of behavior problems but can apply equally well to academic problem assessment (Ysseldyke & Christenson, 2002). Here the consultant tries to see what affects the behavior; what drives it, maintains it, and prompts it; and what makes it potentially valuable or appropriate from the standpoint of the student. In other words, the consultant needs to get inside the reasoning of the student in order to determine the causes of the behavior.

Essentially, functional assessment considers antecedents, behaviors, and consequences, and how they interact (Alessi & Kaye, 1983; Shapiro & Kratochwill, 2000; Watson & Steege, 2003). Antecedent events (themselves often behaviors of teachers or others) might include teacher's directions, earthquake drills, noises by other children, an upcoming social event, and, most important, the client's entire developmental history. Added to this list, especially by cognitively oriented behaviorists, are the student's expectancies and self-monitoring functions. What a student thinks about a situation adds immeasurably to her reaction to it (Hughes, 1988).

Consequences are events that follow the target behavior and influence its future probability of occurrence. We ordinarily think of positive reinforcement, extinction (planned ignoring), and punishment as three major classes of consequences that are used, wittingly or otherwise, by behavior modifiers.

Gresham (1991) believes that some behaviorists do not attend sufficiently to the potential influences of distal antecedents (see Chapter 2). He also suggests that behaviorists tend to focus excessively on the controlling influences of the consequences of behavior, sometimes ignoring the powerful potential of antecedent manipulation.

It is very important to remember that people who practice behavior modification do not directly modify or change the behavior of students. Although these people are regarded by others (and themselves) as behavior-change specialists, they realize that the behavior of a student is a function of the antecedents and consequences that surround it. What can really be controlled or manipulated (it is hoped) are the antecedents and consequences, not the student's behavior itself. In other words, behaviorists manipulate these antecedent and consequent factors and then see what effects these manipulations have on the target behavior. It isn't the behaviorist or teacher who's changing the student's behavior; it's the student who changes it (or doesn't) depending on how alterations in the antecedents and consequences are arranged by the adults who, by and large, control these contingencies.

If behavior is going to change, it will best happen when those who control the antecedents and consequences are willing to change the way in which they set up or deliver these events. The role of the consultant is to understand these controlling contingencies and to build intervention plans designed to alter them. At the end of a functional behavioral assessment, the following groups of questions should have at least tentative answers:

1. What exactly is the behavior of concern? What does it look like, how long does it last, how often does it occur, who else is involved with it, what purpose does it serve, and how serious is it?
2. What seems to prompt it? Does it occur because of some readily identifiable cause or antecedent? Does it seem to be driven by internal events (perhaps hunger or anger)? Have you asked the student why he does it? What does this tell you?
3. What happens after the target behavior that may have a functional relationship to the occurrence of the behavior? Does the student seem to get what he wants as a function of the behavior? In short, what purpose (function) did the behavior seem to have? If no readily discernable consequent event can be determined, do you believe that the reinforcement for the behavior is internal—that is, satisfying in and of itself without any external events needed to justify (reinforce) its future occurrence?

One of the important variables to be determined on the basis of a functional assessment is the function or purpose of the student's behavior. Those conducting a functional assessment directly observe behavior and ecological influences and record these observations using charts or anecdotal notes. On the basis of this information they determine whether the student's behavior is an effort to obtain something (e.g., positive reinforcement) or to avoid something (e.g., some environmental or personal event perceived as being aversive). In practical terms, functional assessment is useful because it allows the observer to make better predictions about the relationships among the student and the antecedent conditions, the probable effect of known consequences, and other variables that may influence the probability that a given behavior will occur. To be able to determine such probabilities, the consultant needs to interview the teacher or parent–consultee very carefully about the details that surround the occurrence of the target behavior(s) in addition to observing the interactions among the consultee, the student, and the student's peers in the classroom or playground.

One possible result of such interviewing and observing is that assumptions about functional relationships may be contradicted by the data. For example, the consultant may believe that a given behavior is controlled by a reinforcement system that she feels is inadequate. Functional assessment may reveal that some antecedent, either distal or proximal, may be controlling the behavior. Gresham and Witt (1987) present evidence in support of the idea that inappropriately arranged antecedents result in more referrals than do inadequate reinforcement (consequent) systems.

Determining the function(s) of the student's behavior may not be an easy task. There may be many competing explanations within the context of the dichotomous "get something—avoid something" paradigm. For example, a student may be noncompliant. What the student may be getting is a chance to demonstrate power. He may also be using noncompliance to avoid disliked tasks or to get attention, which, though negative from the teacher, may be positive from his peers. It may satisfy the needs of a depressed or easily irritated student by allowing him to be left alone. He may feel that others are picking on him, and noncompliance is a way to get even. A student frustrated with his own communication difficulties may be noncompliant rather than trying to explain to a teacher why he can't do an assignment. He may have learned at home that noncompliance serves a number of the needs previously mentioned. Given the multiplicity of possibilities, consultants may have to estimate the most likely functions and build their plans with these functions in mind.

Functional Analysis of Behavior

After behaviorists have assessed behavior and determined its functions, they engage in a functional analysis, which is the deliberate manipulation of variables believed to be controlling or influencing the behavior, in order to see what effects these manipulations have on the behavior. Chandler and Dahlquist (2002) discuss the differences between functional analysis conducted in a natural setting (i.e., a classroom or playground) and that which is done in analogue settings, separate areas where strict control can be placed over all contributing variables. McComas et al. (2000) state that a "functional analysis involves systematic manipulation of events within a single-case design and results in the identification of the behavior-environmental relations, or behavioral mechanisms, that maintain the problem behavior" (p. 80). It is essentially a very refined application of one or more interventions under (preferably) strictly controlled conditions, and the accurate measurement of the effects of these interventions.

Functional assessment and analysis, carefully done, take considerable time and effort. Someone other than the teacher (who is ordinarily too busy teaching) must be the objective observer in the classroom. This person has to be trained to record antecedents, behavior, consequences, setting events, and other aspects of the classroom ecology that may be influencing the target behavior(s), and to give guidance to the teacher in his efforts to apply interventions designed for functional analysis. Although school-based consultants are probably the ideal people for this task, they usually do not have the time to devote to it over an extended period. It is usually necessary to train a paraprofessional to do the functional assessment observations, if such a person is available. If not, the consultant may need to select times when he can do the observations, relying on the teacher (the consultee) to do the rest. Admittedly, this is not the ideal way to conduct a functional assessment, but it is often the best that can be done given the limited resources available in the schools.

Figure 6.1 gives an example of a functional behavioral assessment done by a resource teacher–consultant and the referred student's teacher. Note the attention to the search for causes (functions) of the student's behavior, in addition to efforts to answer the "wh" questions: What is the behavior? When does it happen? Where does it happen? Who is involved? Antecedents and consequences are also addressed in this assessment.

Excellent sources of further information about functional assessment are Alberto and Troutman (1999), Carr (1994), Chandler and Dahlquist (2002), Crone and Horner (2003),

Figure 6.1

Functional behavioral assessment (FBA) example

The following FBA was conducted by a school-based resource specialist with a special education teacher–consultee, whose responses are often represented here.

FUNCTIONAL BEHAVIORAL ASSESSMENT
CONSISTENT WITH IDEA MANDATES

Student: Johnny BeGood **DOB:** 11-11-89 **C.A.** 10-4
School: ABC **Number of students in class:** 12
Teacher(s): Mr. Johnson **Aide:** Ms. Smith
Setting: Special education; special day class

Target behavior(s): Johnny is noncompliant; he does very little schoolwork; he pesters others (i.e., threatens, bullies, extorts money).

What is the current frequency/intensity/duration of the behavior? (1) Johnny refuses to follow teacher directives between 5 and 10 times a day. If the teacher repeats the request he will often become verbally abusive. This refusal/escalation may last between 5 and 50 minutes. (2) Johnny turns in only about 20% of the work assigned; this is mostly math, his best subject. (3) He pesters others with verbal insults and threats between 5 and 20 times a day, largely depending on the reactions of the other students or Mr. Johnson or Ms. Smith. He may persist until he is timed-out; sometimes he just stops, especially if he gets no reaction.

When, and during what activities, does the target behavior occur? Pretty much throughout the day, with fewer problems occurring during math. During recess he is usually against the wall because of these behaviors.

What actions or behaviors of the targeted student or others typically precede the behavior? Teachers have not seen anything the others do to provoke Johnny. They are intimidated by him, and try to avoid doing or saying anything to him. If he sees others getting attention for good student behaviors, he will sometimes insult them for that. Otherwise, it just seems to arise with no specific identifiable antecedent.

What are the typical consequences of the behavior, planned or otherwise? (*Teacher's response*): I usually ask him to desist, and both Ms. Smith and I try to do it positively (e.g., "Johnny, remember our rules about politeness in class. I need you to do your own work at this time"). Sometimes when I'm sick of it, I'll be stronger in my correction ("Johnny, stop insulting/pestering Billy. Mind your business, which is your work"). I never know which correction will or won't work. He seems fairly oblivious to my interventions.

Are there known health issues that could be affecting his behavior? He seems physically healthy. Vision and hearing are apparently OK. The nurse has tried to get a more detailed history, but Mrs. BeGood just says there is nothing wrong with him, and refuses to answer more detailed questions. Certainly (I believe) he is emotionally unhealthy.

What are some desired reinforcers for this student? Mr. Johnson stated that free time works somewhat, but Johnny usually winds up losing it because he uses it unwisely. He seems not to know what to do with himself if he isn't commanding attention by being a nuisance. Teacher has tried stickers, points toward bigger prizes (models, Pokemon cards), but he has earned these only once, and he didn't seem impressed by it. He usually seems to like positive attention. At times, he tells us to "get lost" when we give him verbal reinforcement.

What is the function of the behavior? What is the student trying to get or avoid? Teacher believes he's trying to get attention. We also believe he's trying to avoid doing schoolwork; except math. I think he's seeking power, or maybe revenge. I don't know what for.

What are the desired replacement behaviors? Compliance to task requests; nonhostile behavior toward others; increase in academic output.

Under what conditions/situations are replacement behaviors exhibited? When and where does the student behave well? He's at his best during math. He'll stop provoking (sometimes) when teachers request it. He'll sometimes stop if he gets no reaction from the others.

What has been successful in managing (i.e., replacing) the target behavior(s)? Nothing has been really successful. Perhaps a full day of math would help!? So far, nothing has worked really well.

What has been unsuccessful? Pretty much everything listed above. Success is slippery with him. Sometimes Mr. Johnson thinks he's done or said something that gets to him, but then it doesn't seem to work the next day.

Have there been any recent changes in the school or home environment, daily schedule, medications, and so on? The home environment is characterized by inconsistent discipline; threats are common, as is ignoring deviant behavior, as reported by Mrs. BeGood. Mr. Johnson reports little follow-through regarding schoolwork or notes home. Johnny's not on any medications we know about.

Describe the behavior of others that may be influencing the student's behavior. Other than that of his parents (see above), we don't know what it is. His peers try to avoid him. Could that be it?

Other comments or ideas about the nature or causes of the target behavior(s). Johnny is a very unhappy boy. He has a large chip on his shoulder. He feels responsible to no one, especially when he is upset.

Gresham and Noell (1999), Kaplan (2000), Shapiro and Kratochwill (2000), Watson and Steege (2003), and Wright and Gurman (1998).

ACTIVITY 6.13

Discuss the functional assessment conducted on Johnny BeGood (Figure 6.1). Answer the following questions:

What are some antecedents to Johnny's behavior?

What consequences are presently operating?

What are some likely functions of Johnny's behavior?

What strategies and supports should the teacher/school/home implement in order to improve Johnny's behavior?

Develop a positive behavioral intervention plan that will address Johnny's needs in the least restrictive environment.

The next section discusses the various diagnostic methods used in behavioral assessment, such as charting methods, rating scales, self-report questionnaires, and interviews of teachers and parents.

Charting Methods

When the consultant agrees to observe a particular student or to have someone else do the observation, she needs to obtain a fairly comprehensive description of the behaviors of concern from the teacher. Variables to consider include the type of behavior, frequency, setting events (when it occurs, under what conditions, and so on), duration, intensity, and any other information that will help the observer know what to look for (Alberto & Troutman, 1999; Shapiro & Kratochwill, 2000; Walker & Shea, 1999). The consultant will often need to assist a teacher in carefully defining behaviors of concern. Some teachers have a difficult time being "behavioral"; they tend to describe their concerns in terms of value judgments (such as "bad," "disruptive," or "provocative") rather than in terms of observable actions.

ACTIVITY 6.14

A teacher asks you to observe a girl in her seventh-grade class who she says is aggressive. What questions might you ask the teacher to help clarify what she means by aggressive? Your goal should be to convert what may be a value judgment into a set of observable behaviors.

ACTIVITY 6.15

In pairs of two, have one partner play the role of a teacher who has referred a student for what he calls excessive disruptiveness. The other partner plays the role of the consultant, who tries to get the teacher to be specific about the behavior of concern and to get answers to questions about possible antecedents and consequents, including classroom dynamics and results of interventions the teacher has tried.

There is a wide literature on methods of recording (charting) data as it occurs in the classroom or playground (Alberto & Troutman, 1999; Kratochwill, 1982; Reynolds & Kamphaus, 2004; Skinner, Rhymer, & McDaniel, 2000). The most common method of charting behavior is probably *event (frequency) recording*. Here the observer has determined in advance what the behaviors of concern are and then indicates with a mark on a predesigned form every occurrence of them for a specified period of time. It is also necessary to record duration if they are continuous behaviors in which length of time is an important variable, as in tantrums or time on task. When the amount of time an event occurs is recorded, this is sometimes referred to as *duration recording*. A rate of occurrence can be computed by dividing the number of times the behavior occurred (for discrete behaviors such as cursing) or the total length of time the behaviors occurred (as with tantrums) by the length of the observation period. These methods provide data with which you can compare treatment effects. Figure 6.2 shows a typical event/duration recording form with tallies indicating the occurrence of discrete behaviors and time periods during which continuous behaviors occurred.

Naturally, forms could be designed with multiple behaviors listed. Alberto and Troutman (1999) and Hintze, Volpe, and Shapiro (2002) give examples of forms that allow for a variety of event-recording purposes.

Time sampling (interval recording) is a special case of event recording in which the observer records behaviors if they occur during specified brief periods of time. For example, the observer would note that a behavior occurred if it did so at least once during a specified 15-second interval, using the following 5 seconds to record the note on the form. This process would continue for a given length of time, possibly a half hour, during the same period of time each day for 2 weeks or so. The student observation system form included in the BASC-2 system (Reynolds & Kamphaus, 2004) uses a time-sampling method.

Typical of the available sophisticated behavioral observation (charting) systems is the *Functional Assessment Observation Form (FAO)* (O'Neill et al., 1997). This form allows for the recording of behaviors, proximal antecedents, and consequences. It can be helpful in determining likely predictors of targeted behaviors, as well as functions of the behaviors. Some of these methods require sophisticated approaches and the availability of personnel whose only responsibility is to record behaviors, but most can be adapted for use by a teacher or aide.

The reality in the public schools is that ordinarily there is no one available to do comprehensive behavior charting. The three people with the interest and potential

Figure 6.2
Event/duration recording form

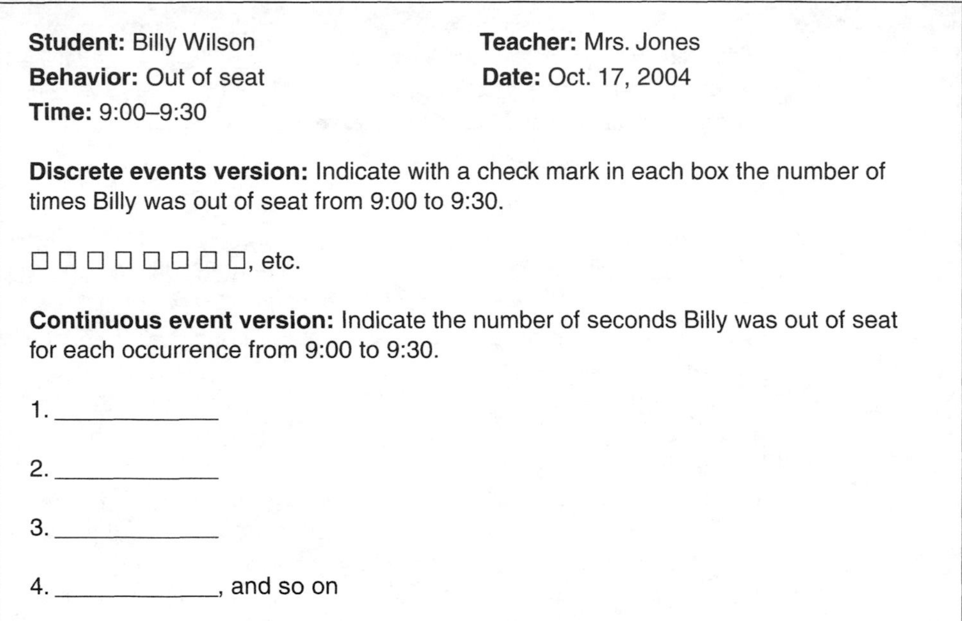

Student: Billy Wilson **Teacher:** Mrs. Jones
Behavior: Out of seat **Date:** Oct. 17, 2004
Time: 9:00–9:30

Discrete events version: Indicate with a check mark in each box the number of times Billy was out of seat from 9:00 to 9:30.

☐ ☐ ☐ ☐ ☐ ☐ ☐ ☐, etc.

Continuous event version: Indicate the number of seconds Billy was out of seat for each occurrence from 9:00 to 9:30.

1. ____________

2. ____________

3. ____________

4. ____________, and so on

sophistication to do this sort of work are the teacher, the teacher's aide (presuming the existence of such a person, a rarity in general education classes), and the school consultant. As I have mentioned, none can devote sole attention to specific disruptive students in order to accurately tally their behaviors and the behaviors of the teachers over extended periods of time. The best we can usually hope for is that the teacher or aide will maintain some sort of tally sheet and will make a conscientious effort to tally behavior for at least brief periods of the day. As potentially unscientific as this may be, it is better than nothing. In my experience as a school consultant, I have often assisted teachers by showing them how to tally behaviors, but rarely have I had the time to sit in a classroom on a regular basis and record behaviors. Often teachers, particularly general education teachers, tire of this data-gathering activity after a few days, especially if they are tallying behaviors to gather baseline information. Teachers want to get on with the interventions and deal with the behaviors rather than count what they feel they already know exists. The consultant has to decide in each case how best to deal with these potential problems.

These realities, among others, mean that trying to do behavior modification in the classroom is not simple. Your results may not be as scientifically defensible as those in the journals devoted to tightly controlled studies (for example, the *Journal of Applied Behavior Analysis*). The authors of articles in this and other journals usually have a staff of graduate students to act as observers/recorders in the classrooms in which their experiments take place. However, knowing this limitation should not deter us from doing what we can. Clearly, somewhat imperfect data are better than no data at all as long as the imperfect data are not invalid.

The consultant's role isn't the same as the scientist's. The consultant has the more mundane but crucial responsibility of helping teachers deal with complicated situations in ways that enhance the school experience for all the students in the class. In the process, the consultant may have to leave some of the niceties of experimental rigor in behavior charting to those with the resources to do so. Further refinements in recording behaviors can be found in Alberto and Troutman (1999); Hintze et al. (2002); Merrill (2003); Repp and Horner (1999); Sattler (2001); Shapiro and Kratochwill (2000); Sugai and Tindal (1993); and Sulzer-Azaroff and Mayer (1986).

ACTIVITY 6.16

Take a behavioral description from a teacher and then construct a charting method based on the teacher's concerns. To make this chart useful for classroom observation, be sure that it has clear definitions of the behaviors of concern, a method for recording each incidence and length of the behavioral episodes (if appropriate to the referral concern), time of day when behaviors occur, and a method for indicating probable antecedents and consequences to the behavior. Also, indicate possible replacement behaviors and a method for recording them. Figure 6.3 gives an example of such a chart, which was custom-designed for a given situation. Describe the behaviors of concern, a recording method, possible antecedents, consequences, the student's reaction to consequences, and other relevant information.

Rating Scales

Another method for determining the type and severity of behavior problems is to have the teacher or parent fill out a rating scale. Several examples are listed below:

Child Behavior Checklist (CBC) (Achenbach, 1991a; Martin, Hooper, & Snow, 1986)

Teacher's Report Form (Achenbach, 1991b)

Behavior Disorders Identification Scale (Wright, 1988b)

Emotional or Behavioral Disorder Scale (McCarney, 1992)

Connors Teacher Rating Scale (Connors, 1997)

Behavior Assessment System for Children-2 (BASC-2) (Reynolds & Kamphaus, 2004)

Children's Attention and Adjustment Survey (Lambert, Hartsough, & Sandoval, 1990)

Devereux Behavior Rating Scale (Naglieri, LeBuffe, & Pfeiffer, 1993)

Adjustment Scales for Children and Adolescents (McDermott, 1993)

Revised Behavior Problem Checklist (Quay & Peterson, 1996)

Behavior and Emotional Rating Scale (Epstein & Sharma, 1997)

Social Skills Rating System (Gresham & Elliott, 1990)

Figure 6.3
Event sampling, with examples

Behavior 1: off task, defined as no apparent progress toward assigned task for at least 1 minute

Time: 9:04
Possible antecedents: reading; he seemed bored
Consequences: teacher prompt
Student's reaction: brief return to reading
Other information: teacher kept track of number of prompts
Possible replacement behavior: Time on task, defined as number of words read or questions answered

Behavior 2: rude verbal comments, defined as comments made to others with the apparent purpose of upsetting them

Time: 9:18
Possible antecedents: Chang bumped him
Consequences: reminder to desist by teacher
Student's reaction: blamed Chang; told teacher to watch Chang instead of him
Other information: conflict has been growing for a few weeks
Possible replacement behaviors: increase in prosocial statements to peers

Note: In regard to behavior 2, rude verbal comments, there will be an escalating set of consequences. Student will be given a reminder to desist from this behavior the first time it occurs. The second time it occurs, the student will be required to meet with the teacher after school to complete a writing task. The third time it happens, the student will be sent to the principal's office and assigned to detention. For each half day of no rude comments to others, the teacher may provide a check mark and a positive comment. Check marks may be turned into a material or activity reinforcer after a predetermined number of points have been accumulated.

These scales provide a basis for determining behaviors on which to focus. The rater judges the student's behavior according to the separate items and rates the student on a three-, five-, or seven-point Likert-type scale, depending on the severity of the behavior.

For example, an item on the *Behavior Disorders Identification Scale* (Wright, 1988b) is "[student] becomes upset when a suggestion or constructive criticism is given." The teacher (rater) indicates the extent to which this behavior is exhibited by giving from one point ("Behavior not exhibited in my presence") to seven points ("Behavior occurs more than once per hour"). In this way, the consultant gets a good idea of the behaviors of concern and their severity. Having more than one teacher rate the child (when appropriate) gives an idea of the situational specificity of the behaviors: A disruptive or withdrawn student may be showing different patterns of behaviors in different settings. This particular instrument also has a home version (Wright, 1988a). There are numerous other home-based rating scales available, such as the Child Behavior Checklist, Parent's Report Form (Achenbach, 1991a), the *Connors Parent Rating Scale* (Connors, 1997), a section of the BASC-2 (Reynolds & Kamphaus, 2004), and the *Children's Attention and Adjustment Survey* (Lambert et al., 1990).

Scales specialized for particular diagnostic categories, such as social skills and ADHD, have also been developed. *The Social Skills Rating System* (Gresham & Elliott, 1990) measures five social behaviors (cooperation, assertion, responsibility, empathy, and self-control) along with three problem behaviors (externalizing, internalizing, and hyperactivity). Another rating scale used for social skills measurement is the *Walker-McConnell Scale of Social Competence and School Adjustment* (Walker & McConnell, 1995), which is connected to a social skills training program developed by Walker, Todis, Holmes, and Horton (1995). Other available rating scales include the *Attention Deficit Disorders Evaluation Scale—School Version* (McCarney, 1995), The Attention-Deficit/Hyperactivity Disorder Test (Gilliam, 1995), the ADHD Symptom Checklist (Gadow & Sprafkin, 1997), the *SNAP Rating Scale* (Atkins, Pelham, & Light, 1985), the Scales for Diagnosing Attention Deficit/Hyperactivity Disorder (SCALES; Ryser & McConnell, 2002), and subscales of the instruments already mentioned (e.g., the Child Behavior Checklist, the BASC-2, and the Quay-Peterson).

As handy and seemingly valid as these rating scales are, there are some disadvantages to their use (Martin et al., 1986; McConaughy & Ritter, 2002; Merrill, 2003). First, the rater may be biased one way or another, and this can affect the way in which he rates the child. Second, it is common for persons reviewing a rating scale or checklist to focus on certain items that seem very important. Remember that individual items usually do not have high reliability, especially when compared to that of the whole test. Given these possible limitations, it is best to use these scales only in conjunction with the other diagnostic methods discussed in this chapter.

Self-Report Rating Scales The rating scales just discussed are all filled out by an informant other than the target student, usually a teacher or parent. It is often very useful to have the student complete one or two of the numerous self-report instruments that are available. As with all structured instruments used in assessment, the consultant has to be aware of the psychometric and developmental characteristics of these instruments. Developmentally immature youngsters may not be able to either read or understand the meaning of the items. Further, they may respond defensively rather than admit to certain behaviors or thoughts. With these caveats in mind, the consultant may have the student fill out a self-report questionnaire and then compare the results to other sources of information. The consultant might also use the student's responses to generate discussion about how the student perceives situations. These discussions might best be conducted by school counselors or school psychologists.

Among the instruments that have respectable norming data are the Children's Personality Questionnaire (Porter & Cattell, 1979); the Millon Adolescent Personality Inventory (Millon, Green, & Meagher, 1982); the Children's Behavior Checklist, Youth

Self-Report Form (Achenbach, 1991c); the *Behavior Rating Profile* (Brown & Hammill, 1990); the *Revised Children's Manifest Anxiety Scale* (Reynolds & Richmond, 1985); the Children's Depression Inventory (Kovacs, 1992); the Self-Esteem Inventory (Coopersmith, 1984); the *Piers-Harris Self-Concept Scale* (Piers, 1996); the Reynolds Adolescent Adjustment Screening Inventory (Reynolds, 2001); the *Reynolds Adolescent Psychopathology Scale* (Reynolds, 1998); the BASC-2 (Reynolds & Kamphaus, 2004); and the Children's Inventory of Anger (Nelson & Finch, 1973).

On these self-report scales, the student typically responds either "yes" or "no" or in some Likert-like manner. Merrill (2003) provides a review of many of these instruments.

Classroom Observations

In addition to those mentioned in the previous section on charting methods, there are a number of other formal methods designed to assist an observer in making classroom observations. Barkley has developed the restricted academic situation (RAS) coding system (Barkley, 1990). Reynolds and Kamphaus (2004) have contributed their student observation system (SOS). In both of these systems, the observer, usually someone other than the teacher, codes behaviors into a variety of categories.

The BASC-2 (Reynolds & Kamphaus, 2004) SOS is based on 15-minute observations of a targeted student using a time-sampling approach. The observer allows 27-second periods to go by, observes the student for 3 seconds, and then uses the next 27 seconds to record what was observed, repeating this process for a total of 30 observations in the 15-minute period. Up to 13 specific behavioral categories are recorded, such as the response to teacher/lesson, inappropriate movement, and aggression. Of the 13 categories, 9 are maladaptive behaviors and 4 are positive/adaptive. Obviously, you want to make repeated observations of a targeted student, particularly when the student is having behavioral difficulties as well as during periods in which the student adapts more positively.

The formal code-based observation systems are ordinarily used in research-based behavior-change programs where interrater reliability and firm operational definitions are required. In the usual school consultation situation, however, the consultant has neither the time nor the necessary staff to do reliability checks or similar activities. Thus, most observation is more informal. Nevertheless, the consultant and the consultee do attempt to establish an operational definition of the target behavior(s). This step is essential and should be taken during the initial discussion with the teacher or after the first observation of the student. Consultants soon discover that most consultees, unless they are used to describing behavior in operationally useful ways, need to be taught how to do so. There are numerous references available to help with this process. Alberto and Troutman (1999); Alessi (1988); Alessi and Kaye (1983); Gresham and Noell (1999); Hintze et al. (2002); Mash and Terdal (1997); Shapiro and Kratochwill (2000); and Ysseldyke and Christenson (2002) have all discussed methods for observing child classroom behavior.

Skinner et al. (2000) have described "naturalistic" observations as those that take place during ordinary classroom sessions. Narrative recording procedures are informal and primarily consist of a neutral observer recording what she sees in the classroom or playground, ordinarily in the form of a log or anecdotal record. Since it is impossible, except with a wide-angle television camera, to record everything, the observer typically records only the antecedents, consequences, and behaviors that are being targeted, and does so in a narrative form.

The following is an example of a narrative recording of a targeted behavior of a 6-year-old boy referred for suspected ADHD:

Date: September 10, 2004

Time: 9:20

Setting: Reading follow-up activity; not teacher-led. Six other boys and girls doing a worksheet having to do with consonant substitutions.

Antecedents: Boy (Will) adjacent to Hans (targeted student) stuck his tongue out at Hans.

Behavior: Hans got up, walked over to the soft toys box, got out a "bopper" (a soft mallet, stuffed with cotton), and went to Will and proceeded to hit him with it.

Consequence(s): Other children laughed. Teacher told Hans to desist. He did, but loudly proclaimed that he was mad because Will stuck out his tongue. Teacher said she would talk to Will and Hans about it at recess break. Hans continued to mutter at Will.

Interviews

The art of interviewing requires all the skills discussed in Chapter 3 and presented in further depth by Benjamin (1987), DeVito (2001), Egan (2001), Lentz and Wehmann (1995), Merrill (2003), and Sattler (1998). I cannot overstress the need to be an effective interviewer in order to be successful as a school consultant. What happens during the interview, both in terms of information transmission and interpersonal bonding between the consultant and the consultee, provides the foundation on which consultation rests.

There are three primary sources of interview data: the teacher(s), the parent, and the referred student. In special cases, agency personnel may also be sources of interview data. The consultant may interview all concerned personnel, depending on the case and time availability. Certainly the most concerned teacher(s) should be interviewed, as should the parents. The amount of time devoted to the parent interview depends somewhat on the age of the student; the younger the student, the more necessary it is to involve the parent in the assessment and treatment process. Interviewing the student can be very useful in terms of understanding her perspective, discussing antecedents and consequences to her behaviors, getting to know her self-perceptions, and reviewing possible reinforcers.

Teacher Interview Step 2 of the SOCS in Chapter 5 deals briefly with the initial discussion (interview) with the teacher, which may occur either before or during an SST meeting, and step 9 of the SOCS reviews ongoing case monitoring efforts, which are largely interview-centered. Rating scales, discussed previously, may be used during an interview, with the rating scale constituting an outline and data-recording system for the interview.

When it becomes clear that you need to interview the teacher(s) about a student who presents with a behavior problem, it is useful to consider at the least the following:

1. What is the problem?
2. What do I want to know?
3. How can I get the most out of the interview?
4. What can I do to make the teacher believe that the interview was worthwhile?

Basic information about the problem has probably come to you in some abbreviated way through the use of a referral form, directed either to you or to the SST. The following are typical questions/comments that the consultant might use in order to elicit information about the problems and classroom context in which they occur:

- Tell me more about your concerns about the student.
- Give me an example of this behavior. What is it like, typically? Who else is involved in it? (Possibly: Show me what he does when he does the behavior.)
- Have you been able to keep data on this behavior? How often and when does it occur?
- What seems to bring it on? What causes it? What circumstances are occurring when it happens?
- What do you typically do when it occurs? What has been your response in the past and currently? What is the response of the other students? What has been the result of these responses?
- You've described settings in which it occurs. Are there times when it does not occur in the same settings? If so, what seems to determine whether or not it occurs?
- When the student behaves appropriately in situations where he usually has trouble, how do you or others react to him?
- What is your goal with this student and these behaviors? How do you want this student to behave? (This may seem like an odd question. Won't the consultee always say, "Like she should; like the other students"? or "I want her to stop acting this way and start acting like she should"? If the consultee responds in this fashion, tell him that the purpose of the question was to give the two of you a goal for this student. How do the two of you want this student to behave? In other words, what behaviors of the student will you reinforce, and what behaviors will you ignore or discourage?)

- What does (Student) do well? What are her strengths socially, academically, or otherwise?
- Given what you know about this behavior and what you've tried up to now, what do you believe would be a good approach to take at this time? What do you believe is the best thing to do at this time?

Be aware that when teachers are asked these questions they may come up with one of two responses other than what you intended. The first might be an attempt to put the burden on you to solve the problem unilaterally—for example, "That's why I referred the student to you. What do you think I should do?" The implication here is that you are the expert and the teacher will do whatever you tell her, or will at least consider it. The second type of response is designed to put the problem in somebody else's lap by requesting that the student be referred to special education (assuming that the student is not already identified as a student with a disability) or at least be removed a few hours a week for counseling. In this case the teacher sees you as the gatekeeper who needs to be convinced that the student's behavior is so difficult that only special education (or counseling) can deal with it. In both cases it is important to keep the focus on the consultee and the student as a part of the classroom. The extended conversation between a teacher and a consultant presented in Chapter 3 (with Ms. H. regarding Sammy) gives an example of how a consultant can encourage this focus. The cases in Chapter 9 also contain examples of how the consultant can deal with these sorts of reactions, which will remain common as long as the teachers with whom you are working see you as either an expert or a gatekeeper. Consultants who stress a collaborative approach to problem solving will notice a decrease in this sort of dependency as their style becomes familiar to the teachers with whom they consult (Allen & Graden, 2002; Davison, 1990; Friend & Cook, 2003). Chapter 3 discusses teacher responses that indicate resistance to the consultation process and ways of dealing with this resistance.

Kratochwill, Van Someren, and Sheridan (1990) have developed a competency-based model for training school-based consultants in the interview skills that are necessary in order to function in a behavioral model of consultation in the schools.

Parent Interview Other than a call from the school to report that their child has been injured, there is probably no phone call parents fear more than the one that says that their child is causing serious behavior problems. The usual message that follows is that the parents need to talk to their child about it, or come to the school to discuss it.

This phone call (or written note) about their child's behavioral issues causes a number of different reactions among parents. School personnel need to be aware of the following possible reactions:

1. *Anger.* The parents may be angry at their child, at the school, or at the teacher in particular. They may also project blame onto others, often onto other students, or even accuse the teacher (directly or indirectly) of poor teaching or inadequate behavior management.

2. *Denial.* The parents may simply deny that there is a problem or try to minimize it, attempting to convince you that it's a temporary thing and will soon go away, even though it may have been noted for years.
3. *Acceptance.* Here the parents are well aware of the behavioral or emotional difficulties their child is having, they agree that these problems are serious, and they want to know what they can do to help. Obviously this is the reaction the teacher or the consultant is hoping for, but it may take some time to appear.

Parents naturally tend to be protective of their children. The goal of school personnel is to work with this tendency, to use it to their advantage by projecting the impression that they, too, are on the side of the child and that they want to work as a team with parents to develop their child's strengths and ability to cope well with their emotional difficulties and interact well with others in the classroom.

When either anger or denial is predominant, you need to approach a parent in the same way a counselor does when faced with an angry or confrontive student: stay calm, don't take the reaction personally, be a good listener, reflect feelings, and take time to develop rapport while supporting the parent during this difficult interaction (Benjamin, 1987; Lehman & Irvin, 1996). Confrontation early in the proceedings will only strengthen the parents' defenses; arguing leads to a win-win mentality that stifles the give-and-take that is often necessary in the beginning stages of an interview with a defensive person.

Teachers and consultants need to have a plan in mind before the parents are called or interviewed face to face. They need to have their facts well organized and must be in a positive, helpful frame of mind. This is not always easy, especially for the teacher who has just finished a difficult day with a student who manifests behavior or emotional difficulties. Here are some issues to think through and plan for before dialing the parents or meeting with them after school, along with some strategies for keeping the interview positive and problem-centered.

1. *Explain your reason for concern.* After spending a few moments building rapport, which always includes some comments about the target student's strengths, the consultee (or the consultant) will spell out the behaviors that need to be discussed. Keep your discussion of both the strengths and the behaviors of concern objective and data-oriented. This impresses the parent positively and indicates a professional approach to observation of the child. Avoid child- or other-blaming approaches.

2. *Ask for the parent's opinion of the situation.* Does she see this behavior at home? What does she think the child's goals are? What does she do about it at home? Focus on replacement behaviors: what can be done to replace the unwanted behaviors with more appropriate behaviors?

3. *Review efforts made to deal with the problem.* Tell the parent what school personnel have tried and what results they have had. Generally, you haven't had good results; otherwise, you probably wouldn't be having this interview. Try, however, to indicate some areas of improvement in order to set a positive tone for the discussion.

4. *At this point you may ask the parent what she thinks the school ought to do about the behavior, or you can suggest a plan for discussion.* Remember the

suggestion that was presented in Chapter 3: Your goal is to get an agreement, not to win an argument. Try not to debate with the parent about every point in your plan; be ready to compromise on small points in order to develop a plan both of you can agree on. Think of the discussion as "win-win" in purpose. Negotiate toward yes (Fisher & Brown, 1988; Fisher & Ury, 1991). Strive to achieve Gordon's (1974) Method III ("nobody loses") results.

5. *Having arrived at some goal-oriented, positive plan that involves action on the part of the school and the home, summarize it to see if there are any further questions or comments that the parent wishes to make.* Then set a date when you will call the parent to review the plan, usually in a week or so. Of course, be sure to follow-through on this promise.

ACTIVITY 6.17

In dyads, one person plays the part of a teacher calling a parent about his child's disruptive behavior. The other person plays the part of the parent, who acts defiant or hostile to the teacher.

In a second scenario (partners switch roles), the parent maintains a denial position; he asserts that his child would not engage in such behavior and that the teacher must be mistaken.

ACTIVITY 6.18

It is worthwhile to do many role-plays of parent–consultant interviews. As a group, discuss the kinds of situations that could come up during a parent interview, review possible strategies for dealing with them, and then take turns role-playing these situations. Also, practice with three persons involved: the teacher, the parent, and the consultant.

Further information about the communication skills necessary to interview parents are contained in Chapters 3 and 5. Procedures for interviewing students are discussed later in this chapter in the section on communication methods.

DETERMINING PRIORITIES FOR INTERVENTION

It is common for a teacher to refer a student for a wide variety of concerns, both academic and in the area of EBD. Students with EBD are rarely displaying only one circumscribed behavior of concern. Depending on the circumstances, it may be best, at least at first, to only work on certain behaviors rather than all the concerns the teacher has expressed. There are at least two good reasons for doing this: (a) It may be just too overwhelming to develop and carry out interventions for a wide variety of behaviors; and (b) if a consultee can have success with a limited number of targeted, key behaviors, she may be more willing to try additional interventions with the remaining behaviors of concern.

Prioritizing which behaviors to work on is a necessary early step in the consultation process. Cooper, Heron, and Heward (1987) list nine factors that should be considered when prioritizing target behaviors. The consultant should determine:

1. If the behavior is of danger to the individual or to others.
2. If the frequency of the behavior or, in the case of a new behavior, the opportunities to use the behavior warrant intervention.
3. The duration of the problem or, in the case of a new behavior, how long the individual's need for the new behavior has existed.
4. If the behavior will produce a higher level of reinforcement for the individual than other behaviors under consideration. Generally, behaviors that produce a high level of reinforcement take priority over behaviors that produce a low level of reinforcement.
5. The impact of the behavior on the individual's skill development and independence.
6. If learning the (substitute) behavior will reduce the negative attention that the individual receives.
7. If learning the (substitute) behavior will increase reinforcement for others in the individual's environment.
8. The difficulty (time and energy) to be expended to change the behavior.
9. The cost involved in changing the behavior.

It is not always easy to determine what should be involved in the conceptualization of these factors, particularly in the early stages of discussing and observing the target behaviors. Among the variables that make certitude difficult are the behaviors of the other students (Do they wittingly or unwittingly provide reinforcement for the problem behaviors?); the ability and willingness of the teacher to implement change; the strength of the behaviors (that is, the value that the student ascribes to these behaviors in her efforts to either obtain reinforcers or avoid aversive situations, or in her belief that these behaviors will support her self-concept and self-perceived role in the classroom); and the degree of parental and cultural support for the desired change.

The decision about which behaviors to focus on and how to prioritize your efforts should be the result of a discussion between the consultant and the teacher, with input from the student's parents and others (e.g., SST) as appropriate. Consultants always need to remember that the consultee will be doing most of the in-class intervention work; therefore, the consultee should take the lead in determining priorities for that setting, taking the factors previously listed by Cooper et al. (1987) into account. The consultant, however, should determine priorities for other settings, such as parent work, the need for medical intervention, school-based counseling, or other outside referrals.

It may be best, depending on the situation, to delay the determination of priorities until the consultant has interviewed the consultee, observed the behaviors of concern, and gathered information through the charting methods or rating scales previously discussed.

GENERAL AND SPECIFIC IDEAS FOR MANAGING CLASSROOM BEHAVIOR

This section presents some general and specific interventions that consultants should be aware of when consulting about students who demonstrate EBD. This information is relatively brief and is intended only to provide some suggestions that can be adapted to particular cases. Interested readers can find a wide array of literature in this area, much of which is indicated in this chapter's reference section. This discussion is limited to general preventive techniques, contingency management and contracting, noncontingency-related interventions, social skills training, and communication methods.

1. General Preventive Techniques

a. Classroom Rules It is a truism that no one has taught school for more than 10 minutes without recognizing the need for rules to govern the classroom. All experienced teachers have a set of rules, which are usually characterized by the following:

1. They are brief, both in the way each one is written and in the total number of rules.
2. They are usually positive.
3. They are relevant and reasonable.
4. They are clear and are usually behaviorally stated.
5. They are capable of being enforced in a firm, fair, and consistent manner.

Alberto and Troutman (1999) suggest the following "rules about rules":

1. Be specific about what is expected.
2. Make as few rules as possible.
3. Be explicit about the relationship between rules and consequences. (p. 466)

Sulzer-Azaroff and Mayer (1986) have provided some additional guidelines for developing classroom rules. They also give examples of negatively stated classroom rules and some positive alternatives to each one. Here are three:

Negative: Don't be late to class.
Positive: Be in your seat when the tardy bell rings.
Negative: Don't waste time.
Positive: Complete your assignments on time.
Negative: Don't touch, hit, or kick others or throw objects.
Positive: Keep your hands, feet, and objects to yourself.

Typical examples of positive rules include the following, which were found on the front wall of a third-grade class:

1. Be polite to each other.
2. Be prepared to follow directions and do your best work.
3. Leave your seat only for schoolwork purposes.
4. Respect everybody's property.

Here are some other suggested positive wordings of class rules:

1. Listen carefully.
2. Follow directions.
3. Work quietly. Allow others to work in peace.
4. Respect others. Be kind with your words and actions.
5. Work and play safely.

ACTIVITY 6.19

In small groups, discuss methods for establishing classroom rules. Have a group devise appropriate rules for primary, middle, junior high, and senior high classes. Review these in light of the criteria for the development of the class rules just given.

Some teachers have a set of rules that they have found to be effective, and they simply announce them the first day of class. Sometimes they give examples of what the rules mean and rehearse examples of their meaning and violations of them. Other teachers believe that students should assist in developing their own class rules. While helping the students to make up their own rules, teachers may subtly direct the students' thinking toward rules they have already considered or previously used. In this way the students feel that they have had a voice in the development of the rules, and the teachers succeed in getting the rules they feel comfortable with.

Rules need to be accompanied by consequences. These can also be stated in writing, although this is not common; teachers often prefer to be able to establish consequences depending on the factors surrounding each rule infraction, a practice that can, unfortunately, lead to inconsistency and bias. Here is a set of rules followed by a brief list of examples of violations and a set of predetermined consequences:

Rule	*Examples of Violations*	*Consequences*
Be polite	Hitting, pushing, saying mean things	Teacher reprimand, time-out, loss of recess
Be prepared to follow directions and do your best work	Not paying attention, turning in poor work	Being asked to repeat directions

Kampwirth (1988) has suggested a list of interventions for rule violations, ranging from mild through moderate, severe, and profound in the degree of intrusiveness. As a general rule, the mildest interventions should be used until it is clear that something more intrusive needs to be tried. Sprick and Howard (1995) have presented a list of 100 behavior problems, with 500 plans for solving them. Their method is to start with the simplest plan to use and then escalate the degree of involvement as the problem proves to be more difficult.

ACTIVITY 6.20

In small groups, arranged according to grade levels from preschool through high school, design lists of consequences that range from the mildest to the most severe. Review each group's list, noting the different consequences that are believed to be appropriate at the different grade levels.

The school-based consultant needs to be aware of the rules the consultee is using and how they are being enforced. Some behavior problems are the result of inappropriate rules or inconsistently enforced rules. This latter problem is especially possible and troublesome in overcrowded classrooms where there are a number of students exhibiting behavior problems simultaneously. Consultees may need help in thinking through their rules and applications. Some students need to know that the rules are meant for them; sometimes a review of the rules with the consultee and the student done in the context of the communication (conference) methods that follow can clarify misunderstandings.

b. Procedural Practices In addition to a set of rules, every teacher establishes rules that govern the customs, norms, and procedures by which the classroom is conducted. Students expect that a teacher will have such procedures to govern everything from how to enter the classroom, getting oriented to assignments, and responding to crises. The following are some aspects of general classroom management that consultants should be sensitive to:

1. Is the teacher prepared to teach? Does it appear that there is a structured system that the teacher is following? Does the curriculum seem appropriate to the developmental needs of the students, as well as being in accord with the standards for the classroom established by the district or state?
2. Are the teacher's methods appropriate for her class? Does she use a variety of techniques designed to motivate her students and achieve her teaching goals?
3. Does the grouping of the students enhance the learning process? Should the class be reorganized in order to better maximize the teacher's goals? Students who may not be able to resist the temptation to be unproductively social or provocative toward each other need to be separated.
4. Rathvon (1999) presents a number of suggestions for having students learn and engage in classroom procedures such as raising hands and waiting to be called

on and moving from one activity to the next. Transition times are a major source of difficult behavior for some students; the relative lack of structure during these times is often not strong enough to contain their impulses.

5. Ysseldyke and Christenson's *Functional Assessment of Academic Behavior* (2002), though devoted to *academic* issues, contains a number of suggestions about teacher behaviors that impact on behavioral issues in the classroom.
6. General texts on classroom organization and teaching skills (Jones, 2001; Jones & Jones, 2004; Kyle & Rogien, 2004; Moore, 1995) and educational psychology (Cooper, 1999; Ormrod, 2000; Slavin, 1997) present a number of practical tips and strategies for dealing with everyday procedural issues.

2. Contingency Management and Contracting

Contingency management refers to the application of the ABC model of behavioral sequences that was previously discussed. As simple as the ABC conceptualization may sound on the surface, further study indicates that it can be very complex. It is not always easy to determine which kind or combination of antecedents may be prompting the behaviors we see, which is why a functional assessment needs to be done. The consultant needs to gather information about a given student from a wide variety of sources in order to accurately determine what the antecedents and consequences may be. Steps 2, 3, and 4 of the SOCS process (discussed in Chapter 5), consisting of interviewing and observing, are the keys to determining antecedents, consequences, and the purposes of the student's behavior.

Another way to conceptualize the nature of contingency management in the classroom is in terms of the "if ... then" rules that the teacher has established: If a student engages in a target behavior, then a certain contingency will apply. This implies that there are classroom rules and preestablished, usually negative, consequences for students who fail to obey the rules. Conversely, there are positive consequences for appropriate, prosocial behavior. Contingencies tend to be more explicit in classrooms for students with special needs because the students in these classes usually need the structure of knowing exactly what the consequences for their behavior, either positive or aversive, will be. Here are some examples of contingency management:

Ms. Rivera has noticed that her fourth-grade students start getting noisy and more active as recess approaches. This behavior has been increasing over the last week. Ms. Rivera tells her students that she has noticed the increase, gives examples of what she means, elicits examples from the students, and then tells them that she will delay their recess for 2 minutes if she notices it again. She has to apply this contingency only once during the following week; the students are no longer behaving inappropriately before recess.

Mr. Smith, a junior high shop teacher, has decided to modify his grading procedures to emphasize neatness in the work space. He tells his students that every now and again he will give a signal, which means that all students should back away from their work stations and projects while he walks through the classroom giving bonus points to those students who have a neat work area and deducting points for a messy area. After he has done this twice, only one boy persists in being messy, and Mr. Smith counsels with him individually. This contingency change has produced a positive effect.

Mrs. Mellow, who teaches a senior high advanced English class, has decided to talk with her students about their apparent boredom and the carelessness in some of their assignments. Her students give her some ideas about ways to make the class materials and discussion more interesting, including a greater effort to relate the older plays and stories they are studying to contemporary problems. She gives each of the three groups the challenge of modifying Shakespeare's *Richard III* to make it more contemporary. Each group should develop its own modifications. Also, students agree as a class to determine the criteria for grading each other's efforts. These changed contingencies regarding student involvement result in a very lively set of activities that make *Richard III* come alive for these bright seniors.

These examples could be multiplied a hundredfold by those who observe classroom practices (Cooper, 1999; Kyle & Rogien, 2004; Metcalf, 1999). The consultant needs to study the contingency practices of teachers who have excellent classes as well as those who have difficulty with behavior management and motivation in order to comprehend the differences in these teachers' approaches.

The primary purpose of observing a class in action should be trying to find ways in which the teacher may be better able to manage the behavior and instructional presentation to enhance learning and improve the socioemotional climate of the room. The Student Observation System from the BASC-2 (Reynolds & Kamphaus, 2004) and the FAAB (Ysseldyke & Christenson, 2002) would be good starting points to give direction to classroom observation relative to a consultee's use of contingency management, as well as many other aspects of student and teacher behaviors.

A contract is a specific form of a contingency management system, an agreement between a teacher or parent and a student that is based on the "if ... then" proposition previously mentioned. In a simple contract, the consultee may say to a student, "If you finish your work, then you can go outside." If the student agrees to this statement, the contract exists. If the student does not agree, no contract has been made since contracting implies mutual agreement. Teachers base most behavior management on a rather informal style of contracting. They often make "if ... then" statements, though they do not always ask for, or expect, any verbal agreement from the students. Agreement is often assumed since the teacher, operating as a benevolent autocrat, as most teachers do, is giving a directive that he expects students to follow.

Teachers are often bothered by the fact that a referred student doesn't follow the implicit contracts that the teacher has been establishing. Because uncooperative students usually do not follow implicit contracts, they may need more explicit contracts that involve more than verbal statements or apparent verbal agreement; the agreement may need to be in writing.

Consultants are often asked to help consultees write explicit contracts until the consultees develop some experience with them. This is an appropriate task for a school-based consultant and one she should welcome, particularly with an inexperienced teacher or a parent.

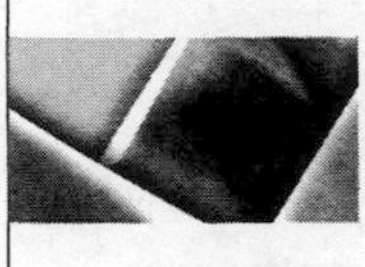

ACTIVITY 6.21

After considering the communication-based approaches just summarized, discuss their pros and cons. When would these approaches be appropriate for a consultee to use? When would they be inappropriate?

Here are some general guidelines for establishing formal (written, explicit) contracts:

1. Keep the contract simple. It should be no more complicated or cumbersome than necessary. Most abandoned contracts met that fate because they were too time- or cost-intensive for the consultee.
2. Tasks and rewards need to be very specific. Spell out exactly what the student is to do, or stop doing, and exactly what the consequences will be.
3. Specify time constraints; for example, when will the contract go into effect, how long will it last, and when must an assignment be completed?
4. Avoid tasks that are too difficult for the student. At first, it is a good idea to make the contract easy for the student to fulfill. In that way the student will become attracted to the idea of contracting; then you can escalate the expectations.
5. Formal contracts are signed by both parties and often witnessed by another teacher, the consultant, the parent, or the principal.
6. Be prepared to have some students fail to carry out the contract. Discuss the reasons for failure with the student and then try again.

Homme (1970) describes a method of transferring control of the contract from the consultee to the student over a period of time. When this occurs, the student tends to become more involved in the contract because she owns more responsibility for it. More details about writing effective contracts can be found in Homme (1970), Gallagher (1988), Jones and Jones (2004), Krumboltz and Thoresen (1969), Levin and Nolen (2004), and Walker and Shea (1999). Kaplan and Hoffman (1990) have produced a book with many examples of contracts that are visually appealing to students. Figure 6.4 gives an example of a contract written for a fifth-grade girl designed to increase her use of prosocial comments to other students. The case of Maria in Chapter 9 gives another example of a written contract.

The following are some additional ideas that involve the use of contingency management:

1. Positive reinforcement, the undisputed best practice in behavior management, is essentially a contingency-based intervention. It is given when students engage in appropriate behavior, if only an approximation to that behavior, with the intention to reinforce or strengthen the behavior that preceded the giving of the positive reinforcement. It may involve a verbal comment ("I really liked the way you handled that situation."), a positive look (implying approval), or the administration of some type of reward (e.g., grades, notes home, phone calls home, certificates, and

Figure 6.4

Behavior contract between a student and a teacher

AGREEMENT

Here's a good deal for both of us!

Ms. Portelo (teacher) agrees to give Sylvia (student) one bonus point for each time Ms. Portelo hears Sylvia make a positive comment to another student. Sylvia can earn up to four bonus points per day for this behavior. Good luck, Sylvia!

This contract begins on: December 11, 2004 at 9:00 a.m.

This contract will be reviewed on: December 20, 2004 at 2:30 p.m.

Signed: ____

MRS. PORTELO SYLVIA SYLVIA'S MOM DATE

access to preferred objects or activities, possibly through the use of a reinforcement menu). The use of "mystery rewards" (Rhodes, Jenson, & Reavis, 1993), which are surprise rewards given in a variety of different situations, serve to keep up a level of intrigue regarding the use of extrinsic reinforcers.

2. Aversive consequences are punishments administered contingent on a student's inappropriate behavior. These usually involve a teacher's directive to desist from the behavior, perhaps a critical comment, a referral to a higher authority (principal, counselor, parent), or the application of some sort of detention or suspension from school. The student may be sent to a "time-out" (or "time-away") area of the room or out of the room, or may lose credit points toward an assignment.

3. Whenever feasible, tie the contingencies to both school and home consequences. Behavioral improvement at school is often contingent on home support (Christenson & Sheridan, 2001).

3. Noncontingency-Related Interventions

Most of the previous discussion regarding behavior problem intervention has been presented from a behavioral point of view because most of the behavior-change literature is presented from that perspective and most research data have been provided by the behavioral school (Bergan, 1977; Bergan & Kratochwill, 1990). This is not to say that other perspectives have no use and should be discounted. The literature contains numerous references to behavior-change procedures that have nothing to do with behavior modification as such (Charles, 2002; Hyman, 1997; Kanfer & Goldstein, 1986; Walker & Shea, 1999). These can be classified as psychodynamic (counseling, including the use of media such as puppets, art, and music), ecological (changing situations or events within the client's environment, either within or outside the classroom), or biophysical (medication, diet, or megavitamin therapy). Behaviorists may argue that many of these treatments have behavioral components: For example, changing an ecological component may be interpreted as antecedent manipulation; medication may be seen as an effort to treat symptoms only rather than some underlying cause. However, most people see them as distinctly different, primarily because they derive from a philosophical position that treats behaviors as symptoms of underlying disorders, not as the disorder itself, which is a hallmark of behavioral thinking (Skinner, 1971; Ullmann & Krasner, 1965).

With the exception of ecological alterations with the classroom, most of the previously mentioned noncontingency-related approaches are done by personnel outside of the classroom, such as counselors and health care practioners. The following are some behavior management techniques that do not rely on a contingency-based approach, and that can be applied by a teacher:

a. Teachers and parents model appropriate behavior, such as ways of entering classrooms, addressing others, or accepting redirects.
b. When interest in the academic material is dwindling and behavior problems seem to be arising, teachers might try these:
    1. *Interest boosting*, which consists of doing or saying something that will regenerate students' interest in the subject matter or assignment. Perhaps a different way of presenting the information, or getting students' ideas about the topic, or relating it to some recent event might stimulate more interest and reduce the frequency of behaviors attributable to boredom.
    2. *Signal interference* is a common teacher technique. It consists of "The Look," wherein the teacher stops or slows instruction to give a brief serious look at an offending student. This usually brings the ordinarily well-behaved student back to the understanding that he should be doing his assignments and not something else.
    3. *Proximity control* is an effort to control a potentially disruptive situation by physically moving closer to the student or students who are misbehaving. Usually this is enough to at least temporarily stop disruptive behavior.
    4. *Temporary reassignments* consist of having students who are causing behavioral disruptions go to a different part of the classroom. It is a mild form of "time-out."
    5. *Gentle reminders* are statements from the teacher about what the students are supposed to be doing. Teachers sometimes preface these reminders with a carrier phrase such as "Maria, I need you to...", or "Cody, We're all doing our math follow-up now. You need to...."
    6. *Hurdle help* consists of detecting times when students are stuck with an assignment and providing direct help, or a reminder to the whole group about how to overcome the problem, or having a peer give timely assistance to the student needing it.

7. *Planned ignoring* is a form of hoped-for extinction (see Chapter 2) in which the teacher tries to avoid giving any recognition for disruptive behavior. Depending on the student involved and the situation, this may be a safe and effective technique. It is best used when a back-up plan that can easily restore order can be put into effect in case the planned ignoring does not work. Numerous other ideas for managing mild, predictable behavior disruptions in the classroom are available in Charles (2002), Jones and Jones (2004), Long and Morse (1996), and Rhodes et al. (1993).

c. Teachers need to increase the ratio of positive to negative interactions they have with students, especially those students whose behavior commonly prompts negative reactions. A positive greeting in the morning, a comment about something the student is interested in, a nod of recognition when things are going well, pointing out the good parts of otherwise inadequate assignments, and making a phone call or writing a brief note to home to deliver some good news are some ways teachers can try to keep the ratio of positive to negative on the positive side.

d. Since purpose-driven individuals tend to control their behavior in the direction of their goals, keeping students focused on the goals of the lesson, for the hour, the day, the week, and so forth, is worth the time it takes to convey those goals, and to convey your expectations for improvement. Setting daily goals and objectives alerts people to what their targets are for that day.

e. At times it may be wise for a teacher to allow a time-out from academic work to get a check from the students about how they are doing, academically or socially. An occasional class meeting devoted to topics of academic expectations, social relationships, or other issues of importance to the students may help the teacher gain a better understanding of what motivates or bothers her students. Glasser (1969, 1992) has presented ideas about the value of class meetings.

4. Social Skills Training

Merrill and Gimpel (1998) have presented 15 definitions of social skills that have been used in the literature, indicating both considerable interest in this area and some difficulty in coming to agreement about the nature of this constellation of behaviors. Gresham (1983) has preferred to use a *social validity* definition that conceptualizes social skills as socially significant behaviors exhibited in specific situations that predict important social outcomes for children and youth.

Over the past 30 years, researchers have become increasingly aware that deficits in social skills are correlated with behavior problems. Indeed, many behavior problems may be seen as symptomatic of a lack of social skills or a failure to apply them. Parker and Asher (1987) have found poor peer relations to be correlated with dropping out of school, crime, and the diagnoses of psychopathology. Some DSM-IV disruptive behavior categories may not be caused so much by internal psychopathologies as by failure to learn more appropriate prosocial behavior. Trower, Bryant, and Argyle (1978) have observed that psychiatric disorders such as anxiety, conduct disorder, personality disorder, and mood disorders are all characterized by limited or ineffective social skills. Gresham (2002) has noted that two of the five criteria specified in IDEA for the category of emotional disturbance are: (a) an inability to build or maintain satisfactory interpersonal relationships with peers and teachers, and (b) inappropriate types of behavior or feelings under normal circumstances. Both of these criteria speak directly to possible problems with social skills acquisition or performance.

Goldstein, Spafkin, Gershaw, and Klein (1983) list six general sets of social skills:

1. Beginning social skills (such as listening and saying "Thank you").
2. Advanced social skills (such as joining in constructively and apologizing).
3. Skills for dealing with feelings (such as expressing one's feelings and understanding the feelings of others).
4. Skill alternatives to aggression (such as negotiating and using self-control).
5. Skills for dealing with stress (such as getting ready for a potentially difficult situation and standing up for a friend).
6. Planning skills (such as gathering information and deciding what caused a problem).

Gresham (2002) indicates that social skills training should have four primary objectives:

1. Promoting skills acquisition
2. Enhancing skill performance
3. Reducing or eliminating competing problem behaviors
4. Facilitating generalization and maintainence of social skills

Although the four objectives just listed suggest a sequence of training considerations, Gresham (2002) points out that a best practice is to incorporate generalization from the outset of any social skills training program. It is too often the case that at-risk or EBD students may be given a sequence of social skills training sessions, but do not generalize these skills to the playground or even to the classroom because the strength of the competing stimuli in those settings overwhelms the situation-specific stimuli presented in the training sessions.

The most common assessment instruments for the measurement of social skills are rating scales, which were mentioned earlier in this chapter. Anecdotal records, as presented in Figure 6.2 as recordings of events, are useful for keeping track of specific examples of social skills deficits. A review of the nature of behavior problem referrals indicates that many of these problems are due either to a social skills acquisition deficit or to a social skills performance deficit. An *acquisition deficit* is the absence of, or failure to have learned, particular social skills, while a *performance deficit* is the failure to perform these skills at the right time and to an appropriate degree (Gresham, 2002).

Merrill (2003) has presented a very extensive text devoted to issues of assessment of social, behavioral, and emotional problems of students. Numerous sources of information and complete curricula in social skills training have recently been developed. Among the sources for this information are Walker et al. (1995), Elliott and Gresham (1992), and Goldstein (1999), whose *The Prepare Curriculum* consists of three major emphases: aggression reduction, stress reduction, and prejudice reduction. Charney (1992) developed the "responsive classroom," an instructional approach that teaches social and academic skills in the general education classroom. Magg (1992) has presented a useful model for integrating consultation service delivery into social skills training in the schools. Sheridan and Elliott (1991) describe how the behavioral model of consultation can be used in the assessment and treatment of social skills, and Colton and Sheridan (1998) demonstrated that a combination of conjoint (i.e., parents and teachers working together) behavioral consultation and social skills training improved the cooperative behavior of elementary-age boys who were diagnosed with ADHD.

5. Communication (Conferencing) Methods

This group of methods is characterized by teachers' efforts to talk with students who present behavior problems about these behaviors, their effects, and their possible consequences. These methods also emphasize efforts to invite cooperation from these students. By using these relatively mild and unobtrusive techniques, teachers hope that they won't have to resort to any of the more serious consequences discussed in the sections on contracts and contingency management.

Consider this scenario. Jason, a sixth-grader, has been passing notes, whispering, and irritating others over the past few weeks. His teacher, Mr. Jacobs, has told him, in front of the whole class, to desist. This has had a temporary effect each time, but overall Jason's behavior problems are increasing. Mr. Jacobs decides he needs to talk with Jason about this situation. How should he do it?

This is another referral that school consultants should welcome. It gives the consultant a chance to assist a consultee at the primary- and secondary-prevention stages of problem solving rather than the tertiary stage, when the consultee has become very irritated with a student. Intervening at the earlier stages might cause the situation to de-escalate. Communication that can be effective at these stages often consists of the relatively benign methods explained by Ginott (1971), Gordon (1989), and Glasser (1969), and as the milder forms of interventions suggested by Sprick and Howard (1995).

Haim Ginott (1971), in *Teacher and Child,* points out that teachers need to exert self-discipline. Otherwise, they may create or escalate the negative interaction between themselves and the student. In other words, "When the children act like children, the adults need to act like adults." This is often easier said than done, particularly when a student's disruptiveness is spoiling the teacher's efforts to teach or when repeated requests to "Behave yourself" have been ignored. According to Ginott, teachers who have lost their self-discipline tend to attack the student instead of focusing on the behavior and its causes, demand rather than invite cooperation, deny students' feelings, use labels and other pejorative comments, lecture excessively, and ignore the student's opinions and feelings. Ginott emphasizes "sane messages" (statements that address the situation without attacking a student's character) and "congruent communications" (when the teacher's statements to a student match the student's feelings about the situation and about himself). Here is an example:

> (Insane message): "Some of you students are acting like animals. This isn't a zoo, you know."
>
> (Sane message): "This is the quiet time for independent reading. Being quiet helps everybody to enjoy their reading."

In his various books, Ginott gives many examples of interactions between adults and students that exemplify his soft approach to inviting cooperation in the classroom.

William Glasser, a psychiatrist, was originally trained in psychodynamic methods of understanding human socioemotional problems. His earliest writings demonstrated methods of talking with individual students and whole classes. For example, Chapter 10 of *Schools Without Failure* (Glasser, 1969) presents a model for classwide discussions of problem situations based on a rational problem-solving method stressing individual responsibility and plan building. Glasser inferred that teachers were able to do this and were generally good at it.

In his later books, Glasser takes schools to task for failures to make an effort to really stimulate students to be the best they can be. He seems to agree with students that schools, particularly high schools, are boring. He points out that students need belonging, power, fun, and freedom. In *The Quality School: Managing Students Without Coercion* (1992), he shows how teachers can evolve from the "boss-teacher" model, which he feels dominates most public school discourse between teachers and students, to a "lead-teacher" approach. In answer to the question "How do we talk with students who are disrupting the educational process?", he suggests a review of the behaviors of concern (such as "What were you doing when I asked you to stop?"), reminders of class rules, and the development of a plan to prevent future occurrences. The purpose of the conference is to find solutions, not to assign blame.

Ginott and Glasser both rely on the following communicative behavior prerequisites: teachers must take a pro-student stance in their conversations with students; they need to be good listeners, not good lecturers; and they need to understand that students may be defensive and may deny responsibility and project blame onto others. None of these reactions should deter teachers from focusing on the behavior, its consequences, and a plan for dealing with it that meets both the teacher's and the student's needs. Charles and Charles (2004) have presented lesson plans for a series of seven whole-class discussions that emphasize a communications-based approach to classroom management. The purpose of these discussions is to develop a set of agreements concerning how the class will operate and how teachers and students will work together to make the classroom a pleasant and productive place.

Here are some general guidelines for consultees when they are planning to confer with individual students about their behavior:

1. It is best to have conferences when no other students are around and you can devote 5 minutes or so to the student without being interrupted.
2. Don't sit behind your desk; trappings of authority are likely to increase defensiveness or forced compliance.

3. Strive to listen more than you talk. Tape-record your conferences from time to time to determine the ratio of your talking compared to the student's. Also try to determine the sources of breakdown in communications that sometimes happen.
4. Use open-ended questions more than closed questions, especially when discussing the student's feelings about her classroom experience. (Chapter 3 gives examples of these types of questions.)
5. Avoid asking why the student has engaged in a deviant behavior. Generally, students will say they don't know, or they will deny their responsibility and try to project blame onto others, or they will give you some socially acceptable reason that they hope will satisfy you and won't get them in further trouble.
6. Try to get the student to take the initiative in coming up with a plan to solve the problem. Realize that her plan may reflect her degree of immaturity, so you may need to facilitate the process of working out the details. This parallels the process of collaborative consultation.
7. If the student is reluctant or cannot come up with a plan, suggest some ideas that are acceptable to you and encourage commitment from the student. Sometimes you may have to wait a day or so before deciding on a plan.
8. Never argue with a student. Arguments often turn into heated exchanges and are detrimental to rational problem solving.
9. Note the student's emotions; these often give clues to her feelings. Avoid trapping the child in a logical or emotional corner. Leave an escape route by suggesting options.
10. If you suspect that the student is emotionally distressed beyond what you would expect in the circumstances, you may want to make a referral to the school-based consultant (that is, the psychologist or the counselor) or to the student's parent who may wish to seek his or her own resources for direct service (counseling) or other assistance in understanding the student.

USEFUL GENERALIZATIONS ABOUT BEHAVIOR MANAGEMENT IN THE CLASSROOM

1. Classrooms with good behavioral management are rule-governed. With a few exceptions (such as a highly charismatic or greatly feared teacher), there is a high correlation between rules enforcement and good behavioral control. Students will test new or inconsistent teachers to determine if the rules mean what they say and under what circumstances. Chaotic classrooms are often characterized by students blurting out anything that comes to mind, and teachers responding inconsistently to these random interruptions.

2. Good behavior managers demonstrate a high ratio of positive to negative statements to students.

3. Students need to perceive that teachers have power and are not afraid to use it. The same power bases that were discussed in Chapter 3 for consultant–consultee relationships apply to teacher–student relationships. Teachers should rely primarily on their legitimate, reward, and informational power bases when dealing with students.

4. Ignoring misbehavior is risky. Using extinction as a sole method for dealing with disruptive behavior may be catastrophic. This method needs to be supported by positive contingencies for appropriate behavior and possibly negative contingencies for disruptive behavior. Since reinforcement for most misbehaviors lies either in the reactions of the other students or because of the self-reinforcing nature of the behavior, a teacher who simply ignores the behavior may see a rapid escalation of it.

5. The major determinant of teacher–student interactions is the relationship between them. A positive relationship coupled with a good curriculum and effective motivational techniques goes a long way toward controlling a student's or class's tendency to engage in off-target disruptive behaviors. A powerful tool to help in building this relationship is the use of the whole-class discussions previously mentioned (Charles & Charles, 2004).

6. Power in the classroom can be obtained by either the teacher or the students. It needs to be earned. Gordon's (1974) Method III (win-win) is based on the subtle power of the teacher to control a conference with a student so that the student feels heard, not demeaned, and believes he has the power to change his own behavior.

7. The teacher is the ultimate reinforcer. If the teacher's favor or approval is reinforcing and she capitalizes on this fact, little else is needed (assuming the emotional and neurological integrity of the student). If the teacher's favor is not reinforcing, the student will need an enticing curriculum, effective motivational techniques, self-discipline, or external controls (fear of aversive consequences).

ACTIVITY 6.22

In dyads, with one person being a teacher–consultee and the other a school-based consultant, role-play discussions in which the teacher wants advice about how to deal with behavior problems in the classroom.

SUMMARY

This chapter has presented information about dealing with students who have classroom behavior problems. We reviewed methods of classifying these problems, diagnostic approaches (rating scales, observations, interviews), and general strategies for dealing with the problems. Chapter 9 presents two cases, one of which centers around a student with behavior problems. You will see how the SOCS approach (Chapter 5) and the information presented in this chapter helped school consultants assist school personnel and parents in both of these cases.

REFERENCES

Achenbach, T. M. (1991a). *Manual for the child behavior checklist and revised child behavior profile.* Burlington: University of Vermont, Department of Psychiatry.

Achenbach, T. M. (1991b). *Manual for the teacher's report form and 1991 profile.* Burlington: University of Vermont, Department of Psychiatry.

Achenbach, T. M. (1991c). *Manual for the youth self-report and 1991 profile*. Burlington: University of Vermont, Department of Psychiatry.

Achenbach, T. M., & McConaughy, S. H. (1996). Relations between DSM-IV and empirically based assessment. *School Psychology Review, 25*(3), 329–341.

Achenbach, T. M., & McConaughy, S. H. (1997). *Empirically based assessment of child and adolescent behavior: Practical applications* (2nd ed.). Newbury Park, CA: Sage.

Alberto, P. A., & Troutman, A. C. (1999). *Applied behavior analysis for teachers* (5th ed.). Upper Saddle River, NJ: Merrill/Prentice Hall.

Alessi, G. (1988). Direct observation network for emotional/behavioral problems. In E. S. Shapiro & T. R. Kratochwill (Eds.), *Behavioral assessment in schools: Conceptual foundations and practical applications* (pp. 14–75). New York: Guilford Press.

Alessi, G., & Kaye, J. (1983). *Behavior assessment for school psychologists*. Kent, OH: NASP.

Allen, S. J., & Graden, J. L. (2002). Best practices in collaborative problem solving for intervention design. In A. Thomas & J. Grimes (Eds.), *Best practices in school psychology IV* (pp. 565–582). Bethesda, MD: NASP.

American Psychiatric Association. (1994). *Diagnostic and statistical manual of mental disorders* (4th ed.). Washington, DC: Author.

American Psychiatric Association. (2002). *Psychiatric effects of media violence*. Retrieved [May 26, 2004] from *http://www.psych.org/public_info/media_violence.cfm*.

American Psychological Association. (1994). *Violence and youth: Psychology's response*. Washington, DC: Author.

Atkins, M. S., Pelham, W. E., & Light, M. (1985). A comparison of objective classroom measures and teacher ratings of attention deficit disorder. *Journal of Abnormal Child Psychology, 13,* 155–167.

Barkley, R. (1990). *Attention deficit-hyperactivity disorder: A handbook for diagnosis and treatment*. New York: Guilford Press.

Bauer, A. M., & Sapona, R. H. (1991). *Managing classrooms to facilitate learning*. Boston: Allyn & Bacon.

Benjamin, A. (1987). *The helping interview*. Boston: Houghton Mifflin.

Bergan, J. (1977). *Behavioral consultation*. Columbus, OH: Merrill.

Bergan, J., & Kratochwill, T. (1990). *Behavioral consultation & therapy*. New York: Plenum.

Brown, L. L., & Hammill, D. D. (1990). *Behavior rating profile*. Austin, TX: Pro-Ed.

Buss, A. H., & Plomin, R. (1984). *Temperament: Early developing personality traits*. Hillsdale, NJ: Lawrence Erlbaum.

Carey, W. B. (1998). Temperament and behavior problems in the classroom. *School Psychology Review, 27,* 522–533.

Carey, W. B., & Jablow, M. M. (1997). *Understanding your child's temperament*. New York: Macmillan.

Carr, E. G. (1994). Emerging themes in the functional analysis of problem behavior. *Journal of Applied Behavioral Analysis, 27,* 393–399.

Chandler, L., & Dahlquist, C. (2002). *Functional assessment: Strategies to prevent and remediate challenging behavior in school settings*. Upper Saddle River, NJ: Merrill/Prentice Hall.

Charles, C. M. (2002). *Building classroom discipline* (7th ed.). White Plains, NY: Longman.

Charles, C. M., & Charles, M. G. (2004). *Classroom management for middle-grade teachers*. Boston: Allyn & Bacon.

Charney, R. (1992). *Teaching children to care: Management in the responsive classroom*. Greenfield, MA: Northeast Foundation for Children.

Chess, S., & Thomas, A. (1996). *Know your child*. New Brunswick, NJ: Jason Aronson.

Christenson, S., & Sheridan, S. (2001). *Schools and families: Creating essential connections for learning*. New York: Guilford Press.

Colton, D. L., & Sheridan, S. M. (1998). Conjoint behavioral consultation and social skills training: Enhancing the play behavior of boys with attention deficit hyperactivity disorder. *Journal of Educational and Psychological Consultation, 9,* 3–28.

Conderman, G., & Katsiyannis, A. (1995). Section 504 accommodation plans. *Intervention in school and clinic, 31*(1), 42–45.

Connors, C. K. (1997). *Connors rating scale—revised technical manual*. Toronto: Multi-Health Systems.

Cooper, J. (Ed.). (1999). *Classroom teaching skills*. Boston: Houghton-Mifflin.

Cooper, J., Heron, T., & Heward, W. (1987). *Applied behavior analysis*. Upper Saddle River, NJ: Merrill/Prentice Hall.

Coopersmith, S. (1984). *Self-esteem inventories*. Palo Alto, CA: Consulting Psychologists Press.

Crone, D., & Horner, R. (2003) *Building positive behavior support systems in schools*. New York: Guilford Press.

Davison, J. (1990). The process of school consultation: Give and take. In E. Cole & J. Siegel (Eds.), *Effective consultation in school psychology* (pp. 53–70). Toronto: Hogrefe & Huber.

Deitz, S. (1982). Defining applied behavioral analysis: An historical analogy. *Behavior Analyst, 5*(1), 53–64.

DeVito, J. (2001). *The interpersonal communication book* (9th ed.). New York: Longman.

DeVoe, J., Peter, K., Kaufman, P., Ruddy, S., Miller, A., Planty, M., Synder, T., Duhart, D., & Rand, M. (2002). *Indicators of school crime and safety*. U.S. Departments of Education and Justice. National Center for Educational Statistics. NCES 2003-009/NCJ 196753. Washington, DC.

Drasgow, E., & Yell, M. (2001). Functional behavioral assessment: Legal requirements and challenges. *School Psychology Review, 30,* 239–251.

Dreikurs, R. (1968). *Psychology in the classroom* (2nd ed.). New York: Harper & Row.

Dreikurs, R., & Gray, L. (1995). *Logical consequences*. New York: Penguin-NAL.

Egan, G. (2001). *The skilled helper* (7th ed.). Boston: Houghton Mifflin.

Elliott, S. N., & Gresham, F. M. (1992). *Social skills intervention guide*. Circle Pines, MN: American Guidance Service.

Emmer, E. T., Evertson, C. M., Clements, B. S., & Worsham, M. E. (1994). *Classroom management for secondary teachers*. Boston: Allyn & Bacon.

Epstein, M., & Sharma, J. (1997). *Behavior and emotional rating scale*. Austin, TX: Pro-Ed.

Evans, I. M., & Meyer, L. H. (1985). *An educative approach to behavior problems: A practical decision model for interventions with severely handicapped learners*. Baltimore, MD: Paul H. Brookes.

Evertson, C. M., Emmer, E. T., Clements, B. S., & Worsham, M. E. (1997). *Classroom management for elementary teachers*. Boston: Allyn & Bacon.

Feldhusen, J., Thurston, J., & Benning, J. (1973). A longitudinal study of delinquency and other aspects of children's behavior. *International Journal of Criminology and Penology, 1,* 341–351.

Fisher, R., & Brown, S. (1988). *Getting together*. Boston: Houghton Mifflin.

Fisher, R., & Ury, W. (1991). *Getting to yes: Negotiating agreement without giving in* (2nd ed.). Boston: Houghton Mifflin.

Forness, S., & Knitzer, J. (1992). A new proposed definition and terminology to replace "serious emotional disturbance" in the Individuals with Disabilities Education Act. *School Psychology Review, 21,* 12–20.

Friend, M., & Cook, L. (2003). *Interactions: Collaboration skills for school professionals* (4th ed.). New York: Longman.

Gadow, K., & Sprafkin, J. (1997). *ADHD symptom checklist (ADHD-SC4)*. Austin, TX: Pro-Ed.

Gallagher, P. (1988). *Teaching students with behavior disorders*. Denver: Love Publishing.

Gilliam, J. (1995). *Attention deficit/hyperactivity disorder test*. Austin, TX: Pro-Ed.

Ginott, H. (1971). *Teacher and child*. New York: Macmillan.

Glasser, W. (1969). *Schools without failure*. New York: Harper & Row.

Glasser, W. (1992). *The quality school: Managing students without coercion* (2nd ed.). New York: Harper & Row.

Goldstein, A. P. (1999). *The prepare curriculum*. Champaign, IL: Research Press.

Goldstein, A. P., Spafkin, R. P., Gershaw, N. J., & Klein, P. (1983). Structures learning: A psychoeducational approach for teaching social competencies. *Behavioral Disorders, 8*(3), 161–162.

Gordon, T. (1974). *Teacher effectiveness training*. New York: McKay.

Gordon, T. (1989). *Discipline that works*. New York: Random House.

Gresham, F. (1983). Social validity in the assessment of children's social skills: Establishing standards for social competency. *Journal of Psychoeducational Assessment, 1,* 297–307.

Gresham, F. M. (1991). Whatever happened to functional analysis in behavioral consultation? *Journal of Educational and Psychological Consultation, 2*(4), 387–392.

Gresham, F. M. (2002). Best practices in social skills training. In A. Thomas & J. Grimes (Eds.), *Best practices in school psychology IV* (pp. 1029–1040). Bethesda, MD: NASP.

Gresham, F. M., & Elliott, S. (1990). *Social skills rating system*. Circle Pines, MN: American Guidance Service.

Gresham, F., & Gansle, K. (1992). Misguided assumptions about DSM-III: Implications for school psychological practice. *School Psychology Quarterly, 7,* 79–95.

Gresham, F. M., & Noell, G. H. (1999). Functional analysis assessment as a cornerstone for noncategorical special education. In D. J. Reschly, W. D. Tilly, &

J. P. Grimes (Eds.), *Special education in transition* (pp. 49–80). Longmont, CO: Sopris West.

Gresham, F. M., & Witt, J. C. (1987, October). Practical considerations in the implementation of classroom interventions. Paper presented at the annual meeting of the Oregon School Psychological Association, Eugene.

Hartmann, D., Roper, B., & Bradford, D. (1979). Some relationships between behavioral and traditional assessment. *Journal of Behavioral Assessment, 1,* 3–21.

Hayes, S., Nelson, R., & Jarrett, R. (1986). Evaluating the quality of behavioral assessment. In R. Nelson & S. Hayes (Eds.), *Conceptual foundations of behavioral assessment* (pp. 463–503). New York: Guilford Press.

Hill, J. L. (1999). *Meeting the needs of students with special physical and health care needs.* Upper Saddle River, NJ: Merrill/Prentice Hall.

Hintze, J., Volpe, R., & Shapiro, E. (2002). Best practices in systematic direct observation of student behavior. In A. Thomas & J. Grimes (Eds.), *Best practices in school psychology IV* (pp. 993–1006). Bethesda, MD: NASP.

Homme, L. (1970). *How to use contingency contracting in the classroom.* Champaign, IL: Research Press.

Hughes, J. (1988). *Cognitive behavior therapy with children in schools.* New York: Pergamon.

Hughes, J. N., & Hasbrouck, J. E. (1996). Television violence: Implications for violence prevention. *School Psychology Review, 25*(2), 134–151.

Hunt, N., & Marshall, K. (1999). *Exceptional children and youth.* Boston: Houghton Mifflin.

Hyman, I. (1997). *School discipline and school violence: The teacher variance approach.* Boston: Allyn & Bacon.

Jones, F. (1987). *Positive classroom discipline.* New York: McGraw-Hill.

Jones, F. (2001). *Fred Jones's tools for teaching.* Santa Cruz, CA: Fredric H. Jones and Associates.

Jones, V. J., & Jones, L. S. (2004). *Comprehensive classroom management: Creating communities of support and solving problems* (7th ed.). Boston: Allyn & Bacon.

Kampwirth, T. J. (1988). Behavior management in the classroom. *Education and Treatment of Children, 11*(3), 286–293.

Kanfer, F., & Goldstein, A. (Eds.). (1986). *Helping people change: A textbook of methods.* New York: Pergamon.

Kaplan, J. S. (2000) *Beyond functional assessment.* Austin, TX: Pro-Ed.

Kaplan, P. G., & Hoffman, A. G. (1990). *It's absolutely groovy.* Denver: Love Publishing.

Kauffman, J. M. (2000). *Characteristics of emotional and behavioral disorders of children and youth* (7th ed.). Columbus, OH: Merrill/Prentice Hall.

Kazdin, A. (Ed.). (1985). *Treatment of antisocial behavior in children and adolescents.* Pacific Grove, CA: Brooks/Cole.

Kovacs, M. (1992). *Children's depression inventory.* Los Angeles: Multi-Health Systems.

Kratochwill, T. R. (1982). Advances in behavioral assessment. In C. R. Reynolds & T. R. Gutkin (Eds.), *Handbook of school psychology* (pp. 314–350). New York: Wiley.

Kratochwill, T. R., Van Someren, K. R., & Sheridan, S. M. (1990). Training professional consultants: A competency-based model to teach interview skills. *Professional School Psychology, 4,* 41–58.

Krumboltz, J., & Thoresen, C. (1969). *Behavioral counseling.* New York: Holt, Rinehart, & Winston.

Kuykendall, C. (2003). *From rage to hope: Strategies for reclaiming Black and Hispanic students.* Bloomington, IN: National Education Service.

Kyle, P., & Rogien, L. (2004). *Opportunities and options in classroom management.* Boston: Allyn & Bacon.

Ladson-Billings, G. (2003). *The dreamkeepers: Successful teachers of African American children.* San Francisco: Jossey-Bass.

Lambert, N., Hartsough, C., & Sandoval, J. (1990). *Children's attention and adjustment survey.* Circle Pines, MN: American Guidance Services.

Lehman, C., & Irvin, L. (1996). Support for families with children who have emotional or behavioral disorders. *Education and Treatment of Children, 19*(3), 335–353.

Lentz, F. E., & Wehmann, B. (1995). Best practices in interviewing. In A. Thomas & J. Grimes (Eds.), *Best practices in school psychology III.* Washington, DC: NASP.

Lerner, J. (2000). *Learning disabilities* (8th ed.). Boston: Houghton-Mifflin.

Levin, J., & Nolen, J. (2004). *Principles of classroom management* (4th ed.). Boston: Allyn & Bacon.

Levin, K., & Shanken-Kaye, J. (2002). *From disrupter to achiever: Creating successful learning environments for the self-control classroom.* Dubuque, IA: Kendall-Hunt.

Lieberman, C. (1994). Television and violence. Paper presented at the Council of State Governments Conference on School Violence, Westlake Village, CA.

Long, N., & Morse, W. (1996). *Conflict in the classroom.* Austin, TX: Pro-Ed.

Magg, J. W. (1992). Integrating consultation into social skills training: Implications for practice. *Journal of Educational and Psychological Consultation, 3*(3), 233–258.

Martin, R. (1996). *The temperament assessment battery for children.* Austin, TX: Pro-Ed.

Martin, R., Hooper, S., & Snow, J. (1986). Behavior rating scale approaches to personality assessment in children and adolescents. In H. M. Knoff (Ed.), *The assessment of child and adolescent personality* (pp. 309–351). New York: Guilford Press.

Mash, E., & Terdal, L. (Eds.). (1997). *Assessment of childhood disorders* (3rd ed.). New York: Guilford Press.

Mathews, F. (1992). Re-framing gang violence: A pro-youth strategy. *The Journal of Emotional and Behavioral Problems, 1*(3), 221–230.

McCarney, S. B. (1992). *Emotional or behavior disorder scale.* Columbus, MO: Hawthorne Educational Services.

McCarney, S. B. (1995). *Attention deficit disorders evaluation scale—School version.* Columbus, MO: Hawthorne Educational Services.

McComas, J. J., Hoch, H., & Mace, F. C. (2000). Functional analysis. In E. S. Shapiro & T. R. Kratochwill (Eds.), *Conducting school-based assessments of child and adolescent behavior* (pp. 78–120). New York: Guilford Press.

McConaughy, S. H., & Ritter, D. R. (2002). Best practices in multidimensional assessment of emotional or behavioral disorders. In A. Thomas & J. Grimes (Eds.), *Best practices in school psychology IV* (pp. 1303–1320). Bethesda, MD: NASP.

McDermott, P. (1993). *Adjustment scales for children and adolescents.* Philadelphia, PA: Edumetric and Clinical Science.

Merrill, K. W. (2003). *Behavioral, social, and emotional assessment of children and adolescents* (2nd ed.) Mahwah, NJ: Lawrence Erlbaum Associates.

Merrill, K., & Gimpel, G. (1998). *Social skills of children and adolescents: Conceptualization, assessment and treatment.* Mahwah, NJ: Lawrence Erlbaum Associates.

Metcalf, L. (1999). *Teaching toward solutions.* West Nyack, New York: The Center for Applied Research in Education.

Millon, T., Green, C. J., & Meagher, R. B. (1982). *Millon adolescent personality interview manual.* Minneapolis: National Computer Systems.

Moore, K. (1995). *Classroom teaching skills* (3rd ed.). New York: McGraw-Hill, Inc.

Naglieri, J. A., LeBuffe, P. A., & Pfeiffer, S. I. (1993). *Devereux behavior rating scale—School form.* San Antonio, TX: Psychological Corporation.

National Association of School Psychologists. (1990). *School Psychology Review, 19*(2), whole issue.

National Association of School Psychologists. (1996). *School Psychology Review, 25*(3), whole issue.

Nelson, W. M., III, & Finch, A. J., Jr. (1973). The children's inventory of anger. Unpublished manuscript, Xavier University. Cincinnati, OH.

O'Neil, J. (1991). A generation adrift? *Educational Leadership, 49,* 4–10.

O'Neill, R., Horner, R., Albin, R., Sprague, J., Storey, K., & Newton, J. (1997). *Functional assessment and program development for problem behavior: A practical handbook.* Pacific Grove, CA: Brooks/Cole.

Olds, D., Hill, P., Mihalic, S., & O'Brien, R. (1998). *Blueprints for violence prevention, book seven: Prenatal and infancy home visitation by nurses.* Boulder, CO: Center for the Study and Prevention of Violence.

Olweus, D., & Limber, S. (1999). Bullying prevention program. In S. Elliott (Ed.), *Blueprints for violence prevention.* Boulder, CO: Institute of Behavioral Science, Regents of the University of Colorado.

Ormrod, J. (2000). *Educational psychology: Developing learners* (3rd ed.). Upper Saddle River, NJ: Merrill/Prentice Hall.

Parker, J. G., & Asher, S. R. (1987). Peer relations and later personal adjustment: Are low-accepted children at risk? *Psychological Bulletin, 102,* 357–389.

Patterson, G. R., Chamberlain, P., & Reid, J. (1982). A comparative evaluation of parent training procedures. *Behavior Therapy, 13,* 638–650.

Patterson, G. R., Reid, J., Jones, R. R., & Conger, R. (1975). *A social learning approach to family intervention.* Eugene, OR: Castalia.

Piers, E. V. (1996). *Revised manual for the Piers-Harris children's self-concept scale.* Los Angeles: Western Psychological Services.

Poland, S., Pitcher, G., & Lazarus, P. (2002). Best practices in crisis prevention and management. In A. Thomas & J. Grimes (Eds.), *Best practices in school psychology—IV.* (pp. 1057–1080). Bethesda, MD: NASP.

Porter, R. B., & Cattell. R. B. (1979). *What you do and what you think.* Champaign, IL: Institute for Personality and Ability Testing.

Prasse, D., & Schrag, J. (1999). Providing noncategorical, functional, classroom-based supports for students with disabilities: Legal parameters. In D. Reschly, W. Tilly, & J. Grimes (Eds.), *Special education in transition* (pp. 259–284). Longmont, CD: Sopris West.

Quay, H. C., & Peterson, D. R. (1996). *Manual for the revised behavior problem checklist–PAR version.* Odessa, FL: Psychological Assessment Resources.

Rathvon, N. (1999). Effective school interventions. New York: Guilford Press.

Rehabilitation Act of 1973, Section 504, (1973), 29 U.S.C., 706, 1996; 504 [30 C.F.R.. Part 104].

Reid, J., Eddy, J., Fetrow, R. & Stoolmiller, M. (1999). Description and immediate impacts of a preventative intervention for conduct problems. *American Journal of Community Psychology,* 24(4), 483–517.

Repp, A., & Horner, R. (Eds). (1999). *Functional analysis of problem behavior: From effective assessment to effective support.* Belmont, CA: Wadsworth.

Reynolds, C. R., & Kamphaus, R. W. (1990). *Handbook of psychological and educational assessment of children: Personality, behavior, and context.* New York: Guilford Press.

Reynolds, C. R., & Kamphaus, R. W. (2004). *Behavior assessment system for children-2 (BASC-2).* Circle Pines, MN: American Guidance Service.

Reynolds, C. R., & Richmond, B. O. (1985). *Revised children's manifest anxiety scale (RCMAS).* Los Angeles: Western Psychological Services.

Reynolds, W. (Ed.) (1992). *Internalizing disorders in children and adolescents.* New York: Wiley.

Reynolds, W. M. (1998). *Adolescent psychopathology scale (APS).* Odessa, FL: Psychological Assessment Resources, Inc.

Reynolds, W. M. (2001). *Reynolds adolescent adjustment screening inventory (RAASI).* Odessa, FL: Psychological Assessment Resources, Inc.

Rhodes, G., Jenson, W., & Reavis, H. (1993). *The tough kid book.* Longmont, CO: Sopris West.

Ryser, G., & McConnell, K. (2002). *Scales for diagnosing attention deficit/hyperactivity disorder.* Austin, TX: Pro-Ed.

Sattler, J. (1998). *Clinical and forensic interviewing of children and families.* San Diego, CA: Sattler Press.

Sattler, J. (2001). *Assessment of children: Behavioral and clinical applications* (4th ed.). San Diego: Sattler Press.

Shapiro, E., & Kratochwill, T. (Eds.). (2000). *Conducting school-based assessments of child and adolescent behavior.* New York: Guilford Press.

Sheridan, S. M., & Elliott, S. N. (1991). Behavioral consultation as a process for linking the assessment and treatment of social skills. *Journal of Educational and Psychological Consultation, 2*(2), 151–173.

Skinner, B. (1971). *Beyond freedom and dignity.* New York: Knopf.

Skinner, C. H., Rhymer, K. N., & McDaniel, E. C. (2000). Naturalistic direct observation in educational settings. In E. S. Shapiro & T. R. Kratochwill (Eds.), *Conducting school-based assessment of child and adolescent behavior.* New York: Guilford Press.

Slavin, R. (1997). *Educational psychology: Theory and practice* (5th ed.). Boston: Allyn & Bacon.

Smith, G. (Ed.). (1993). *Public schools that work: Creating community.* New York: Routledge.

Snell, J., MacKenzie, E., & Frey, K. (2002). Bullying prevention in elementary schools: The importance of adult leadership, peer group support, and student social-emotional skills. In M. Shinn, H. Walker, & G. Stoner (Eds.), *Interventions for academic and behavior problems II* (pp. 351–372). Bethesda, MD: NASP.

Sprick, R., & Howard, L. (1995). *The teacher's encyclopedia of behavior management.* Longmont, CO: Sopris West.

Stoff, D., Breiling, J., & Maser, J. (Eds.). (1997). *Handbook of antisocial behavior.* New York: Wiley.

Sugai, G., & Tindal, G. (1993). *Effective school consultation.* Pacific Grove, CA: Brooks/Cole.

Sulzer-Azaroff, B., & Mayer, G. (1986). *Achieving educational excellence.* New York: Holt, Rinehart, & Winston.

Trower, F., Bryant, B., & Argyle, M. (1978). *Social skills and mental health.* Pittsburgh, PA: University of Pittsburgh Press.

Ullmann, L., & Krasner, L. (1965). *Case studies in behavior modification.* New York: Holt, Rinehart, & Winston.

Walker, H., Colvin, G., & Ramsey, E. (1995). *Antisocial behavior in school: Strategies and best practices.* Albany, NY: Brooks/Cole Publishing Co.

Walker, H., & McConnell, S. (1995). *The Walker-McConnell scale of social competence and school adjustment.* Austin, TX: Pro-Ed.

Walker, H., Todis, B., Holmes, D., & Horton, G. (1995). *The Walker social skills curriculum: The ACCESS program.* Austin, TX: Pro-Ed.

Walker, J., & Shea, T. (1999). *Behavior management: A practical approach for educators* (7th ed.). Upper Saddle River, NJ: Merrill/Prentice Hall.

Watson, T., & Steege, M. (2003). *Conducting school-based functional behavioral assessments.* New York: Guilford Press.

Webster-Stratton, C. (1998). Preventing conduct problems in Head Start children: Strengthening parenting competencies. *Journal of Consulting and Clinical Psychology, 66*(5), 715–730.

Widom, C. S. (1989). Does violence beget violence? A critical examination of the literature. *Psychological Bulletin, 106*(1), 3–28.

Wright, D. B., & Gurman, H. B. (1998). *Positive intervention for serious behavior problems* (2nd ed.). Sacramento, CA: RISE.

Wright, F. (1988a). *Behavior disorders identification scale: Home version.* Columbia, MO: Hawthorne Educational Services.

Wright, F. (1988b). *Behavior disorders identification scale: School version.* Columbia, MO: Hawthorne Educational Services.

Ysseldyke, J., & Christenson, S. (2002). *Functional assessment of academic behavior.* Longmont, CO: Sopris West.

Ysseldyke, J., & Marston, D. (1999). Origins of categorical special education services in schools and a rationale for changing them. In D. Reschly, W. Tilly, & J. Grimes (Eds.), *Special education in transition.* Longmont, CO: Sopris West.

Zirpoli, T., & Melloy, K. (2001). *Behavior management: Applications for teachers* (3rd ed.). Upper Saddle River, NJ: Merrill/Prentice Hall.

Consulting About Students with Academic Learning Problems

OBJECTIVES

1. Delineate important variables in school learning.
2. Review the most important reasons for poor learning, and list specific interventions applicable to each reason.
3. Discuss the role of the school consultant in understanding problems in learning, and in developing appropriate interventions.
4. Present a brief example of consulting about problems in learning.
5. List numerous general and specific ideas for interventions in the area of problems in learning.

It is December, and Mrs. Kim, the third-grade teacher, is very concerned about the lack of academic success of four of her students, three boys and a girl. What factors may be causing these four students difficulty in keeping up with their peers and grade-level standards?

Ms. Lopez, the principal at Crossroads Middle School, asks you to talk with her about what she calls the "generalized underachievement" of many students in her school, particularly those students from minority backgrounds. She wants to know what can be done to remedy this situation. How might you, as a school-based consultant, assist Ms. Lopez?

INTRODUCTION

The term *academic learning problems* is used here to refer to any student deficit in academic production that concerns the teacher. The deficit may be in the students' rate of learning, their skill attainment, or the amount and quality of work they produce. It is usually the teacher (but sometimes a parent) who determines whether or not a learning problem exists. Given the wide variations in achievement patterns among U.S. schools, it is quite possible that one teacher could be very concerned about a child who earns a percentile of 40 on a nationally normed test, whereas another teacher could be very pleased with students who earn that score, and certainly would not refer them. Parents, of course, have an important role to play in the referral process, and their influence can determine whether or not a student is referred. There are communities in the United States in which a meeting of the local board of education would be swamped with phone calls from concerned parents if the annual achievement scores reported in the local newspaper indicated a slight drop. In other neighborhoods, however, this level of concern would not be evident. Does this imply that there are more learning problems in the former school district than in the latter? Hardly. It is merely a reflection of the sensitivity of some parents to these issues compared with the more casual, perhaps even passive, acceptance approach found in other communities. This chapter reviews information about variables that contribute to school learning, possible causes for academic learning problems, suggestions for how school-based consultants can help teachers and parents understand these problems, and ideas for what can be done about them, particularly within general education classrooms.

IMPORTANT VARIABLES IN SCHOOL LEARNING

What factors really make a difference in whether students learn well or not? Consultees and other school personnel expect consultants to know about the reasons why some children learn easily while others do not. These reasons may be useful when trying to determine intervention plans.

In an effort to determine variables that influence learning, Wang, Haertel, and Walberg (1993) used three methods—content analysis, expert ratings, and results from meta-analyses—to quantify the existence, importance, and consistency of these variables. Borrowing from the "effective schools" literature (Bickel, 1999; Edmonds, 1979; Purkey & Smith, 1983), Wang et al. (1993) looked at the effects of distal variables (such as school restructuring, types of school organization, and state and local policies) and proximal variables (such as instructional strategies and practices, as well as student aptitudes). In general, their three methods of analysis suggest that the following six theoretical constructs account for the greatest effects on school learning, from most influential to least influential:

1. Student characteristics.
2. Classroom practices.
3. Home and community educational contexts.
4. Design and delivery of curriculum and instruction.
5. School demographics, culture, climate, policies, and practices.
6. State and district governance and organization.

According to Wang et al. (1993), the key proximal variables that influence student learning are psychological, instructional, and home environment. Psychological variables include aptitudes such as cognitive, metacognitive, motivational, and affective. Instructional variables include classroom management techniques and the amount and quality of teacher–learner academic and social interactions. Significant home environment variables are parent attitudes and activities that support school learning and behavior, participation in school activities, and high expectations for student success. The authors summarize their findings by emphasizing the significance of the proximal variables:

> Two major findings from the present review suggest important policy implications: the actions of students, teachers and parents matter most to student learning; policies at the program, school, district, state and federal levels have limited effect compared to the day-to-day efforts of the people who are most involved in students' lives. Knowing that proximal variables have a greater impact on school learning than distal ones, educators, when formulating policies, should be mindful of where they can make the biggest difference in terms of the student, the classroom and the home. (p. 279)

Cohen (cited in Brandt, 1991) maintains that schools should begin restructuring to solve problems by addressing proximal variables, such as curriculum, instruction, and assessment, that emphasize student outcomes. Wang et al. (1993) would certainly agree. These problems are commonly brought to the attention of the school-based consultant, although at the initial referral the emphasis may be elsewhere.

Consider this referral statement: "This student has a learning disability. He needs to be in special education." Once the consultant sorts through this statement, she discovers that it is essentially a request for assistance in curriculum, instruction, and assessment. What is needed is an evaluation of the learning environment, along with an assessment of the student's needs. When the results of both pieces of information are available, the consultant, the consultee, and the school can best assess the consultee's statement that the student needs to be in special education.

Bossert (1985), in reviewing data deriving from the body of research known as the "effective schools research" (Bickel, 1999), indicated that effective schools for all students are characterized by the following:

- A school climate conducive to learning—one free of disciplinary problems and vandalism.
- An expectation among teachers that all students can achieve.
- An emphasis on basic skills instruction and high levels of student time-on-task.
- A system of clear instructional objectives for monitoring and assessing student performance.
- A school principal who is a strong programmatic leader and who sets school goals, maintains student discipline, frequently observes classrooms, and creates incentives for learning. (p. 39).

It is clear that all of these characteristics are closely aligned with what Wang et al. (1993) refer to as proximal variables.

POOR SCHOOL ACHIEVEMENT: NINE REASONS AND SUGGESTED INTERVENTIONS

The goals of assessing an academic problem are to determine the reasons for the problem and to suggest remedial strategies. There is extensive literature on the reasons for school failure (Bloom, 1964; Glaser, 1977; Good & Brophy, 1984; Gordon, 1984; Kampwirth, 1981; Kelly, 1999; Messick & Associates, 1976; Oakes, 1999; Rosenfield, 1987). Nine reasons are presented as to why some students do poorly in school. Consultants should consider each reason as they listen to the consultee and other specialists discuss the student's learning problem and as they progress through the consultation process. Usually more than one of the reasons are responsible for, or related to, the referral problem. The first seven of these reasons are characteristics of individual students; the last two reasons are more closely related to school or community variables that impact on school learning. Following each of the nine reasons are suggested interventions that may assist consultees in dealing with these reasons.

1. Slower-Than-Average Rate of Intellectual Development

It has been long established that individuals differ in their ability to perform the cognitive skills related to academic achievement (Gustafsson & Undheim, 1996). Further, it has been demonstrated for some time that cognitive ability and school achievement are strongly, though not perfectly, related (Brody, 1997). Correlations of 0.6 to 0.7 are commonly found when comprehensive intelligence tests are compared to academic achievement (Salvia & Ysseldyke, 2004; Sattler, 2001). Obviously other factors also play a part in school achievement (Neisser et al., 1996), but students who manifest slower-than-average rates of conceptual understanding, as measured by well-normed intelligence tests, generally have lower academic achievement (and school grades and school completion) across all socioeconomic groups (Reynolds, Lowe, & Saenz, 1999; Sattler, 2001). This is not to imply that there are not problems with the use of IQ tests; their limitations are freely acknowledged in the literature (Figueroa, 1990; Neisser et al., 1996; Reschly & Grimes, 2002; Sattler, 2001; Valde & Figueroa, 1994). Suffice it to say, for the purposes of this discussion, that knowing a student's level of mental ability, whether measured by standard, norm-based instruments or by any of a number of alternative assessment methods (Kaufman, Lichtenberger, & Naglieri, 1999; Lidz, 1987; Reschly & Grimes, 2002), helps us to understand one possible cause for academic difficulties and may be useful in planning for that student.

Suggested interventions:

- Simplify verbal instructions.
- Provide for repetition, review, and rehearsal under varying conditions.
- Use manipulatives, visuals, and concrete aides.
- Increase "wait time," the span of time given to students to respond before moving on to another student.
- Remind students of their past knowledge.
- Model all responses before expecting students to respond.
- Group students heterogeneously, so slower learners can profit from the modeling provided by more adept students.

2. Health and Sensory Factors

Poor vision, hearing, or general health should certainly be looked at as possible contributors to academic deficiencies. The screenings done by school nurses should detect these problems, but in some cases a more thorough evaluation needs to be done. Lynch, Lewis, and Murphy (1993) have demonstrated that children with medical problems are often passive, inattentive, and withdrawn, adding an emotional and motivational issue to their medical condition. If the consultant believes the academic problem may be related to these factors, a physical evaluation of the student should be conducted by qualified personnel.

Suggested interventions:

- Refer to the school nurse and possibly to other health providers.
- Inform parents.
- Accommodate seating and other variables for the student.
- Inquire about food for students who are nutritionally deprived.

3. Motivation

Some students don't do well in school because they are not interested in the curriculum or in the way it is presented, do not believe they can be successful with schoolwork, do not feel a sense of support from home for the importance of school or success in learning, and believe that school success is not as important as success in other aspects of life.

When trying to determine the reasons for academic difficulties, teachers and students often agree that the problem is one of motivation (Hidi & Harackiewicz, 2000). Teachers state that underachievers often do not indicate any interest in the subject matter or with the work required to be successful in that subject; students often comment that they find the work boring or useless, or, in a word, "unmotivating."

Evidence demonstrates that there is a high correlation between motivation and school achievement (Wang et al., 1993; Weinstein, 1998). As with all correlations, it is not clear which variable accounts for most of the correlation. Do children who achieve well do so because of their high motivation, or is some part of their motivation the result of their success in school?

All of us can remember how an inspired teacher made us take an interest in a subject we thought was going to be boring. We can also remember another teacher who took what we thought was going to be an interesting subject and ruined it with a stultifying presentation and/or onerous requirements.

There are numerous reasons for poor motivation:

- Less-than-average mental ability, resulting in difficulty keeping up with the material and a subsequent desire to quit attending to material that seems overwhelming.
- Poor models at home or in the community; parents, siblings, or peers who show little or no interest in school achievement.
- Poor teaching (discussed later in this section).
- Depression (discussed later in this section).
- A poor match between the student's inherent interests and the required curriculum.
- Personal distaste for schooling in general or for particular subjects or teachers.
- Little perceived reinforcement for success.

This last reason for poor motivation has been very influential in the thinking of behaviorists, who take the view that behavior is a function of its antecedents and consequences: If there is little learning, it might be because there is either an inadequate set of antecedent conditions (i.e., curriculum, materials, method, review of previously learned material, encouragement, goal setting, and so on) or no effective reinforcement for it (i.e., meaningful success, acknowledgement for work well done, sensible grading policies, goal attainment, and so on). If the learner does not believe that the consequences of learning are strong enough or immediate enough, she may produce poorer quality work and have less success. Poorer work leads to even less reinforcement, and so the cycle continues.

When education is looked at from a student-centered point of view, the important questions become: What motivates the students to do the work? Why should they do it? Why do some do it and others don't? The usual explanation is that there is an inherent human tendency to want to master the environment, which is the result of a natural curiosity about the ways of the world that can only be satisfied by the accumulation of facts and skills. The expression "Curiosity killed the cat," which is sometimes used to squelch students' desires to understand their world, has a redeeming retort: "But satisfaction brought it back." Further, most students are encouraged by their parents to do well in school; indeed, this seems to be a fairly reliable cultural and developmental expectation that students accept (McLoyd, 1998). Lastly, many teachers have observed a crowd instinct in classrooms: If they can get the class leaders to do the assignments, many other students follow their lead. In other words, some students do schoolwork only because others are doing it. Being gregarious, children tend to do what their peers are doing. For teachers in some schools, the secret to effective work production is to figure out which students hold power among their peers and to get this group to work with them in terms of effort and behavior; then the rest will follow. When these sources of motivation do not seem operative, the teacher may have to resort to the kinds of extrinsic reinforcers previously mentioned.

Suggested interventions:

- Review the subject matter and teaching methods with the student (or the whole class) to determine if there is an apparent problem in either area from their point of view.
- Find ways of getting students involved in the learning tasks; in what ways could the tasks be more meaningful? Pressley (1998) and Gambrell, Morrow, Neuman, and Pressley (1999) indicate that students tend to willingly participate in academic activities that are closely aligned with the social context of their lives.
- Provide a variety of interesting visual material to accompany the ordinary auditory–verbal discussion.
- Provide for cooperative and other group-oriented learning experiences. Allow students choices among different ways of reaching the same educational goals.
- Frequently reinforce efforts, possibly with extrinsic (activity, social) reinforcers.
- If you believe that your failing students are attributing the failures to external causes (e.g., bad luck, teacher discrimination) or to internal causes (e.g., low ability, ethnic heritage), talk to them about these mistaken notions (Marsh & Craven, 1997). Your school counselor may be able to conduct group sessions with underachievers to help them explore their reasons for poor achievement.
- Teach study skills and learning strategies. Pressley and Woloshyn (1995) discuss numerous cognitive-strategy tactics that may be appealing to youngsters who do not automatically construct these strategies for themselves.
- Try to balance the use of anxiety: Some anxiety spurs efforts; too much discourages people from trying.

4. Inability to Concentrate

Attention deficit disorder, with or without hyperactivity as one of its components, is increasingly recognized as a valid and relevant psychoeducational diagnosis (Barkley, 1998). It often accompanies other disabilities such as learning disabilities and emotional disturbance (Hardman, Drew, & Egan, 2002). Although experts and practitioners may disagree about numerous aspects of this condition (Armstrong, 1995), there is little doubt that most educators and psychologists agree that there are some students who don't do well in school because they find it very hard to concentrate and to focus attention on the relevant stimuli in the classroom. This condition is certainly not new; it has been described in the literature for at least 50 years (Barkley, 1998). In the DSM-IV, a diagnosis in this area may result in one of three possibilities: a predominantly inattentive type, a predominantly hyperactive-impulsive type, or a combined type (American Psychiatric Association, 1994).

Any teacher can point to some students in her class who do not attend, have a difficult time concentrating, want to be "on the go" all the time, and often act impulsively. They do not learn well because they aren't attending to the curriculum or classroom expectations. Whether they are able to attend and simply choose not to, perhaps because they would rather be somewhere else (motivational problems), must be decided by those who know the student best and have seen her in a variety of learning situations. If the student appears unable to attend or to remain calm enough to profit from instruction even after modifications to the regular program have been attempted, she should be referred for a medical evaluation, preferably to a pediatrician familiar with the ADHD condition. Perhaps a medical approach to this problem is appropriate and may be a most effective strategy to take along with in-class modifications (Barkley, 1998). Extended suggestions for interventions for students with ADHD and similar conditions can be found in DuPaul and Eckert (1998), Munden and Archelus (2001), and Silver (1999).

Suggested interventions:

- Place students in environments where there are a minimum of distractions.
- Keep the lessons highly structured.
- Use materials that draw attention to the relevant stimuli.
- Have students repeat instructions before getting started on assignments.
- Assign highly distractible or inattentive students to study-buddies who can assist in keeping them on task.
- Find activities that will give hyperactive students something to do, within the confines of task expectations.
- Teach organizational and study skills.
- Try organizing the material into smaller chunks, if feasible.
- Use technology that serves an instructional purpose and doesn't become yet another source of distraction.
- Reinforce all efforts at concentrated work.

5. Emotional and Behavioral Disorders (EBD)

Emotional disturbance has been codified as a category of exceptionality (IDEA, P.L. 108-446). As a category, it requires that a student be identified as eligible for special education and related services only when the IEP team believes that the condition is quite severe and adversely affects educational performance. Students with behavioral disorders that are caused by emotional disturbance are also eligible for services. Some students, due to their constitutional makeup and the circumstances they have endured, seem consistently upset, depressed, or angry with specific people or situations or with the world in general (Bauer & Shea, 1999; Costenbader & Buntaine, 1999; Kauffman, 2001; Long & Morse, 1996; Quay & Werry, 1986; Wicks-Nelson & Israel, 2000). This student typically does not do well in school. He is unable to focus his energies on learning because he is obsessed by whatever is bothering him or determined to flaunt the standards of the classroom. Abused and neglected students, those experiencing the trauma of family conflict and possible divorce, those who have not attained an appropriate level of social skills, and those being raised by parents who have passed on their own disturbed view of the world to their children are all at risk for school failure because of their behavior disorders and/or emotional disturbance (Erickson, 1998; Kauffman, 2001).

More extended information about EBD was presented in Chapter 6.

Suggested interventions:

- Try to maintain a conflict-free classroom; do not let students bully others. Excellent sources of ideas on bullying can be found in Garrity, Jens, Porter, Sager, and Short-Camilli (1994), as well as Rhode, Jenson, and Reavis (1992).
- The teacher may need to find ways of giving students who disturb the classroom a nonpunitive time-out from whatever stress is causing the student to become agitated or withdrawn.
- Refer the student to a school counselor, school psychologist, or perhaps to a local mental health agency.
- Chapter 6 contains many other suggested interventions for students who exhibit behavior disorders.

6. Study Skills and Learning Strategies Deficiencies

When teachers are asked why they think certain students aren't doing well academically, they often respond, "Well, if she'd just study, she'd do fine." Or a parent might say, "He's so disorganized. He can't find anything. Even when he reads the material he doesn't know what to do with it. To him it's all just a big bundle of confusion." Failure to apply oneself through study, or possibly not knowing how to study, has been identified as a major reason for poor academic production, particularly as students enter junior and senior high school (Barron & Associates, 1983; Gleason, Archer, & Colvin, 2002; Perkins, 1995; Phye, 1997). Some study problems may be due to ADD, poor motivation, or emotional disturbance, as previously indicated. School-based consultants need to include some study of a referred student's study methods and habits in order to determine the extent to which problems in this area could be contributing to academic learning difficulties.

Beyond study skills, good learners are characterized by strategic approaches to academic competence. The ability to acquire, memorize, organize, and transform information is typical of those who are academically competent. Students strong in these areas are able to monitor how they study and learn. They are able to process their own cognitive activity, or engage in what is known as metacognition or executive control. Students who have difficulties in these areas are typically low-achieving students.

Suggested interventions:

- Along with teaching content, all teachers should be teaching students how to study the content to ensure integration and retention. Archer and Gleason (2002) list a number of specific suggestions for helping students break down individual polysyllabic words and written material into comprehensive segments. Harvey (2002) has presented a number of suggested interventions in this area, in addition to a list of study skills curriculum materials.
- Note-taking is a skill that is both poorly understood and poorly practiced among underachievers. Kiewra (1991) provides a set of suggestions, including providing skeletal notes before a lecture or chapter reading.
- Have students underline (or copy down) the one or two most important sentences in a body of content. Also, have them write down, after every paragraph or so, one sentence that summarizes what they have just read.
- Stress the necessity of finding quiet time in the class for content study. Parents should also require a quiet time and place for homework.
- Teach your students the *PQ4R* method (Anderson, 1995; Thomas & Robinson, 1972), which is an update of the SQ3R method. The PQ4R method (preview, question, read, reflect, recite, and review) is a valuable aid to those whose approach to textual content is generally disorganized. Friend and Bursick (1999) also recommend the *KWL Plus,* which is a method for helping students think through an assignment based on what they already *know,* what they *want* to know, and, at the end of an assignment, what they have *learned.*
- There is no required curriculum in metacognition in our public schools, although some programs for at-risk students are including this content in their course scheduling for these students. Each teacher, however, is required to teach these skills indirectly by extending the subject material to assist students in learning how to learn the material. Deshler and Schumaker (1988) have developed the Strategic Instruction Model (SIM), which is designed to teach students how to learn, rather than what to learn. Schumaker, Deshler, and McKnight (2002) have presented numerous ideas and strategies to assist students to become more competent learners.

7. Learning Disabilities or Disorders

In this book I am not concerned with the numerous questions and issues that surround the learning disabilities concept, nor do I present refined techniques for diagnosis. There are numerous other sources that are valuable in that area (Bos & Vaughn, 1998; Hallahan & Mercer, 2001; Lerner, 2000).

What will be stressed here is that of all the reasons for poor learning in school, learning disabilities is probably the best-known reason and the one most often cited. Children identified as learning disabled (LD) have now reached up to 4.49% of the total school population (with a range of 2.39% in Kentucky to 7.35% in Massachusetts) and make up more than 50% of all U.S. children identified as having disabilities (Smith, Polloway, Patton & Dowdy, 2004). Growth patterns like this suggest that many children who aren't doing well in school may be considered for, and found to have, a learning disability (Heward, 2000; Lerner, 2000). Advocates for the learning disabled are pleased with this growth because they see it as a recognition of the reality of the condition and an acknowledgement of the needs of these children. Others, however, see this diagnosis as fraught with confusion and inconsistency, and some also believe that special education for children with these mild sorts of learning problems is a convenient escape route for regular educators (Reschly & Ysseldyke, 2002; Salvia & Ysseldyke, 2004; Skrtic, 1991).

There doesn't seem to be any argument about the existence of learning disabilities; the bigger questions today concern how they should be determined, whether or not there is an increase in this diagnosis for social or political reasons, and how and where students with these disabilities should be educated (Baker & Zigmond, 1990; Lerner, 2000; Smith et al., 2004; Will, 1986; Zins, Curtis, Graden, & Ponti, 1988).

Suggested interventions:

- Modify the curriculum to adapt to the student's particular style of learning and responding, to whatever extent this is feasible. Break down tasks, use visual aids, use mnemonics, try study-buddies, apply technology, utilize advance organizers, consider opportunities for cultural infusion, and individualize whenever possible.
- Utilize peer assistance, cooperative groupings, and non-special education school programs designed to remediate learning problems (e.g., Project Read, Reading Recovery).
- Review your concerns with the student's parents and encourage them to assist their child in highly structured ways.
- Reinforce approximations to complete success; don't require perfect papers from those for whom this goal is stress-inducing.
- After the faithful implementation and failure of interventions designed to ameliorate or compensate for a student's academic learning problems, the teacher, consultant, or parent should make a formal referral for assessment in order to determine if the student meets the eligibility criteria for the category of learning disabilities.

8. Cultural, Socioeconomic, and Linguistic Differences

Students from minority backgrounds, particularly those who are English language learners, usually have more difficulty with academic achievement than do Eurocentric or Asian students (Grossman, 1995; Knapp, 1995; McLoyd, 1998; Mullis, Dossey, Foertsch, Jones, & Gentile, 1991). In some inner cities, more than half of the minority students drop out of high school (Rumberger, 1995). Green (2001) has shown that in 1998, the overall graduation rate from American high schools was 74%.

Although 78% of whites graduated, only 56% of African Americans and 54% of Latinos graduated. Asian American students are the major exception to generalizations about the lower achievement of minority students; they typically achieve better than all other minority groups in American schools (Levine & Havighurst, 1989).

McLoyd (1998) suggests that the following factors, which are more common among families of lower socioeconomic status, are related to poor academic achievement:

- Poor health care
- Low expectations—low self-esteem
- Learned helplessness
- Peer influences and resistance cultures
- Tracking
- Child-rearing styles
- Home environment and resources

Two of the previously listed factors, low expectations—low self-esteem and learned helplessness (which is a belief that no matter what one does he is doomed to failure), seem to be reactions to a learning history characterized by negative feedback (Seligman, 1975). As a counter to these reactions or beliefs, Slavin (1997) suggests that teachers accentuate the positive; eliminate the negative; go from familiar to the new, using advance organizers or guided discovery; and create challenges in which students actively create problems and solve them using their own knowledge and skills.

If they are to be successful, consultees who teach students from cultural/ethnic groups different from their own need to determine ways that teachers can use to capitalize on the diverse ways in which their students prefer to learn. Three recent studies (Gunn, Biglan, Smolkowski, & Ary, 2000; Linan-Thompson, Vaughn, Hickman-Davis, & Kouzekanani, 2003; Quiroga, Lemos-Britton, Mostafapour, & Berninger, 2002) have all shown positive effects of instructional interventions with ELL primary-grade students. Nieto (1996) discusses some culture-specific educational accommodations, such as using groups of the same sex with Navajo children, developing more interactive as opposed to didactic methods with African American students, and developing collective responsibility and using peer tutoring and mentoring among Latino youths.

Caplan, Choy, and Whitmore (1992) have shown how home influences on achievement are related to the general success of Asian students. Caplan et al. found that Indo-Chinese high schoolers spent twice as much time on homework than did their native-born American counterparts. Home support for learning can be encouraged by assisting parents who wish to work with their children but aren't sure how. Successful home-based efforts to improve academic achievement can be found in Mehran and White (1988) and Thurston and Dasta (1990).

It is interesting to note, however, that there are exceptions to these generalizations about achievement and cultural/ethnic-SES issues (Baruth & Manning, 1992; National Research Council, 2004). Gleitman, Fridlund, and Reisberg (1999) have shown that when students from different ethnicities and racial groups are compared across SES, their scores are much more similar. There is some evidence that some of the commonly observed differences exist because the instruction given to minority students is not compatible with their cultural backgrounds (Boykin, 1994; Lee, 2001; Vasquez, 1993). Teachers from the middle class may be conditioned to believe that students from lower-SES backgrounds aren't going to be able to achieve well in school. There is evidence showing that teachers who are personally committed to equity and racial justice are less likely to have low expectations and more willing to adjust their instructional methods to meet the needs of their students while still insisting on academic rigor (Ball, 2000; Stodolsky & Grossman, 2000). Trueba, Jacobs, and Kirton (1990) have shown that high school teachers of English have low expectations of Latino students. Their study shows that these students were quite capable of higher-level work when they saw the connection between the assignments and their out-of-school lives.

The data on reading and math presented by the National Assessment of Educational Progress (NAEP) indicated that, on average, Latino and African American 17-year-olds read about as well as white 13-year-olds (National Center for Educational Statistics, 2002). The current results in math are very similar. Most recently, the U.S. Department of Education secretary, Rod Paige, expressed his dismay at the widening gap between the best and worst fourth-grade readers based on the NAEP results for the year 2000, which indicated that virtually no change has been made in the scores of the poorest readers, who tend to be African Americans and Hispanics. These results prompted Secretary Paige to say, "After spending $125 billion [of assistance to schools in the area of remedial reading]...over 25 years, we have virtually nothing to show for it" (Helfand & Groves, 2001).

Suggested interventions:

- When working with English language learners, make sure that oral presentations to them are comprehensible. Repeat key phrases and emphasize important vocabulary. Increase wait time.
- Increase the use of visual aids.
- Adapt materials as appropriate.
- Accept answers based on content, not perfection of English grammar.
- Use examples from all the different racial and ethnic groups represented in the classroom.
- Avoid tracking, which can lead to resegregation (Schofield, 1995; Slavin, 1995).
- Use cooperative learning as often as possible. It can lead to greater participation of minority students.
- When grouping students from different racial and ethnic groups for classwork, provide a structure and common goals that will require the various groups to work together. Proximity alone does not ensure social harmony (Slavin, 1997).
- Peer tutoring has been found to be of great assistance in helping at-risk students from all SES groups (Greenwood, Delquadri, & Carta, 1997; Topping & Ehly, 1998).

9. Attendance at Schools with Chronic Underachievement

One of the major thrusts of the No Child Left Behind legislation (2001) is to provide support for schools that consistently underperform. It is an unfortunate reality that most of these schools are in neighborhoods that consist largely of students of minority backgrounds. One of the options given to parents in underachieving schools is to move their children to better schools in the community within guidelines established by each state and district. This legislation is designed to encourage districts to take strong action to improve their schools, with the goal being that no parent should feel the need to move his or her child to a different school. This is where the work of school consultants can have a powerful impact: To what extent is a consultant able to help a school that is underachieving? Given all the roles, skills, and activities described in this text, it should be clear that a school consultant can be at the forefront of assistance both at the individual teacher/student level, and, as described in Chapter 8, at the systems improvement level.

Wang, Haertel, and Walberg (1995) indicate four research-based practices that are characteristic of schools that promote resilience, a characteristic of students who are successful in spite of adverse environmental conditions. These are:

- High and uncompromising academic standards;
- Strong personal bonds between students and teachers;
- Order and high structure; and
- Opportunities for participation in after-school activities.

One of the reasons for poor achievement and motivation is what some students and parents regard as poor teaching. If a student comes to school with a poor foundation for learning because his parents either couldn't or didn't provide a good set of pre-school experiences at home or in a formal preschool, that student may get off to a poor start and may have difficulty catching up with curriculum expectations.

Some students learn well only when being very carefully taught. This was the whole basis for the separate special education system that dominated the education of students with disabilities for many decades (Smith, Polloway, Patton, & Dowdy, 2004). It was believed that if children weren't learning well in the general program, they would do better if they had a modified curriculum, specially trained teachers, and, if necessary, special equipment. Now, however, many leaders in the special education field are saying the opposite: The thrust is to keep all children in the general education program and to require general and special educators to collaboratively design and carry out effective programs in the general education setting (Heron & Harris, 2001; Smith et al., 2004; Stainback & Stainback, 1987). The implications are tremendous: Excellent teaching of all students will now be required, and those who need modifications will no longer be assigned to either self-contained or part-time special education classes. General education teachers will be expected to keep students with learning problems in their classrooms. How will they learn to be successful with them? We hope these teachers will learn through changes in preservice education and a wider acceptance of consultants, who can assist them in finding ways to modify their curriculum, expectations, and methods (Dettmer, Dyck, & Thurston, 1999; Friend & Cook, 2003; Heron & Harris, 2001; Idol, Nevin, & Paolucci-Whitcomb, 2000; Mayen, Vergason, & Whelan, 1996; Rosenfield & Gravois, 1996; Salend, 1998).

Whether the student is in general or special education, what she will get from the experience depends on the skills and knowledge base of the teachers. In addition to knowing their content areas and child/adolescent development, teachers need to be aware of and utilize effective teaching practices. Darling-Hammond (1996) has summarized seven necessary practices of good teachers:

1. Provide work that is regarded as meaningful to the students.
2. Give students choices that are within the limits of the curriculum goals and behavioral constraints of the classroom.
3. Give equal thought to student output as well as teacher input.
4. Assess, monitor, and teach to the student's strengths, and review.
5. Utilize learning experiences that scaffold or mediate students' learning.
6. Build strong relationships with students and their families.
7. Develop students' confidence.

At the level of the individual lesson, Slavin (1997) recommends the following steps:

1. State learning objectives and orient students to the lesson.
2. Review prerequisites.
3. Present new material.
4. Conduct learning probes (i.e., pose questions to students to assess their level of comprehension and to modify your presentation accordingly).
5. Provide independent practice.
6. Assess performance and provide feedback.
7. Provide distributed practice and review.

Suggested interventions:

- Assist the teacher by reviewing his methods, materials, and goals. The FAAB system (Ysseldyke & Christenson, 2002), described later in this chapter, gives a highly structured outline for making classroom observations that can lead to positive improvements in teacher behavior.
- Introduce the teacher to a variety of good ideas that are relatively simple to use.
- Assist the teacher by modeling lessons or engaging in cooperative activities with the teacher or through collaborations with other teachers.
- Consider obtaining the assistance of others, such as the principal, mentor teachers, or a curriculum specialist.

Additional ideas about improvements in curriculum and method are found later in this chapter.

ACTIVITY 7.1

The reasons given previously may not cover all possible reasons for poor learning. Readers may be aware of others that are not included or implied by the previous list. What are some other reasons for poor school achievement? What interventions might be appropriate?

SORTING THROUGH REASONS FOR POOR ACHIEVEMENT

The school consultant looks at these nine somewhat overlapping reasons for poor learning to see what possible contribution they may be having to the referral problem. As the cases in Chapter 9 demonstrate, our ability to understand referral problems and ameliorate them may lie in our understanding of the interplay of these reasons, as well as the influences of psychodynamic, ecological, or biophysical factors that can have a strong effect on behavior and academic learning. Also, our own philosophical beliefs influence how we approach referrals. Some people look to psychodynamics almost exclusively. Others are wedded to curriculum-based measurement to the exclusion of other assessment considerations. Others prefer rational–emotive behavior therapy (Ellis, 1995) or behavior modification or process training. I hope that school-based consultants will keep an open mind regarding causes and assistive strategies and will not become overly restrictive in their views.

Together, the consultant, teachers, and parents of the referred student evaluate the relative contribution of the nine reasons for poor learning previously given. Consider, for example, these referrals from a third-grade teacher. She has two students of the same age with reading problems. The standard scores in total reading for these two students are about 85, in a school in which the average standard score is about 100. The consultant may find that, in one case, the student is of somewhat limited mental ability (verbal and nonverbal IQs are both about 85), demonstrates a moderate and uncorrected hearing loss in both ears, achieves poorly in all academic areas, and comes from a home in which neither parent graduated from high school and neither worries too much about academic success since everyday problems of economic coping have a higher priority. In the second case, the student has an IQ of about 115 (verbal 100, performance 130), is hyperactive and impulsive, but does very well in math and art. His parents, both college graduates, have insisted on no special education assistance for their boy since the first grade. It is clear from the information that we have on these two referrals that the reasons for poor achievement in reading vary considerably, as should the interventions suggested for each case.

ACTIVITY 7.2

How might a school-based consultant approach each of the two situations just described? What other information would he need before he could help the SST and the parents deal with each child's below-grade-level reading achievement?

Chapter 1 discusses the consultee as a variable in the consultation process. I pointed out that consultees manifest both expectations and preferences (Brown, Pryzwansky, & Schulte, 2001). When working on cases involving academic problems, the consultant needs to consider the preferences of the consultees. De Mesquita and Zollman (1995) discuss possible intervention strategies in mathematics and indicate that some consultees prefer one or a combination of instructional interventions. One possibility they studied with primary-grade teachers was a cognitive approach (having the student use manipulatives, engaging in self-talk, using real-world props, and so on). Another was a behavioral approach (largely manifested by manipulation of reinforcers: material, activity, or social). A third was a cooperative/peer learning approach (grouping arrangements, peer assistance). In contrast to consultation for behavior/adjustment problems, in which behavioral approaches are generally favored, consultee preferences about academic problems in this study were primarily for cognitive and cooperative/peer learning approaches. Although much work has been done regarding consultee preferences for dealing with behavioral problems, we need more research evidence for consultee beliefs about the reasons for academic problems and their preferences for dealing with these problems (Johnson & Pugach, 1996; Rosenfield, 1987; Rosenfield & Gravois, 1996).

ASSESSMENT OF THE CLASSROOM AS A LEARNING ENVIRONMENT

One of the reasons for poor learning previously discussed is a student's attendance at a school that doesn't foster high achievement. A school consultant, when making classroom observations or interviewing teachers about their teaching practices, may come upon situations that suggest that at least part of the student's difficulties may be due to poor classroom practices. Consulting about the classroom ecology, including the instructional process, has gained increased interest since the publication of Sylvia Rosenfield's (1987) *Instructional Consultation* and her subsequent *Instructional Consultation Teams* (Rosenfield & Gravois, 1996). Rosenfield believes that mismatches between the learner's capabilities and the curriculum constitute the basis for most learning problem referrals. Rather than viewing the problem as one inherent to the student (such as LD, or minority status), she believes it is more useful to examine the dynamic interaction of the learner, the setting, teaching methods, and the curriculum. As such, this is primarily an ecologically oriented approach to assessment and intervention. She stresses classroom observation and curriculum-based assessment as opposed to extensive norm-based assessment. Her teacher interview style is similar to Bergan and Kratochwill's (1990). The tasks that are collaboratively designed and carried out by the teacher and the consultant are task analysis, process analysis, error analysis, designing instructional interventions, and managing the learning environment for the student.

Questions to be answered when observing a classroom might include the following:

- What are the students doing during instructional time? What demands or expectations does the teacher have for their performance? How do they communicate their understanding of the material?

- When teaching is not teacher-directed, what are the students doing, individually or with others? What keeps them on task? What can be done when they are off task?
- What does the classroom look like? Are child products prominently displayed? Are there many different prompts or motivators for reading? Are activity areas kept fresh and inviting?

A second source of information about ways to approach classroom diagnosis is presented by Ysseldyke and Christenson (2002) in their *Functional Assessment of Academic Behavior* (FAAB) which can serve as a framework for studying the interaction between a student and her learning environment. In this system, the consultant uses a set of interview and observation forms designed to gather information on 12 instructional environment components, 5 home-support-for-learning components, and 6 home–school-support-for-learning components.

After a FAAB evaluation has been conducted, the steps for using the information are similar to the steps used in all consultation models, including SOCS, presented earlier in this text. FAAB results in a set of statements about the extent to which the student is being exposed to an effective and supportive instructional system, both at school and at home. It results in a global picture of what is happening to assist the student's learning. Based on this information the teacher and consultant can begin to develop interventions that may be student specific or be more directed to how the classroom or home environment can be modified to support the student's learning.

A third source of ideas about how to assess classroom instruction is provided by Slavin (1997), who borrowed his ideas from a very important, albeit dated, model of school learning presented by Carroll (1963). Slavin uses the acronym QAIT to refer to the four alterable aspects of Carroll's model:

- ***Q****uality of Instruction.* Does the presentation offer a challenge while ensuring students' ability to learn the material?
- ***A****ppropriate Levels of Instruction.* Is the material neither too hard nor too easy?
- ***I****ncentive.* How does the teacher ensure that the students are motivated to learn the material?
- ***T****ime.* Is sufficient time devoted to instruction and skill-building activities?

Numerous texts and journal articles have been devoted to issues regarding classroom dynamics as they relate to student learning. Interested readers may want to see Eggen and Kauchak (2004), Freiberg and Driscoll (1992), Gettinger and Stoiber (1999), Moore (1995), and Ormrod (2000, especially Chapter 15).

ASSESSMENT OF THE STUDENT AS A LEARNER

The degree to which a school consultant will do an individual assessment of a referred student is dependent on a number of factors, such as the consultant's other roles in the school, the availability of other professionals to do assessments, time considerations, and other variables of the setting in which one works. The following model, the RIOT, breaks the assessment process into four subparts.

Each consultant decides for himself or herself which parts of the following are appropriate in each case.

RIOT is an acronym that stands for:

***R**ecords review.* The consultant often starts an analysis of a referral with a look at the cumulative folder, and the special education folder if there is one. These documents should give some indication of the student's past history of grades, standardized test scores, and teacher comments. Portfolio materials may also be available. In the case of a student assigned to special education, there may be documentation of functional behavioral assessments and positive behavioral intervention plans, in addition to previous formal assessments and the IEP itself.

***I**nterview.* Techniques for interviewing consultees and other adults were discussed in Chapter 3. A student referred for difficulties in learning and/or achievement can also contribute to the database regarding causes, symptoms, and possible interventions by providing information through a structured or informal interview. Figure 7.1 indicates some possible questions that might be asked in the case of an achievement problem. Sattler (1998) provides an extensive interview format for children and adolescents with learning problems (pp. 942–944),

Figure 7.1

Sample interview questions for a student referred because of an achievement problem

Hello ____________; my name is ____________.

I am the ____________ here at ____________ school.

I'd like to talk to you about school, especially about ways that we can help you get better at some of your schoolwork.

If I ask you a question that you don't understand or can't answer, tell me and I'll try to ask it in another way.

Tell me about school in general. What are some of the parts of school that you like the best?

What are some subjects you don't like so well? What is it you don't like about ____________?

(Focusing on the referral areas): What happens when you try ____________?

What are some of the parts of ____________ that seem difficult for you?

What are some things people have done to help you with ____________?

Do you feel they helped you?

What are some ways you have found that make ____________ go better or easier for you?

What would you like us at school to do to help you with ____________?

Are there any questions you want to ask me about school?

as well as a sentence completion technique for generating hypotheses about students' feelings about their academic work (p. 410).

Observation. Look at the student's efforts at work completion and the whole-class atmosphere for learning. The referring teacher(s) can provide samples of the student's work. These are particularly helpful if an historical pattern can be generated. Schools' increasing use of portfolios should be a rich source of archival data for students as they progress through the grades. The consultant will also want to make one or more classroom observations in order to see the referred student as she goes through her efforts to accommodate to expectations. The observation is also intended to give the consultant a picture of the ecological aspects of the classroom setting. The FAAB instrument, previously reviewed, is an excellent tool for giving structure to this aspect of assessment.

Testing. This may be both formal and informal. Although it is entirely possible that a referral for a learning problem may be resolved without test data, it is not common. Usually all parties will need to know specifies about a student's achievement levels, specific skill deficits, and approaches to academic tasks before being able to generate effective interventions. A blend of norm-based and informal (e.g., informal reading inventories, classroom-based assessments, curriculum-based assessments) methods may be chosen, depending on the situation. Details about testing procedures can be found in Cohen, Swerdlik, and Smith (1992), Salvia and Ysseldyke (2004), Sattler (2001), Shapiro (1989), and Shinn (1998).

Here is an outline of questions and suggestions for conducting the RIOT assessment, which may apply to either a learning or a behavior/adjustment problem.

1. Refine the reason for referral. What do the consultees really want to find out? What exactly are the learning or behavior adjustment problems? Get diagnostic information (for example, typical in-class behaviors; typical behavioral difficulties) from the referring party.

2. Is this referral a 3-year reevaluation? If so, update the progress of the student in the special education program that has been provided during the last year and since the last complete evaluation. Data should be available on the student's attainment of the IEP goals and objectives. Use an interview plus a review of the student's records and whatever testing data are necessary.

3. What are the goals of this assessment? These are usually the goals of the referring person and other interested parties (the parent, yourself, the student). Some systems put goal statements in their reports—for example, "The purpose of this assessment is to determine the reasons for the student's slow reading progress" or "One of the purposes of this assessment is to determine the amount of improvement in the student's math ability." These goal statements add focus to the assessment.

4. Once you've determined what the problems and goals are, determine sources of information that will clarify the problems and achieve the goals. Again, use all four aspects of the RIOT.

5. You probably should start with some observation of the student in an important area without letting the student know you are observing her. Discuss with the teacher how he wants you to observe in his classroom. If he has no preference,

observe as a participant: Circulate around the room, observing how all the students react to the materials. This gives you a frame of reference against which to judge the behavior/responses of the referred student.

If possible, try to get the teacher to show you what is being done currently to deal with the student's learning problem. Again, try to have this done unobtrusively.

Be sure to have something positive to say to the teacher about his work after every observation. This requires you to become a good observer of what people are doing well. Be sincere, of course.

6. Discuss your observations with the teacher. Was this a typical day? If not, what is? How is the current intervention working? If not well, how does the teacher want to change it? What else is needed?

7. Presumably the referral (if original, not a 3-year) is made because the student isn't progressing adequately. This stimulates questions such as:

a. What are the interventions the teacher is trying?
b. How well are they being done?
c. How might they be improved?
d. Is the teacher amenable to assistance? Is she willing to try things?
e. What can you offer? This is the point at which consultation often spins off from assessment and becomes the collaborative problem-solving process described throughout this text.

CONSULTATION ABOUT ACADEMIC PROBLEMS: A BRIEF EXAMPLE

Chapter 9 contains an extensive case study (Maria) demonstrating how a school-based consultant might deal with a complicated case of academic problems using the SOCS format described in Chapter 5. The following is a brief example demonstrating how consultants can help teachers in simpler and more typical referrals.

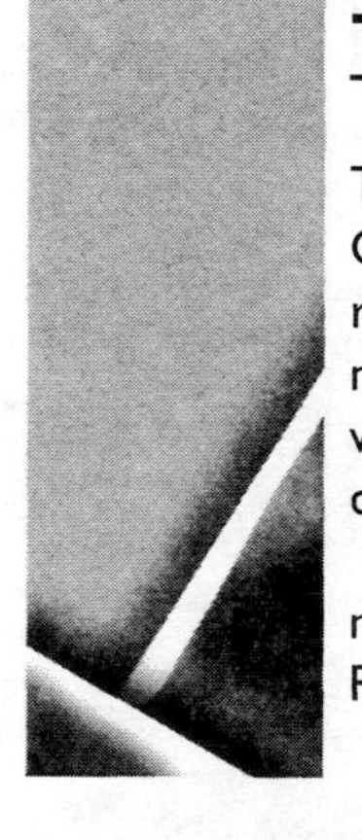

Third Grade: Poor Reading

The teacher–consultee, Ms. DeSousa, refers a boy, Ahmed, to the school SST in October because he is lagging in his reading development. The coordinator of the SST refers the case to Mr. Lee, the resource specialist, and appoints him to be the case manager (consultant). In this district, the case manager attempts to solve the case without having to refer it to the whole SST but will refer back to the team when it is clear that he cannot solve it without assistance.

Mr. Lee visits with Ms. DeSousa and reviews the facts. Ahmed has always been near the bottom of his class (cumulative folder information). He was given some Reading Recovery assistance in first grade, which seemed to provide some temporary help, but no other help since. Now he is in the bottom of Ms. DeSousa's three groups and is not doing well. He is becoming reluctant to read. Together, the consultant and the consultee decide that Mr. Lee will do an informal reading assessment (IRI, CBA, and a phonics survey) and a review of Ahmed's health and family status.

Mr. Lee finds that Ahmed knows most of his phonics facts but seems slow at blending known sounds. He is at a frustration level of 3.1 and an instructional level of 2.1, about a year behind his age expectancy. He is considered to be of about average ability (based on the conversation with him and his math achievement) and has no sensory or other health problems. His family is intact and concerned.

Based on this information, the consultant does not suspect a learning disability but believes that Ahmed may be what Stanovich (2000) refers to as a "garden-variety poor reader," one who has a developmental delay that will most likely remit with age and extra attention but does not constitute a serious problem requiring special education. The consultant (Mr. Lee) and consultee (Ms. DeSousa) decide to try the following:

1. Specify the phonics rules still unmastered, locate materials for teaching them, and enlist the aide of a cross-age tutor to spend 15 minutes a day three times a week with Ahmed (and two others who need similar help) in Mr. Lee's room.

2. Review the referral and Mr. Lee's findings with Ahmed's parents and enlist their aid with structured reading practice at home using books at Ahmed's instructional level (Christenson & Conoley, 1992; Swap, 1993). Appropriate books can be determined from a list provided by Ms. Carlo and are available either from the local library or from her (Monson, 1985). Mr. Lee will work with Ahmed's mother on methods for assisting the child at home (Callahan, Rademacher, & Hildreth, 1998). Ahmed's dad works the evening shift but agrees to help on the weekend with this problem.

3. Ms. DeSousa agrees to find materials with which her lowest group can be more successful—for example, stories geared toward a beginning second-grade level. She is put in contact with the district curriculum director for assistance with this task. She also appoints one of her more mature students, who is a good reader, to monitor the seatwork activities of this low group while Ms. DeSousa is working with her other groups. One of the tasks of this monitor is to keep a record of all the words this group has trouble with. These are then put on flashcards, and Ms. DeSousa designs a series of games to reinforce the practice of these words (Ekwall, 1988; Lerner, 2000). The monitor and the cross-age tutor play the games with the group.

Two months later, the parents, the teacher, and Ahmed all report that there has been much improvement. Most of the members of the low group have increased their reading levels and speeds. The cross-age tutor is assigned to another classroom; the low group monitors itself; parents continue helping at home and provide weekly library trips; and the consultant writes a summary statement for Ahmed's cumulative folder and reports to the SST coordinator that this case is on hold for now. No further interventions are planned.

GENERAL IDEAS ABOUT INTERVENTIONS FOR PROBLEMS IN ACADEMIC LEARNING

The school-based consultant is often asked to assist consultees in planning programs for students who are at risk for academic failure. These students may be in general or special education. No matter the setting or circumstance, these students are not doing well academically relative to their peers or their own expected levels of performance based on their measured or estimated ability. The hope is that their teachers will ask for help from the school-based consultant and work collaboratively with her, the SST, or other service delivery personnel or systems to ensure the development of new approaches for these students. The consultant should be working to get past the attitude that the problem always lies within the child (or his parents), and to replace that with the idea that modifications of curriculum, method, and motivational strategies can be very effective in assisting students to do better in school.

Earlier in this chapter, in the section on reasons for poor achievement, there were many specific ideas following each of the nine reasons discussed. Additional ideas that consultants have found useful in their work with consultees who are working with underachieving students follow. These ideas have been taken from a wide variety of sources (Berninger, 2002; Bos & Vaughn, 1998; Choate, 1993; Eggen & Kauchak, 2004; Fisher, Schumaker, & Deshler, 1996; Jones, 1987; Mayen et al., 1996; McCarney & Cummins, 1988; Munson, 1987; Rathvon, 1999; Salend, 1998; Shinn, Walker, & Stoner, 2002; Zins et al., 1988).

Curricular modifications:

1. Select content that matches the local curricular standards and the interests and needs of the students.
2. Clarify daily, weekly, and monthly goals.
3. Use enrichment activities designed to heighten interest.
4. Design expectations so that students can be successful 70 to 100% of the time.
5. Avoid reading material that is at the students' frustration level unless others (for example, peer-assisted learning, cooperative groups, and so on) are able to assist them.
6. While holding high standards, avoid overwhelming at-risk students with work requirements that appear too difficult or too much.

Modifications of teaching methods:

1. Try to increase what is variously known as academic engaged time, academic learning time, or time on task (TOT). These phrases all refer to the necessity of keeping students actively engaged with the curriculum. One way of ensuring increased TOT is close monitoring of what the students are doing. Greenwood (1996) and Gettinger and Seibert (2002) have found that high rates of monitoring correlate well with academic achievement in all grades.

2. Focus attention on the relevant stimuli. Determine the key elements of any lesson and stress them. Teach at-risk students the LISTEN approach (Bauwens & Hourcade, 1989): When the teacher says, "Listen, please," the students should do the following:

Listen to the teacher.

Idle their motor.

Sit up straight.

Turn toward the teacher.

Engage their brain.

Now . . . [follow instructions and so on].

3. Use outlines, semantic organizers, webs, highlighted materials, think-pair-share, visual aids, interactive methods, and so on (Cooper, 1999; Eggen & Kauchak, 2004).

4. Provide taped lessons, calculators, computer-assisted instructional materials, overheads, and other technology as available.

5. Provide easy access to cues (for example, there = a place (usually); *their* = ownership).

6. Give more examples before starting work (for example, "For those ready to begin, go ahead; if you want more examples, LISTEN").

7. Think of concrete examples that are relevant to the students' experience and ask the students for examples.

8. Alter your voice to emphasize points. When students get noisy, speak in a quiet voice; this often (but not always) encourages students to quiet down.

9. Demonstrate (model) correct responding; have students do the same.

10. Always use at least two modalities (for example, visual and auditory) and, when appropriate, others. For example, when teaching about the colonial states, tell the students about them, show them on a map, have the students draw their own maps, and then have different students represent different states and stand together (kinesthetic modality) to show their geographical relationship to one another.

11. Give students more time to respond. In some cultures, rapid responding is not a value. Also, remember that many at-risk students process information slowly; don't rush them. Further, students who are anxious tend to block when they feel rushed. Give them time to respond. Tobin (1987) reviewed the findings on wait time, the time that elapses between a teacher's questions and a student's opportunity to respond. Teachers who require at least a 3-second wait time receive more thorough answers and get more students to respond. The answers also tend to be correct more often and be more sophisticated. Good and Brophy (2000) have reviewed the literature in this area.

12. Allow many ways to report information: oral, written, acted out, conveyed through another person, multiple choice, essay, tape-recorded, computer-generated, and so on.

13. Be explicit in the use of reinforcement. Tie it to specific actions and identify the actions. For example, "I like the way you were careful with your paper heading. It looks good. Would you like to show it to the rest of the class?" Remember, accept a "no" answer; not all students like to show off their work.

14. Many poor learners lack the metacognitive skills that seem to automatically occur among good learners: for example, study skills, attending to relevant stimuli, keeping on task, being organized, thinking about how they are thinking, having materials, proofreading, skimming, identifying important information, using reference skills, and so on. These need to be identified and, very often, directly taught.

15. Task-analyze your lesson plans by breaking down your expectations and thinking through the steps you'll need to cover, the sequence of these steps, the skills the students need to have mastered in order to be able to do each of the steps, and the possible trouble points, those places in the task that are most likely to produce a breakdown in the process.

16. Design the classroom to avoid traffic problems and enhance your ability to get from one part of the class to another to provide support and avoid behavioral problems. Jones (1987) gives numerous examples of recommended seating plans for different subjects and groupings of students.

17. Use cooperative learning whenever possible, especially in the content areas of social studies, science, and English. There is considerable evidence indicating the benefits of this approach (Dugan et al., 1995; Fantuzzo, King, & Heller, 1992; Greenwood, Maheady, & Delquadri, 2002; Haynes & Gebreyesus, 1992; Nastasi & Clements, 1991; Slavin, 1995).

Placement options:

1. Always consider the general education class ideal unless proven otherwise.
2. Special education should be considered as an option only when the possible range of methods that can be used in the general education program have been demonstrated to be insufficient for a student. The IEP team may admit a student to special education with the full intention of continuing his education in a general setting with collaborative help from a school consultant.
3. Grade-level retention does not have a good track record. Usually, students held back a year do not do any better academically than students of equal achievement levels who are promoted. Often, retained students do poorer socially than do their promoted peers, especially in the junior high years (McCoy & Reynolds, 1999; Rafoth, 2002).
4. Short-term, pull-out remedial programs seem beneficial for some students but not for others. It is not clear why this is so. For any student who manifests skill deficiencies, these programs (for example, Reading Recovery, Project Read, LANGUAGE!) are worth trying, but at-risk students also need to receive the benefit of many of the curricular and methodological modifications mentioned in this chapter that can be utilized in the general education setting.

SUMMARY

This chapter has reviewed some of the variables (for example, psychological, instructional, and home environment) that interact to influence students' academic status. Also reviewed were reasons for poor learning, the role of the school-based consultant, and instructional environment and home-support components of school learning. A brief example of instructional consultation was presented, and the chapter concluded with a list of recommendations that school-based consultants will find useful.

REFERENCES

American Psychiatric Association. (1994). *Diagnostic and statistical manual* (4th ed.). Washington, DC: Author.

Anderson, J. (1995). *Cognitive psychology and its implications* (4th ed.). New York: Freeman.

Archer, A., & Gleason, M. (2002). *Study skills for school success (teacher guides and student workbooks, grades 3–6).* North Billerica, MA: Curriculum Associates.

Armstrong, T. (1995). *The myth of the ADD child.* New York: Dutton.

Baker, J., & Zigmond, N. (1990). Are regular education classes equipped to accommodate students with learning disabilities? *Exceptional Children, 56,* 515–526.

Ball, A. (2000). Preparing teachers for diversity: Lessons learned from the U.S. and South Africa. *Teaching and Teacher Education, 16,* 491–509.

Barkley, R. (1998). *Attention-deficit hyperactivity disorder: A handbook for diagnosis and treatment.* New York: Guilford Press.

Barron, B. G., & Associates. (1983). Study skills: A new look. *Reading Improvement, 20,* 329–332.

Baruth, L. G., & Manning, M. L. (1992). *Multicultural education of children and adolescents.* Boston: Allyn & Bacon.

Bauer, A., & Shea, T. (1999). *Learners with emotional and behavioral disorders.* Upper Saddle River, NJ: Merrill/Prentice Hall.

Bauwens, J., & Hourcade, J. J. (1989). Hey, would you just listen? *Teaching Exceptional Children, 21,* 61.

Bergan, J. R., & Kratochwill, T. R. (1990). *Behavioral consultation and therapy.* New York: Plenum.

Berninger, V. (2002). Best practices in reading, writing, and math assessment-intervention links: A systems approach for schools, classroom, and individuals. In A. Thomas & J. Grimes (Eds.), *Best practices in school psychology IV* (pp. 851–866). Bethesda, MD: NASP.

Bickel, W. (1999). The implications of the effective schools literature for school restructuring. In C. Reynolds & T. Gutkin (Eds.), *The handbook of school psychology* (3rd ed., pp. 959–983). New York: Wiley.

Bloom, B. (1964). *Human characteristics and school learning.* New York: Wiley.

Bos, C., & Vaughn, S. (1998). *Teaching students with learning and behavior problems* (4th ed.). Boston: Allyn & Bacon.

Bossert, S. (1985). Effective elementary schools. In R. M. J. Kyle (Ed.), *Reaching for excellence: An effective schools sourcebook.* Washington, DC: E. H. White.

Boykin, A. (1994). Harvesting culture and talent: African American children and educational reform. In R. Rossi (Ed.), *Schools and students at risk* (pp. 116–130). New York: Teachers College Press.

Brandt, R. (1991). On restructuring schools: A conversation with Mike Cohen. *Educational Leadership, 48*(8), 54–58.

Brody, N. (1997). Intelligence, schooling, and society. *American Psychologist, 52,* 1,046–1,050.

Brown, D., Pryzwansky, W. B., & Schulte, A. C. (2001). *Psychological consultation: Introduction to theory and practice* (5th ed.). Boston: Allyn & Bacon.

Callahan, K., Rademacher, J., & Hildreth, B. (1998). The effect on parent participation in strategies to improve the homework performance of students who are at risk. *Remedial and Special Education, 19*(3), 131–141.

Caplan, N., Choy, M., & Whitmore, J. (1992). Indochinese refugee families and academic achievement. *Scientific American, 266*(2), 36–42.

Carroll, J. (1963). A model of school learning. *Teachers College Record, 64,* 723–733.

Choate, J. (1993). *Successful mainstreaming: Proven ways to detect and correct special needs.* Boston: Allyn & Bacon.

Christenson, S. L., & Conoley, J. C. (Eds.). (1992). *Home-school collaboration: Enhancing children's academic and social competence.* Silver Spring, MD: NASP.

Cohen, R., Swerdlik, M., & Smith, D. (1992). *Psychological testing and assessment.* Mountain View, CA: Mayfield Publishing Company.

Cooper, J. (Ed.). (1999). *Classroom teaching skills.* Boston: Houghton Mifflin Company.

Costenbader, V., & Buntaine, R. (1999). Diagnostic discrimination between social maladjustment and emotional disturbance. *Journal of Emotional and Behavioral Disorders, 7,* 2–10.

Darling-Hammond, L. (1996). The right to learn and the advancement of teaching: Research, policy of practice for democratic education. *Educational Researcher, 25,* 5–17.

De Mesquita, P. B., & Zollman, A. (1995). Teachers' preferences for academic intervention strategies in mathematics: Implications for instructional consultation. *Journal of Educational and Psychological Consultation, 6*(2), 159–174.

Deshler, D., & Schumaker, J. (1988). An instructional model for teaching students how to learn. In J. Graden, J. Zins, & M. Curtis (Eds.), *Alternative educational delivery systems: Enhancing instructional options for all students* (pp. 391–411). Washington, DC: NASP.

Dettmer, P., Dyck, N., & Thurston, L. (1999). *Consultation, collaboration, and teamwork for students with special needs.* Boston: Allyn & Bacon.

Dugan, E., Kamps, D., Leonard, B., Watkins, N., Rheinberger, A., & Stackhaus, J. (1995). Effects of cooperative learning groups during social studies for students with autism and fourth grade peers. *Journal of Applied Behavioral Analysis, 28,* 175–188.

DuPaul, G., & Eckert, T. (1998). Academic interventions for students with attention deficit/hyperactivity disorder: A review of the literature. *Reading and Writing Quarterly, 14,* 59–82.

Edmonds, R. (1979). Effective schools for the urban poor. *Educational Leadership, 37*(1), 15–27.

Eggen, P., & Kauchak, D. (2004). *Educational psychology: Windows on classrooms* (6th ed). Upper Saddle River, NJ: Merrill/Prentice Hall.

Ekwall, E. (1988). *Locating and correcting reading difficulties* (5th ed.). Upper Saddle River, NJ: Merrill/Prentice Hall.

Ellis, A. (1995). Changing rational-emotive therapy to rational-emotive behavioral therapy. *Journal of Rational–Emotive and Cognitive–Behavioral Therapy, 13,* 85–90.

Erickson, M. (1998). *Behavior disorders of children and adolescents.* Upper Saddle River, NJ: Prentice Hall.

Fantuzzo, J., King, J., & Heller, L. (1992). Effects of reciprocal peer tutoring on mathematics and school adjustment. A component analysis. *Journal of Educational Psychology, 84,* 331–339.

Figueroa, R. A. (1990). Best practices in assessment of bilingual children. In A. Thomas & J. Grimes (Eds.), *Best practices in school psychology II* (pp. 93–106). Washington, DC: NASP.

Fisher, J. B., Schumaker, J. B., & Deshler, D. D. (1996). Searching for validated inclusive practices: A review of the literature. In E. L. Meyen, G. A. Vergason, & R. J. Whelan (Eds.), *Strategies for teaching exceptional children in inclusive settings* (pp. 123–154). Denver, CO: Love Publishing.

Freiberg, H., & Driscoll, A. (1992). *Universal teaching strategies.* Boston: Allyn & Bacon.

Friend, M., & Bursick, W. (1999). *Including students with special needs: A practical guide for classroom teachers* (2nd ed.). Boston: Allyn & Bacon.

Friend, M., & Cook, L. (2003). *Interactions: Collaboration skills for school professionals* (4th ed.). New York: Longman.

Gambrell, L., Morrow, L., Neuman, S., & Pressley, M. (1999). *Best practices in literacy instruction.* New York: Guilford Press.

Garrity, C., Jens, K., Porter, W., Sager, N., & Short-Camilli, C. (1994). *Bully-proofing your school: A comprehensive approach for elementary schools.* Longmont, CO: Sopris West.

Gettinger, M., & Seibert, J. K. (2002). Best practices for increasing academic learning time. In A. Thomas & J. Grimes (Eds.), *Best practices in school psychology IV* (pp. 773–788). Bethesda, MD: National Association of School Psychologists.

Gettinger, M., & Stoiber, K. (1999). Excellence in teaching: Review of instructional and environmental variables. In C. Reynolds & T. Gutkin (Eds.), *The handbook of school psychology* (3rd ed., pp. 933–958). New York: Wiley.

Glaser, R. (1977). *Adaptive education: Individual diversity and learning.* New York: Holt, Rinehart, & Winston.

Gleason, M., Archer, A., & Colvin, G. (2002). Interventions for improving study skills. In M. Shinn, H. Walker, & G. Stoner (Eds.), *Interventions for academic and behavior problems II* (pp. 651–680). Bethesda, MD: NASP.

Gleitman, H., Fridlund, A., & Reisberg, D. (1999). *Psychology* (5th ed.). New York: Norton.

Good, T., & Brophy, J. (2000). *Looking in classrooms.* (8th ed.) New York: Longman.

Good, T. L., & Brophy, J. E. (1984). *Looking in classrooms* (3rd ed.). New York: Harper & Row.

Gordon, E. W. (1984). *Human diversity and pedagogy.* Pomona, NY: Ambergris Family Press.

Green, J. (2001). *High school graduation rates in the United States.* New York: Center for Civic Innovation at the Manhattan Institute.

Greenwood, C. (1996). The case for performance-based instructional models. *School Psychology Quarterly, 11,* 283–296.

Greenwood, C., Delquadri, J., & Carta, J. (1997). *Together we can! Classwide peer tutoring for basic academic skills.* Longmont, CO: Sopris West.

Greenwood, C., Maheady, L., & Delquadri, J. (2002). Classroom peer tutoring programs. In M. Shinn, H. Walker, & G. Stoner (Eds.), *Interventions for academic and behavior problems II* (pp. 611–650). Bethesda, MD: NASP.

Grossman, H. (1995). *Teaching in a diverse society.* Boston: Allyn & Bacon.

Gunn, B., Biglan, A., Smolkowski, K., & Ary, D. (2000). The efficacy of supplemental instruction in decoding skills for Hispanic and Non-hispanic students in early elementary school. *Journal of Special Education, 34*(2), 90–103.

Gustafsson, J., & Undheim, J. (1996). Individual differences in cognitive functioning. In D. C. Berliner & R. C. Calfee (Eds.), *Handbook of educational psychology.* New York: MacMillan.

Hallahan, D., & Mercer, C. (2001). *Learning disabilities: Historical perspectives.* Paper presented at the 2001 LD Summit: Building a Foundation for the Future. Available online from *www.air.org/ldsummit.*

Hardman, M., Drew, C., & Egan, W. (2002). *Human exceptionality* (7th ed.). Needham Heights, MA: Allyn & Bacon.

Harvey, V. (2002). Best practices in teaching study skills. In A. Thomas & J. Grimes (Eds.), *Best practices in school psychology IV* (pp. 831–850). Bethesda, MD: NASP.

Haynes, N., & Gebreyesus, S. (1992). Cooperative learning: A case for African-American children. *School Psychology Review, 21,* 577–585.

Helfand, D., & Groves, M. (2001). *Poor readers have gotten worse, U.S. study shows.* Los Angeles, CA: Los Angeles Times.

Heron, T., & Harris, K. (2001). *The educational consultant* (4th ed.). Austin, TX: Pro-Ed.

Heward, W. L. (2000). *Exceptional Children: An Introduction to Special Education,* (7th ed.). Upper Saddle River, NJ: Prentice-Hall.

Hidi, S., & Harackiewicz, J. (2000). Motivating the academically unmotivated: A critical issue for the 21st century. *Review of Educational Research, 70*(2), 151–179.

Idol, L., Nevin, A., & Paolucci-Whitcomb, P. (2000). *Collaborative consultation* (3rd ed.). Austin, TX: Pro-Ed.

Johnson, L., & Pugach, M. (1996). Role of collaborative dialogue in teachers' conceptions of appropriate practice for students at risk. *Journal of Educational and Psychological Consultation, 7,* 9–24.

Jones, F. (1987). *Positive classroom instruction.* New York: McGraw-Hill.

Kampwirth, T. J. (1981). Diagnosing poor learning: Some considerations. *Journal for Special Educators, 17*(2), 142–149.

Kaufman, A., Lichtenberger, E., & Naglieri, J. (1999). Intelligence testing in the schools. In C. Reynolds & T. Gutkin (Eds.), *The handbook of school psychology* (3rd ed., pp. 307–349). New York: Wiley.

Kauffman, J. (2001). *Characteristics of emotional and behavioral disorders of childhood and youth* (7th ed.). Upper Saddle River, NJ: Merrill/Prentice Hall.

Kelly, K. (1999). Retention vs. social promotion: Schools search for alternatives. *Harvard Educational Letter, 15*(1), 1–3.

Kiewra, K. (1991). Aids to lecture learning. *Educational Psychologist, 26,* 37–53.

Knapp, M. (1995). *Teaching for meaning in high poverty classrooms.* New York: Teachers College Press.

Lee, C. (2001). Is October Brown Chinese? A cultural modeling activity system for underachieving students. *American Educational Research Journal, 38*(1), 97–142.

Lerner, J. (2000). *Learning disabilities* (8th ed.). Boston: Houghton Mifflin.

Levine, D. V., & Havighurst, R. S. (1989). *Society and education* (7th ed.). Boston: Allyn & Bacon.

Lidz, C. S. (Ed.). (1987). *Dynamic assessment: An interactional approach to evaluating learning potential.* New York: Guilford Press.

Linan-Thompson, S., Vaughn, S., Hickman-Davis, P., & Kouzekanani, K. (2003). Effective reading instruction for English language learners with reading difficulties. *Elementary School Journal, 103*(3), 221–238.

Long, N., & Morse, W. (1996). *Conflict in the classroom* (5th ed.). Austin, TX: Pro-Ed.

Lynch, E., Lewis, R., & Murphy, D. (1993). Educational services for students with chronic illnesses: Perspectives of educators and families. *Exceptional Children, 59,* 210–220.

Marsh, H., & Craven, R. (1997). Academic self-concept: Beyond the dustbowl. In G. D. Phye (Ed.), *Handbook of classroom assessment: Learning, achievement and adjustment.* San Diego: Academic Press.

Mayen, E., Vergason, G., & Whelan, R. (1996). *Strategies for teaching exceptional children in inclusive settings.* Denver, CO: Love Publishing.

McCarney, S. B., & Cummins, K. K. (1988). *The prereferral intervention manual.* Columbia, MO: Hawthorne Educational Services.

McCoy, A., & Reynolds, A. (1999). Grade retention and school performance: An extended investigation. *Journal of School Psychology, 37,* 273–298.

McLoyd, V. (1998). Socioeconomic disadvantage and child development. *American Psychologist, 53,* 185–204.

Mehran, M., & White, K. (1988). Parent tutoring as a supplement to compensatory education for first-grade children. *Remedial and Special Education, 9*(3), 35–41.

Messick, S., & Associates. (1976). *Individuality and learning.* San Francisco: Jossey-Bass.

Monson, D. L. (Ed.). (1985). *Adventuring with books: A booklist for pre-K–grade 6.* Urbana, IL: National Council of Teachers of English.

Moore, K. (1995). *Classroom teaching skills.* New York: McGraw-Hill.

Mullis, I., Dossey, J., Foertsch, M., Jones, L., & Gentile, C. (1991). *Trends in academic progress.* Washington, DC: U.S. Department of Education, National Center for Educational Statistics.

Munden, A., & Archelus, J. (2001). *The ADHD handbook: A guide for parents and professionals.* New York: Jessica Kingsley.

Munson, S. M. (1987). Regular education teacher modifications for mainstreamed mildly handicapped students. *Journal of Special Education, 20*(4), 489–502.

Nastasi, B., & Clements, D. (1991). Research on cooperative learning: Implications for practice. *School Psychology Review, 20,* 110–131.

National Center for Educational Statistics (2002). *The Condition of Education* (Rep. No. NCES 2002–025). Washington, DC: U.S. Department of Education.

National Research Council. (2004). *Engaging schools: Fostering high school students' motivation to learn.* Washington, DC: The National Academies Press.

Neisser, U., Boodoo, G., Bouchard, T., Boykin, A., Ceci, S., Halpern, D., Loehlen, J., Perloff, R., Sternberg, R., & Urbina, S. (1996). Intelligence: Knowns and unknowns. *American Psychologist, 51,* 77–101.

Nieto, S. (1996). *Affirming diversity: The sociopolitical context of multicultural education* (2nd ed.). White Plains, NY: Longman.

No Child Left Behind Act. 2001. 34 CFR Part 200.

Oakes, J. (1999). Promotion or retention: Which one is social? *Harvard Education Letter, 15*(1), 8.

Ormrod, J. (2000). *Educational psychology: Developing learners.* Upper Saddle River, NJ: Merrill/Prentice Hall.

Perkins, D. (1995). *Outsmarting IQ: The emerging science of learnable intelligence.* New York: Free Press.

Phye, G. (Ed.). (1997). *Handbook of academic learning: Construction of knowledge.* San Diego: Academic Press.

Pressley, M. (1998). *Reading instruction that works: The case for balanced teaching.* New York: Guilford Press.

Pressley, M., & Woloshyn, V. (1995). *Cognitive strategy instruction that really improves children's academic performance* (2nd ed.). Cambridge, MA: Brookline Books.

Purkey, S. C., & Smith, M. S. (1983). Effective schools: A review. *Elementary School Journal, 83,* 427–452.

Quay, H. C., & Werry, J. S. (Eds.). (1986). *Psychopathological disorders of childhood* (3rd ed.). New York: Wiley.

Quiroga, T., Lemos-Britton, Z., Mostafapour, E., & Berninger, V. (2002). phonological awareness and beginning reading in Spanish, ESL first-graders: Research practice. *Journal of School Psychology, 40,* 85–111.

Rafoth, M. A. (2002). Best practices in preventing academic failures and promoting alternatives to retention. In A. Thomas & J. Grimes (Eds.), *Best practices in school psychology IV* (pp. 789–802). Bethesda, MD: NASP.

Rathvon, N. (1999). *Effective school interventions.* New York: Guilford Press.

Reschly, D. J., & Grimes, J. P. (2002). Best practices in intellectual assessment. In A. Thomas & J. P. Grimes (Eds.), *Best practices in school psychology IV* (pp. 1,337–1,350). Bethesda, MD: NASP.

Reschly, D., & Ysseldyke, J. (2002). Paradigm shift: The past is not the future. In A. Thomas & J. Grimes (Eds.), *Best practices in school psychology IV* (pp. 3–20). Bethesda: MD: NASP.

Reynolds, C., Lowe, P., & Saenz, A. (1999). The problem of bias in psychological assessment. In C. Reynolds & T. Gutkin (Eds.), *The handbook of school psychology* (pp. 549–596). New York: Wiley.

Rhode, G., Jenson, W., & Reavis, H. (1992). *The tough kid book: Practical classroom management strategies*. Longmont, CO: Sopris West.

Rosenfield, S. (1987). *Instructional consultation*. Hillsdale, NJ: Lawrence Erlbaum Associates.

Rosenfield, S. A., & Gravois, T. A. (1996). *Instructional consultation teams*. New York: Guilford Press.

Rumberger, R. (1995). Dropping out of middle school: A multilevel analysis of students and schools. *American Educational Research Journal, 32,* 583–626.

Salend, S. (1998). *Effective mainstreaming: Creating inclusive classrooms*. Upper Saddle River, NJ: Merrill/Prentice Hall.

Salvia, J., & Ysseldyke, J. E. (2004). *Assessment* (9th ed.). Boston: Houghton Mifflin.

Sattler, J. (1998). *Clinical and forensic interviewing of children and families*. San Diego: Sattler Publishing.

Sattler, J. M. (2001). *Assessment of children* (4th ed.). San Diego: Sattler Publishing.

Schofield, J. (1995). Promoting positive intergroup relations in school settings. In W. D. Hawley & A. W. Jackson (Eds.), *Toward a common destiny: Improving race and ethnic relations in America*. San Francisco: Jossey-Bass.

Schumaker, J., Deshler, D., & McKnight, P. (2002). Ensuring success in the secondary general education curriculum through the use of teaching routines. In M. Shinn, H. Walker, & G. Stoner (Eds.), *Interventions for academic and behavior problems II* (pp. 791–824). Bethesda, MD: NASP.

Seligman, M. (1975). *Helplessness: On depression, development and death*. San Francisco: Freeman.

Shapiro, E. (1989). *Academic skills problems: Direct assessment and intervention*. New York: Guilford Press.

Shinn, M. (Ed.). (1998). *Advanced applications of curriculum-based measurement*. New York: Macmillan.

Shinn, M. R., Walker, H. M., & Stoner, G. (2002). *Interventions for achievement and behavior problems II*. Bethesda, MD: NASP.

Silver, L. (1999). *Attention deficit hyperactivity disorder: A clinical guide to diagnosis and treatment for health and mental health*. Washington, DC: American Psychiatric Press.

Skrtic, T. M. (1991). The special education paradox: Equity as the way to excellence. *Harvard Educational Review, 61,* 148–206.

Slavin, R. (1995). *Cooperative learning: Theory, research and practice*. Boston: Allyn & Bacon.

Slavin, R. (1997). *Educational psychology: Theory and practice*. Boston: Allyn & Bacon.

Smith, T., Polloway, E., Patton, J., & Dowdy, C. (2004). *Teaching students with special needs in inclusive settings*. Boston: Allyn & Bacon.

Stainback, W., & Stainback, S. (1987). Educating all students in regular education. *TASH Newsletter, 13*(4), 1–7.

Stanovich, K. (2000). *Progress in understanding reading: Scientific foundations and new frontiers*. New York: Guilford Press.

Stodolsky, S., & Grossman, P. (2000). Changing students, changing teachers. *Teachers College Record, 102*(1), 125–172.

Swap, S. M. (1993). *Developing home-school partnerships: From concepts to practice*. New York: Teachers College Press.

Thomas, E., & Robinson, H. (1972). *Improving reading in every class: A sourcebook for teachers*. Boston: Allyn & Bacon.

Thurston, L., & Dasta, K. (1990). An analysis of in-home parent tutoring procedures: Effects on children's academic behavior at home and in school and on parent's tutoring behavior. *Remedial and Special Education, 11*(4), 41–51.

Tobin, K. G. (1987). The role of wait-time in higher-cognitive-level learning. *Review of Educational Research, 57,* 69–95.

Topping, K., & Ehly, S. (1998). *Peer-assisted learning*. Mahwah, NJ: Lawrence Erlbaum Associates.

Trueba, H., Jacobs, L., & Kirton, E. (1990). *Cultural conflict and adaptation*. New York: Falmer.

Valde, G., & Figueroa, R. (1994). *Bilingualism and testing: A special case of bias*. Norwood, NJ: Ablex.

Vasquez, J. (1993). Teaching to the distinctive traits of minority students. In K. M. Cauley, F. Linder, & J. McMillan (Eds.), *Annual editions: Educational psychology 93/94*. Guilford, CT: The Dushkin Publishing Group.

Wang, M. C., Haertel, G. D., & Walberg, H. J. (1993). Toward a knowledge base for school learning. *Review of Educational Leadership, 63*(3), 249–294.

Wang, M. C., Haertel, G. D., & Walberg, H. J. (1995). *Educational resilience: An emerging concept*. Paper presented at the annual meeting of the American Educational Research Association, San Francisco.

Weinstein, R. (1998). Promoting positive expectations in schooling. In N. Lambert & B. McCombs (Eds.), *How students learn: Reforming schools through learner-centered education* (pp. 81–111). Washington, DC: American Psychological Association.

Wicks-Nelson, R., & Israel, A. (2000). *Behavior disorders of childhood*. Upper Saddle River, NJ: Prentice Hall.

Will, M. (1986). *Educating students with learning problems: A shared responsibility*. Washington, DC: U.S. Department of Education.

Ysseldyke, J., & Christenson, S. (2002). *Functional assessment of academic behavior*. Longmont, CO: Sopris West.

Zins, J. E., Curtis, M. J., Graden, J. L., & Ponti, C. (1988). *Helping students succeed in the regular classroom*. San Francisco: Jossey-Bass.

Systems-Level Consultation: The Organization as the Target of Change

OBJECTIVES

1. Orient the reader to the basic concepts involved in organizing changes within a school or school system.
2. Delineate the factors that influence change efforts.
3. List the steps to guide the implementation of systems-change efforts.
4. Provide a brief case example demonstrating how the principles discussed in this chapter were applied in a school situation.

The district superintendent has noticed a general decline in achievement over the past 5 years. The more people she talks to, the more ideas she gets about causes and cures. She appoints three people—the school psychologist, the general education teacher who is the head of the teachers' union, and a special education teacher—as co-chairs of a task force to look into possible ways of dealing with this issue of declining achievement. How should these three proceed?

The district director of special education has issued a call for more inclusion of special education students in the regular classes. Most, but not all, of the special education teachers support this idea; the general education staff is split about 50–50 on the issue, favoring inclusion for the mildly/moderately disabled, but drawing the line strongly on inclusion for students with more severe disabilities. What should the district do to clarify the meaning of the legal, philosophical, and practical issues involved in inclusion? How should they seek support for it?

ACTIVITY 8.1

Analyze the two scenarios just presented and indicate how an internal school consultant might approach each of them. What are some issues to consider in entry (How can you get started?) and diagnosis (How should you go about getting information to analyze the problem?)?

WHY SYSTEMS-LEVEL CONSULTATION?

The previous seven chapters of this book have mainly been concerned with consultation involving individuals or small groups of students, with teachers and parents as the consultees. This is appropriate since most of the work of school consultants centers around referrals by consultees who wish to obtain some assistance in dealing with students who manifest difficulties in behavior, adjustment, or academic achievement. I hope that the material in the first seven chapters will help you deal with everyday important issues that affect the futures of the referred students and let you assist teachers in achieving their goals for all students.

When consulting about individual cases, the school consultant will often encounter situations in which it is apparent that something about the way the individual school or the whole district deals with persistent problems in the delivery of its services to students may be contributing to these problems. These are "systemic" reasons, examples of which are presented in the case studies in Chapter 9.

In this chapter we examine the reasons why a school consultant needs to be aware that the learning and adjustment of students is a systems-wide issue. Student difficulties do not reside only within the students themselves or because of the nature of their classrooms or homes. Although not nearly as influential as the actions of individual teachers and parents, the policies that emanate from large government entities, local school boards, and district and school levels do affect student learning and behavior (Wang, Haertel, & Walberg, 1993). These policies and beliefs can influence the decisions that classroom teachers and schools make regarding curriculum, methods, class size, and other important variables. The No Child Left Behind (NCLB) mandate for annual nationwide assessments of achievement has school districts reassessing how the instructional day should be spent, given the high-stakes nature of these assessments.

We will examine the influence of the school or district organization on teachers, parents, and students. The scope will be limited primarily to the school or district level as opposed to studying the influences of the county, state, or federal government. A systems-change process and steps to guide this process will be discussed. Finally, I present a format for the study of systems change, along with a brief case example demonstrating how school-based consultants were able to assist a district in improving selected aspects of service delivery.

School districts and individual schools operate under a set of explicit and implicit rules not all that different from the rules teachers establish for their classes. Employees are expected to be at work on time, to carry out their responsibilities, to cooperate, and to strive toward achieving the mission of the district or school. These global expectations, readily understood by all employees, are certainly a good starting point for the kind of mutuality of purpose that is essential for organizational health (Illback & Zins, 1995; Illback, Zins, & Maher, 1999). However, when people are expected to adhere to the details that stem from these global expectations, which may involve interpretation of, and cooperation with, the mission, problems can arise. The two scenarios presented at the beginning of this chapter give examples of possible conflicts between various constituencies, along with a question that derives from each and that indicates the need for some degree of consultation.

DISTRICT/SCHOOL ORGANIZATION FACTORS THAT INFLUENCE CHANGE EFFORTS

Knoff (2002, adapted from Egan, 1985) describes four characteristics of an operating school district that contribute to an understanding of the dynamics of districts and individual schools. These four characteristics operate in a holistic and ecological condition of interdependency.

The Receiving System

The traditional receivers of service were K–12 students. Recently, however, schools have expanded their service base to include preschoolers and families through the innovation of full-service schools that utilize community advisory committees. Since these service receivers are our clients, we need to address their needs. What do they want from the schools? What are their goals? How can we integrate their unique interests with the other missions of the schools, especially in times of budget uncertainty?

The Performance System

Five elements define the performance system: a mission statement, goals that derive from the mission statement, activities that lead toward the goals, materials and resources needed, and specific outcomes compatible with the goals and the mission statement.

A mission statement gives overall guidance to the whole educational enterprise and sets the tone for everything that follows. Goals, activities, the need for resources, and specific outcomes can be specified within time frames. Toward the achievement of broad goals, a school might set annual goals that are more modest but headed in the intended direction. These should be stated in behavioral, observable terms and, of course, should be derived from the collaborative input of all constituencies, including the receiving system.

ACTIVITY 8.2

Does your school or district have a mission statement? If so, what long-term or short-term goals can be derived from that statement? Consider something in your school that needs improvement (e.g., attendance, reading achievement, playground behavior, "morale"). Devise a long-term goal that addresses this need.

The Human Resources and People System

This system includes the entire staff: teachers, aides, administrators, specialists, cooks, secretaries, bus drivers, campus security, and so on. A major task here is to hire the most competent people available. Once hired, people need to be developed: Inservice, mentoring, coaching, encouraging, and team building are all activities that can contribute to development. The need for a constant renewal of skills, knowledge, attitudes, and enthusiasm is recognized by every well-functioning school system. Assuming that the staff will always keep up professionally without being required to do so may be naïve (Basham, Appleton, & Dykeman, 2000; Friend & Cook, 2003; Sparks & Hirsh, 1997).

Knoff (2002) points out that any person with the skills and knowledge to serve in a staff development capacity should be encouraged and allowed to do so. A resource teacher, for example, may be the best person to assist a new teacher in matters of classroom management; a team of three people, two ancillary and one regular-grade teacher, may be the best group to plan an evaluation program for the school; a psychologist or counselor may be in the best position to offer staff development in the area of conflict management, anger management, and social skills training, all of which are designed to improve the school climate.

ACTIVITY 8.3

What are some areas in which a resource teacher, special day class teacher, counselor, or school psychologist could have an impact on a whole school, other than through direct contact with students and IEP functions? Review the material in Chapter 2 on inservice staff development, then put together an inservice program for addressing an identified need.

The Pervasive System Variables

Building, district, and community influences are considered to be macro-level variables that can have positive or negative influences on service delivery. Knoff (2002) identifies six specific variables that are, to some extent, controlled at the macro level:

Incentive and reward factors: Certainly personal pride should be the primary determinant of professional effort, but other, more extrinsic variables can also be influential. Salary, contract negotiations, building- or district-level recognition, and released time for professional development activities are some of the specific ways in which districts provide incentives. How each is handled can affect morale and the desire to do one's best.

Quality-of-life and climate factors: Quality-of-life and climate factors are both tangible and intangible. Certainly books and other materials need to be provided, but teachers and students need to know that the environment is safe, welcoming, and encourages high achievement. Parent involvement and support that lead to student involvement are essential, as are dedicated teacher efforts and harmonious race relations.

Quality and climate of schools varies immensely across the United States. To get a taste of some situations that detract from high quality in some neighborhoods, one should read Kozol's (1992) *Savage Inequalities,* an exposé of the dreadful conditions that exist in some schools in inner cities. To read about inner-city schools that are providing a healthy climate for their students, see *Engaging Schools* (National Research Council, 2004), which details the methods and attainments of high-achieving inner-city schools.

Environmental factors: Environmental factors include a wide variety of influences that are community-based (for example, socioeconomic status, government and police support, and neighborhood conditions) and those that are related to the natural or social environment, especially when the environment becomes threatening (for example, during hurricanes, earthquakes, floods, or terrorist threats or attacks). A series of adverse environmental events can depress the ability of citizens to perform to their best potential.

Political factors: Political factors include the potential impact of leaders at all ends of the spectrum, from the federal government to the local school board. Business leaders, the PTA, and other influential groups can become willing and valuable partners in reform efforts if you make an effort to include them.

Cultural factors: These factors include the values, beliefs, assumptions, norms, and so on that can affect the productivity of a school or a district. Shifting demographics, new personnel, new dictums from the federal or state departments of education (e.g., NCLB), and other events have an impact and may cause subtle or serious changes in how people relate to each other and to their jobs. Reform efforts that fail to consider the cultural norms of a school are likely to be given a poor reception (Brubacher, Case, & Reagan, 1994; Fullan, 1991; Knoff, 2002; National Research Council, 2004).

Nonrational factors: Systems resist change, just as people do. People develop a vested interest in what they are doing and how they are doing it and often resist change even when they see the need for it. Reformers need to understand that change does not happen overnight, even when the participants seem interested; habits die hard. All the factors mentioned in Chapter 3 about resistance to individual consultation can apply to reform efforts. Chapter 3 details a list of causes, manifestations, and possible remedies for resistance both at the individual consultee and whole-system levels. Friend and Cook (2003), Dougherty (2000), Erchul and Martin (2002), and Heron and Harris (2001) have also contributed information about the causes for resistance and strategies for minimizing the influence of resistance.

WHO INITIATES SYSTEMS CHANGE? WHERE DOES IT COME FROM?

In the typical school, as in other organizations, the formal leaders are generally expected to decide what changes are needed and how the school or organization should implement them. Although this traditional model of paternalistic leadership is still honored, the trend over the past few decades has been toward a decentralization of power and authority. This decentralization is a common characteristic of schools undergoing reform. Today both the formal leaders (superintendents, principals, and so on) and other constituency groups (teachers, parents, and so on) have powerful voices, if not equal ones, in matters of organization, philosophy, method, and goals (Fullan, 1991). This change follows the spirit of collaboration that has been stressed throughout this text.

Given the current model of dispersed authority, it is common for the impetus for change to come directly and strongly from those people who are closest to the problem, the constituents who sense a need for a different approach to conceptualizing and solving the everyday problems that arise in schools' efforts to deal with *A Nation at Risk* (National Commission on Excellence in Education, 1983) and NCLB. This grassroots impetus has arisen from two divergent strands: (1) there is a growing understanding that change is needed and may best be generated from those closest to the problems, and (2) change that emanates from the top down is often subtly if not overtly rejected by those closest to the problems because these individuals don't feel that they were a part of the problem-solving process. Since they often have had no ownership of the solutions, they may not have personally needed to see that these solutions were carried out correctly or successfully (Fullan, 1995; Heifitz & Laurie, 1997; Safran & Safran, 1997).

Principals, as constituents of a change process, have considerable power in determining whether or not a given change is sustained beyond some mandated (that is, funded) lifetime. Hall, Rutherford, Hord, and Huling (1984) look at the role and style of the local school principal in the determination of the staying power of an innovation. In doing so they categorize principals as responders, those who do as the district office says; managers, those who adapt innovations to their own schools; and initiators, those who design their approaches to change around the interests, skills, and needs of their schools. Hall et al. find that change is more common and of higher quality in schools led by initiators.

But principals are not the only ones who decide what works, what stays, and what disappears. McLaughlin and Marsh (1978) find that federally funded innovative programs remain part of the school routine only when teachers believe that the innovation has made a difference in the lives of the students.

An interest in change, therefore, can come from a variety of sources and for a variety of reasons. *A Nation at Risk* (National Commission on Excellence in Education, 1983) spurred American educators to think about the need for change, although it did not necessarily result in a wide unanimity of beliefs about the direction or extent of changes. What that report did was remind us that we, as a nation, had somehow lost the gains that seemed to occur after the USSR's launch of *Sputnik* in 1957 prompted America to bolster its science and math teaching. After the key trigger event of *Sputnik,* the federal government poured unprecedented amounts of money into the schools with some impressive, though temporary, results. Unfortunately, scores on the SAT and ACT continued to decline in the 1970s. This led to more calls for reform, culminating in GOALS 2000. GOALS 2000 served as a trigger event on the national scale because it informed the states and districts that the federal government was once more committed to making a massive effort to reform or revitalize public education.

More recently the federal government has passed the No Child Left Behind Act, which was signed by President Bush in January 2002. This act provides the states with the largest increase in the history of federal aid to school districts. It will require annual testing of students in grades 3 through 8 in reading and math, starting no later than the year 2005. A sizable percentage of these additional funds will be targeted for schools with low achievement, with the funds intended to help these schools to improve their test scores. Schools not showing improvement over a period of years could be subject to consequences.

Thus, for the first time, the federal government is not only offering carrots, but it is also threatening with sticks. Whether the lofty goals of these federal government efforts can or will be achieved will depend on the efforts of local individuals working at the grassroots level. As I have implied, these people are likely to embrace reforms if they feel that they have been part of the reform process and that their ideas have been heard and valued. Otherwise, the reform movement may fail, predictably, as Sarason (1990) says, for at least the following reasons (Knoff, 1995):

1. Many reform enthusiasts and plan developers do not work in the schools or they have positions that are only distally related to classroom realities. They do not understand what it takes to effect change; they do not consult collaboratively.

2. America's educational problems are far too complex to be solved with quick fixes. The diversity of the school population creates realities that require input from a variety of nonstandard sources: parents, community leaders, teachers, and even students.

3. Reform leaders need to understand the difference between power and influence. Because of their positions, those in charge of many reforms have the power to establish reform policies and to fund them, but they may not know how to, or be able to, influence those who need to carry out the policies at the classroom level.

4. True collaboration and shared decision making require a massive change in the existing traditional power structure and relationships among the various constituencies: administration, teachers, ancillary staff, parents, and so on. Although we have seen evidence that this change can occur, it is now more the exception than the rule.

5. As long as those most responsible for the needed changes at the student–teacher level feel powerless about their roles in the reform process, they will tend to avoid a serious implementation of handed-down ideas, they will engage in the process in minimal ways, and they will avoid real change. Habit, after all, is comforting. The desire to change emerges best from within. As McAdams (1997) indicates, "Convincing a critical mass of teachers to adopt a major reform project, especially one directly affecting instruction, is a time-consuming process fraught with practical and political difficulties" (p. 240).

In summary, change can arise from anyone who has an idea and is willing to put it forward. It comes from the warnings issued by national studies and from thoughtful persons who see a need for system improvement (reform) and want to respond to it. The form (reform) that change takes will depend on a host of variables, some tangible (money, facilities, personnel) and some intangible (felt needs, zeal, comfort level, need for achievement or power, resistance, and so on). It would appear, overall, that reform in American schools has had a checkered history. As Tyack and Cuban (1995; quoted in Glazer, 2003, p. 158) put it, in reference to the common early enthusiasm and early demise of so many reform movements, it appears that such efforts "...often resembled shooting stars that spurted across the pedagogical heavens, leaving a meteoric trail in the media but burning up and disappearing in the everyday atmosphere of the schools."

STEPS TO GUIDE THE IMPLEMENTATION OF SYSTEMS CHANGE: THE DECIDE APPROACH

Welch (1999) has provided a set of general guidelines to assist schools or districts to make decisions and to problem solve in order to improve a system's ability to provide effective service delivery to all schoolchildren. Welch uses the acronym DECIDE to remind consumers of the steps in this method, which, in modified form, are outlined in the following section.

D: Define the Situation

What is currently taking place? Are you concerned about achievement scores? About a rise in the incidence of bullying behaviors? Describe in behavioral terms what the problem/issue/challenge is, and state who is involved in it and impacted by it (i.e., the constituents/stakeholders).

E: Examine the Environment

1. The focus here is on the "where" questions, but the other questions (what, who, when, why, and how) may resurface when the environment in which the behaviors of concern appear is studied.
2. An ecological analysis should be done at this point. What is there about the surroundings in which the behaviors of concern occur that could be contributing to these behaviors?

C: Create a Goal Statement

1. Give this statement (include as many as may be necessary) focus and specificity. Use these four components:
   a. *Behavior:* Describe actions and events that are concrete, observable, and measurable (Alberto & Troutman, 1999).
   b. *Condition:* Where and under what circumstances will the change occur?
   c. *Criterion:* Include a requirement for acceptability by setting a level or standard that the change must meet.
   d. *Duration:* For how long will the change be carried out? If a target student meets the goal for one day, is that acceptable?

I: Invent an Intervention Plan

1. This is where the emphasis shifts from process (how something is done) to content (what will be done, under what conditions, by whom, when, how, and where).
2. Welch (1999) suggests five subareas to be considered in the development of the plan:
   a. *Brainstorming:* This was discussed in Chapters 2 and 5; it consists of getting stakeholders to generate ideas in a freewheeling, noncritical atmosphere.

Egan (1998), Friend and Cook (2003), and Welch and Sheridan (1995) give suggestions for the proper conduct of brainstorming.

b. *Resource allocation:* There are five types of resources to be considered: human (who will do it?); informational (what do we need to know in order to proceed?); technological (what tools are needed?); physical (where will this change occur?); and financial (can we afford it?). Another resource not mentioned by Welch (1999) but which needs to be considered is time. If the intervention takes someone's time, what will be given up in order to have the time to engage in the intervention?

c. *Timelines:* When will the various steps begin, for how long will they be operative, and when will they end?

d. *Cost-benefit analysis:* It may be necessary to attempt to determine if the benefit associated with this change will be worth the costs of the change. Difficult as it is to answer questions of value when it comes to human services, there may be times when the intervention planning team will need to face some hard realities: Not all interventions can be fiscally supported.

e. *Cross-referencing the goal and action plan:* In the development of the intervention plan, it is necessary to go back one more time to determine if there is a close alignment between the original goal statement and the current version of the intervention plan.

D: Deliver the Action Plan

This is the moment of truth in consultation regarding individual or small groups of students, and in systems-improvement efforts as well. All of the steps previously outlined are used to provide guidance as the intervention team implements the intervention(s).

E: Evaluate the Intervention Action Plan

1. What is your formative evaluation telling you? Where are the bottlenecks or breakdowns in delivery of the intervention? Are the consultees and other involved personnel implementing the interventions correctly? Are the reactions of those whose behavior is the target of the intervention appropriate for the goal? Are the planned-for resources available and being used advantageously?

2. The final step of DECIDE is a summative evaluation. To what extent was the goal actually met? Since the purpose of an evaluation is to determine the value of an intervention, what was the value of the activities taken by everyone in the name of systems improvement? What was learned from this experience?

Zins and Illback (1995) point out that any systems-change process is usually conceptualized as consisting of the following phases: diagnosis, planning, initiation, implementation, and institutionalization. Chapter 5 contains information about other ways of conceptualizing the stages or phases of the change process as they pertain to individual consultee and client situations. However, the change process is fairly similar in the case of systems change, with the exception of the need for more group interactions, the extended length of time it takes to affect a systems change, and the possible need for greater resources (e.g., money) in systems change. The change process may best be described as linear circularity. While it generally moves forward, it does so in a recursive, circular fashion; for every two steps forward, there may be one or one-and-a-half steps backward or sideways.

FORMAT OF THE SYSTEMS-CHANGE CASE EXAMPLE

The case example that follows is presented in a series of stages that give coherence and order to the change process. These stages are modifications of those presented by Brown, Pryzwansky, and Schulte (2001) and Parsons (1996). They consist of the following:

1. A problem statement.
2. A brief history of the concern that has developed around this problem.
3. A list of the concerned parties.
4. A statement about key trigger incidents that prompted action.
5. Developing initial plans for change.
6. A description of a fermentation period when issues and concerns were dealt with.
7. A list of the specific interventions agreed on.
8. The implementation of the interventions.
9. Monitoring and evaluation of the interventions.

1. Problem Statement

Systems change (reform, renewal, restructuring) starts with an identified problem. For our purposes, a situation becomes a problem to be solved when someone in authority decides that it (the situation) is impeding her goals for the system. Although there may be many situations that someone is unhappy about, it is not likely that any strong, organized effort to fix them will occur until someone with the authority to command resources, direct people, and focus energy decides to do so.

Academic underachievement, for example, has been identified as a major problem in some schools by a number of constituents for a long time. When officially recognized as a problem to be solved by those in authority, as it has been by GOALS, GOALS 2000, and NCLB, it becomes the focus of formal change efforts. In the example to be presented much of the impetus for change came not from the federal or any other government agency, but from teachers, particularly a resource teacher who acted as a consultant to the principal. Without her support, and the support of the principal, the idea would not have been pursued.

ACTIVITY 8.4

List some problems in the schools with which you are familiar, and indicate the amount of effort that has gone into improving them. What happened to make the reality become a problem (opportunity) that people felt deserved attention?

2. History of Concern

Every problem has a history. Problems don't just spring up out of nowhere, though some may strike us that way (e.g., gang killings, terrorist attacks). When examining the history of a problem, one often finds sporadic efforts to deal with it in the past, but probably there hasn't been a sustained effort, or perhaps the interventions were inappropriate, or, when leadership changes (as so often happens in government and schools), interest in solving the problem diminishes.

ACTIVITY 8.5

For one of the problem areas mentioned in Activity 8.4, recall the history of the problem. When did it seem to start, how did it develop, when did people really begin to take notice of it, and how did they start the process of problem resolution?

3. Concerned Parties

Also known as constituents, stakeholders, or parties at interest, concerned parties are individuals who are affected by the problem or who will be affected by changes to the situation. For example, a change in the dress code of a school district affects the parents, the stores who specialize in the latest fashions, stores that sell uniforms, and the students and their behavior at school. Most generally, the constituents are teachers, parents, administrators, students, and ancillary staff.

ACTIVITY 8.6

Alpha School has experienced a steady decline in achievement scores over the past decade. Who are the constituents of this problem? Who will be affected by any change in policy or practice vis-à-vis the students' achievement efforts?

4. Key Trigger Incidents

These incidents are often something that cause influential people to take notice of the situation and decide that it is a problem (or opportunity or challenge). The event can be dramatic, such as a student committing suicide, which prompts the school principal to organize a crisis response team and to consider hiring another school counselor. Or it might be the state's announcement of a serious drop in math scores, prompting the board of education to order a review of the math curriculum. Some trigger events simply happen in the minds of influential people; these people decide on their own, usually after information about a situation has been brought to their attention, that something should be done about it. It is then officially a problem.

ACTIVITY 8.7

There have been many trigger incidents in the brief history of the full-inclusion movement. At the national level, these incidents have consisted of statements from leaders in the field and court judgments. At the local level, they typically have consisted of a parent requesting that her child who is disabled be enrolled in the regular education classes for all or most of the school day. Since the courts have generally supported this request, districts needed to react when these requests (trigger events) were made. When this phenomenon first began to occur, many districts were not ready, and they reacted in a wide variety of ways.

Recall how your district reacted to these requests for full inclusion when they first started to develop and how the district policy toward future requests has evolved. How has your district responded to this challenge?

5. Developing Initial Plans for Change

Although the source for initial plan development can vary, usually the local school administration or district-level personnel develop the framework for this stage in the systems-change process. There is a wide literature that they can follow in their efforts to develop a rational approach to this and all other stages of the process (Adelman & Taylor, 1997; Bacharach, 1990; Borgelt & Conoley, 1999; Egan, 1998; Miles & Lewis, 1990; Sarason, 1990; Snapp, Hickman, & Conoley, 1990; Valentine, 1991; Wehlage, Smith, & Lipman, 1992). Fashola and Slavin (1998) and the National Research Council (2004) present a summary of reform models and discuss commonalities among those that have been successful.

Whoever is developing the initial plans probably will want to start with a needs assessment (Block, 1981; Harvey, 1990; Illback et al., Nagle, 2002), with "need" being defined as a discrepancy between a current unsatisfactory situation and a more desirable one. Just how do the constituents see this problem? What do they think should be done about it? What specific actions will reduce the discrepancy?

ACTIVITY 8.8

Imagine that your district has decided to explore the possibility of changing from a pull-out RSP special education service delivery model to one based on a collaborative consultation model. How do you think the district might go about exploring the possibility and potential of this newer model? Who would the constituents be? What methods of initial data gathering might they use?

6. Fermentation Period

During this period there will be discussions about various dimensions of the problem, data gathering will proceed, and other activities designed to define and remedy the problem will take place. In poorly organized or immature systems, there will be suggestions for quick fixes; reliance on old, previously used remedies; efforts to bury the problem; or the generation of excuses about why nothing can be done. Resistance within the system can occur at this time; those who see the possible solutions as a threat may want to deny the reality of the problem.

In a well-functioning system, constituents will be interviewed, records will be reviewed, task-specific groups will consider what is known, and tentative plans will be discussed. The purpose of these plans is to improve the way in which the system operates vis-à-vis the problem now and in the foreseeable future.

The fermentation period allows people to take the time to look at the problem from a broad perspective. Very often what seems like a localized problem has ramifications that were not considered initially. A gang violence problem, for example, reveals a need to examine closer ties to the community and its leaders (including the police, social welfare agencies, and the parents), gang members in the student body, drug and weapons traffic, dress codes, the counseling program, and so on.

At the end of the fermentation period, the study groups will have reported to the authorities, and together they can decide on implementation plans.

ACTIVITY 8.9

Imagine that your school has decided to strengthen its prereferral intervention process in an effort to slow the placement rate of students in special education programs. A committee of interested special and regular education teachers, administrators, and ancillary staff develops some possible methods. The committee presents these to the whole school for consideration. What problems or issues might be raised that will extend the fermentation period?

7. Selection of Interventions

This part of the process consists of listing the interventions to be used; their sequential order (if appropriate); who is responsible for what parts of the plan; how the plan will be accomplished; where it will occur; and other details such as how it will be paid for, if that is a consideration. If the planned changes cannot be funded, the team studying the problem needs to apply pressure to get it paid for, seek outside funding, or rethink the plan.

This is often the period in a change process that generates the most enthusiasm. Anger and confusion about the problem have passed, potential difficulties about developing a plan have been resolved, and now the group has agreed on specifics. As long as there are no funding problems, energy and a sense of purpose should be at a peak.

ACTIVITY 8.10

In your high school two major reform efforts have been developing concurrently. One has to do with a move toward implementing the General Education Initiative by giving support to regular education class teachers in their efforts to mainstream or include students with disabilities. The other has to do with modifying the structure of the day so that more flexible times can be given to subject areas as the semester progresses. What possible problems could arise as a result of trying to implement both of these reform efforts at the same time?

8. Implementation of Interventions

Under the direction of the appropriate administrator or designee, the program begins. Some beginnings may not directly affect the targeted students or the problem itself but may consist of activities that are preliminary to the main or major events that will influence the problem more directly. For example, if a system wants to utilize a computer-based instructional system, the computers have to be bought and installed and more electricity may have to be funneled into the building, which may take more time and money than was planned for. After the preliminary activities are successfully accomplished, the more direct systems-change activities begin. If planning has been competent and if the change participants carry out their assigned duties, there is reason to expect some degree of initial success. This success creates a honeymoon effect: Participants believe that the plan is perfect and that nothing can go wrong. Such perfection hardly ever happens, however, in any comprehensive systems-change process; there are simply too many factors that can intrude and lessen enthusiasm during a middle period of the implementation process.

9. Monitoring and Evaluating the Interventions

The degree to which these problems are worked out determines the fate of the remainder of the process. Some of the problems may be mechanical (equipment breaks down), financial (other demands intrude, state funding decreases, inflation increases), personal (resistance becomes evident when the plan is finally implemented), or administrative (the administration decides that another problem is more important and decides to pull back its support). The characteristics of the system, described previously in this chapter, exert their influence at this point. The hope is that the system is strong enough to withstand these potentially destructive factors and can proceed with a successful change effort.

Other possibilities include the fact that the interventions are being implemented correctly but are not having the desired effect. Your formative evaluation suggests that some aspects of the interventions need to be changed. This is often very discouraging to those who designed and/or are implementing the interventions. Getting past the all-too-common finding that plans need to be changed in midstream is a major challenge to those who are personally involved in wanting to see the interventions be successful. If the planners and implementers are willing to change the interventions, you may hope to see an improved product.

Example: Changing to a Consultation-Based System of Service Delivery for General/Special Education

In this project a school district changed its special education service delivery system from one dominated by a pull-out resource specialist model to one characterized by general education placements with a consultation support system. This project is not based on an actual example; rather, it is a composite of various change efforts that I have observed. Goldberg (1995) provides an actual example of a case with a similar goal. Rosenfield and Gravois (1999) discuss a long-term system-improvement process that acknowledges the necessity of change within the school culture as a prerequisite to change in the work of individuals or separate classrooms.

PROBLEM STATEMENT

The teachers and administrators at King Elementary, a K–6 school in the Middletown School District, had been concerned for some time about the efficacy of their pull-out oriented special education delivery service for the approximately 6% of their 900 students who had been identified as having a specific learning disability (SLD), predominantly in the area of reading and written language. The concerns included the following:

1. the *scheduling* results in too many students missing too much of their general education program;
2. the *achievement* of the students being pulled out doesn't seem to justify the time spent away from the general education curriculum; and
3. the *stigma* attached to being in the program is problematic for many of the targeted students.

King is in many ways a typical elementary school. It is located in an urban neighborhood consisting mainly of working-class people. Of its students, 62% are Anglo-American, 24% are Latino, 10% are African American, and the remainder are primarily Asian American or Middle Eastern American. Of the teachers, 80% are Anglo-American females; there are two Latino males and one African American female. Of the 54 students identified as learning disabled, 55% are Anglo-American, 30% are Latino, and 12% are Black.

HISTORY OF CONCERN

Schools, like all well-established large institutions, have a culture, a set of norms and habits that guide their everyday activities. Since pull-out programs for students with mild-to-moderate degrees of disabling conditions, primarily in the category of learning disabilities, have been part of that culture, people have come to expect that this system will exist and will provide some extra, or "special," education for students with disabilities. Parents are generally comforted to know, and sometimes are very insistent, that their child will get this special treatment. At the same time, there have always been voices within the system that have questioned the value of this form of special education (Dunn, 1968; Howe & Miramontes, 1992). Over the last decade, the number and strength of the voices questioning the status quo in special education have grown steadily (Goodlad & Lovitt, 1993; Lewis & Doorlag, 1999; Lloyd, Singh, & Repp, 1991; Salend, 1998; Stainback & Stainback, 1996), partly because of a lack of supporting empirical evidence, and partly because of a strict interpretation of the intent of the "least restrictive placement" provisions of IDEA (P.L. 108-446).

The history of the concern at King School is based only somewhat on these national concerns about special education as a separate system. The school staff members at King are more concerned about their own students than about national agendas. They feel that students attending the RSP are missing out on the general education curriculum and may not be making enough gains in the resource classes, in spite of competent teachers in those classes, to justify the continued existence of this program.

CONCERNED PARTIES (CONSTITUENTS)

Any change in service delivery affects both general and special education. Thus, it is no exaggeration to say that all persons concerned with the school will be potentially affected by a change in this area. Naturally the students will be affected, as will their parents. All teachers and ancillary staff can expect a significant change in how they work. For example, general education teachers used to the idea that there is a program "out there" for dealing with students who manifest learning (and possibly behavior) problems need to consider the fact that these students may no longer go "out there" but will stay in the general education classes. The teacher will be expected to deal with the students' learning problems with the help of a collaborating staff of administrators, special education teachers (who may no longer have a classroom of their own), and ancillary staff. If this plan is to be successful, these ancillary staff (school psychologists, counselors, and speech and language specialists) will also experience a major change in their expected daily activities. The thought of all this change, based on what many consider to be an unsubstantiated premise—that students with mild disabilities will do better in the mainstream if given accomodations and modifications—seems overwhelming to some staff but signifies positive potential to others.

KEY TRIGGER INCIDENT(S)

In this case, three incidents occurred simultaneously and together served as triggers for this systems-change project:

1. The principal attended a district workshop in which the idea of more mainstreaming of students with mild disabilities was briefly discussed.
2. The school psychologist attended a national convention in which she heard about resource teachers without classrooms who spent the majority of their time in general education classes.
3. One of the resource teachers (the "hidden" consultant in this example), fully expecting to be discouraged by her general education peers, found a number of them supportive of the idea.

In a few weeks, an idea once regarded as unlikely to flourish rapidly became a hot topic. The impetus for change had formed. It just needed to be promoted and nurtured. It was from this point on that the special education teacher (consultant) found herself having many "nurturing" discussions with the principal.

DEVELOPING INITIAL PLANS FOR CHANGE

Following up on the trigger events, the principal called a meeting to discuss how King school could meet the challenges inherent in this change. At the meeting were the two special education (resource) teachers, the district director of special education, the ancillary staff, and a representative teacher from each of the grade levels. This group developed the following list of concerns and questions:

- This new model calls for "collaborating." Who exactly is going to do the collaborating? Will it be others in addition to the two resource teachers?
- What about those learning disabled students who are probably somewhat ADHD and manifest behavior problems? They have a very difficult time maintaining themselves for 5 hours in a general education class. How will not giving them an "escape valve" (that is, the special education room) be helpful to them?
- There are 30 classes at King school. How are these two resource teachers going to be able to serve 15 classes each? Aren't they going to be spread too thin?
- Just what is this collaborative model going to look like? How will any given child get the assistance he needs, according to his IEP, while being in a general education classroom?
- What about the parents of the identified students? Aren't they going to be bothered when they hear that their children aren't going to be getting "special" education (i.e., resource teacher assistance) anymore?

The committee realized that developing answers to some of these questions would require careful deliberation. The principal asked for volunteers to work on subcommittees to develop some tentative answers and then to meet together again in 2 weeks. Based on the answers received from the subcommittees and discussed by the whole committee, they decided that the idea was worth pursuing. They put together a statement to be sent to the parents of the children who would be involved. Another meeting was held in 2 weeks. Prior to then the letters to the parents were sent, and some parents responded, some (with alarm) to members of the board of education. Also, the board of education met, and some questions about this proposal came up at their meeting. (The superintendent had briefed the board. Their response to questions from citizens was that a new service delivery system was being studied but that it was only in the preliminary stages; no decisions had yet been made.)

FERMENTATION PERIOD

This is that period between official meetings when people air their views in the lunchroom, the hallway, the parking lot, and the neighborhood. Three different unofficial groups developed: one in favor of the inclusion of all students with mild-to-moderate disabilities into the regular program with consultative support to the general education teachers, one opposed to it, and a small offshoot of "middle-road" people who thought that inclusion might be good for some of the students with SLD but not for all of them. The questions and problems just mentioned were discussed, with each group answering the questions from its point of view. Each group claimed to be advocating for the best interests of the children; and, like the blind man and the elephant, each supported its own perspective, unable or unwilling to admit that the other side might have a better perspective. It was clearly time for the leaders to take control, clarify issues, and seek consensus. Otherwise, the groups would continue to polarize, and the proposal would die.

Two weeks after its initial meeting, the committee—now expanded to include any interested staff member and three parents who want to be included (requiring the meeting to be held in the evening, distressing some of the teacher members)—convened again for a 2-hour meeting that was structured and coordinated by a small subcommittee (consisting of the consultant, two teachers, two parents, and the principal) organized by the principal. The meeting lasted 2 hours. At the end, after summarizing what she heard, the principal asked for a straw vote from the group. She asked, "Should we pursue this proposal further or continue providing service in our current model?"

The vote was 16 to 5 in favor of moving forward with the proposal. The principal said that she was prepared to move ahead to the plan-development stage, with September of the following year as the target date of implementation. She asked for volunteers to serve on the planning committee; eight people, including two parents, volunteered.

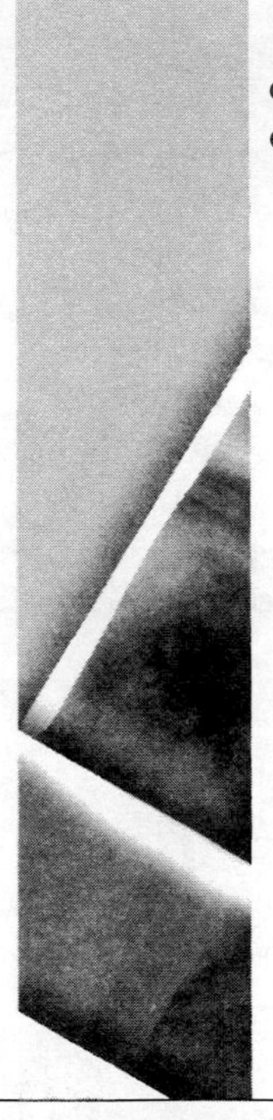

All things considered, this was a very effective meeting. Although there was not complete unanimity (there rarely is in public education), there was enough support to encourage the principal to go forward.

Now the real work began and consisted of the following elements:

1. Planning the logistics: job descriptions, possible time allocations, possibility of additional staff time, materials purchasing, and so on.
2. Contacting all constituents with information on an ongoing basis.
3. Holding IEPs this academic year for all involved students to indicate that services will be provided in the general education classroom with consultative assistance to the regular teacher.
4. Creating a series of staff development workshops on inclusion issues.
5. Contacting the special education department of the local state college to see if the faculty was interested in working collaboratively on this project. One faculty member was delighted to do so and waived his fee for permission to use this project as a case example for his textbook.
6. Networking with other districts to see which had moved toward a collaborative model; find out how they did it.
7. Seeking possible outside funding to cover anticipated costs.

ACTIVITY 8.11

Comment on the steps taken during the fermentation period. What effective things happened? What might have been done differently? What potential problems have not been dealt with adequately?

SELECTION OF INTERVENTIONS

During the remainder of the academic year, the committee, with some changes in composition and now usually including five concerned parents, met monthly to put the final touches on the plan scheduled to start in the fall of the next school year. All parents of students with SLD were asked to attend an IEP meeting about their child. There the following philosophy and plan for full inclusion with consultative help was outlined to them:

1. We believe we can meet the needs of your child without having to remove her from her peers in the general education class. We can do this by having the special education teachers and other staff assist the general education teachers with ways of accommodating the curriculum and other classroom expectations to the ability level of your child in those subject areas affected by your child's SLD. In this

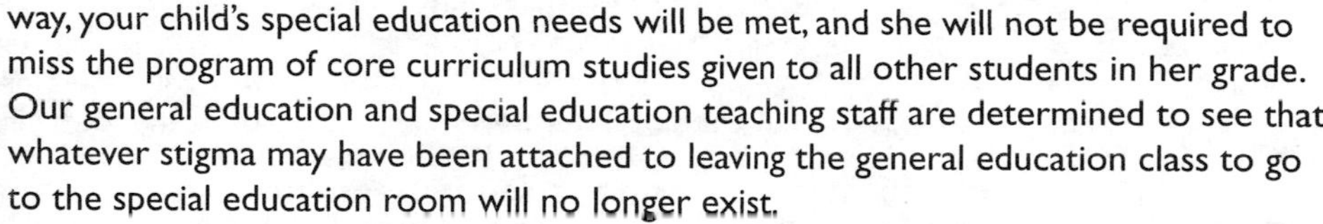

way, your child's special education needs will be met, and she will not be required to miss the program of core curriculum studies given to all other students in her grade. Our general education and special education teaching staff are determined to see that whatever stigma may have been attached to leaving the general education class to go to the special education room will no longer exist.

2. Your child's regular education teacher will be assisted by anyone on staff who has the expertise to provide consultation (assistance, advice, specific skills) to the general education teacher. Although this person will usually be one of the special education teachers, consultants may also include the school counselor, school psychologist, or other general education teachers. As the parent, you are invited to take part in whatever consultative services you want from our staff (such as homework hints, discipline, ways of supporting your child, and so on).

3. Your child's specific program will be determined by the general education teacher in consultation with the individuals just mentioned and with the student study team (SST). These people will meet at least bi-monthly to discuss your child's progress, more often as needed. You will be given a copy of the plan for your child's special education program on a bi-monthly basis. Of course, you will be invited to these SST meetings when they are held.

4. We anticipate that we will be able to hire two more floating aides to assist us in implementing some of the accommodations necessary for some students. We are also going to hire a teacher who will act as a substitute teacher in classes when your child's teacher needs to attend a meeting (SST or otherwise) concerning our inclusion program.

IMPLEMENTATION OF INTERVENTIONS

The program as just outlined was implemented in September. All but three parents supported the new plan. The IEPs on the students whose parents supported the change were modified the previous spring to reflect their children's full inclusion with consultative assistance on a regular basis. The three parents who refused this change were offered a transfer to a more traditional pull-out program in another school. The SST meetings designed to formalize the plans for each currently identified student were held Monday through Thursday from 8:00 to 8:45, with three students discussed at each meeting. Although the structure of these 15-minute sessions varied somewhat depending on needs, the general plan was to devote 5 minutes to a review of the current plan and 10 minutes to the development of a new bi-monthly plan, copies of which are sent home to the parents. This allowed for all 51 involved students to have their plans reviewed on a regular basis. When more students enter the program, or the population of identified students goes down, this schedule can be adjusted.

Once every 2 months, during a student-free day, the inclusion program staff takes part in inservice activities related to inclusion for half the day. For the rest of the day, they get together and share success stories and discuss problems under the leadership of a local university faculty member who is knowledgeable about inclusive programs.

MONITORING AND EVALUATING THE INTERVENTIONS

The question of plan evaluation had been discussed throughout the plan's development. Teachers and parents were concerned about the following:

1. Will these students profit academically as much from an inclusion program as they will from the traditional pull-out program?
2. How well-accepted will these students be when fully integrated into general education classes?
3. How will included students feel about themselves when they are in the general education classes full time? How do these feelings compare to those they held about themselves when they were in the pull-out program?

To answer question 1, staff members give all students with SLD achievement tests, both norm-based and curriculum-based, in reading, writing, and math in January and June of the planning year. These data are used as a baseline growth rate and are to be compared to data gathered during the same 2 months during the first year of the plan's implementation.

Question 2 was answered using a sociometric measure in which children are asked to select students they would most like to work on school projects with and would be most likely to invite to a party. Gresham and Elliott (1989) have reviewed the use of these techniques with students with SLD.

Question 3 has two parts. The first was measured by a simple questionnaire to be administered to all included students and an equal number of nondisabled students from the same classes asking for opinions about their acceptance in classes. The second part in question 3 required that the included students be given a self-report questionnaire modified from Piers and Harris (1996) during the last 6 months of the planning year and then again a year later when they were fully included. The district director of research was consulted about appropriate minimally intrusive procedures to use and was responsible for data analysis.

SUMMARY OF CASE EXAMPLE:

This example indicates how a school, under the direction of a strong leader, a resource teacher-consultant, and a cooperative staff, was able to develop a plan for the termination of a resource program based on the pull-out model and replace it with an inclusion model that returned almost all students identified as SLD to age-appropriate general education classes. It also allowed for planning time, collaborative efforts, and continued staff development. The primary hurdles overcome by the staff were (1) the typical resistance that accompanies any change effort, (2) concern about the ability to find the funds for hiring a floating substitute teacher, and (3) getting agreement from parents who may have become comfortable with the pull-out program. A brief description of a plan for program evaluation was also provided.

ACTIVITY 8.12

Review the plan just described. How effective do you think it will be? What are some possible problems that may arise? How might you design a program differently?

SUMMARY

This chapter has reviewed some general considerations for consultants and others in the schools who are interested in systems change (reform). It is crucial that the constituents of the problem are involved at every step beyond initial discussions so that they will feel some ownership of the solutions that are determined to be the best for the local situation.

An example of a school (and district) engaging in a systems change was presented. It demonstrated how a school consultant, operating closely with a school principal, monitored a structured approach that considered all the important elements discussed earlier in the chapter.

REFERENCES

Adelman, H. S., & Taylor, L. (1997). Toward a scale-up model for replicating new approaches to schooling. *Journal of Educational and Psychological Consultation, 8*(2), 197–230.

Alberto, P. A., & Troutman, A. C. (1999). *Applied behavioral analysis for teachers* (5th ed.). Upper Saddle River, NJ: Merrill/Prentice Hall.

Bacharach, S. B. (1990). *Educational reform: Making sense of it all.* Boston: Allyn & Bacon.

Basham, A., Appleton, V., & Dykeman, C. (2000). *Team building in education.* Denver, CO: Love Publishing.

Block, P. (1981). *Flawless consultation.* San Diego, CA: Pfeiffer.

Borgelt, C., & Conoley, J. (1999). Psychology in the schools: System intervention case examples. In C. R. Reynolds & T. B. Gutkin (Eds.), *The handbook of school psychology* (pp. 1,056–1,076). New York: Wiley.

Brown, D., Pryzwansky, W. B., & Schulte, A. C. (2001). *Psychological consultation: Introduction to theory and practice* (5th ed.). Boston: Allyn & Bacon.

Brubacher, J., Case, C., & Reagan, T. (1994). *Becoming a reflective educator.* Thousand Oaks, CA: Corwin.

Dougherty, A. M. (2000). *Psychological consultation and collaboration.* Belmont, CA: Wadsworth/Thomson Learning.

Dunn, L. M. (1968). Special education for the mildly retarded: Is much of it justified? *Exceptional Children, 35,* 5–24.

Egan, G. (1985). *Change agent skills in helping and human service settings.* Monterey, CA: Brooks/Cole.

Egan, G. (1998). *The skilled helper* (6th ed.). Monterey, CA: Brooks/Cole.

Erchul, W., & Martin, B. (2002). *School consultation: Conceptual and empirical bases of practice.* New York: Kluwer Academic/Plenum Publishers.

Fashola, O., & Slavin, R. (1998). Schoolwide reform models: What works? *Phi Delta Kappan, 79,* 370–379.

Friend, M., & Cook, L. (2003). *Interactions: Collaboration skills for school professionals* (4th ed.). New York: Longman.

Fullan, M. (1991). *The new meaning of educational change.* New York: Teachers College Press.

Fullan, M. (1995). *Change forces: The sequel.* Levittown, PA: Falmer.

Glazer, N. (2003). The american way of school reform. In D. Gordon & P. Graham (Eds.), *A nation reformed? American education 20 years after* A Nation At Risk (pp. 153–164). Cambridge, MA: Harvard University Press.

Goldberg, I. (1995). Implementing the consultant teacher model: Interfacing multiple linking relationships and roles with systemic conditions. *Journal of Educational and Psychological Consultation, 6*(2), 175–190.

Goodlad, J. I., & Lovitt, T. C. (Eds.). (1993). *Integrating general and special education*. Upper Saddle River, NJ: Merrill/Prentice Hall.

Gresham, F. M., & Elliott, S. N. (1989). Social skills assessment technology for LD students. *Learning Disability Quarterly, 12,* 141–152.

Hall, G. E., Rutherford, W., Hord, S., & Huling, L. (1984). Effects of three principal styles on school improvement. *Educational Leadership, 41*(5), 22–31.

Harvey, T. R. (1990). *Checklist for change: A pragmatic approach to creating and controlling change.* Boston: Allyn & Bacon.

Heifitz, R., & Laurie, D. L. (1997). The work of leadership. *Harvard Business Review,* 75, 124–134.

Heron, T., & Harris, K. (2001). *The educational consultant: Helping professionals, parents, and students in inclusive classrooms*. Austin, TX: Pro-Ed.

Howe, K. R., & Miramontes, O. B. (1992). *The ethics of special education.* New York: Teachers College Press.

Illback, R., & Zins, J. (1995). Organizational interventions in educational settings. *Journal of Educational and Psychological Consultation, 6*(3), 217–236.

Illback, R. J., Zins, J. E., & Maher, C. A. (1999). Program planning and evaluation: Principles, procedures, and planned change. In C. Reynolds & T. Gutkin (Eds.), *Handbook of school psychology* (3rd ed., pp. 907–932). New York: Wiley.

Knoff, H. (1995). Facilitating school-based organizational change and strategic planning. In A. Thomas & J. Grimes (Eds.), *Best practices in school psychology IV* (pp. 239–252). Bethesda, MD: NASP.

Knoff, H. M. (2002). Best practices in facilitating school-based organizational change and strategic planning. In A. Thomas & J. Grimes (Eds.), *Best practices in school psychology IV* (pp. 235–254). Bethesda, MD: NASP.

Kozol, J. (1992). *Savage inequalities: Children in America's schools.* New York: Crown.

Lewis, R. B., & Doorlag, D. H. (1999). *Teaching special students in general education classrooms.* Upper Saddle River, NJ: Merrill/Prentice Hall.

Lloyd, J. W., Singh, N. N., & Repp, A. C. (Eds.). (1991). *The Regular Education Initiative: Alternative perspectives on concepts, issues, and models*. Sycamore, IL: Sycamore.

McAdams, R. P. (1997). A systems approach to school reform. *Phi Delta Kappan,* 78, 138–142.

McLaughlin, M., & Marsh, D. (1978). Staff development and school change. *Teacher's College Record, 80,* 70–95.

Miles, M. B., & Lewis, K. S. (1990). Mustering the will and skill for change: The findings from a four-year study of high schools that are experiencing real improvement offer insights into successful change. *Educational Leadership, 47,* 57–61.

Nagle, R. J. (2002). Best practices in planning and conducting needs assessments. In A. Thomas & J. Grimes (Eds.), *Best practices in school psychology IV* (pp. 265–280). Bethesda, MD: NASP.

National Commission on Excellence in Education. (1983). *A nation at risk: The imperative for educational reform.* Washington, DC: U.S. Government Printing Office.

National Research Council. (2004). *Engaging schools: Fostering high school students' motivation to learn.* Washington, DC: National Academies Press.

Parsons, R. D. (1996). *The skilled consultant.* Boston: Allyn & Bacon.

Piers, E. V., & Harris, D. B. (1996). *The Piers-Harris children's self-concept scale.* Los Angeles: Western Psychological Services.

Rosenfield, S. A., & Gravois, T. A. (1999). Working with teams in the school. In C. Reynolds & T. Gutkin (Eds.), *The handbook of school psychology* (3rd ed., pp. 1,025–1,040). New York: Wiley.

Safran, S. P., & Safran, J. S. (1997). Prereferral consultation and intervention assistance teams revisited: Some new food for thought. *Journal of Educational and Psychological Consultation, 8*(1), 93–100.

Salend, S. J. (1998). *Effective mainstreaming: Creating inclusive classrooms.* Upper Saddle River, NJ: Merrill/Prentice Hall.

Sarason, S. B. (1990). *The predictable failure of educational reform: Can we change before it's too late?* San Francisco: Jossey-Bass.

Snapp, M., Hickman, J. A., & Conoley, J. C. (1990). Systems intervention in school settings. In T. B. Gutkin & C. R. Reynolds (Eds.), *The handbook of school psychology* (2nd ed., pp. 922–936). New York: Wiley.

Sparks, D., & Hirsh, S. (1997). *A new vision for staff development.* Alexandria, VA: Association for Curriculum and Development.

Stainback, W., & Stainback, S. (Eds.). (1996). *Controversial issues confronting special education: Divergent perspectives* (2nd ed.). Boston: Allyn & Bacon.

Tyack, D., & Cuban, L. (1995). *Tinkering toward Utopia: A century of public school reform*. Cambridge, MA: Harvard University Press.

Valentine, E. P. (1991). *Strategic management in education: A focus on strategic planning*. Boston: Allyn & Bacon.

Wang, M. C., Haertel, G. D., & Walberg, H. J. (1993). Toward a knowledge base for school learning. *Review of Educational Leadership, 63*(3), 249–294.

Wehlage, G., Smith, G., & Lipman, P. (1992). Restructuring urban schools: The new futures experience. *American Educational Research Journal, 29*, 51–93.

Welch, M. (1999). The DECIDE strategy for decision making and problem solving: A workshop template for preparing professionals for educational partnerships. *Journal of Educational and Psychological Consultation, 10*(4), 363–377.

Welch, M., & Sheridan, S. (1995). *Educational partnerships: Serving students at risk*. Fort Worth, TX. Harcourt Brace.

Zins, J. E., & Illback, R. J. (1995). Consulting to facilitate planned organizational change in schools. *Journal of Educational and Psychological Consultation, 6*(3), 237–245.

Case Studies in Consultation: Behavior and Academic Problems in the Classroom

OBJECTIVES

1. Present two cases utilizing the SOCS approach where the primary concerns are either behavior or academic problems exhibited by students at two different grade levels.
2. Ask the readers a set of questions about the process and interventions used by the consultants and consultees in these cases.
3. Reflect on the content of previous chapters, especially Chapters 5 (where the outline for these case studies, SOCS, was presented) and 6 and 7 (which discussed issues in consultation regarding behavior and academic problems), and demonstrate how a consultant can use the ideas and information presented in these chapters.

ORIENTATION TO THE CASES

The SOCS system helps the consultant and the consultee follow an organized system designed to generate solutions for referrals and to persist in consultative activities until the situation has improved to a reasonable degree.

The following two cases are not presented as perfect examples of how consultation should be done. Depending on one's theoretical orientation, and the process one chooses to follow, it is certainly possible that these cases could have been handled quite differently with different possible results. What I have tried to do is follow a set of steps (SOCS) primarily embedded in a behavioral approach and to represent typical realities in schools, including both positive and negative aspects of these realities. The cases were gleaned from my experiences as a special education teacher and a school psychologist/consultant. None of the names of the students or any other participants are real; think of them as composites of students and school personnel who could very well be in the schools you are, or will soon be, working in.

Sequential numbers in brackets within the cases refer to questions or comments designed to stimulate discussion about the consultative process. The reader is encouraged to respond to these questions and comments in light of his or her own perceptions of these cases and others with which he or she may be familiar.

The first case in this chapter concerns a 14-year-old boy (Todd) who presents with a serious problem with defiance. In this case a school psychologist combines his consultative work with some counseling of Todd. There is a good degree of success in this case, though perhaps not as much as he and the teachers might have hoped for.

Case 1: Defiance

Todd Jackson, who is now 14 years, 2 months of age, was referred in November of his seventh-grade year because of his defiant behavior, particularly toward his social studies and English teachers, who "have had it up to here with him." A review of the referral with his other teachers revealed that he was a fair student with them, not an academic star but not a major problem. They would not have referred him.

Two years ago, Todd's fifth-grade teacher noticed this problem. She suspended him twice, referred him to the school counselor, and also referred him to SST. Todd was somewhat better in grade 6, where he was under the thumb of a particularly forceful male teacher. Now in the seventh grade, Todd has six different teachers and reacts differently to each of them, being particularly difficult in the classrooms of the two referring teachers, Mrs. Hansen and Ms. Jones.

Todd was retained in grade 1. In grade 3 he was referred for learning disability placement but was not found eligible under his district's strict guidelines. The district has no other funded source of help for poor achievers, so parents are advised to find whatever tutoring they can on their own. Todd apparently did get some tutoring during grade 3, and his reading and writing skills improved. However, he has remained a poor academic student, typically earning Cs and Ds [1].

Todd is the younger of two children in an intact family. His father is a machinist, steadily employed, and his mother works full time as a department store clerk. English is the only language spoken at home. Todd's older brother, now 18, dropped out of high school in his junior year and is employed for 20 hours a week at McDonald's. He has gang affiliations but has not been arrested. Todd admits to not liking his brother; in fact, he may be afraid of him.

Todd's mother, Mrs. Jackson, states that Todd has been increasingly defiant toward her, also. He is not this way toward his father. Mrs. Jackson would like help in dealing with Todd, since she is afraid he will turn out like his older brother if somebody doesn't do something about it soon.

RECEIPT OF A REFERRAL AND INITIAL THOUGHTS ABOUT IT

My name is Bill Casey. I'm the school psychologist at Kennedy Junior High, which has 1,000 students in grades 7, 8, and 9. At Kennedy we use a consultation-based service delivery model, which means that we try to work collaboratively with one another to help solve the learning or behavior problems of our students. All initial referrals come to the grade-level counselor, who decides how to deal with them. Learning problem referrals are usually sent to the SST or the RSP teacher-consultant, but behavior or adjustment problems are often sent to my office unless the referring teacher or a school administrator believes they should go directly to the SST for some reason. I usually refer cases to the SST if my efforts to resolve them have not been successful. In serious cases I refer the parents to appropriate outside agencies.

I learned about Todd last May when our counselors and I took our annual trip to the K–6 feeder school to consult with its counselor about "at-risk" students. Of the 60 students coming from that school, Todd's name was among the 5 identified as potential dropouts based on his fifth- and sixth-grade teachers' comments and the fact that his older brother had dropped out. My procedure is to call all at-risk students into my office during the first week of the semester and get to know them. Our counselors do the same. Then we discuss the ones who appear the most in need of our services. I remember Todd from that meeting; in my notes I wrote that he was sullen and uncommunicative, very defensive, and eager to get out of my office. When the referral came last week, I wasn't surprised [2].

Our teachers are expected to contact students' parents prior to referring students to us, to see if a resolution can be effected at that level. In this case they have noticed no good results from those discussions. When submitting their referrals they are asked to try to define their concerns behaviorally: to give concrete examples and to avoid inferences. Mrs. Hansen and Ms. Jones put in the referral together since their lunchroom conversation convinced them that Todd was acting the same way in each of their rooms. His other teachers say he is a poor student but not a major problem.

My initial impressions are that Todd is too old (too mature physically) for seventh grade (the ghost of first-grade retention has come back to haunt us [3]), that he seeks out nice (which he interprets to mean that they are weak or defenseless) women to humiliate, and that he feels that his main chance at recognition is to act the role of a rebellious teen and to lead his less-mature peers into the joys of adolescent nonconformity. The referring teachers may have different views. Let's see.

INITIAL DISCUSSION WITH THE TEACHERS

Both consultees came to see me at lunchtime today. I've known each of them for at least 3 years. They are both competent; Mrs. Hansen tends to be much less outgoing than Ms. Jones. After brief pleasantries we got into our discussion. They defined Todd's problems (behaviors of concern) as refusal to follow directions, verbally provoking others, and talking back to both teachers with an attitude that says, "Hey, Teach, make me." Both have spoken to him about these concerns; he acts disinterested, bored, and condescending. Both have called home. Mrs. Hansen talked to Mr. Jackson, who told her that she has to be firm with him. Ms. Jones talked to Mrs. Jackson, who said that she would talk to Todd about it but was putting up with the same behavior herself.

I asked both consultees to demonstrate for me what he did, while I played the part of a teacher. They were quite forthcoming in their portrayal of an arrogant pop-off, the kind you're glad isn't your child. I then asked about their reactions to him. They agreed that it varied depending on the situation, but usually they gave him a frown of disapproval, asked him to apologize, or threatened to send him to the office. Mrs. Hansen had sent him twice, but Ms. Jones hadn't, pending advice from me. I asked them about the frequency of these defiant behaviors. They estimated that they occurred once or twice a day, depending on their need to interact directly with him. His behavior toward the other students tended to be bullying. He's bigger than almost everybody else, seems sexually more mature, and flaunts it. He probably says suggestive things to some of the girls because they are often heard telling him to shut up. All in all, he isn't liked, but he is given a rather wide berth. In short, Todd is an unpopular student who is increasing the behaviors that make him unpopular. He seems to be the kind of student that Dreikurs, Grunwald, and Pepper (1982) had in mind for the category "power seekers." If you use the DSM-IV, you might say that he has an oppositional defiant disorder; according to Quay's (1986) system, Todd would be classified as having a conduct disorder [4].

With time being short as usual, we decided to keep track of Todd's defiant behavior for 1 week, during which I would call him into my office and discuss the problem with him. Mrs. Hansen said she wanted to do more; she was burning out fast. I asked her what she had in mind. She suggested detention contingent on his refusal to follow her directions, if only to get his attention. Ms. Jones readily agreed but was concerned that detention might make him worse. What did I think? I said that each of them had the right to invoke the detention contingency; it was available. However, the school principal and the counseling staff discouraged its use, preferring to deal with disruptive behavior in nonpunitive ways until it is clear that something stronger is needed.

The teachers each decided to keep track of Todd's defiant acts and then, after class every day, have him stay long enough for them to tell him what they had observed. I asked them to consider telling him about any positive things he might have done, but they both looked at me as if to say "You haven't been paying attention." Then they both rushed off to class [5].

CLASSROOM (ECOLOGICAL) OBSERVATION

Ordinarily I try to do classroom observations, especially if I don't know the teacher very well, if the teacher asks me to, or if the behavior is so strange that it has to be seen. In this case I thought I knew what I would see in both classes. After all, I had seen other students in the past, both boys and girls, engage in this sort of behavior. I decided to forego the visit and instead have Todd come in to see me.

I hoped that by going to a direct-service approach with Todd instead of the usual indirect approach of consultation, I would be able to get a deeper understanding of the dynamics that might account for Todd's behavior. I wanted to confront him with its importance, just as the consultees were doing. This was about to become Todd's week in the hot seat [6].

USING PARENTS AS ALLIES IN THE CONSULTATION PROCESS

I reached Mrs. Jackson by phone at work for one of those 1-minute phone calls that are often all you can get with working people. I reviewed our concerns; she understood. I asked her how we might be able to help. She said she thought he needed to be dealt with firmly. She wasn't able to be firm with him because he often ignores her or yells at her. She couldn't talk any more, a customer was waiting. What time could she call me? Tomorrow between 8:30 and 9:00? I agreed. Good, she'd call. Good-bye [7].

GETTING TEACHERS AND PARENTS TOGETHER: THE SST MEETING

As I have indicated, I rarely go to the SST with a behavior problem unless it is very severe and is definitely impeding academic progress or disrupting the progress of the other students. It is possible, of course, that SST members might come up with some ideas beyond what my consultees and I can come up with, but in this case I didn't think so. Rather than take members' time at this point, I opted to not go to SST; perhaps we'll come back to it later.

ASSESSMENT OF THE STUDENT

Psychological Assessment

Todd had been evaluated in an earlier grade when referred for possible eligibility for special education and related services under the category of learning disability. At that time his cognitive ability was found to be in the average range with no significant deviations in his pattern of scores. No serious difficulties in information processing were noted. Although his achievement was not strong, he was not found eligible for special education. As implied earlier, Todd is not strong academically, but his achievement, according to the group tests, is not seriously deficient. He can hold his own academically when he chooses to do so. I did not plan for any further academic assessment at this time. Also, no formal personality tests (see Chapter 6) were administered at the time of his earlier assessment or at the present time. If Todd's behavior becomes indicative of a serious emotional disturbance, such tests may be given at that time. For the present, a behavioral approach will be emphasized.

Psychodynamic, Ecological, and Biophysical Factors

We know that Todd comes from a home in which the disciplinary power seems to belong primarily to the father; his mother admits this. We have also learned that Todd has an older brother who had school difficulties and possibly engages in antisocial behaviors. Although Todd does not seem to identify strongly with his brother, he is at a stage in which he may resort to a lowest common denominator as a temporary model, primarily because it makes him feel more powerful. Clearly his mother is concerned about this. One wonders if she hasn't made reference to Todd about his turning out like his brother, a future scenario that she fears.

In an effort to understand the dynamics that support and drive Todd's behavior and to suggest ways in which Mr. and Mrs. Jackson might be able to work together in helping Todd through his adolescence, I decided to arrange a meeting with one or, preferably, both parents along with Todd. Pending that meeting, I reviewed with the two consultees what I thought were the dynamics so far and mentioned my concerns about stopping their apparently successful intervention after only a week. With my encouragement they agreed to continue with the present plan.

Mr. and Mrs. Jackson agreed to come to the school at 7:30 the following morning. We could have 15 minutes together. I asked them to bring Todd with them [8]. When they arrived, we spent a few minutes with small-talk rapport building and then got into our mutual interests. When I talked about the concerns of both consultees, Mrs. Jackson nodded a lot, and Mr. Jackson looked very unhappy, glancing first at me and then at Todd. I also revealed the latest turnaround that the consultees had reported, emphasizing Todd's prosocial actions. This gained a smile from everybody except, unfortunately, Mr. Jackson. Deciding to focus on the negative only, he pinned Todd down with an angry look and told him he won't have that sort of behavior and this is the last he wants to hear of it. (Wouldn't it be nice if that's all it took, I thought!) Mr. Jackson didn't comment on the prosocial part. Todd's response was that he was doing fine in all the other classes; these two were just boring. To my surprise, Mrs. Jackson said that if that was true, couldn't Todd be moved out of those classes? I thought all of these comments were telling in regard to the family dynamics: Mr. Jackson gives an order and focuses on the negative, and Mrs. Jackson makes an excuse and seeks an escape route for Todd. I responded by saying that Todd and I were discussing his behavior in social studies and English. I felt that we had made some good progress over the past week and that we should continue to try to have Todd meet his responsibilities in all his classes since I felt confident that he could. I asked Todd what he thought, and he said, "Yeah, I guess." I thought that answer kept him OK in the sight of both parents: He's passively promising to behave to satisfy his father, and he's leaving the door open for continued complaints about these boring classes in case he needs to use this ploy again with his mother. I suggested that we talk about ways in which Todd's parents could help him with his schoolwork, and both parents sat up to listen. Todd looked bored.

I mentioned the following four ways that parents can help:

1. Set aside a homework time.
2. Ask to see what the assignments are before and after they are done.
3. Give help and encouragement as needed.
4. Check periodically with Todd's teachers to see how he is doing.

I reminded them of the teachers' room phone numbers and the time of each teacher's free period. We concluded the conference by reassuring each other that Todd could do well and that we would work together closely to see that he does [9].

The biophysical possibilities were not brought up at this meeting because there was no reason to suspect that Todd has any difficulty in this area. He has always been healthy, he's never shown any of the symptoms of ADHD, and his vision and hearing are normal. In this case there do not seem to be any significant biophysical contributors to his behaviors.

I asked both consultees to meet with me after school for 10 minutes to review the conference. They were both pleased with me for taking the time to have the conference, and they felt that things looked good. We briefly discussed their classroom situations (task expectations, class format, seating arrangements, grouping, and so on) and any ways we could think of to change Todd's role image in the classroom. We had already decided to continue monitoring his defiance and to give him daily feedback. Now we decided to put more emphasis on whatever prosocial things we see him doing. I said I would find an excuse for getting him to help me on some task in my office and to chat with him while he was doing it.

I decided that I would do a functional behavioral assessment after I met with Todd and heard again from the teachers. Todd and I met for 15 minutes the next morning. Initially he acted like he had before: closed-mouthed, sullen, mildly hostile, and generally uncooperative. I tried all my reflective techniques, but there wasn't much forthcoming from him except denial and apparent distortion. Here is a transcript of our conversation:

Consultant: Todd, I've asked you to come in to see me again because I'm concerned about your relationship with two of your teachers, Mrs. Hansen and Ms. Jones.

Todd: What're you talking about? I didn't do nothing.

Consultant: What these two teachers have told me is that you sometimes refuse to follow their directions, you provoke others and get them angry with you, and you talk back to these teachers.

Todd: [silence]

Consultant: [after 20 seconds] I've hit you with some pretty bad news. I'm wondering what you think about what I've said.

Todd: Yeah, well, they're all like picking on me, you know. There's plenty of guys screwing off in there, and I'm the one who's in trouble.

Consultant: You're concerned that they're picking on you and you're in some sort of trouble for it?

Todd: Yeah.

Consultant: You're probably right that there are some others who also give the teachers grief, and you are right about being in some trouble with your teachers. After all, they don't like it when students don't behave well in class. Do you see how they could be bothered by your behavior?

Todd: Yeah, but they're always bugging me about, you know, like, "Do this, do that." I do my work. The other teachers ain't complaining, are they?

Consultant: I'm glad you brought that up. You're right. I've asked all your other teachers, and they tell me you're doing OK in their classes. So obviously you're not a troublemaker. What is it about these two classes? That's what I'd like to know.

Todd: They're a drag. The stuff's boring. Who cares about history anyway? And in English we only write and listen to everybody read. What a bore.

Consultant: Not all of your work is exciting to you. What subjects do you like this semester?

Todd: Phys ed, home ec; math's a drag, but Mr. Simpson's cool. Shop's got too many rules. They're all OK, I guess. I gotta get back to class now.

Consultant: I realize this sort of conversation isn't your favorite thing to do, but I need you to stay longer. We still haven't worked out this problem with Ms. Jones and Mrs. Hansen. Let me tell you what is going to be happening this week, and I want to hear what you think about it. Mrs. Hansen and Ms. Jones are going to be keeping notes on your behavior, and they're—

Todd: [interrupting] Yeah, yeah. Mrs. Hansen already bugged me about it. She's all, like, going to send me to Club Med [the students' name for detention]. You tell her to do that?

Consultant: No, but if she or Ms. Jones decides to do it, I would support them. I'm feeling that you may not realize what impact your behavior has on them.

Todd: [grinning] Yeah, I bug 'em a little. It's no big deal. What're you telling me? I gotta, like, kiss up to 'em?

Consultant: Kissing up is one thing I don't think I could talk you into. You're not that kind of guy. I'm more concerned about what we can do to make your time with these teachers more interesting so you won't feel the need to bug them. What I'd like you to be thinking about, and what I'll be thinking about also, are ways that we could make your time in their rooms more enjoyable for everybody, without this business of bugging people being such a big part of what you do.

Todd: Hey, I think if everybody just got off my back and didn't make such a big deal about a little teasing we'd get along just fine. Can I go back to class now?

Consultant: I know this isn't comfortable for you, but we need to come to some sort of agreement on a plan. What I'd like to do is meet with you again next week after the teachers have shown me their data for this week. In the meantime I'll be thinking of some ways to make your experience in their classes better for everybody, and I'd like you to be doing the same. What do you say, partner?

Todd: Huh? Yeah, OK, I dunno. They gonna be showing you all the stuff they're writing down?

Consultant: Yes, I asked them to so that I would have a better idea of what their concerns are. What I'd like you to do is to be thinking about some ideas about how these classes can be better for you and for everybody [10].

Todd: Yeah, all right. Maybe I should be writing down what they do. When will I see you again?

Consultant: You know, that's not such a bad idea, you writing down what they do. Why don't you, as long as it doesn't get in the way of your assignments? I'll call for you next week, probably during a different period. What don't you want to miss?

Todd: Phys ed.

Consultant: OK. Before you go, is there anything else you'd like to talk to me about?

Todd: Nah.

Consultant: OK. I'll see you in a week. Bye.

As the week went by, I saw Todd in the hallway a couple of times. He didn't look at me.

The teacher-consultees met with me at the agreed-on time and showed me their data. In both cases there had been a dramatic decrease in the rate of defiance relative to their memory of preceding weeks. One problem of starting an intervention before getting solid baseline data is that it is sometimes difficult to know if you are making any headway. In this case, as in many others in the schools, teacher-consultees do not want to put off interventions pending solid baseline data; their classes are often being ruined by these behaviors. They know about how often the behaviors occur, so they will often start intervening with or without your approval. In this case, they were determined to do something, so they did.

Their treatment, as I have mentioned, was to keep a record of Todd's transgressions and to inform him of them after each period. I asked that they also inform him of good behaviors they had observed, and both thought I was putting them on: After all, Todd never did anything right. As it turned out, they were both surprised to find that not only had his defiance calmed down, but they were actually able to point out something nice he had done in both classes. He helped a slow learner correct his spelling in English, and he commented positively on a nice map-coloring job a student had done in social studies. They wondered what magic I had performed in my meeting with him. So did I, but I deflected the praise to their strategy, while also wondering if the threat of Club Med may have been influential. It seemed almost too good to be true. I suggested that we decide how to proceed. They wanted to drop the written record of his negative behaviors because he seemed to have learned his lesson and also because it was tiresome. So what should we do?

This sort of decision point is very common in consultation. The consultant has established good rapport with the consultees, they are eager to start an intervention, and within a week they are singing your praises because the intervention seems to be working. You're often amazed yourself. But your experience tells you to be aware of the honeymoon phenomenon. Todd's behavior has a long history; to expect it to be extinguished in favor of more prosocial behavior on the basis of a few interventions is asking for too much too soon. What very often happens, especially if you believe the problems are solved and therefore terminate with the consultees or agree to put the issue on the back burner, is that the consultees call you back in another few weeks to tell you that the student has regressed to his old self.

Functional Behavioral Assessment/Analysis

In terms of a functional assessment of Todd's behavior, I believe the antecedents were directions from the teacher or another student telling him to do something, or something internal that prompted him to defy convention or to stir up some

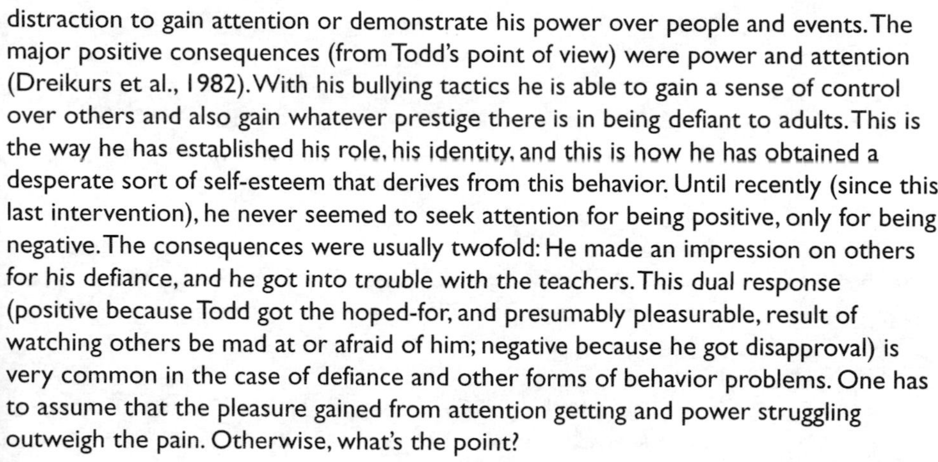

distraction to gain attention or demonstrate his power over people and events. The major positive consequences (from Todd's point of view) were power and attention (Dreikurs et al., 1982). With his bullying tactics he is able to gain a sense of control over others and also gain whatever prestige there is in being defiant to adults. This is the way he has established his role, his identity, and this is how he has obtained a desperate sort of self-esteem that derives from this behavior. Until recently (since this last intervention), he never seemed to seek attention for being positive, only for being negative. The consequences were usually twofold: He made an impression on others for his defiance, and he got into trouble with the teachers. This dual response (positive because Todd got the hoped-for, and presumably pleasurable, result of watching others be mad at or afraid of him; negative because he got disapproval) is very common in the case of defiance and other forms of behavior problems. One has to assume that the pleasure gained from attention getting and power struggling outweigh the pain. Otherwise, what's the point?

PLANNING OR MODIFYING INTERVENTIONS

In this case, the plan (that is, the interventions the consultees will take to correct the problem) has already been in effect for more than a week. As I have mentioned, violating the sequential nature of the steps in the SOCS process described in Chapter 5 is common. Consultees are anxious to try something, and they will do so, if only unwittingly. Remember that when the consultee refers a student to the consultant, a plan is already in effect. It probably isn't working—hence the referral. Given this reality, this section of the SOCS may consist of planning interventions or modifying those already in effect. In either event, at this point we take all the information we have and decide what to do.

The collaboratively derived plan we adopted consists of keeping track of defiant episodes and prosocial behaviors and reviewing them with Todd at the end of each social studies and English period. This requires some time investment from the teachers, but so far they have accepted it. At the same time they are not reprimanding Todd when he is defiant but are treating his behavior with benign neglect. Of course, this reaction can have its limits: Todd may push his behavior to a point where the consultee is required to take stronger steps in order to keep classroom decorum. Fortunately, this hasn't happened yet. The purpose of this approach is to let Todd know, with only a slight delay of feedback, what he is doing that irritates others and what prosocial behaviors have been observed. Hopefully he will get the point and give up the irritating behaviors.

Why should Todd give up this behavior? It has been his calling card, his identity, for a long time and has certain gains associated with it. Why risk giving that up when there is no assurance that its substitute will yield the same gains? One possible answer comes from the Dreikurs et al. (1982) notions of power and attention. Dreikurs et al. refer to these as "mistaken goals of behavior," activities a student engages in when "he has lost his belief that he can find the belonging and recognition that he desires, and erroneously believes that he will find acceptance through provocative behavior by pursuing the mistaken goals of behavior" (p. 14). The appropriate method suggested is to give the student the attention he seeks when he engages in prosocial behavior (as when the behaviorist rewards good behavior while ignoring inappropriate behavior; Alberto & Troutman, 1999; Walker & Shea, 1999), to avoid power struggles by not confronting the student who is trying to pull you into one, and to find some way to give the student a prosocial power base. In cases of both attention seeking and power, the consultee must let the student know what the purpose of the behavior is: to be noticed, and to be part of the social group by negative rather than by positive means. (For further suggestions about this technique, see Albert, 1996; Ferguson, 1995.) The consultee must also suggest how the child can have his needs for attention and power met in ways that do not disrupt the rights of others to learn.

My concern at this point is threefold: (1) Will it work? (2) If it doesn't, what's next? (3) If it does, how do we phase it out? Also, I'm wondering what sort of stress these new expectations are having on Todd. We're asking him to change a behavior of long duration; how does he deal with the temptation to revert to his old self, especially if provoked by someone? One way to assist a client with a behavioral transition is to use some "stop and think" cognitive behavior-modification techniques (Brigham, 1989; Durrant, 1995; Hughes, 1988; Kendall & Braswell, 1985; Larson, 1992; Larson & McBride, 1990; Murphy & Duncan, 1997). Essentially, these techniques consist of getting a cooperative client to analyze his thought processes in order to see where anger or irrational thinking (Robinson, Smith, Miller, & Brownell, 1999) or mistaken goal problems (Dreikurs et al., 1982) can get him into trouble.

Who has the time or skill to provide such training? In the best of all possible worlds, it would be readily available at the school, in a local clinic, or through a cooperative arrangement with some mental health treatment source. Going outside the school requires major parental commitment and possibly some financial resources. Would Todd's parents think this was worth the investment? I didn't ask, so I never found out. Instead, I thought I'd start with a resource right here: our own school counselor, Ms. Marks. I'd ask her if she might be interested in this problem.

She was. Not only did she see this as a very good use of her time, but since she knew of at least five other students who could benefit from the same sort of training, she decided to start a group for cognitive behavior modification centering on aggressive, defiant behaviors. Wow! What a stroke of luck! It's amazing what you can come up with right in your own staff if you look for it. She wrote a brief description of what she wanted to do with the group based on some combination of the Kendall and Braswell (1985) model, and that of Murphy and Duncan (1997). She called the parents of the six boys she had in mind (including Todd's parents), got phone approval from all six, and sent official permission forms to them the same day. Five were returned, and she started with these five the next week. Ms. Marks does not waste time.

ISSUES IN THE IMPLEMENTATION OF INTERVENTIONS

Because of the usual round of crises in the life of a junior high school psychologist, I lost touch with Todd for a week. Mrs. Hansen stopped by to see me and asked what had happened. I showed her my desk full of pink slips (calls to be returned), referrals, behavioral intervention plans to be monitored, and so on, and she understood. She said that Todd was slipping somewhat. He had smarted-off to her that morning and she wondered what we were doing about it. At that point, so did I.

I called a meeting of the two consultees and our school counselor, Ms. Marks. We spent some time reviewing what had happened over the past week or so, what was going on in the group counseling with Ms. Marks, and what we should do at this point. Ms. Jones reflected some frustration: The honeymoon of our initial treatment plan seemed to have ended. Why? Was this common? Is all this effort worth it? She was showing signs of depression, somewhat seconded by Mrs. Hansen. They were in the mood for revenge. Ms. Jones suggested that we proceed with detention.

Students like Todd often have this effect on teachers. Todd's defiance flies in the face of everything teachers stand for. Students who flaunt their ability to spoil teachers' efforts are very challenging. Consultants need to be aware of this. Teachers have their ego needs satisfied by teaching, watching students progress, and feeling that they are making a valuable contribution to their students and to society through their efforts. They are achieving Maslow's (1968) stage of self-actualization when they are teaching well; students who get in the way of that achievement frustrate teachers and can cause them to regress in their behavior in the classroom. They need an objective outsider who can work with their feelings of discouragement, help them to see what role the defiant student is playing, and help them cope with that role and (we hope) successfully turn it around. This is an excellent opportunity for a school-based consultant.

One of the first things that consultees need to understand is that behavior problems are rarely remediated in a short period of time. They usually have a long reinforcement history; they have been meeting the client's needs at some level, and for a student to give them up may require the application of resources and influences not entirely controlled by the school. A review of the reasons for poor behavior (see Chapter 6) shows some of the issues important in creating and sustaining a behavior problem that may require the assistance of nonschool personnel: parents, medical practitioners, and counselors who have time to engage in relatively long-term therapy. But let's see what our team has to say.

Ms. Marks, our counselor, reported that Todd came to the counseling group and tried to jeopardize it. He acted silly, wouldn't take part in the activities, and said he wanted to quit. Ms. Marks kept him after the others had gone and listened to his concerns. He was afraid of being identified as a crazy who had to see a shrink. He saw no point in taking part in the group since his behavior had improved. Ms. Marks explained that the purpose of the group was to help youngsters learn to understand themselves and why they react the way they do. She reminded Todd of his long history of defiance, what effect it had on others, and its likely long-term consequences. Apparently Todd softened and agreed to come back to the group. Ms. Marks described Todd as having a hard-shell finish but a much softer interior [11]. (For an interesting discussion of the use of cognitive-behavioral techniques with students like Todd, see Robinson et al., 1999.)

Mrs. Hansen wants to have an after-school conference with Todd and lay down the law to him. She will use after-school detention the next time he smarts off and have him call his parents in her presence so he can explain to them (preferably the father) why he got detention. That's it. She's had it.

Both consultees want to drop the daily monitoring. It's a bother, and Todd doesn't seem to care about it. Ms. Jones was able to report some good news, however. In her social studies class, Todd hadn't really been a problem for the past week. He had been doing his work adequately and had turned in a project report that he had done at home. She was favorably impressed. She complimented Todd on it, and he said that his parents were on him about his homework, so he had to do it. Ms. Jones sensed, however, that he really was proud of himself for having done a job on time. I suggested that Ms. Jones call Todd's parents and reinforce their efforts in the homework area.

We discussed the problem further and decided on the following:

1. I would call Todd in to review where we were, compliment him on his behavior in Ms. Jones's class and on getting the paper in on time, and get some commitments from him regarding the issues we have discussed.
2. Ms. Marks would continue her counseling group with him.
3. Mrs. Hansen would see him after school and tell him that she would be calling his dad and sending Todd to after-school detention if he refused to obey requests or used any defiant language toward her.
4. Ms. Jones would keep her fingers crossed, hoping that his cooperative behavior in her room wasn't just a fluke. She would also find ways to make him feel part of the group whenever she could. She said she would make the call home to reinforce the homework effort.

My conversation with Todd went very well. He apologized to me for giving Mrs. Hansen a hard time; he won't apologize to her, however, because he doesn't like her. He says she's too bossy. We discussed ways in which he could make himself a useful contributor in Mrs. Hansen's class, such as volunteering to help another child or just learning to keep his hostile comments to himself. He said that he was working on that in Ms. Marks's group. He was learning to put a roadblock between his brain and his mouth and to count to three before responding whenever he thought he was going to say something somebody wouldn't like. He said that he misses the laughs he used to get from the other students. I commented that it must feel good to know that he is able to control himself when he wants to. He smiled and said that he was having fun learning how to talk to himself about his emotions. He didn't know he could do that. I told him that not trying to entertain the other students was a tradeoff on the road to maturity. He thought his father ought to take some lessons, and his brother, too! I went on to tell him that Ms. Jones had told me about his good behavior in her room and that she was impressed that he had gotten his paper in on time. Todd told me that seven kids were late with theirs. I had the sense that he was proud to be on the good side for a change.

Mrs. Hansen had her conference with him. Surprisingly, he did apologize to her, even before she had a chance to tell him about the consequences he would suffer if he was defiant with her. She did anyway, not trusting him to turn over a new leaf without the threat of some punishment consequence attached to it, which would be intended to serve as firm reminders of the negative effects of his defiant behaviors. When he left the conference with her, he said that she wouldn't get a chance to send him to detention "even if she wanted to." We didn't know what to make of that comment.

I called Todd's mom at work and had about 1 minute to boost her spirits by reporting the good news. She was ecstatic, of course. I also complimented her on being sure that Todd had done his social studies homework. She said that Mr. Jackson had stepped in and insisted that Todd do homework from 6:30 to 8:00 in the evening, whether he had any or not. This simple intervention apparently has sent a message to Todd that we all agree that he will have to become a real student rather than a hanger-on, a troublemaker. I think the Jacksons' experience with their older son has taught them a lesson; they aren't going to let Todd slip away, too.

MONITORING INTERVENTIONS

I decided to put Todd's case on the back burner for awhile. Two weeks later, Mrs. Hansen was in to see me about another boy in her class, and I asked about Todd. She said he was much improved. She had to send him to detention only once, and he handled it very well. She expected an angry outburst from him but got none. I told her to mention the matter to Ms. Marks; she said she would. I haven't heard from Ms. Jones, but I think things are going well in there. I'll check in another week or so. Ms. Marks is bursting her buttons over her success with her group, Todd included. While she was in such a good mood, I brought up a continual problem, which is very significant for first-time parents of teenagers: communicating with teens. Anybody who has had teens or worked with them knows what they can be like. She took an immediate interest and said that she would like to try the STEP-Teen program with a small pilot group. Who would I recommend? I suggested that we put a notice in the school–home newsletter and announce it, including a clip-out sheet interested parents could return. We should offer it once during the daytime hours and again during an evening for working parents, about four sessions each. OK? Good, Ms. Marks commented. She'll talk to the newsletter editor about it. I plan to make a personal call to Mrs. Jackson and a few others I'm aware of to personally invite them to attend.

EVALUATION AND CLOSURE

I did not do any formal evaluation. We had gathered no real data; the exact dates of the different types of interventions were not accurately recalled, and so many interventions were going on at the same time that it didn't seem as if the project could be formally evaluated. Who knows what effect the daily record keeping, the threats from Mrs. Hansen and Mr. Jackson, and the group counseling program had on the behavior? Further, in the ordinary school psychologist's day, there is no time for anything but the most cursory record keeping. I'm not a laboratory with tightly controlled procedures.

All constituents agree that this is a successful case, at least so far. Todd has dropped his defiant act, he's more cooperative, and he's doing more academically. As an interesting spin-off, we will soon be starting two parent groups titled "Talking with Your Teen." I plan to sit in on the daytime one.

As you learned in Chapter 5, evaluation has as its goal the determination of the value of something. I think this consultation project was very valuable for all concerned. Although our goals were only loosely set (reduction in defiant acts and verbalizations; increase in academic work production), I think it's fair to say we met them. Someday, when the pink slips are only an inch thick and I don't have too many 3-year reevaluations staring at me, and ... well, you know what a psychologist's office is like, I'd like to do one of those tightly designed studies we used to read about in grad school. However, right now, I have to see Mrs. Overdue about the behavior of some gang-involved kids in her class.

NOTES AND COMMENTS ON CASE I

This was a generally successful case characterized by a considerable amount of collaboration among the various consultees. From a scientific point of view, the results are difficult to discuss because not much attention was devoted to the analysis of discrete data. In the everyday hubbub of activities that constitute the work of school psychologists and other school consultants, careful data analysis is a luxury.

The following is a list of questions and comments derived from the various events in this case, indicated by the bracketed numbers in the narrative.

1. Except for special education, Todd's school has no source of help for students who manifest academic problems. What other kinds of resource programs for assistance are present in the schools with which you are familiar? If you were asked to develop such a resource, how might you go about it? Chapter 8 discusses procedures for engaging in systems-level consultation.

2. Each school-based consultant has to develop a plan for dealing with at-risk students, however they are locally defined. These students are typically considered unlikely to graduate from high school because of a higher-than-normal number of dropout indicators, such as dysfunctional families, learning problems, antisocial

behavior, truancy, and a history of dropping out among older siblings (Walker, Colvin, & Ramsey, 1995). It is very easy to let our good intentions in this regard get lost in the everyday shuffle of students and papers. Generation of an "at-risk committee" headed by an assertive person who is committed to this problem is a first step toward dealing with it. How does your junior high or high school deal with this issue?

3. The question of the value of grade-level retention has been discussed for many years. What is the research evidence concerning this topic? If there are generalizations that result from the research, how might they lead to some guidelines a school could use to decide its own grade-level retention policy (see Jimerson, Carlson, Rotert, Egeland, & Sroufe, 1997; Rafoth, 2002)?

4. Does the use of these labels help anything? Do they explain why the student engages in the target behaviors, or are they just a convenient way for professionals to communicate with each other? These questions are more than rhetorical. As discussed in Chapter 6, the mental health and special education fields have always had lively discussions about the purpose and usefulness of labeling or diagnosing (Bratten, Kauffman, Bratten, Polsgrove, & Nelson, 1988; Reynolds, Wang, & Walberg, 1987; Ysseldyke, Algozzine, & Thurlow, 1992). It appears that there will always be people who think they know more about a student if a label has been attached. Other people stick to the behaviors. Does a student have ADHD because she doesn't like to sit still for long, is very inquisitive, and often seems lost in the classroom? Or do we simply call her ADHD because the label is needed in order to get special education assistance, accommodations under Section 504 of the Vocational Rehabilitation Act, medical intervention, or insurance reimbursement? See the very interesting discussion of these issues in Goodman and Poillion (1992).

5. What do you think of this intervention? The point is to alert the student to the fact that the teacher is paying attention to the student's behaviors (to positive behaviors also, we hope) and to encourage the student to curb the negative behaviors. What might you do to encourage teachers to try this relatively simple approach?

6. The image of the hot seat seems possibly negative. The consultant is responding to a sense of urgency from the teachers and has arranged so far for two interventions: the teachers' daily reporting to Todd about their observations, and time with the counselor, which will be followed with a parent conference by phone. How might you structure this discussion with Todd? Remember that this case could be dealt with by any of a number of school-based consultants. How might a resource teacher deal with the situation at this point?

7. Although less than ideal, this sort of rushed conference is often the best a consultant can get. We hope that all concerned parties will have more time later to sit down and have a thorough conference. This should be the goal of all collaborative consultants.

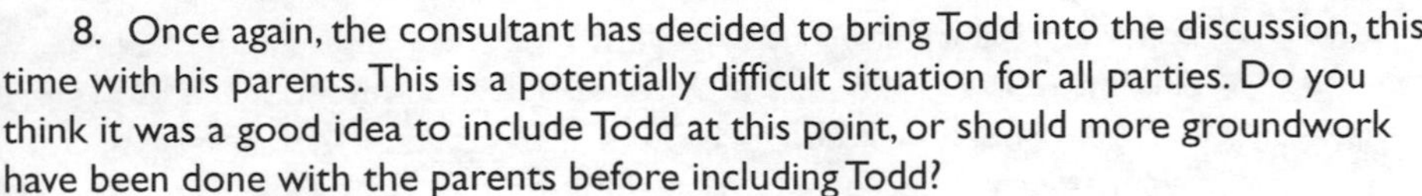

8. Once again, the consultant has decided to bring Todd into the discussion, this time with his parents. This is a potentially difficult situation for all parties. Do you think it was a good idea to include Todd at this point, or should more groundwork have been done with the parents before including Todd?

9. This conference seems to have gone well. School personnel are sometimes concerned about having conferences with parents because they fear being rejected, ignored, or subtly threatened. Develop a list of hopes and fears that teachers have for a conference; do the same for parents. Discuss ways of ensuring that consultee hopes are realized (through effective planning, for example) and that their fears can be managed (for instance, by converting negative thoughts to positive).

Negative: The parents may scowl throughout the conference.

Positive: Scowling indicates their discomfort, not their evaluation of me. I have to try to make them more comfortable.

Chapter 5 presents ideas about conferencing and collaborating with parents, as do Christenson (1992); Elizalde-Utnick, (2002); O'Shea, O'Shea, Algozzine, and Hammitte (2001); Sheridan, Kratochwill, and Bergan (1996); and Turnbull and Turnbull (1997).

10. Note the consultant's effort to bring Todd into the planning process. Instead of using only interventions done to students, it makes good sense to bring students into the planning to give them a sense of self-determination and control over what happens to them. Students, like consultees, are much more likely to follow plans that they have had a voice in determining. How might you structure this process of student self-determination for Todd to be sure it has a good chance of working?

11. The consultant was very pleased that the school counselor had this conference with Todd and worked through this crisis. It would have been easy for the counselor to dismiss Todd from the group. Nobody was surprised that Todd acted the way he did in the group; that behavior was fairly predictable. See the previous discussion on the functional assessment of behavior.

Case 2: Academic Motivation

Maria Fuentes does not care for school. In fact, if her parents didn't insist that she go, she wouldn't. She is 15 now and a sophomore in the general education program at Carter Senior High. She was identified in the third grade as a student with a learning disability in the area of reading. Her writing skills were not at grade level, and her spelling was also not strong. She had been seen by special education teachers on primarily a consultation-based model until the seventh grade, at which time she was found to be no longer eligible for special education, since her literacy skills had improved.

Credit-wise, Maria's still a freshman. At the rate she is going, it will take her another 3 years to graduate. I doubt she will last that long. It is November, and her teachers are very worried about her. Her social studies (history) teacher put in the referral. Maria is presently taking math fundamentals, social studies (American history), general science (for the second time), family studies (home economics), and P.E. She is failing the first three and barely passing the other two.

RECEIPT OF A REFERRAL AND INITIAL THOUGHTS ABOUT IT

My name is Ms. Suiter, and I am one of two resource specialist teachers here at Carter. I've been here for 9 years. During that time I've seen our school population change from primarily a college-bound white middle-class student body to a much more diverse population. Whereas 9 years ago 75% of our students went on to some sort of postsecondary education, that figure is now down to about 40%, and almost all of these students are community-college bound. Also, our dropout percentage has risen from about 15% to 32%. Maria seems, in many ways, typical of these changes; she comes from a home where neither parent graduated from high school. Her one older brother transferred from here to our continuation school a year ago. Maria's family is bilingual. Her parents were born in the United States; her grandparents immigrated from Mexico about 50 years ago. Maria and her family make occasional visits to Mexico to visit their relatives. Maria and her brother are fluent in both Spanish and English.

Our teachers vary in their reactions to our current realities. Some of the older teachers still act as if nothing has changed, and they teach as they did a decade ago: largely verbal lectures, not many class activities, and written assignments that are expected to look like college-level work. They believe their job is to separate the chaff from the wheat and let the chips fall. Other teachers, many of them younger and some (fortunately) from cultural and linguistic backgrounds similar to those of our newer students, have a mission to work with the students where they are and to present materials in a way that provides for much more student involvement. You can see why these differences among our teachers result in some heated discussions. However, even with these differences we as a faculty generally get along, at least as long as no one makes too much out of the contrasting methods and philosophies [1].

At Carter, the teachers send all referrals to the assistant principal (AP), but they indicate on the referral the specialist to whom they really want it to go. The AP screens them and decides whether to send them to the position or person indicated or to send them elsewhere. Maria's history teacher referred her at my suggestion, and the AP sent the referral to me since it might have special education implications.

INITIAL DISCUSSION WITH THE TEACHERS

Since I know Maria is in academic trouble in more than just her history class, I decide to hold a case conference and invite all five of her teachers to come. All five come to the meeting and inform me that she is failing math, history, and science and barely passing family studies and P. E. My question to each is, "Why is she failing?" Her history teacher (Mr. Petrullo, a great old guy who loves kids and loves history, and who will be my main teacher–consultee) says it's simple: Maria is often absent, and when she's there, she may as well not be since she hasn't read anything and doesn't know what chapter they're on. His efforts to get her involved have been met with an expression of disinterest on her part. The math teacher laughs and says, "Ditto." The science teacher says that Maria has failed every test she has taken this semester and acts as if she couldn't care less. He thinks she is depressed, obsessed with boys, and will probably be a dropout. Family studies gives a slightly better report, as does P. E. Both of these last two teachers are female, but so is the science teacher. All five want me to see her and find out what's going on. Should they bother with her or not? How can they motivate her when she appears to be so indifferent? Of course, she's not the only student like that, they unnecessarily inform me. They want to know if I care to hear about some others. I suggest we focus on Maria. What we learn from her may help us deal with the others.

I ask them to answer their own questions about motivation. What do they think will make a difference with her? What methods have they found that work with other low-motivation students? Answers are not forthcoming. Mr. Petrullo says that he is trying to get close to her when she is in class, but she has erected a barrier of indifference and he doesn't have time in class to get around it. The science and math teachers inform me that they didn't come to the meeting to be asked to try harder. They see her as a future dropout, and it is up to her to turn herself around. Could I refer her to her counselor so he could counsel her into trying harder [2]? The science teacher asks about special education. He knows she used to be in that program and was wondering if she doesn't belong in there again.

I respond that the records indicate that Maria was dismissed from special education 3 years ago. I would be glad to review the idea with the school psychologist, Ms. Yates, who wasn't able to come to the meeting, but I personally don't see this as a special education issue or responsibility. The history teacher and the science teacher both agree that it isn't a question of her ability to read the material or do the written work; they have both had her read to them in private and her portfolio materials from last year indicate that she can write fairly well. I think we all see it as motivational. How can we deal with that problem? Again, answers are not forthcoming. The teachers wonder, "Aren't counseling and special education the only approaches?"

Time is running out and we aren't getting anywhere. I ask the teachers to think about this question of motivation. I will focus on one teacher, Mr. Petrullo, to begin with and see where we go from there. Obviously, this has been a challenging meeting. I have noticed that group meetings such as this case conference are often frustrating. It is sometimes difficult to get a group of teachers to come up with ideas. They can tend to get tied up in some group conspiracy of either passivity or "It's us versus them (the students), and we have standards to uphold." They are also eager to see problems such as this as belonging to the counseling office, or special education, or even our continuation and alternative education programs, which are increasing in size annually. As I have indicated, this reluctance to accommodate nontraditional learners, multiplied by the apparent nonacademic orientation of many of our current students, seems to be at the core of an increasing number of referrals [3].

The questions I believe I need to answer in this case are in two categories: immediate concerns about Maria, and long-term questions about how this school and the faculty need to come up with solutions designed to keep up with the shifting demographics. Regarding Maria specifically, I have the following questions and concerns:

1. What is she like as a person, and how does this affect her schoolwork?
2. What are her academic levels? Is she able to read the 10th-grade texts, as the history and science teacher have said?
3. What happens in her classrooms to either encourage or discourage her participation?
4. Should we make program changes that will be more appropriate for her? What does "appropriate" mean?

CLASSROOM (ECOLOGICAL) OBSERVATION

I ask Mr. Petrullo when he would like me to visit. He thinks that the second half of a period would be best because that is when the discussion usually gets lively. I tell him I can't wait to make the visit, knowing how much fun he and his students seem to have when freewheeling about historical issues and their current relevance. We decide on next Tuesday, assuming that Maria is at school. She has missed about 50% of the Mondays this semester and some Tuesdays also.

The students at Carter, especially the sophomores, know me from my consultative work, so my visiting a classroom is not regarded as remarkable or suspicious. Mr. Petrullo's classes are always fun. He has a lot of energy, and his classes are characterized by lively interactions, brave arguments, and the kind of enthusiasm that is characteristic of turned-on adolescents. His style has earned him accolades from a variety of sources over the years. He's a bit of a ham, and it works. He used to dress up like Lincoln and other famous figures, but he doesn't do that anymore. Still, if I were a student, I'd like to be in his class. Students rarely complain that he is boring. I worry about those who do.

On Tuesday, Maria is very uninvolved with the discussion on tariffs. Mr. Petrullo calls on her once (probably for my sake), and one of her friends tries to get her involved in the discussion, but she demurs. After class Mr. Petrullo puts his big paw around her shoulder (we don't do that much anymore, but Mr. Petrullo sometimes forgets) and says he wants to see her after school. No problem, just a brief talk about her work. I ask if I can sit in; Maria looks at me suspiciously, but passively agrees. When she leaves, I ask Mr. Petrullo if he can see me before the afternoon meeting. He is eager to.

USING PARENTS AS ALLIES IN THE CONSULTATION PROCESS

Before the after-school meeting I call Maria's mom, Mrs. Fuentes. She is at home. She works 3 days a week as a domestic and is able (and eager) to come to school to discuss Maria. She is glad I have called since she and her husband are both very worried about Maria. Mr. Fuentes works as an auto mechanic all day and can't come to a daytime meeting, but she will be glad to come in on Thursday at 11:10, Mr. Petrullo's free period. I'll inform him of the meeting.

GETTING TEACHERS AND PARENTS TOGETHER: THE SST MEETING

At this point I think it's best to keep the case simple and not involve the SST until I know how the team can help. I decide to follow-up my initial discussions with Mr. Petrullo to see what he thinks. When we meet, I ask him what might be effective in getting Maria more involved with his class. He says he has been thinking about the problem since our last meeting and wants to run three ideas past me:

1. Contact her parents and see what they can do about it.
2. Set up some sort of contract with her that spells out very clearly what she has to do to earn a passing grade.
3. See her after school today and tomorrow to review the material with her and give her some sort of boost.

I tell him that every one of his ideas has merit and is worth pursuing; in fact, I've moved forward on his first idea already by arranging the parent meeting. He's pleased by this. He then asks for some ideas about how he might develop a contract that will meet her needs and to which she will respond. I ask what has worked for him in the past. He says he has only used a few, which spelled out how work was to be done and what grades would be given. "Nothing fancy," he says.

I suggest, "We are talking about a student whose present level of involvement is so low that we probably ought to stick to very basic 'acting like a student' behaviors such as attendance, having requisite materials, and responding at least once per period." He agrees and says we should talk to Maria about it after school [4].

I ask him what his goals are for the after-school meeting. He mainly wants to let Maria know that he cares about her, that he is concerned for her when she doesn't come to class, and that he wants to see if there is anything that he can do to help her with what might be bothering her. I say that I think those are excellent goals. He is apparently trying to meet Maria where she is emotionally, rather than act out the role of the angry, demanding teacher, which would almost certainly turn her away. You can see what sort of person Mr. Petrullo is: caring, empathetic, and fatherly. I say that I want to be at the meeting because I need to get to know Maria better but that Mr. Petrullo should do most of the interacting.

I've learned how to do this job better over the past few years. Before, I used to take over meetings like this and thereby give the impression that I was the main person there and that it was all right for the teacher to take a back seat and let me do all the work. Now I make it clear that the meeting is between the teacher and the child (and/or parent). I monitor and facilitate as necessary, but I'm in a secondary role.

I close our meeting by asking Mr. Petrullo if he feels OK about the contract or wants to discuss it further. He says he is ready to go with it, so we part company until the after-school meeting with Maria. Note that I'm not telling him how to write the contract. I could, and I used to. Now if teachers say they can do it, I let them. I'm not always thrilled by what they do, but that's all right. It's all part of my effort to empower teachers by staying out of the decision-making process as often as possible and letting them try things their way. Of course, if I see that they are very far off base, I'll make suggestions, and I'll give them some examples, but only if necessary. The after-school meeting goes as I expect. Mr. Petrullo is very friendly, encouraging, and enthusiastic. Maria is reticent, quiet, and compliant, but generally noncommittal. She denies that there is any real problem, then says that the work is too hard, and then asks to get out of math and science. At this point Mr. Petrullo looks at me for help.

I say that we are here to start a process of helping Maria be successful in her classes that is going to involve her teachers, myself, her parents (she looks at me with astonishment and concern when I mention her parents), and especially herself. Is she willing to work with us to help her be more successful in school? This can be a risky question. Some children will say no or talk around the question. I gamble with Maria because she seems to be basically compliant. I am right.

Maria says that she is willing but doesn't know why her parents have to be involved. Mr. Petrullo replies, "We always try to get parents involved, even if the student is a senior. You're lucky to have parents who want to get involved."

Maria looks dark; I think she sees this business of getting her parents involved as a dirty trick on our part.

Mr. Petrullo says that for now he wants Maria to look at the contract that he has handwritten during his prep period. If she agrees, she can sign it.

CONTRACT

I, Maria Fuentes, agree to come to class each day (unless excused for illness by my parents). I will be sure to have my book and a notebook and a pencil for taking notes. I will also make at least one relevant comment or answer at least one question during each class period. I will study the material and do my best on the weekly exam on Thursdays.

Each week, on Friday, Mr. Petrullo will give me a weekly report card based on these behaviors. I will bring it home and have my parents read and sign it. I will return it to Mr. Petrullo on the following Monday.

For every signed form Mr. Petrullo receives, I will receive five bonus points toward my next class grade.

Signed: Mr. Petrullo ______________________________

Maria Fuentes ______________________________

Ms. Suiter (witness) ______________________________

It's funny about contracts. You never know how students are going to respond to them. I've had students who act like lawyers; they want to haggle with me over every word. I've had other students agree to everything and then do nothing to comply with the contract. And I've seen simple ideas like this one turn students around when I thought the contract wasn't going to be effective. Much of the literature on contracting seems to be written for younger students. Most high school teachers are not about to ask a student what she would like to earn for being a good student. Grades and mild praise are the reinforcers in high school for those who are not invested in learning as a goal in itself. So Mr. Petrullo has stuck with grades as his reinforcer in this case, and I see no reason to object. I'll discuss it later with Maria when I see her myself [5].

Maria seems pleased with the contract. I believe she thought it was going to be something awful, but it isn't. She signs it and then wants to know what we are going to talk about with her mother. Mr. Petrullo tells her that we are going to ask her to talk with Maria every day about her schoolwork, ask her what her homework is, see to it that Maria has a good place to do her homework, verify that she actually does it, and review and sign the weekly contract. We will give a copy of the contract to Mrs. Fuentes on Thursday, and it will go into effect the following Monday.

Mr. Petrullo then asks Maria why she misses school so often on Monday. She says she is sick a lot. He suggests that she come to school even if she isn't feeling like it, that we want her here and that we will talk to her mother about it. She then says that sometimes she goes with her mother on Mondays to help clean a really big house.

She doesn't want us to tell her mother that she told us that, but that's the way it is. Besides, Maria gets 15 dollars for the job, and she needs the money. We say that we will keep the confidence but that we will encourage Mrs. Fuentes to be sure that Maria is in school every day. The meeting ends [6].

Mr. Petrullo and I have no time to meet before Mrs. Fuentes comes in on Thursday. Since we have only about 15 minutes for this conference, my main goal is to keep the discussion solutions-oriented. Mrs. Fuentes admits that Maria is becoming more difficult to deal with at home. Defiance and noncompliance are on the rise, just as they are with Maria's older brother. I mention that our local child guidance clinic has a family counselor who is very helpful to parents dealing with exactly that sort of behavior. I say that I would be glad to get the clinic's number for Mrs. Fuentes. She wants it, though she doubts if Mr. Fuentes will approve of their going to the clinic. Mr. Petrullo is anxious to get on with the contract, so he brings it out and gives Mrs. Fuentes a copy. She says that Maria has shown it to her and that she thinks it's fine. She wants Maria to finish regular high school and will support anything we want. We mention to her about talking every day with Maria about her work, checking the homework, and so on. "What about the absences?" I ask. Mrs. Fuentes says that she often gives in to Maria when she says she is too sick to go to school. Sometimes Mrs. Fuentes has to go to work early and doesn't know until she gets home that Maria hasn't gone to school.

Two years ago, our school instituted a computerized home-calling system that informed parents that their children were absent. Unfortunately, many of our parents didn't get the calls because they either weren't home and didn't have an answering machine or because their children answered the phone or intercepted the answering machine message and the message got lost. Now, if the parents don't call back, the call is repeated in the evening, which works better.

Nothing is said by either party about Maria's allegation that she helps her mother at her job instead of coming to school on Mondays. We're hoping that we'll never have to mention it and that Maria's attendance will improve on the basis of what we're currently doing. The meeting ends with each side vowing to support the other.

ASSESSMENT OF THE STUDENT

Psychological Assessment:

I don't believe that Maria has a learning disability related to some information-processing difficulty that prevents her from doing well academically. My feeling is that this is more of a production deficit: resistance to school tasks because of boredom, a reluctance to invest oneself in learning tasks, or a sense of futility. Possibly it's a symptom of learned helplessness (Maier & Seligman, 1976). However, I think it's best to check with the school psychologist who did the reevaluation 3 years ago. We meet in her office for 10 minutes, and she reviews her report. She gave Maria the WISC-III, on which Maria earned a verbal IQ of 83, performance of 92, and full-scale of 87. Ms. Yates's notes indicate that she offered to have Maria tested in Spanish but that Maria said she preferred English. The Wechsler Intelligence Scale for Children-III (WISC-III) scores were regarded as valid—that is, not contaminated by health, environmental, motivational, or primary-secondary language issues. At that time her achievement standard scores on the Woodcock-Johnson were all in the mid-80s, up from the low 70s she obtained when first evaluated in third grade. Essentially, she was doing about as well as the IQ tests predicted.

I'm sure we could get into a discussion about the meaning of all this for students like Maria, but I simply want to know if Ms. Yates thinks Maria can read and comprehend the 10th-grade texts she is expected to read. Ms. Yates answers, "She probably could, but not well—probably somewhere between the instructional and frustration levels. She would probably be reading very slowly, with somewhat below-average comprehension." That's what I was afraid of.

Ms. Yates goes on to say that this situation is becoming the norm for our sophomores. She is appalled at how many of our faculty still haven't accommodated themselves to this reality. She says she has talked with the principal about it but feels like she hasn't made much impact. She asks, "Would you be willing to help bring our administration and faculty to the realization that the old days are gone and that we need to make curricular and teaching-method changes if we are to provide our current students with the kind of school experiences that will be meaningful to them?"

Wow! That's quite a statement! I tell her that I, along with many others on the faculty, have been sensitive to this problem. Then I set a time with her for next week to discuss it. Who knows? Maria could be a catalyst for some meaningful changes around here. Ms. Yates goes on to caution me that there is not always a one-to-one correspondence between test results and actual textbook competence. This is especially likely to be true with test data that are 3 years old. What I really should do is see Maria and listen to her read aloud from her books. This will give me a better grasp of her current abilities to succeed. In addition, Ms. Yates suggests having Maria bring in her recent schoolwork and reviewing it with her. Her teachers might also have some things to show me. In our district, the idea of portfolio-based assessment has recently begun in the elementary schools but so far has been avoided at the high school level by a very reluctant staff. We'll get to that next year, maybe.

Ms. Yates's comments prompt me to have Maria come in to see me about her schoolwork and the contract. I ask Maria to bring her social studies and science books for her appointment tomorrow. She passively agrees.

Unfortunately, Maria's ability to read and comprehend the two texts she brings with her is somewhat less than Ms. Yates predicted. Maria reads slowly, doesn't recognize about every 15th word, and doesn't seem to care to organize what she reads into comprehensible information. She reads these books at about instruction-to-frustration level; she can get through them, but it's not easy or enjoyable. It's not surprising that she doesn't read them very much. And if she doesn't read the material, how can she engage in the classroom discussions? Some students do, especially those who pick up context clues from the other students and are basically interested in the material. Others, like Maria, who seem to be moving into the learned helplessness syndrome, simply avoid the discussions, especially if they are whole-class interactions.

Ms. Yates wrapped up our conversation by telling me she doesn't believe Maria ever really had a learning disability. She probably got off to a slow start in school and simply took a longer time than most students to master the fundamentals of the literacy requirements in English than do most bilingual students. Her rate of progress improved during fourth grade, possibly because of the pull-out program help she received through special education. Ms. Yates also commented that she didn't see Maria as having any serious psychological problems when she saw her 3 years ago, and believes that now she may be defeated more by the requirements of school, rather than intrapersonal depression. She said she would be glad to assess Maria for depression if our efforts at motivational tactics and increased parental requirements didn't seem to be helping. Given her too-busy schedule, she suggested that we consult with Ms. Spears, the school counselor, who may have more time to see Maria.

While Maria is with me, I ask about the contract and how it is going. She says her parents have been on her case about it and keep bugging her to do her homework and show it to them. I silently thank them for showing this concern and say, "I think that's a sign of their concern for you." She passively agrees and then adds that she isn't going to be allowed to go on the Monday job from now on until her grades get better, all because of the contract. (They usually don't have that much impact!)

I review my concerns about Maria's reading limitations with her and wonder if there is someone at home who can help her with her reading. She says her brother reads well, but she knows he won't want to help her. "He's too stuck up," she says.

I gamble, asking if she thinks he might agree to help if I ask him. I knew her brother, Rudi. He left us a year ago to go to the continuation school, but I remember him as a neat kid who just might help out if asked. She declines, I think for matters of personal pride. Too much sibling stuff, I'm afraid. I inquire about either of her parents helping. She thinks maybe her mother; her father doesn't read much. She's not sure he can, "At least not 10th-grade books," she says with a sigh.

"So," I say, "would you ask your mother to sit with you for a half hour every night and go over your schoolwork with you?"

"Yeah, OK, I'll ask her," says Maria.

Great! I say to myself, even while I know that many students will promise anything to get out of a difficult situation.

When Maria leaves, I make a note to call Mrs. Fuentes and tell her of our new plan and to encourage her involvement in it. I'm somewhat concerned that Maria has been going along with this plan just to get me off her case. I really don't get a strong feeling of any serious commitment on Maria's part to improving her schoolwork as yet. I do think that Mrs. Fuentes will be very cooperative, however, because I think she'll see this as having a positive potential for a number of reasons. It will get her closer to Maria, whom she feels she is losing to the alienation of adolescence; it will give her something constructive to do to help her daughter; and it will relieve some of the guilt she feels about having Rudi drop out of the regular high school.

Psychodynamic, Ecological, and Biophysical Factors:
I don't profess to be an expert in any of these three areas, but I think I understand enough of the surface behavior and events to make some good judgments about what is going on with Maria and her situation. At the psychodynamic level, based on my conversations with her, I believe Maria sees herself as nonacademic. She's eager to leave school and get on with her life, which she sees as work- and boyfriend-oriented. She plans to be a mother, probably in her early 20s. I hope not earlier, but if it happens, it will be accepted. She does not plan on a career since her husband will support her. She does not plan to go on to college, but it will be nice if her children do. A dream deferred. Should we interrupt this image for her? Making a potentially long story short, I'll say yes. Maria's boyfriend and future husband will just have to wait his turn. I want to ENABL Maria: education *n*ow *a*nd *b*abies *l*ater.

Let's look at the ecological aspects from two perspectives: home and school. Her home and community tend not to give education as high a priority as they give family issues. A view too often expressed is that a girl like Maria who isn't very good at school shouldn't worry about it; there are more important things. A high school diploma would be nice, but, after all, many of the adults in the community didn't graduate, and many of them are doing all right. But there is something else in Maria's family: a mother who says she will help. I find this out when I call to ask about the plan just described. Mrs. Fuentes says she would have started doing this a long time ago if she thought she knew enough to help. But she thought parents weren't supposed to interfere. She doesn't really know what they do in school, and her children haven't been very forthcoming ever since fifth or sixth grade. I say that the main purpose of this plan is to ensure that Maria reads the material and to assist her with both word recognition and comprehension.

Mrs. Fuentes laughs, saying that she hopes she understands it herself; after all, she never finished high school.

I say, "I think you'll do very well. The main thing is your interest and your willingness to show Maria that you feel that education is very important."

Mrs. Fuentes says she'll try. We thank each other and promise to check back in a few weeks to see how everything is going.

Can cultural expectations be changed one case at a time? Maria and her mother will help us find out [7]. The school ecology has already been mentioned somewhat. Essentially, I see our task as one of changing both attitudes and methods. My plan is to work with Ms. Yates and the others (faculty, administrators, parents, and students) who have a stake in this problem to organize a study group to analyze the changes in our student body and our community. What can we do to turn around the steadily declining success rate that we have witnessed over the past decade? It isn't just our faculty and administrators who need to take a look at themselves; it's our students, too. We are becoming used to students who are trying to convince us that the educational process is a sham. They float through without any real commitment and claim that school has only a minimal impact on them. I'm sure there is literature out there that describes programs that make a difference to the educationally alienated, and I'm sure that our students and faculty have ideas about how we might restructure our school to meet the needs of our students. Pie in the sky? Maybe, but no more so than every other good idea that people think can't work because ... well, because [8].

I don't believe there are any important biophysical factors that have an impact on this case. I'm fairly certain now that Maria's absences are not due to any health problem. Her vision and hearing are fine, and she's in good health.

Functional Behavioral Assessment:
The antecedents to Maria's behaviors of concern seem to be: (a) being asked to get up to go to school; (b) arriving in a classroom; and (c) being asked and expected to produce schoolwork, expecially when it is based on textbooks that are somewhat difficult to read. The functions of Maria's school behavior seem to be (a) to avoid engaging in academic work because it is too difficult for her; (b) to substitute social interests for academic pursuits; and (c) to put in one's time, as if school is a jail sentence, until she is old enough to leave, at which point she can get on with important and less-threatening activities. The reinforcers that keep this behavior alive seem to be (a) negativity toward school makes teachers avoid you and expect little from you; (b) an occasional piece of luck in getting somebody else to do some assignments for you; and (c) the belief that every day she becomes more attractive to the boys, so who needs school? These largely belief-system (internal) reinforcers have arisen from years of listening to older, poorly achieving girls, and her need to have some goals other than success that is dependent on hard work in school.

PLANNING OR MODIFYING INTERVENTIONS

We've identified six overlapping, related problem areas, some having to do directly with Maria and her behavior, and some that influence her due to the behavior of others or the nature of the system. Listed next are the six areas and some possible interventions.

Maria Is Failing in Three Subjects

Interventions:

1. Conference with Maria. We've already done this, apparently with good preliminary results.

2. Provide academic tutoring, at school or at home. Mrs. Fuentes's agreement to monitor Maria's work might not be considered tutoring, but it is a solid step in the right direction. Other than special education, our high school doesn't have a formal system of tutoring designed to remediate specific deficiencies in basic skills. Maria could benefit from a peer tutor. Who, when, where, using what materials? This is a problem we haven't faced historically, so we need to talk about this when we have our hoped-for discussions with the school administrators about reforming our system for today's students.

Maria Manifests a Serious Motivational Problem

Interventions:

1. *Conference with Maria.* We need to talk about her lack of interest and effort. We know that uninvolved teens have their minds elsewhere. Perhaps Ms. Spears, our school counselor, can find some time to visit with Maria. Ms. Yates had suggested that earlier. We'll have to get a permission form signed by Mrs. Fuentes regarding this. Among the things they can discuss are study skills, time management, and her self-talk regarding her status as a student. It might be best to develop a list of students who seem similar to Maria and have small-group meetings about these topics. I need to handle this referral to Ms. Spears carefully so that the teachers don't get the idea that they no longer have any ownership of the problem because Maria has been referred to counseling.

2. *Child guidance clinic.* I hope Mr. and Mrs. Fuentes will follow-through on this. We'll see.

3. *Contract.* Mr. Petrullo's contract may boost Maria's efforts to participate. If so, extend this contract idea to other classes.

4. Improve reading. Sometimes motivation is connected to a student's perception of her ability to be successful. We know that Maria's reading skills are marginal. Perhaps if we can improve her reading, she will show more interest in being productive.

5. *Study-buddy system.* A study-buddy system is used in some classes at different times. Perhaps this would help in some of Maria's classes.

6. *Change her self-concept.* Try to change Maria's self-concept as a silent, know-nothing student by giving her answers before a question-and-answer time and then calling on her to answer these questions. If she will cooperate, this plan could nudge her out of her general reticence to speak in class.

7. *Written record.* Have Maria keep a written record of her assignments, due dates, and so on in an effort to get her more structured and aware of her responsibilities. This record will need to be checked often at first. Will the teachers accept this responsibility?

8. *Plan for success.* Try to find at least one way every day that Maria can be successful in every class. Again, will the teachers be cooperative about this?

9. *Modify presentations.* Emphasize the possible use of cooperative learning strategies and other alternatives to the lecture-discussion method that still dominates our content-area methods.

Maria May Be Depressed

We hear the word *depression* a lot in regard to teens nowadays. I don't know if this is just a fashionable way of saying that teens are sometimes down in the dumps due to the numerous pressures of social relationships, sex, school expectations, parent–child dynamics, and extracurricular activities, which has always been true, or if there may really be an increase in clinical depression due to the complexities of modern life. In any event, Maria often seems down, at least at school. Her parents haven't noticed it at home. Or are they, like many parents who feel threatened by its implications, apt to deny it even when it seems obvious to others?

Interventions:

I hope Ms. Spears will be able to make a determination about depression when she sees Maria for counseling. If we believe she truly is depressed, not just down because she sees little hope or need for school, then I will encourage her parents to bring her to the child guidance clinic.

Maria Is Often Absent

Interventions:

1. We'll try to find out what the reasons are, other than her helping her mother on Mondays. It's probably her general antipathy toward school. I'll ask Ms. Spears to talk to her about it during counseling.
2. Being present in class is written into Mr. Petrullo's contract. We'll see if that helps. The school office keeps data on attendance, so we will have a permanent record in this area.
3. If the problem persists, we will discuss with Maria and her parents our policy on excessive absences.
4. Is it possible that Maria may respond to a "wake-up buddy" system, in which a peer (a friend, preferably) comes to her house every morning to get her up and out the door for school? This has been successful elsewhere.

Teachers Project the Blame onto Maria and Believe the Best Solution Is Counseling

Interventions:

1. I plan to hold another meeting with Maria's teachers to discuss these possible solutions. When doing so, I hope they will see that part of the solution lies with them. If they will make Maria a priority among all the students they are concerned about, I believe she will start to take notice and reciprocate by being more attentive and responsive in class.
2. I will ask Ms. Spears to review her counseling goals with the teachers and indicate how they have a part, also. Counseling by itself rarely solves a multifaceted problem such as this one.

Teachers Are Not Adapting to Our School Population

Maria is just one of many students for whom the curriculum, expectations, and resources are inappropriate.

Interventions:

1. Discuss the issue with staff members and get their ideas about what is needed to meet these realities.
2. Put together a staff interest group to plan how to present this concern to the principal.
3. Review this situation with the principal, listing problems and possible solutions.
4. With the support of the principal and key staff members, develop a committee to discuss the situation and devise a plan for dealing with it.

A few days later I meet with Mr. Petrullo. We talk only briefly about Maria because I want to present the ideas I've just listed. As I expect, he is in favor of the items concerning staff adaptation to the school population, and he mentions three other faculty members who are also interested. We are on our way to developing a systems-improvement plan. However, let's not forget Maria. We still need to follow-through with her.

ISSUES IN THE IMPLEMENTATION OF INTERVENTIONS

After both Mr. and Mrs. Fuentes sign the approval form for counseling services, Ms. Spears starts to see Maria twice a week to implement the plans we've just discussed. Maria is reluctant to go to counseling at first, but I am assertive with her and also lean on our parent support system. Mr. and Mrs. Fuentes tell her to see the counselor, so she does. It is interesting to note that Maria may have given both her parents and me more resistance if we had been operating independently about her. Now that she knows we are working collaboratively, she is more compliant. Also, when she sees that Ms. Spears is not a shrink planning to delve into her innermost secrets, she is relieved. Most students and parents don't know that in high schools there is no time for in-depth counseling of any length; Ms. Spears seeing her for two sessions a week is very much the exception.

Mr. Petrullo reports that the contract is successful. Maria is producing more work of better quality, and her attendance is now almost 100%. Her Thursday exam grades are now at the C level for the first time this year. Mr. Petrullo has so far sent home three weekly report cards, all of which have been signed and returned, twice by both parents. With the bonus points they have agreed to, Maria could earn a B for this quarter. Mr. Petrullo says that he is willing to share his results with Maria's other teachers. Perhaps we will be able to come up with a contract that will be useful in all classes.

I've talked to Mrs. Fuentes only once in the past 2 weeks. She is holding firm on the homework monitoring. She has even received support from an unlikely source, her son, who tells Mrs. Fuentes that she should have made him do his homework when he was in regular school. She's not sure if he's serious or not. So far she and her husband are still thinking about the referral to the child guidance clinic. They want to see if things get better without taking that step.

A hallway conversation with Maria's math fundamentals teacher results in a cursory review of our progress with Maria and a promise to organize another staff meeting on her. It also develops this teacher's interest in the study-buddy idea and a desire to know more about how to structure it. I say we'll discuss everybody's experience with this sort of grouping as well as other cooperative-teaching methodologies, along with our interest in doing more of these strategies schoolwide. The teacher says she is interested in joining these discussions. She also notes that since Maria is showing up more often now, she finds herself attending to her more readily. Still, Maria has fundamental skill deficits in arithmetic that somebody ought to do something about. "What about special education?" the teacher asks. I review Maria's history in the special education program and tell her that Maria doesn't presently meet the criteria for that program. I say, "We're thinking this is more of a motivation problem." The teacher laughs. "If you want to see a motivation problem, just come to my class sometime."

I don't find her comment so funny, and it's just another example of the need for some form of system improvement.

MONITORING INTERVENTIONS

A month after our initial staff meeting on Maria, I call another meeting to review our progress. Mr. Petrullo gives an enthusiastic summary of his efforts; Ms. Spears reviews her counseling goals (and the goals for the other three students who now meet together with Maria in the small group format) and we discuss the role of Maria's parents. The math and science teachers report that Maria is now doing better, largely because she is coming to school and, for some reason, seems more involved. She is also turning in some homework, although it is often not done carefully. She is showing concomitant improvements in family studies and P.E.

I explain that I want to spend the rest of our 15-minute meeting on the subject of cooperative learning and other alternative methods of teaching, just to get their opinions. I review, briefly, material I have learned from classes, workshops, and the literature. I also bring up the notion of culturally appropriate materials. As expected, I am reminded of the Cinco de Mayo celebration and Black history month. We need to move forward in this area, past the celebrations approach to multiculturalism.

But how? I don't have the time or expertise to restructure our school. As I have indicated, we need to get at least part of the staff to draw up some tentative plans, tell the principal of our resolve, and move forward. I believe we are going to need some outside expertise in this area, and that means spending money. In today's budget realities it may be a real obstacle. But there I go again; my budget-crisis conditioning needs to be reversed. I need to give up my learned depression and exchange it for learned optimism (Seligman, 1991).

EVALUATION AND CLOSURE

As you can tell, I'm not a data-oriented person. I haven't presented graphs showing how each of our behavioral objectives were met. I could, but who has the time to prepare these things? In the high school I work in, simply finding the time to deal with a noncrisis, non-special education student such as Maria is a luxury. As for graphing data, asking swamped teachers to do the same, and applying statistical tests to these data, forget it; let the university researchers do that [9].

For my part, I'm happy with our efforts for the following reasons:

1. Maria is now coming to school more. Since data about attendance are easy to come by, courtesy of our office staff and computers, we know that she has increased her attendance 27% over the past month. That's great.

2. She is doing more work in class, especially history, and is turning in more assignments and more homework in all classes. That's also great. We have not yet made much progress on remediating her deficit skills; that will be next month's target.

3. We have established a strong working relationship with Maria's parents, and it has paid off very well in terms of attendance and homework monitoring.

4. We have stirred up interest in school reform here at Carter, at least among some of the staff. I have already heard the negative rumors about this; I should have moved forward more quickly with the plan development and consultation with our principal. I'll work on that next week.

In general, I believe this collaborative consultation effort has been very effective. We have not yet solved some of the basic problems that underlie the development of a student like Maria in our schools, but I think we have helped her and her family and have been able to use her case as a springboard for making some fundamental changes in how we do business here at Carter. I have no idea what we'll look like a year from now or, more likely, 3 years from now since these restructuring efforts, if serious, take about that long to work their way into an entrenched system (Knoff, 2002; National Research Council, 2004; Rosenfield & Gravois, 1996; Zins, Curtis, Graden, & Ponti, 1988; Zins & Illback, 1995). I know we are in for some tough times. Giving birth to new ways of doing things is not easy; resistance is going to occur. It's either that or stagnation. I'll start by reviewing the references that follow the notes for this case.

NOTES AND COMMENTS ON CASE 2

1. What are the implications for dealing with a changing school population? How does this influence teaching styles, class size, support services, staff development needs, and so on?

2. It is interesting that some of these teachers believe that a counseling approach is the way to improve academic achievement. What is the evidence to suggest that a counseling approach or technique will increase academic motivation? What are some other ways of improving motivation toward academic improvement? See Ames and

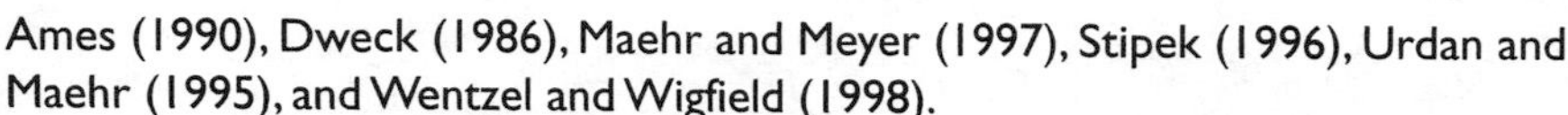

Ames (1990), Dweck (1986), Maehr and Meyer (1997), Stipek (1996), Urdan and Maehr (1995), and Wentzel and Wigfield (1998).

3. What are some methods for getting teachers to generate ideas at an SST meeting or case conference? Why might they be resistant to doing so? Chapter 5 reviews some strategies for generating ideas within SST meetings. See also Bay, Bryan, and O'Connor (1994); Evans (1990); Gutkin and Nemeth (1997); Iverson, (2002); Kovaleski, (2002); Margolis, Fish, and Wepner (1990); Meyers, Valentino, Meyers, Boretti, and Brent (1996); Powers (2001); Ross (1995); Thomas, Correa, and Morsink (1995); and Whitten and Dicker (1995).

4. Chapter 5 has information about contracting. Remember that a common problem with contracting is the tendency to make the contract either too complicated or too labor-intensive for the teacher. Either of these concerns is especially true for high school teachers. How might you develop an inservice meeting to review contracting to make it appealing to teachers? Epanchin, Townsend, and Stoddard (1994); Jones and Jones (2004); Maher (1987); and Miller and Kelley (1994) suggest some useful techniques for implementing contracting in classrooms.

5. In pairs, devise a learning problem for which a contract might be useful. Then draft a simple positive contingency contract. Discuss these contracts in class.

6. If this Monday-absence pattern continues, what should the school do about it? What systems do your local schools use to deal with excessive absences?

7. Is there a potential cultural clash developing here? The school is trying to create some discomfort within Maria and her family by encouraging Maria to change her perspective and encouraging her parents (especially her mother) to change the family's approach to schooling by insisting on homework, checking weekly reports, and requiring Monday school attendance. Could these changes exacerbate the rift already developing between Maria and her parents? Or might these changes heal that rift and pull the parents and child closer together?

8. What programs for dealing with schoolwide underachievement, particularly at the high school level, have been found successful? See Bergerud, Lovitt, and Horton (1988); Bossert (1985); Epstein, Jackson, Salinas, and Associates (1991); Horton and Lovitt (1989); Lenz, Alley, and Schumaker (1987); Molnar (2002); National Research Council (2004); and Teddlie and Stringfield (1993). Teddlie and Stringfield report the following six characteristics associated with effectiveness in low-SES schools: (a) promotion of high educational expectations; (b) hiring of principals who are initiators and innovators; (c) increasing the external reward structure for academic achievement; (d) focusing on basic skills; (e) evaluating the effects of the community on achievement—if the community doesn't support it, try to buffer the school from the effects of the community; and (f) hire younger, possibly more idealistic teachers.

9. What do you think of the consultant's stance regarding the possibility or necessity of gathering data? Are there ways to do this that are not obtrusive and burdensome? How might you gather some objective data, other than the attendance data, in this case?

REFERENCES

Albert, L. (1996). *A teacher's guide to cooperative discipline* (Rev. ed.). Circle Pines, MN: American Guidance Service.

Alberto, P., & Troutman, A. (1999). *Applied behavior analysis for teachers*. Upper Saddle River, NJ: Merrill/Prentice Hall.

Ames, R., & Ames, C. (1990). *Research on motivation in education* (vol. 3). New York: Academic Press.

Bay, M., Bryan, T., & O'Connor, R. (1994). Teachers assisting teachers: A prereferral model for urban educators. *Teacher Education and Special Education, 17,* 10–21.

Bergerud, D., Lovitt, T. C., & Horton, S. V. (1988). The effectiveness of textbook adaptations in life science for high school students with learning disabilities. *Journal of Learning Disabilities, 21*(2), 70–76.

Bossert, S. (1985). Effective elementary schools. In R. M. J. Kyle (Ed.), *Reaching for excellence: An effective schools sourcebook*. Washington, DC: E. H. White.

Bratten, S., Kauffman, J., Bratten, B., Polsgrove, L., & Nelson, C. (1988). The Regular Education Initiative (REI): Patent medicine for behavioral disorders. *Exceptional Children, 55,* 21–27.

Brigham, T. (1989). *Self-management for adolescents: A skills-training program*. New York: Guilford Press.

Christenson, S. L. (1992). *Home-school collaboration*. Washington, DC: NASP.

Dreikurs, R., Grunwald, B. B., & Pepper, F. C. (1982). *Maintaining sanity in the classroom: Classroom management techniques*. New York: Harper & Row.

Durrant, M. (1995). *Creative strategies for school problems*. New York: Norton.

Dweck, C. S. (1986). Motivational processes affecting learning. *American Psychologist, 41,* 1,040–1,048.

Elizalde-Utnick, G. (2002). Best practices in building partnerships with families. In A. Thomas & J. Grimes (Eds.), *Best practices in school psychology IV* (pp. 413–430). Bethesda, MD: NASP.

Epanchin, B. C., Townsend, B., & Stoddard, K. (1994). *Constructive classroom management: Strategies for creating positive learning environments*. Pacific Grove, CA: Brooks/Cole.

Epstein, J. L., Jackson, V. E., Salinas, K. C., & Associates. (1991). *Manual for teachers: Teachers involve parents in schoolwork (TIPS)*. Baltimore: Johns Hopkins University, Center on Families, Communities, Schools, and Children's Learning.

Evans, R. (1990). Making mainstreaming work through prereferral interventions. *Educational Leadership, 47,* 73–77.

Ferguson, E. (1995). *Adlerian theory: An introduction*. Chicago: Adler School of Professional Psychology.

Goodman, G., & Poillion, M. (1992). ADD: Acronym for any dysfunction or difficulty. *Journal of Special Education, 26,* 37–56.

Gutkin, T., & Nemeth, C. (1997). Selected factors impacting decision making in prereferral intervention and other school-based teams: Exploring the intersection between school and social psychology. *Journal of School Psychology, 35,* 195–216.

Horton, S. V., & Lovitt, T. C. (1989). Construction and implementation of graphic organizers for academically handicapped and regular secondary students. *Academic Therapy, 24*(5), 625–641.

Hughes, J. (1988). *Cognitive behavior therapy with children in schools*. New York: Pergamon.

Iverson, A. (2002). Best practice in problem-solving team structure and process. In A. Thomas & J. Grimes (Eds.), *Best practices in school psychology IV* (pp. 657–670). Bethesda, MD. NASP.

Jimerson, S., Carlson, E., Rotert, M., Egeland, B., & Sroufe, L. A. (1997). A prospective, longitudinal study of the correlates and consequences of early grade retention. *Journal of School Psychology, 35,* 3–25.

Jones, V., & Jones, L. (2004). *Comprehensive classroom management* (7th ed.). Boston: Allyn & Bacon.

Kendall, P., & Braswell, L. (1985). *Cognitive behavioral therapy for children*. New York: Guilford Press.

Knoff, H. (2002). Best practices in facilitating school reform, organizational change, and strategic planning. In A. Thomas & J. Grimes (Eds.), *Best practices in school psychology IV* (pp. 235–254). Bethesda, MD: NASP.

Kovaleski, J. (2002). Best practices in operating prereferral intervention teams. In A. Thomas & J. Grimes (Eds.), *Best practices in school psychology IV* (pp. 645–656). Bethesda, MD: NASP.

Larson, S. (1992). Anger and aggression management techniques utilizing the Think First curriculum. *Journal of Offender Rehabilitation, 18,* 101–117.

Larson, S., & McBride, S. (1990). *Think First: Anger and aggression management for secondary level students.* VHS tape. Milwaukee, WI: Milwaukee Board of School Directors.

Lenz, B. K., Alley, G. R., & Schumaker, J. B. (1987). Activating the inactive learner: Advanced organizers in the secondary content classroom. *Learning Disability Quarterly, 10,* 53–67.

Maehr, M., & Meyer, H. (1997). Understanding motivation and schooling: Where we've been, where we are, and where we need to go. *Educational Psychology Review, 9,* 371–409.

Maher, C. (1987). Involving behaviorally disordered adolescents in instructional planning: Effectiveness of the GOAL procedures. *Journal of Child and Adolescent Psychotherapy, 4,* 204–210.

Maier, S., & Seligman, M. (1976). Learned helplessness: Theory and evidence. *Journal of Experimental Psychology: General, 105,* 3–46.

Margolis, H., Fish, M., & Wepner, S. (1990). Overcoming resistance to prereferral classroom interventions. *Special Services in the Schools, 6,* 167–187.

Maslow, A. (1968), *Toward a psychology of being* (2nd ed.). Princeton, NJ: Van Nostrand.

Meyers, B., Valentino, C. T., Meyers, J., Boretti, M., & Brent, D. (1996). Implementing prereferral intervention teams as an approach to school-based consultation in an urban setting. *Journal of Educational and Psychological Consultation, 7*(2), 119–149.

Miller, D., & Kelley, M. (1994). The use of goal setting and contingency contracting for improving children's homework performance. *Journal of Applied Behavior Analysis, 27,* 73–84.

Molnar, A. (Ed.). (2002). *School reform proposals: The research evidence.* Tempe, AZ: Arizona State University, Education Policy Research Unit.

Murphy, J., & Duncan, B. (1997). *Brief intervention for school problems.* New York: Guilford Press.

National Research Council. (2004). *Engaging schools: Fostering high school student's motivation to learn.* Washington, DC: The National Academies Press.

O'Shea, D., O'Shea, L., Algozzine, R., & Hammitte, D. (2001). *Families and teachers of individuals with disabilities.* Boston: Allyn & Bacon.

Powers, K. (2001). Problem solving student support teams. *The California School Psychologist, 6,* 19–30.

Quay, H. (1986). Classification. In H. C. Quay & J. S. Weery (Eds.), *Psychopathological disorders of childhood* (3rd ed., pp. 35–72). New York: Wiley.

Rafoth, M. (2002). Best practices in preventing academic failure and promoting alternatives to retention. In A. Thomas & J. Grimes (Eds.), *Best practices in school psychology IV* (pp. 789–802). Bethesda, MD: NASP.

Reynolds, M., Wang, M., & Walberg, H. (1987). The necessary restructuring of special and regular education. *Exceptional Children, 53,* 391–398.

Robinson, T., Smith, S., Miller, M., & Brownell, M. (1999). Cognitive behavior modification of hyperactivity/impulsivity and aggression: A meta-analysis of school-based studies. *Journal of Educational Psychology, 91,* 195–203.

Rosenfield, S., & Gravois, T. (1996). *Instructional consultation teams.* New York: Guilford Press.

Ross, R. P. (1995). Best practices in implementing intervention assistance teams. In A. Thomas & J. Grimes (Eds.), *Best practices in school psychology III* (pp. 627–637). Washington, DC: NASP.

Seligman, M. E. P. (1991). *Learned optimism.* New York: Knopf.

Sheridan, S. M., Kratochwill, T. R., & Bergan, J. R. (1996). *Conjoint behavioral consultation: A procedural manual.* New York: Plenum.

Stipek, D. (1996). Motivation and instruction. In D. C. Berliner & R. C. Calfee (Eds.), *Handbook of educational psychology.* New York: Macmillan.

Teddlie, C., & Stringfield, S. (1993). *Schools make a difference: Lessons learned from a 10-year study of school effects.* New York: Teachers College Press.

Thomas, C. C., Correa, V. I., & Morsink, C. V. (1995). *Interactive teaming: Consultation and collaboration in special programs.* Upper Saddle River, NJ: Merrill/Prentice Hall.

Turnbull, A., & Turnbull, H. (1997). *Families, professionals, and exceptionality: A special partnership.* Upper Saddle River, NJ: Merrill/Prentice Hall.

Urdan, T. C., & Maehr, M. L. (1995). Beyond a two-goal theory of motivation and achievement: A case for social goals. *Review of Educational Research, 65,* 213–243.

Walker, H., Colvin, G., & Ramsey, E. (1995). *Antisocial behavior in school: Strategies and best practices.* Pacific Grove, CA: Brooks/Cole.

Walker, J. E., & Shea, T. M. (1999). *Behavior management: A practical approach for educators* (7th ed.). Upper Saddle River, NJ: Merrill/Prentice Hall.

Wentzel, K., & Wigfield, A. (1998). Academic and social motivational influences on students' academic performance. *Educational Psychology Review, 10,* 155–175.

Whitten, E., & Dicker, L. (1995). Intervention assistance teams: A broader vision. *Preventing School Failure, 40,* 41–45.

Ysseldyke, J., Algozzine, B., & Thurlow, M. (1992). *Critical issues in special education.* Boston: Houghton Mifflin.

Zins, J., Curtis, M., Graden, J., & Ponti, C. (1988). *Helping students succeed in the regular classroom: A guide to developing intervention assistance programs.* San Francisco: Jossey-Bass.

Zins, J., & Illback, R. (1995). Consulting to facilitate planned change in schools. *Journal of Educational and Psychological Consultation, 6*(3), 237–245.

Index